RSAC

2009

INSIDE JIHADISM

THE YALE CULTURAL SOCIOLOGY SERIES

Jeffrey C. Alexander and Ron Eyerman, Series Editors

PUBLISHED

Triumph and Trauma, by Bernhard Giesen (2004)

Myth, Meaning, and Performance: Toward a New Cultural Sociology of the Arts, edited by Ron Eyerman and Lisa McCormick (2006)

American Society: A Theory of Societal Community, by Talcott Parsons, edited and introduced by Giuseppe Sciortino (2007)

The Easternization of the West, by Colin Campbell (2007)

Culture, Society, and Democracy: The Interpretive Approach, edited by Isaac Reed and Jeffrey C. Alexander (2007)

Changing Men, Transforming Culture: Inside the Men's Movement, by Eric Magnuson (2007)

Do We Need Religion? On the Experience of Self-Transcendence, by Hans Joas (2007)

A Contemporary Introduction to Sociology: Culture and Society in Transition, by Jeffrey C. Alexander and Kenneth Thompson (2008)

Inside Jihadism: Understanding Jihadi Movements Worldwide, by Farhad Khosrokhavar (2009)

FORTHCOMING

Making Los Angeles: How People Create Place Out of Ordinary Urban Space, by Christopher D. Campbell

Setting the Stage for a "New" South Africa: A Cultural Approach to the Truth and Reconciliation Commission, by Tanya Goodman

Meaning and Method: The Cultural Approach to Sociology, edited by Isaac Reed and Jeffrey C. Alexander

INSIDE JIHADISM

UNDERSTANDING JIHADI MOVEMENTS WORLDWIDE

FARHAD KHOSROKHAVAR

Paradigm Publishers

Boulder • London

To my father and mother, to my wife

The author would like to thank Jeffrey Alexander, Hélène Monot,
Beth Wright, Ann Delgehausen, and Carol Smith for the efforts they contributed
to publishing this book. He would also like to thank Yale University
for the opportunity it gave him as a visiting professor to pursue his research.
He also is grateful to the École des Hautes Études en Sciences Sociales
and the Centre d'Analyse et d'Intervention Sociologiques
for providing him an academic environment
in which he could pursue his research.

All rights reserved. No part of this publication may be transmitted or reproduced in any media or form, including electronic, mechanical, photocopy, recording, or informational storage and retrieval systems, without the express written consent of the publisher.

Copyright © 2009 Paradigm Publishers

Published in the United States by Paradigm Publishers, 3360 Mitchell Lane, Suite E, Boulder, CO 80301 USA.

Paradigm Publishers is the trade name of Birkenkamp & Company, LLC, Dean Birkenkamp, President and Publisher.

Library of Congress Cataloging-in-Publication Data

Khosrokhavar, Farhad.
    Inside jihadism : understanding jihadi movements worldwide / Farhad Khosrokhavar.
        p. cm. — (Yale cultural sociology series)
    Includes bibliographical references and index.
    ISBN 978-1-59451-615-3 (hardcover : alk. paper)
    ISBN 978-1-59451-616-0 (paperback : alk. paper)
    1. Jihad. 2. Islamic fundamentalism. 3. Terrorism—Religious aspects—Islam.
I. Title.
  BP182.K52 2008
  363.325—dc22
                                                                2008026672

Printed and bound in the United States of America on acid-free paper that meets the standards of the American National Standard for Permanence of Paper for Printed Library Materials.

Designed by Straight Creek Bookmakers.

13 12 11 10 09 1 2 3 4 5

363.325 K528i 2009
Khosrokhavar, Farhad.
Inside jihadism :
understanding jihadi movement

Contents

Introduction

Jihadism, a radical version of Islam, is wreaking havoc in almost every part of the world. A Jihadist group is any group, small or large, for which violence is the sole credible strategy to achieve Islamic ends.[1] Al Qaeda is the major group within the Jihadist constellation. The nature of Jihadist groups is not the same all over the world. One can distinguish many types and many generations. We shall see that two major Jihadist movements exist, one rooted in the Islamic (mainly Sunni) world and the other in the West, mainly Europe. They are linked globally through many networks. But still, major differences separate the two movements, not least the ideology and the social roots of those involved in it. In Europe, there are uprooted people who are religiously separated from mainstream Islam, particularly the second- and third-generation sons (and marginally, daughters) of migrants. Even though many leaders are from lower middle classes, they still are culturally uprooted and feel socially stigmatized. In the Muslim world, there is more continuity in religious terms, and Islam is part of daily life, in spite of the emergence of secular minorities.

Jihadism is the largest violent utopian, anti-Western, and anti-democratic movement in the world. It has extended to all continents, with the partial exception of Latin America, where it is still a minor phenomenon. At the same time, it attracts many non-Muslims, who convert and adopt a Jihadist view of the world. It combines many ideological items of the extreme left (the fight against American "arrogance" and imperialism among others) and of the extreme right (the restoration of the "virtuous" family, sending women back to the task of motherhood, and eradicating all the social "vices" like homosexuality and alcohol consumption).

Jihadism indulges in extreme violence.[2] One subcategory of its sympathizers goes to the extreme and promotes a sectarian, cultic representation of religion where death looms large. These groups can indulge in activities that lead not only to indiscriminate death but promote death as the central value of their version of Islam.

Jihadism has been faced with two types of denial. One consists in rejecting Jihadists as not being Muslims: those who reject them tend to be devout Muslims, outraged by the excesses in the name of Jihad. According to these pious people, Jihadists are not Muslims but mere criminals who disfigure Islam and distort its message and values. Another group believes that Islam is nothing but Jihadism and therefore its very nature prevents its integration within democracy. These are either people of Muslim background who reject it violently or Western ideologues who believe that the central message of Allah's religion is violence against unbelievers and rejection of secular values.

In my view both these groups are wrong. Jihadism is a movement based on a specific version of Islam, but it is only one way of looking at Allah's religion and certainly not the only one. There are many others that are much closer to political pluralism and tolerance, promoted by Islamic Reformists, who are in a minority position institutionally and culturally. The crisis of the Muslim world—the domination of Muslim religious institutions by fundamentalist religious authorities and heedless, erratic American policies in the Muslim world—have given Jihadism credibility in Muslims' eyes.

Prominent in Jihadism is a warrior culture that was first established in Islam in its first century and then developed during its conquest of other lands, including the Byzantine and Persian Empires, North Africa, and part of Spain. The tradition of Jihad became much less combative after the establishment of the Muslim empire in its stabilized state. This tradition was not actively renewed until European colonialism, when Muslim leaders invoked the necessity to fight against Western invaders as an individual duty, incumbent upon every able-bodied believer (*fardh al eyn*). With the new Jihadists in the second half of the twentieth century, holy war acquired a new feature that could be called an offensive. For modern Jihadists, it is not enough to throw out Western invaders from the land of Islam. It is necessary to expand Islam to the entire world as the sole legitimate religion. The novelty in Jihadism is the irredentism of its proponents, who dream of spreading the religion of Allah to the entire world not by persuasion and through winning hearts and minds of non-Muslims (which is the characteristic of Muslim Fundamentalists), but by imposing it through physical violence and intimidation.

The Jihadist interpretation of *Tawhid* (Allah's uniqueness, the first pillar of Islam) is characterized by a lack of a fear of death, acceptance of one's fate as being in the hands of Allah, and a willingness to sacrifice oneself for Allah. Jihadists develop an entire psychology of selflessness in the fight against the godless world order within a dissymmetric military system, one in which they are at a major disadvantage, being unable to fight on equal terms against the West.

The regeneration of Jihad is directly related to the renewal of Jihadist production by a new generation of scholars, ages thirty to late fifties, who bring new ideas, new interpretations, and new stamina to Jihad[3] as a major duty—in fact, as the most important duty for Muslims. Jihadism as an ideology is, after the collapse of communism, the most comprehensive—and in a way, cogent—set of notions, rules for action, and propaganda that the last twenty-five years of the twentieth century and the beginning of the twenty-first century have witnessed so far. It is naïve to undervalue or belittle this creative yet destructive ideology, as do most Western critics, or depreciate it as a mere "mental construct" with little effect on reality, as do many prominent writers on Jihad nowadays. The new generation of Jihadist intellectuals and their websites, the most important being undeniably *Minbar al Tawhid wal Jihad*, are renewing Islamic radicalism by injecting it with modern Western ideas from the extreme left to the extreme right and by adjusting Jihad to the new global reality of our age. It is about time we took this ideological movement seriously in order to find appropriate solutions to deal with it. In this respect, repressive acts are only of limited scope. Understanding, responding, and even finding outlets for dialogue or new intellectual creations in order to counter Jihadism are long overdue.

In the West, Jihadists change rapidly. The new generations take the place of the older ones, who were Afghan veterans trained in Afghanistan, mainly in Al Qaeda camps, before and during the Taliban regime. The young Jihadists in the West are computer addicts in search of their parents' roots, looking for heroism and thrill, sick of the permanence of social prejudice and old colonial clichés against the Muslims. In the Muslim world, repression of Muslim Fundamentalists in the political arena favors Jihadists. In this way, an understanding of Jihadism, in spite of the global network, must always be two-pronged, incorporating the version in the Muslim world and the other mainly in Europe.

This work intends to address the significance of Jihadist intellectual creation and the little echoes it has found in the Western world or even in Islamic countries where authorities are satisfied to repress it or integrate part of it into the political arena rather than cope with its root causes. Among major Jihadist intellectuals, four have been chosen as sources for assessing the following statements. First of all, Jihadism is a powerful current in which many intellectuals share a common vision of reality. Their dissent is on minor issues, whereas their consensus extends to the following issues: the necessity for holy war, the rejection of democracy as a false Western religion, their condemnation of any compromise not only with the West but also with the prevailing power structure in the world, their diabolic picture of the West and the Muslim world, and their defense of blind violence against all those who oppose them. These topics and some others make them a very powerful minority within the Muslim world, with offshoots in the West, mainly through the London connection.

This book is also an attempt to show the multifaceted nature of Jihadism—its diversity, religious foundations, intellectual basis, and social bedrock in the Muslim world and the West, mainly Europe. Moreover, this work aims to understand Jihadists from within by letting them explain their motives. Understanding is not justifying: it is another way of reaching the goal of opposing violence. Of course, this violence is not only one-sided. Western and particularly American policies have had a major influence on the Muslim world, and Jihadism is, in part, a reaction to it.[4] Undeniably, the politics of the dominant Western countries and more especially the United States have induced a defiant reaction from the Muslim world, an element of which is Jihadism. Since the war in Iraq began in 2003, Jihadism has been reinvigorated, mainly in two distinct ways. In Iraq, a new generation of Jihadists has been trained, distinct from Afghanistan's generation; there are far fewer Western Islamists than in Afghanistan, but still, more than a few dozen can be traced to the West with certainty, and some of them might return incognito to the West and cause havoc there. In the West, tiny groups among indignant Muslims have enrolled in Jihadism and are becoming more and more autonomous toward their forerunners in Afghanistan and Bosnia. They are aware of Iraqi, Palestinian, and Afghan plights through the new global media and are incensed over the fate of their fellow Muslims. Their involvement in Jihadism through the Internet and other modern means of communication makes them a Western phenomenon, largely autonomous from the Muslim world, instituting what is commonly called "homegrown terrorism." They are building up the third generation of Jihadists, after the groups trained by Al Qaeda in Afghanistan and Bosnia.[5]

Nevertheless, Jihadism cannot be reduced to a "reaction" to Western imperialism or oppression. It has at least four other causes. First of all, it is deeply rooted in a minority current among Islamic movements that is theologically inspired by a radical group among the followers of the Prophet after his death. This type of movement emerges every now and then in the Muslim world since the beginning of the religion, in order to restore Islam to its primal purity. Moreover, when the fall of the Berlin wall in 1989 closed the door to leftist radicalization, and communist-inspired movements and parties largely disappeared from the Muslim world, Islam gained prominence as the major anti-Western, anti-liberal, and anti-imperialist ideology in both the West and the Muslim world. Jihadism is also partially rooted in the creation of the State of Israel and the perception of Israel as an offshoot of Western imperialism, implanted in the heart of Muslim land to destroy Islam and humiliate Muslims. The unsettled Palestinian question contributes to the legitimacy of Jihadism in the eyes of many Muslims.

Major differences distinguish the study of Jihadism from most other social fields. To begin with, those who work on urban sociology "go and see" what is happening on the ground. No one expects sociological or anthropological research on an urban district to be done without observing it in person, analyzing its streets, landmarks, and other features. Studying Jihadism, in the overwhelming majority of the cases, means working on secondhand documents, mostly produced or published by intelligence agents; consulting data on the Internet; or analyzing statistics put at scholars' disposal by government authorities. Only a tiny number of people have had the opportunity to meet Jihadists, and even then, the number they have encountered is insignificant. In my case, I interviewed in French prisons in 2003 a dozen people condemned for having taken part in Al Qaeda terrorist activities. Jihadists can be found in jails, in wars, or plotting in Europe or in the Muslim world at large. Still, as a rule scholars cannot meet them but only can get in touch with those Jihadists who have renounced violence, their friends and family members, or their colleagues, if they are even willing to talk. Jihadist studies include reports based on aggregate data and journalists' insights—but not in-depth studies. The wide varieties of Jihadism in the world make it impossible for a single person to have a comprehensive view of it worldwide. It is probably the first time in history that a radical movement has such a worldwide scope. In the past violent movements, such as the European working-class movement in the nineteenth century before its institutionalization, the anarchist movement in Russia in the late nineteenth century and beginning of the twentieth (the Decembrists), and the leftist movement in Europe in the 1970s,[6] were found only in Europe and marginally in the United States and Asia; nowadays, almost all continents are outposts of Jihadism.

Jihadism is the result of what can be called "perverse modernization" in the Muslim world and its transmission to a minority of Islamic radicals in the West. By perverse modernization I mean the dismantling of traditional communities through state action and a new market economy but without the positive side effects of the latter, namely the promotion of individual freedoms, the individual capacity to assure social and economic upward mobility by positive involvement in society, the opening up of the political system, and the creation of a new role for government as the defender of social liberty rather than the instigator of blind repression. Jihadism is the result of a political and economic development where the individual is partially freed from traditional ties without being vouchsafed the positive aspects of his or her insertion into new social nexuses. Jihadism promotes "individualism through death" by making the holy war a personal duty and not a collective one. It gives a new definition to the old Muslim community (*umma*) by making it an organic entity that never existed before in such a coercive form, akin to the fascist entity of the "Volk" directed by an Islamic leader (be it called imam, emir, or caliph) and contrary to the traditional Islamic community, within which the hierarchy made it impossible for a single person to claim political and religious absolute supremacy.[7] While the old Umma is seen as "cold" and impersonal, the neo-Umma marketed by Jihadists is "hot," even effervescent and "boiling," personalized to the extreme through charismatic prominent figures like Bin Laden and other local actors. Many other characteristics of Jihadism as a perverse modernization will emerge in this book.

To understand the "perverse modernization" point of view—which does not uniquely apply to the Muslim world—one has to understand the notion of "cultural distance." When the distance between two cultures is too great, understanding social phenomena becomes difficult without long-term familiarity with each of them. Analyzing Jihadism requires haunting the Islamic world and culture, particularly its languages. Otherwise, the cultural distance between the West and the Muslim world makes it very hard to understand major events without automatically grasping them through the patterns of one's own culture. Therefore, many studies of Jihadism are flawed because of a lack of understanding of Islamic culture, history, and society. Still, understanding Islam from within does not warrant a good book on Jihadism. On the other hand, lack of understanding from within certainly yields a bad book, unless one wields an exceptional imagination or an immense ability for empathy. Without living from time to time in the Muslim world, without reading texts directly in at least some of its different languages, and without haunting some Fundamentalist or pro-Jihadist circles in Islamic societies, the study of Jihadism runs the risk of being at best one-sided, at worst deeply flawed. The same holds true for Muslim diasporas in the West. Here, too, anthropological knowledge of the diasporas, mainly in Europe, is necessary for understanding their version of Jihadism.

NOTES

1. All the Arabic and Persian texts quoted in the following chapters are my translations, unless otherwise stated. The Koranic verses are mainly quoted from the Saudi translation of the King Fahd Complex. The overwhelming majority of the Jihadist writings are quoted from the Internet, mainly the *Minbar al Tawhid wal Jihad* (http://www.tawhid.ws), founded by the major Jihadist intellectual Maqdisi. The pagination is not consistent, and therefore pages are not indicated in my translations. The words of reverence that come after the name of the Prophet (Peace and Benediction of Allah upon him) or respected religious people (Allah be content of him) and the like are ignored in my translation, because they unduly burden it, without any specific content other than the respect paid to them. The dates are usually not available but can be approximately situated between the 1990s and today, unless otherwise stated.

2. The terms "Islamic terrorism," "Islamist terrorist," and "Jihadism" are subject to scholarly disputes and disagreements. Most social scientists agree that "Islamic terrorism" is per se a deleterious phenomenon, morally, socially, and internationally, but some avoid using the word because the condemnation it implies would prevent an objective analysis of the phenomenon. Still, for lack of a better word, I will sometimes use it.

3. The word *Jihad* is used only four times in the Koran, while the word *qital* (combat) is often used. In more frequent use is the verb phrase "to accomplish the Jihad" (*jahada*), appearing twenty-seven times, with a related phrase, "the people performing jihad" (*Mujahidun*) appearing four times. All in all, 35 of the 6,235 verses of the Koran contain a word derived from the root j-h-d, only 10 of the 35 occurrences having an exclusively warlike meaning. See Jean-Pierre Filiu, *Les frontières du jihad* (Paris: Fayard, 2006).

4. See François Burgat, *Face to Face with Political Islam* (London: Tauris, 2003).

5. See Marc Sageman, *Leaderless Jihad: Terror Networks in the Twenty-First Century* (Philadelphia: University of Pennsylvania Press, 2008).

6. See David Rapoport, "The Four Waves of Modern Terrorism," *Current History* (December 2001).

7. Even the so-called qazi-caliphs in the Middle Ages, the caliphs in the Umayyad or Abbasid dynasties, and the sultans in the Ottoman Empire did not have the kind of absolute power bestowed upon the imam by modern Jihadists. See Michael Bonner, *Jihad in Islamic History* (Princeton: Princeton University Press, 2006).

I

Explanatory Approaches
to Jihadism

There are many explanatory approaches to Jihadism, a large body of literature having appeared after September 11 (more than fifteen hundred books and articles up to 2007). Some stress psychosocial factors, cultural determinants, international crisis, the media's role, and the Internet as well as the breakdown of social bonds as causes of Jihadist terrorism. There are, as well, those who explain Jihadism through the crisis of the state (weak or failed states) combined with some of the above factors. Some sociologists explain Jihadism as a social movement or a campaign. From this perspective, Jihadists frame social demands as opportunities for violent action, networking among themselves, forging collective identities, building up cells and informal organizations, making specific claims against the state and other institutions, and encouraging their members to accept sacrifices and other costs even though in most cases the success is not guaranteed by the action.[1] For some researchers, accounting for terrorism in terms of global conditions (political, economic, cultural, or demographic) is inadequate. Terrorist activity may rise or decline with otherwise constant global conditions; the important factor is the intent and purpose of small groups and their representation of reality.[2] These scholars insist on organizational dynamics,[3] and many focus on the statistical data available on Jihadists and their terrorist cells to learn their general characteristics. Leiken and Brooke have made a quantitative analysis of terrorism and immigration.[4] Using the biographical data of 373 terrorists, they outlined the following features:

- Global Jihad is not restricted to the Middle East: 41 percent of the sample is nationals of the West and a quarter, Europeans.
- Converts play an important role within Jihadist movement in regard to their proportion in Western societies.
- There is a link between immigration and terrorism: although the overwhelming majority of Muslim immigrants are not terrorists, most terrorists are immigrants.
- Jihadist cells are based on anthropological characteristics rather than skills: the role of the family, nationality, and immigration status are by far more important than other factors.

THE ROLE OF SOCIAL NETWORKS AND GROUP DYNAMICS

Bakker studied individuals and networks involved in Jihadist terrorist activities in Europe, specifically in the thirty-one foiled and successful plots and attacks between September 2001 and September 2006. He identified about 250 terrorists and their networks, and investigated circumstances under which they joined the violent Jihad. He drew the following conclusion:

> Most of the networks are active in Western Europe and differ in size, target selection, geographical background, and other variables. However, *within* networks there is homogeneity. Members of the network often are about the same age and come from the same places. This may be explained by the way these networks are formed, which often is through social affiliation. Many consist of people that are related to each other through kinship or friendship.
>
> Our analysis of the characteristics of the 242 individual jihadi terrorists leads to the following general picture. They are mostly single males that are born and raised in Europe; they are not particularly young; they are often from the lower strata of society; and many of them have a criminal record. . . . Given the fact that more than 40 percent of them were born in Europe and an additional 55 percent have been raised in European countries or are long-term residents, the label "home-grown" is very appropriate to this group.
>
> If we look at the circumstances in which these individuals became involved in jihadi terrorist activities, a picture emerges of networks including friends or relatives that do not seem to have formal ties with global Salafi networks; that radicalise with little outside interference; and that do so in the country in which they live, often together with family members or friends.[5]

Many of his conclusions are in agreement with Leiken and Brooke's study, namely that Jihadist cells are formed in relation to ties of family, friendship, local residence, and kinship relations. Sageman has also noted this phenomenon.[6]

In their study of the 2004 Madrid bombings, Atran and Sageman using the social network analysis conclude that Jihadist groups are moving from a hierarchical organizational model toward a "leaderless resistance model."[7]

Insistence on group dynamics in the West seems to be pertinent even in some parts of the Muslim world, such as Afghanistan, according to Hegghammer: "Many of those who went to Afghanistan had a relative or a friend who had gone previously. Most people made travel preparations as well as the journey itself together with friends or relatives. In some cases, political and religious motivations seem to have been completely subordinated to group dynamics and peer pressure."[8] The strength of this type of reasoning resides in the fact that it accounts for Jihadist cells, particularly in the West, and proposes a legitimate model to predict some of their future shapes. Its weakness lies in the fact that it systematically underestimates ideology and the larger social setting, which is difficult to quantify and therefore even more difficult to assess in statistical terms or in formal modeling.

Those who work on statistical data study the social origin of Jihadists, and more generally terrorists, including the role of religion. Pape gathered data about a total of 315 terrorist attacks and sociological data on 462 suicide attackers.[9] According to his research, religion is rarely the root cause of suicide terrorism, and the main goal of suicide terrorist attacks is "to compel modern democracies to withdraw military forces from territory that terrorists consider to be their homeland." Another conclusion he draws is that suicide attacks have a high success rate (54 percent). Among terrorists analyzed by Pape, only 17 percent were unemployed or members of the lower classes, considerably less than the lower classes' proportion in their respective societies, where they made up about one-third overall. These conclusions have been partially called into question. Moghadam points to an alternative analysis that puts the success rate at 24 percent. He notes that Pape exaggerates the link between occupation and suicide terrorism, especially with regard to the case of Al Qaeda, which has a global pattern of action rather than a localized (national or ethnic) one.[10]

Studies like Pape's point to some basic features that might stimulate Jihadism (like the occupying Western army in the Muslim world), but it totally ignores the possibility that culture, social setting, and historical background play any major role in Jihadist mobilization. Some studies combine many levels of social structure but focus on organizations and their recruitment capacities. Pedahzur proposes an analytical three-stage model in which suicide terrorism is explained through the interaction between the decision making among the elites of terrorist organizations, the militants' individual motivations, and the organizational process of recruitment and socialization of the terrorists.[11]

Jihadist groups have a life cycle of their own. Repression and prevention operate in the long term, but once a group is built up, it becomes independent of the external world. Once the group has been declared illegal by the authorities, the members' clandestine lives separate them from the outside world. For the most determined ones, preserving the existence of the group as such becomes the major, perhaps sole purpose. Therefore, "dormant" cells in Europe or elsewhere become dangerous because their active members intend to maintain the group in its underground life.

ECONOMIC ISSUES AND JIHADIST MOVEMENTS

The role of micro- and macro-economic variables is a subject of debate among researchers. For the so-called deprivation school, there is no strong correlation between poverty and radicalization, both at the level of the country of origin and the individual terrorists. Still, the same researchers find that the setting of historical terrorist attack is, on average, marked by low economic openness, high demographic stress, and a high level of international disputes (in the case of transnational terrorist activity).[12] Analyses of the period 1997–2004 confirm for some scholars the fact that the number of terrorist incidents is negatively associated with levels of development, literacy, and ethnic divisions and positively related to mineral reserves (mainly oil), nondemocratic political regimes, and participation in international organizations.[13] Still, some studies underline the relation between poverty and terrorism. According to Ahmed Rashid, the rise of Islamist radicalism in Central Asia is related to youth unemployment there.[14] Khashan found similar results in Palestine.[15]

The economic variable cannot be neglected in Jihadism, although its role, as we shall see, has to be contextualized in the West as in the Muslim world. Still, economy is embedded in culture and society, and explanations giving primacy to economics do not explain why in so many other societies the same economic variables do not give birth to the same type of radical action. By ignoring the role of Islam as a culture and a religion, these studies give at best a one-sided account of Jihadism.

Sociological studies throw light on the role of economic marginalization combined with cultural factors to explain terrorism, for example, in the case of the Spanish enclaves of Ceuta and Melilla in North Africa. The culture that can promote terrorism alongside economic exclusion is the so-called "broken windows": the excluded believe that everything is allowed, in the absence of institutional control and fragile intercultural links with Spanish Christians. In this situation, a culture of urban violence develops among adolescents.[16]

CULTURE AND RELIGION

Beside quantitative and micro-level studies, others stress the role of culture, religion, and macro-level phenomena like globalization and international politics as well as the media to explain Jihadism. Morgan mentions the emergence of religious and millenarian terrorists in contrast to political terrorists who made up the "old terrorism."[17] Esposito refers to religion as an indigenous mind-set that populations will understand better than Western frames, which are largely alien to them even though their objectives are purely political.[18] Michel, in the 1990s, stressed the fact that globalization induced a political crisis and therefore the religious frame is more and more used to compensate for the vacuum thus created.[19] Pedahzur, Eubank, and Weinberg believe that the variety of causes for terrorism has decreased in the last decade. Social revolutionary, secular nationalist, and radical right-wing organizations and ideologies have given way to organizations with religiously grounded agendas, in particular Islamists.[20]

These studies have merit in bringing up subjective factors and human agency as determined by the lack of political options after the collapse of the communist movement worldwide. But this type of explanation is at best unilateral. Jihadism is in part related to the absence of a protest movement, but why it takes this shape rather than any other one cannot be explained away by ignoring Islam and its cultural, political, and historical dimensions.

Stern argues that, in situations of deep frustration and humiliation, religion links a personal cause to the social and political goals of militant groups. In Pakistan, "inspirational leaders" transcribe poverty, repression, and humiliation into an Islamic register.[21] The problem is that explanation by humiliation is part and parcel of a general framework, and humiliation per se does not assume the same meaning in the West and in the Muslim world.[22] At the same time, humiliation even within a religious framework does not necessarily lead to Jihadism, without the ideological and historical background that makes it pertinent to violent mobilization.

Whereas for some scholars religion and culture fill in the gaps of politics or give legitimacy to social claims, others stress their role as autonomous variables, radicalizing conflicts or giving them a specific turn. For Juergensmeyer, religion is susceptible to contributing to a "culture of violence," and violence has become a defining issue in the identity of militant groups. Entering into a political conflict, religion radicalizes it, making compromise more difficult. He talks about the "cosmic war" in this case.[23] Religion offers to some researchers like Hafez a "tool kit" of myths and notions from which terrorist groups draw some notions to build up strategies of action, like the Palestinian suicide bombers.[24] This perspective is put into question by some researchers, who stress the situation of humiliation and repression by the Israeli occupation that pushes many Palestinians toward radicalism for lack of any credible solution offered by their own governments and the Jewish state, incomparably stronger in economic and military terms.[25]

To what extent reality or symbols are effective in mobilizing people—whether culture and religion play an autonomous role or whether they uniquely serve as means of expressing social conflicts—is a disputed issue. In this book I take the position that Jihadism mobilizes through different symbols and meanings in the Muslim world compared to the West; we are facing two different types of movements, connected to each other through intellectuals and networks.

Some scholars consider the nature of the culture to be just as important in radicalizing people. Weinberg and Eubank compare "collectivist" cultures and "individualist" ones. In a survey of IBM employees in forty different nations, they found that individuals in collectivist cultures are more likely to sustain attacks against foreigners.[26] This theory has found indirect confirmation in the studies of Post, Sprinzak, and Denny on Middle Eastern Jihadists.[27]

Hofstede proposes a five-factor model of cultural features that might favor terrorism: power distance, lack of individualism, masculinity, uncertainty avoidance, and long-term orientation. In Arab countries there are high levels of power distance, uncertainty avoidance, and masculinity and a low degree of individualism.[28] In these explanations, culture looms justifiably large, but the lack of an integrated view and the dissection of the culture into separate characteristics make the issue at best abstract. Islamic culture has to be taken into account in its historical continuity in the Muslim world and its discontinuity in the West, and only a phenomenological view can bind these dimensions together into a meaningful whole.

Why does Jihadist ideology find sympathy within sizeable minorities among Muslims in Europe? For Paz, global Jihad has been a successful attempt that has enabled millions of Muslim youngsters to create a new sense of identity as members of the worldwide Umma.[29] Coolsaet finds that within immigrant Muslim communities in Europe rigid interpretations of Islam (mainly by organizations like Tabligh and Salafists) provide a set of credible rules in times of rapid change.[30] In Europe Petersen places the justification for violence within the history of Islamic activism since the 1980s. Salafism or other similar currents reject the integration of Muslims in host societies, aim at the creation of an Islamic state in Europe, and provide justifications for terrorism.[31] These studies underline the imagined, utopian dimension of Jihadism and the reference to a new type of effervescent Islamic community that fills the vacuum created by rapid change. Still, the nature of this new Umma and its embeddedness in the two worlds of Jihad (the West and the Muslim world) remain problematic.

RATIONAL CHOICE THEORY

Rational choice theory proponents have also tried to make sense of terrorist action: it is a conscious, calculated, and rational decision to make this type of action the optimum strategy to accomplish certain socio-political goals. Many scholars try to determine whether Jihadist suicide bombers are religious zealots and unbridled, irrational radicals or whether their action is motivated by a logic that can be explained in rational terms. According to one view, suicide bombers fight an unequal war with an adversary that is much more powerful. They influence their opponent and public opinion in a way that can at least symbolically give them some advantage against the enemy. They recruit as well through the mechanism of self-sacrifice and push the more powerful enemy into a situation in which it might not be ready to sacrifice as much as the suicide bombers. Human bombs are also low-cost and give an advantage to the weaker party to fight the stronger enemy with meager means. In this respect and in many others one might surmise that Jihadist suicide actions are "rational" and based on a strategic and tactical view that yields its own logic.[32] Religion is thus instrumentalized in order to give sense to this type of rationality.

This perspective ignores manipulation by Jihadist organizations and the effects of imitation and emulation within the Muslim world. Jihadism has its own rationality, but the manifestation of a subculture of death within it is based on a deep alienation, manipulation, and perverted sense of life that are difficult to entirely explicate using rational choice theory. Organizationally, it is true that martyrdom and Jihad are weapons of the poor against a stronger and richer enemy, but those who accept death act through a logic of deep conviction that goes beyond any kind of utility appraisal. The subjective side has to be understood culturally, politically, psychologically, and socially, and the framework of rational choice theory is too restrictive to permit this type of complex explanation.

NOTES

1. See Mohammed M. Hafez, *Suicide Bombers in Iraq* (Washington, DC: United States Institute of Peace Press, 2007), who mainly follows the social movement framework set up by Donatella della Porta and Mario Diani, *Social Movements: An Introduction*, 2nd ed. (Malden, MA: Blackwell, 2006).

2. See Martha Crenshaw, "Political Explanations," in *Addressing the Causes of Terrorism*, Club de Madrid Series on Democracy and Terrorism, vol. 1, ed. Peter R. Neumann (Madrid: Club de Madrid, 2005), 13–18; D. Della Porta, "Research Design and Methodological Considerations," in *Political Violence and Terrorism: Patterns of Radicalization in Political Activism*, ed. D. Della Porta and C. Wagemann (Florence: EUI, 2005).

3. See J. Allahwin, "Review Essay: What Must We Explain to Explain Terrorism," *Social Movement Studies* 3, no. 2 (October 2004).

4. R. Leiken and S. Brooke, "The Quantitative Analysis of Terrorism and Immigration: An Initial Exploration," *Terrorism and Political Violence* 18 (2006).

5. Edwin Bakker, *Jihadi Terrorists in Europe: Their Characteristics and the Circumstances in which They Joined the Jihad: An Exploratory Study* (The Hague: Clingendael Institute, 2007), 52–53; emphasis in original.

6. Mark Sageman, *Understanding Terror Networks* (Philadelphia: University of Pennsylvania Press, 2004).

7. Scott Atran and Mark Sageman, *Global Network Terrorism: Comparative Anatomy and Evolution*, Briefing to the National Security Council, Washington, DC, April 28, 2006.

8. T. Hegghammer, "Terrorist Recruitment and Radicalisation in Saudi Arabia," *Middle East Policy* 13, no. 4 (2006).

9. Robert Pape, *Dying to Win: The Strategic Logic of Suicide Terrorism* (New York: Random House, 2005).

10. See A. Moghadam, "Suicide Terrorism, Occupation and the Globalization of Martyrdom: A Critique of *Dying to Win*," *Studies in Conflict & Terrorism* 29 (2006).

11. A. Pedahzur, "Toward an Analytical Model of Suicide Terrorism—A Comment," in *Terrorism and Political Violence* 16, no. 4 (October–December 2004).

12. See K. Drakos and A. Gofas, "In Search of the Average Transnational Terrorist Attack Avenue," *Defense and Peace Economics* 17, no. 2 (2006).

13. See A. Bravo and C. Dias, "An Empirical Analysis of Terrorism: Deprivation, Islamism and Geopolitical factors," *Defense and Peace Economics* 17, no. 4 (2006).

14. A. Rashid, *Jihad: The Rise of Militant Islam in Central Asia* (New Haven: Yale University Press, 2002).

15. H. Khashan, "Collective Palestinian Frustration and Suicide Bombings," *Third World Quarterly* 24, no. 6 (2003).

16. See J. Jordan and F. M. Manas, *Indicios externos de la radicalizacion y militancia yihadista*, Universidad de Granada, Jihad Monitor Occasional Paper no. 4, 2007, http://www.jihadmonitor.org.

17. M. J. Morgan, "The Origins of New Terrorism," *Parameters* (US Army War College Quarterly) 34, no. 1 (2004).

18. J. L. Esposito, *Unholy War: Terror in the Name of Islam* (New York: Oxford University Press, 2002).

19. Patrick Michel, "Internationalisation, conscience nationale, religion," *Social Compass* 41, no. 1 (1994).

20. A. Pedahzur, E. Eubank, and L. Weinberg, "The War on Terrorism and the Decline of Terrorist Group Formation: A Research Note," *Terrorism and Political Violence* 14, no. 3 (2002).

21. J. Stern, *Terror in the Name of Allah: Why Religious Militants Kill* (New York: Harper Collins, 2003).

22. See Farhad Khosrokhavar, *The Suicide Bombers: The New Martyrs of Allah*, trans. David Macey (London: Pluto Press, 2005), for an explanation of different types of humiliation in Jihadism.

23. M. Juergensmeyer, *Terror in the Mind of Allah: The Global Rise of Religious Violence* (Berkeley: University of California Press, 2003).

24. M. Hafez, *Manufacturing Human Bombs: Strategy, Culture and Conflict in the Making of Palestinian Suicide Terrorism*, National Institute of Justice, Suicide Terrorism Conference, Washington, DC, October 2004.

25. P. Larzillière, *Etre Jeune en Palestine* (To Be Young in Palestine) (Paris: Balland, 2004); Laetitia Bucaille, *Générations Intifada* (Paris: Hachette, 2002).

26. L. Weinburg and W. Eubank, "Cultural Differences in the Behavior of Terrorists," *Terrorism and Political Violence* 6 (1994).

27. J. Post, E. Sprinzak and L. Denny, "The Terrorists in Their Own Words: Interviews with 35 Incarcerated Middle Eastern Terrorists," *Terrorism and Political Violence* 15 (Spring 2003).

28. G. Hofstede, *Culture's Consequences: Comparing Values, Behaviors, Institutions and Organizations Across Nations* (Thousand Oaks, CA: Sage Publications, 2001).

29. R. Paz, "Global Jihad and WMD: Between Martyrdom and Mass Destruction," *Current Trends in Islamist Ideology* 2 (2005).

30. R. Coolsaet, *Radicalisation and Europe's Counter-Terrorism Strategy*, Royal Institute for International Relations (Brussels) and Ghent University, Transatlantic Dialogue on Terrorism, The Hague, 2005.

31. P. Petersen, "On 9/11 and the Problem of Immigration: Fight Club and Glamorama as Terrorist Pretexts," *Orbis Litterarum* 60, no. 2 (2005).

32. See Diego Gambetta, ed., *Making Sense of Suicide Missions* (Oxford: Oxford University Press, 2005).

2

Jihadist Ideology

One commonly held belief is that Jihadist ideology is perfunctory and at best inconsistent and incoherent. Nothing is further from the truth. There is a solid body of literature behind the Jihadist enterprise, mainly in Arabic, which is based on the reinterpretation of religious traditions and their renewal in light of the contemporary world. More than a dozen major writers, hundreds of minor ones, and thousands of small scribes account for its vitality. The Internet has largely facilitated the undertaking, making the work of core Jihadist intellectuals widely accessible. There is no "leaderless ideology" in Jihadism; highbrow intellectuals provide it with solid Islamic credentials. Jihadists' longevity is assured through an Islamic tradition in which religious radicalism has almost always existed, though as a minority phenomenon. Because of the lack of a unique authoritative religious body in Islam (even among the Shi'ites, in spite of Iran's theocracy, the hierarchy is not monolithic), radicals have always been present—marginal, but still present.

Jihadism's ideology is perhaps the most comprehensive, anti-modern, and anti-liberal of any in the world after the demise of communism. It is solidly argued in terms of ideas and cogency, and its content is by far the broadest one in the postcommunist era. It has its defenders and its scope is much wider than what most of the observers in the West could guess. Many groups are involved in it: the close circle of devoted Jihadists who are ready to sacrifice their lives for the Sake of Allah; the much wider circle of hyper-Fundamentalists who are ready to cooperate with the Jihadists financially and sometimes logistically and politically, but not in their military enterprises; the even much wider circle of Islamic Fundamentalists who refuse to get involved in the Jihadist enterprise or to help them directly, financially or politically, but who, indirectly, are ready to facilitate some of their undertakings in those parts of the world they deem necessary to actively engage in. There is also a minority among the Muslim diasporas in Europe that is attracted toward Jihadist action because of what they suffer (mostly poor people with no hope for the future)—Islamophobia and racism in conjunction with the memory of colonialism. Many of their leaders are from the lower middle classes, but they identify with the humiliations and distress of the Muslim underclass in Europe, in much the same way as the extreme left middle-class intelligentsia in 1970s Europe identified with the plight of the working class (Red Brigades in Italy, Action Directe in France, Rote Armee Fraktion in Germany). Finally, among the converts in the West are a few who embrace the Jihadist version of Islam for lack of any alternative ideology (since the traditional extreme left groups in Europe are in decay) or because of their close identification with the Muslim plight and their own sense of victimization.

THE RENEWAL OF JIHADIST THOUGHT

Loyalty and Disavowal as the Pillars of Jihad

Current radical Islam has a fivefold root. The first goes back to the beginnings of Islam, after the death of the Prophet and the rule of the four major caliphs, called *rashidoon* (the "well-guided") namely, Abu Bakr, Umar, Uthman, and Ali, whose reign extended from 602 to 660. Under the caliphs, Islam expanded to part of the Byzantine Empire, to Persia (Iran), and North Africa. During the reign of the last caliph, Ali, dissension among Muslims came out in the open. A group of radical, puritanical Muslims, the Kharijites ("those who exited" from the right path), opposed him and declared war on other Muslims, whom it accused of being infidels. A member of this group killed Ali in 661. Their conduct was marked by fanaticism, heroism, economic egalitarianism, inflexibility, and violence against those whom they deemed bad Muslims. The Kharijites survived as a minority during the first centuries of Islam but eventually died out. Their legacy still shapes radicalism in the name of Islam, although the term "Kharijite" itself is derogatory.[1]

The second source of Islamic radicalism goes back to the eighteenth century and the advent of Wahhabism in Arabia, under the leadership of Muhammad ibn Abd il Wahhab. The modern Saudi state was founded on the alliance between the Wahhabi religious movement and the House of Saud. Although Jihadists oppose Wahhabi officials, they are in agreement with them on many major issues related to interpreting Islam.

The third source of Jihadism goes back to a reform movement in the late nineteenth century, which intended to modernize Islam under the leadership of Al Afghani, Muhammad Abduh, and many other Islamic intellectuals but ended up with a return to the Islamic Golden Age and indirectly favored radicalism in Islam.

The fourth source of Islamic radicalism goes back to the first half of the twentieth century, particularly with the new intellectuals in the Muslim world, namely Hassan al Banna (1906–1949) and Seyed Qutb (1906–1966) in Egypt, Abul Ala Mawdudi (1903–1979) in Pakistan, Ali Shariati (1933–1977) and Ayatollah Khomeini (1902–1989) in Iran, and other thinkers all over the Muslim world. These leading figures set a new tone in Islamic radicalism by modernizing and connecting it directly to politics.

The fifth group is made of new Jihadists; among the most important are Abdullah Azzam (1941–1989), Abu Mohammad Maqdisi, Abu Basir al Tartusi, Abu Mus'ab al Suri, and Abu Qatada al Filistini.[2] Below are brief profiles.

The Jordanian-Palestinian Maqdisi, born in 1959, is one of the most prominent.[3] He is the founder of the major Jihadist website *Minbar al Tawhid wal Jihad*, where many Jihadist intellectuals have their work published and publicized. He mainly travels within the Muslim world. He lives in Jordan, alternately in prison and out of prison under surveillance. He has a theological education, and his writings are some of the most authoritative among Jihadists around the world.

The Syrian al Suri was born in 1958 in Aleppo, Syria, where he studied mechanical engineering.[4] He has been in Afghanistan and in Europe, has lived a long time in Spain and England, and has been in close touch with Western culture and society. He is imprisoned in one of the CIA's secret prisons, after Pakistani forces arrested him in the city of Queta in Pakistan in 2005 and handed him over to the United States. His encouragement of a third Jihadist wave after Afghanistan and September 11 makes him the most prominent Jihadist intellectual with a bent toward social sciences. He preaches tactics that would empower new Jihadist cells—namely, renouncing the kind of large organizations like that which monitored the September 11 attacks, building up small, highly decentralized, and loose cells acting in an autonomous manner, and organizing a leaderless resistance.[5]

Abu Qatada al Filistini (also called Abu Omar) is another Jihadist cleric. He was born in 1960 in Bethlehem, which was part of Jordan at that time. He has been accused of involvement in Al Qaeda activities by a number of countries. He went to the United Kingdom in 1993 on a forged passport and was granted asylum. Like others Jihadists, he insists on the fact that Muslims' individual duty (and not a looser, collective duty) is to fight against the infidels and secular governments in Muslim land. Condemned by Jordan to life imprisonment in absentia, he lives in Britain.

The Syrian-born Abu Basir al Tartusi is a theologian residing in London. He is the most moderate of the Jihadist thinkers. He condemned the London bombings of July 2005 as well as some others in the Muslim world. He is rejected by the more radical elements of the Jihadist movement.

One major characteristic of these new intellectuals is that many of them (in the list above, three out of four) have been in touch with the Western world, living there, starting families, and establishing a line of heirs and followers. Maqdisi is a notable exception. Their contribution to Jihad is not groundbreaking in terms of mere ideas but is paramount in adapting Jihad to the world, making it operational and convincing Muslims of its legitimacy in the fight against the West and Muslim governments that are dominated by depraved pro-Western leaders.

Jihadist intellectuals have many features that distinguish them from their forefathers, recent and long ago, although they share many characteristics as well, namely the prominence of politics, the absolute animosity toward the West, and an anti-modernist outlook. The new ideology is split into different tendencies, but the intellectuals build up a major unified current (*tayyar*), and their unity of inspiration is beyond doubt.[6] Their main tenet is the first pillar of Islam reinterpreted in a peculiar manner, through what can be called "obsessive unitarism." For them, the first Islamic pillar, the Unity of Allah (*Tawhid*) makes it compulsory for Muslims to wage the Jihad against infidels. The status of the holy war and of the infidels[7] is radicalized in the same fashion as among extremist currents within Islamic history. The new interpretation brings new twists to the tradition in terms of "revisiting" it through the key concept of *Al Wala' wal Bara'*[8] (Loyalty and Disavowal). It literally means friendship toward those who worship Allah and enmity toward those who adore any other god.

Traditionally there are five pillars to Allah's religion: testimony to the Uniqueness of Allah (*Tawhid*, that is: "There is no god but Allah"), performance of the daily prayers, fasting during the month of Ramadan, paying Islamic tax or alms (*zakat*), and making the pilgrimage to Mecca for those who can financially afford it. Jihad is not mentioned among them. Jihadists sidestep this obstacle in two different yet correlated ways. Either they flatly state that Jihad is the sixth pillar because of the insistence on fighting the infidels in the Koran, the spirit of the Prophetic traditions, and the behavior of the Prophet and his close followers;[9] or they circumvent the lack of Jihad among the five pillars of Islam by deducting it directly from the *Tawhid*, the first principle in the Islamic faith.

For the Jihadists, *Al Wala' wal Bara'* means not only the recognition of Allah as the unique god but also absolute war against any other god. The motto of the first pillar of Islam, namely, "There is no god but Allah," is divided into two parts. The first one begins with a denial through a negative statement, namely, "There is no god," and is followed by a second part, which wields a positive content, that is, Allah is the real god.[10] The Jihadists firmly believe that the dual aspect of Islam's first pillar results in the rejection of any sacred principle other than Allah. From their perspective, other gods and religions are nothing but idols, and embracing the Islamic faith induces an inescapable war against them. This idea has far-reaching consequences.

To begin with, it results in an endless fight against other religions in the name of Loyalty toward Allah's worshippers (*Al Wala'*) and Disavowal of any other believer (*wal Bara'*). In the twentieth century, one of the first to insist that Islam entails its imposition on humanity was Seyed Qutb, one of the modern forefathers of Jihadism (he was executed by the Egyptian government under Nasser in 1966). He stated that Islam summons to worship no one else but Allah (the negation followed by an assertion).[11] This implies the relentless fight against all idols until Allah's reign is set up on earth:

> Islam is not only faith, Islam is the public declaration for the liberation of the people from the worship of human beings and its aim was from the beginning to wipe out the systems and the political powers that act on the basis of the domination of man over man and the worship of man by man. It frees people to choose the faith they want, after having removed the political pressures on them, attempting at talking to their soul and their reason. But this experience does not mean that they set up as god their own desires or that they choose to be the worshippers of other human beings! The system that should command humanity should be on its principle the worship of Allah alone.[12]

The war on idolatry (*taqut*) is, in his interpretation, the most important part of Islam, taking precedence over the other principles. From this view, all of modernity is based on the worship of idols and, therefore, illegitimate, necessitating that Jihad wipe out its idolatrous tendencies.

Under the influence of Western extremist ideologies, he states that Islam is permanent Jihad and the "permanent revolution."

The late traditional interpretation of Islam stipulates Jihad as a personal duty enforced on the faithful in defensive situations in which Muslims are being attacked.[13] The Egyptian Seyed Qutb rejects this vision in the name of the first principle that implies the war on idolatry: "He who understands the nature of this religion as already mentioned understands the necessity of promoting a movement for Islam in the form of the Jihad by sword accompanied by the Jihad by words. He also understands that this is not a defensive Jihad as declared by the defeatists under the pressure of the current times and the attacks by the cunning Orientalists [*mostashreqin maaker*]."[14] According to this view, Islam is constantly at war with disbelievers, and peaceful coexistence with non-Muslims can be established only while dominating them (e.g., non-Muslims would pay taxes) or if they are apprehensive of Islam and tied to it through a nonegalitarian peace treaty. Islam accepts no other alternative with non-Muslims:

> Jihad is necessary for *da'wa* (proselytizing, calling the others to join Allah's religion). . . . Although Islam aims at peace, it does not seek it at a cheap price. . . . Islam wants a peace in which religion is totally Allah's, the worship of the people is entirely directed towards Allah, and people do not take each other for god (as in Western political systems). . . . As Ibn Qayyim says: the relation with Infidels is of three kinds: those who fight Islam, those with whom a peace treaty has been concluded and those who are under the protection of Islam by means of a tax [*zimmah*]. Those who have concluded a peace treaty fall into two kinds: those who fight Islam but are frightened of Islam and the Muslims, and (at the same time) protected by Islam [*zimmah*]. The population of the earth falls therefore into three kinds: devout Muslims, people of whom Muslims are sure—and they are people of *zimmah* (Christians and Jews who pay taxes to Muslims)—and those who (would like to) fight Islam but are fearful of it (through a peace treaty imposed on them).[15]

Within this viewpoint, only a nexus based on subservience or fear can regulate the relation between Muslims and non-Muslims. No egalitarian relation is accepted between different faiths. The West is rejected for not accepting the nonegalitarian relationship and, on the contrary, imposing unequal relations in which Muslims are treated as inferior. This means total war against a world that is ruled by the "domination" of one people over another instead of Allah's, a world where the "wrong" dominates the "right": "This is a permanent situation, not an incidental one because Right and Wrong cannot coexist on this earth until Islam succeeds in its declaration of Allah's rule in the two worlds [this world and the world of the afterlife] and emancipates man from the worship of people. Usurpers fight against the rule of Allah on earth and do never make peace with it and therefore, they defend the rule of man on earth, this usurper of power. This situation is permanent and the emancipating movement of Jihad does not stop until religion is only Allah's [on earth]."[16]

According to this conception we are in a situation of permanent Jihad, and there is no peace with other contenders of power: they reject Allah's rule on earth, and therefore they are enemies of Islam. This "maximalist" interpretation of Jihad is partially founded on Islamic tradition and the triumphalist first centuries of Islam, but also has many innovative dimensions related to modern nondemocratic ideologies. The definition of Islam as freeing human beings from the yoke of other human beings is close to Marxism: it is universal, and it is theological-political (the Marxist definition was economical, but its universal message was the freeing of people from the yoke of other people in the name of the class war). We have a war wrapped in religious garb but structured in the same fashion as within the totalitarian ideology of vulgar Marxism (in contrast, fascism contradicts radical Islamic tenets because it is not "universalistic," being based on race or an exclusive nation).

In this situation, there is no escape: the war against the wrong in order to impose the law of Allah is calling Muslims, and they are not free to choose another path, freedom being here synonymous with disbelief. The war cannot be avoided; it is imposed by Islam on a pagan world, which has been subdued by the criminal disavowal of Allah: "This religion is the principle [*manhaj*] of Allah for the life of humanity and not a principle [concocted by] human beings, nor the religion of a group of people, nor the system of nationality. . . . It is not possible for man to know this gigantic truth and then look for another justification as regards Islamic Jihad! . . . Islam forces to engage in the fight and there is no freedom in this situation, due to its mere existence and the existence of societies of Godlessness [*jahiliya*] that attack it by necessity."[17]

Another major Jihadist ideologue is Abdallah Azzam, who was killed in Pakistan in 1989. For this Palestinian who prompted Muslims to fight against the Soviets in Afghanistan, the defense of Islamic territories constitutes the individual duty within the defensive Jihad. In a traditional manner, he distinguished two types of Jihad:

(1) The offensive Jihad (*jihad talab*) or attacking infidels in their own country: this is a collective Jihad, and the least that can be

done is to preserve the frontiers of the Muslim world and to frighten enemies by sending an army to them, at least once or twice a year. If Muslims do not help in this enterprise, they are sinners.

(2) The defensive Jihad (*jihad al daf'*) or throwing the enemy out of Islamic land: this is an individual duty and compulsory. It applies when non-Muslims occupy Muslim land, have Muslim prisoners, are fighting the Islamic army, and so forth. Even if infidels occupy a span of Muslim territory, Jihad as a personal duty is an obligation for those who inhabit that land or those who are close to it.

In his book *Join the Caravan!* Azzam proposes the following justifications for Jihad: "to prevent Heresy to win, to escape the punishment of Hell, to fulfill a pressing duty, to respond to Allah's appeal, to follow the example of the pious ancestors, to establish a solid base for the further expansion of Islam, to defend the Oppressed (*mustadh'afin*) or to embrace martyrdom."[18] For him, the sins of the Muslims will never be erased while an Islamic territory is in the hands of infidels, and only the Muslim who fights against them will have his sins wiped out. A Muslim who does not engage in defensive Jihad is as if he broke off his fasting during Ramadan without any religious authorization. Azzam's originality lay in the awakening of Muslims rather than in the innovation of the doctrine of Jihad. His main ideological motive was to restore Islam to its past glory and recapture Muslim land lost to Israel and the Soviet Union (in 1979 the Soviet army occupied Afghanistan). His world is filled with sin, Hell, and fear of being thrown into Hell, as well as the hatred of the infidels and the desire to walk in the footsteps of the "pious ancestors," that is, followers of the Prophet and his immediate successors (traditionally, the three centuries after the death of the Prophet). Azzam's universe is imbued with religious traditionalism but is less anti-modern than that of Qutb, who viewed Islam as the only world religion and, therefore, to be imposed through Muslims' individual duty irrespective of any other consideration, rejecting the notion of defensive Jihad and promoting the offensive one as the only legitimate form. Azzam's vista is more modest: fighting against the infidels who occupy Islamic land (Soviets in Afghanistan, Israelis in Palestine) rather than engaging in a world war against the infidels. These two trends (traditionalism and confinement to the Muslim world versus anti-modernism and direct address of the entire world) are hallmarks of the two major trends of Jihadism since the 1930s.

From Azzam's point of view, Jihad is the apogee of Islam, and genuine Muslims accede to it through emigration for its preparation (*hijra*—Azzam himself "migrated" to Afghanistan for the purpose of fighting against the Soviets), then military preparation (*i'dâd*), then guarding of the frontiers of Islam (*ribât*), and finally combat (*qital*).

In his "Customs and Jurisprudence of Jihad" Azzam assigns a universal function to the holy war by identifying it with the expression "fighting in the path of Allah" from the Koran.[19]

Ayman al Zawahiri is another major Jihadist intellectual. He was born in 1951 in Egypt and is the key ideologue of Al Qaeda. He is a surgeon, speaks Arabic and English, and belongs to a prominent middle-class family, his father being a pharmacologist and a descendant of a large family of doctors and scholars. For him, "Loyalty and Disavowal" is the keystone to Jihad: "It is clear from the calamities of this war [against American crusaders] and its consequences that there is a dire emergency to understand the significance of the principle *Al Wala' wal Bara'* in Islam and the extent of neglect and carelessness for preserving this fundamental principle of the Islamic faith. Consequently, [one should grasp] the imposture of enemies of Islam and their followers and supporters, even among the people of the Islamic community who aim at disfiguring the features of this essential foundation, express their adversity in the guise of Custodians [of the Two Holy Mosques, that is, the Saudi regime] and condemn innocent people by accusing them of being bombers."[20] This view opens the way to its politicization: rituals become less important than the fight against *Taqut* (idolatrous political regimes), and Islam becomes the linchpin for the fight against Western imperialism, called "arrogance" (*isitkbar*) by the Shi'ites as well as the Sunnis.

The followers of idolatry intend to weaken the Muslims by blurring the dividing line between right and wrong: they cover up their subservience to Western governments. "The attacks [against Jihadist people] intend to erase the frontiers between Right and Wrong so that friends and foes intermingle. In their fierce attempt at fighting the expanding forces of Islamic Jihad, they intend as well to embellish the reality of servility and submission [to the West]. They follow another principle than Allah and another commandment than His law, disfiguring at the same time the call to Allah and Jihad and its dignity [as well as those who] propose the standard of Jihad to the combatant Muslim community, their supporters, and all those assembled around them."[21] Who is behind the evil crusaders who fight Islam? For al Zawahiri, the answer is the Jewish powers: "Those enemies [of Islam] embark upon intellectual and religious attacks in parallel to their crusading military attacks, in order to mend the bleak reality represented by the ruling regimes in our [Muslim] countries with all their corruption and corrupting effects and their servility toward the worldwide Crusading Jewish oppressive powers."[22] Jihadists intend to return to Islam by tracing clear-cut frontiers against idolatrous rulers and people and by enrolling in Jihad according to Allah's commandment: friendship and obedience toward those Muslim rulers who practice and promote genuine Islam and enmity toward those who are only Muslims by name and toward Western crusaders.

Abdolrazzaq Afifi, another radical intellectual, wrote the foreword to *Loyalty and Disavowal in Islam* by Muhammad Saeed al Qahtani. According to Afifi, "the topic *Al wala wal Bara'* is the most important principle of Islam. It is the expression of sincere love toward Allah, His prophets, and the devoted people. Disavowal is the expression of hatred toward the Wrong and its followers. This is a principle of faith, and its importance from the viewpoint of present times is [as follows]: they mix up everything, and people are forgetful of the characteristics of the devoted Muslims that distinguish them from the others."[23] The militant meaning accorded to the Uniqueness of Allah (*Tawhid*) is one of the characteristics of Fundamentalist and Jihadist Islam. For Qahtani, this principle necessitates Jihad for its fulfillment: "The essence of this eternal calling [of Islam] is the word *Tawhid*: 'There is no god but Allah and Mohammad is His Prophet.' This is a major word, as says Ibn Qayyim [a famous Islamic jurist, 1292–1350]. According to it, rules have been set, and organizations have been established, and the ways toward paradise and hell [have been determined] and the Muslim ruler (*khalifah*) distinguishes according to it believers and disbelievers, innocent and guilty people. This is the founding principle of the faith, and according to it the sword is drawn for the sake of Jihad, and this is the right of Allah over all the Creatures."[24] Radical Muslims make Jihad coeval with *Tawhid* (Uniqueness of Allah): the assertion of Allah as the sole legitimate god in a confrontational attitude toward all other faiths, considered Unbelief. This understanding of the faith is far from that of many Muslims, who do not attribute any meaning to *Tawhid* other than a strictly religious one, without any activist political implication.

Like Qutb, Qahtani sees the deviation from this principle as the cause of the decay of the Muslims:

> The Islamic Umma became the leader of mankind for a long period when it spread this faith that glued [the members of Umma] in different parts of the inhabited world and pushed out people from the worship of the creatures to the worship of the God of the creatures and from the confined world to the wide one [including] the Other world. Then what happened?
>
> This Umma regressed to the sidelines after it left Jihad for the misdeeds of the cattle!
>
> It moved backward after it went away from Jihad, which is the apogee of Islam. . . .

It followed other communities by relying on a life of meekness, luxury, welfare, and dissipation. . . . Its ideas became confused after it mixed up its pure sources with philosophies of godlessness (*Jahiliya*) and heterodoxies of humanity. . . . It started obeying Disbelievers, trusted in them, and looked for the benefits of this world by giving up its religion, losing thus this world and the other.[25]

Without Jihad and devotion to the cause of Islam, Muslims have been subdued by others and lost their leadership of the world:

Instead of fighting godless people through Jihad, Muslims showed Loyalty to them (*al Wala'*), which is the opposite of what should have been done [*al Bara'*, Disavowal]. And the different expressions of Loyalty toward Disbelievers were shown in many fields. They showed their love for Disbelievers, were subservient to them, and helped them in their fight against the Followers of Allah. They set aside the law of Allah in exchange for the government of this world, justifying their rejection and negligence by pretending that Allah's laws were not adapted to our time and to the ascending march toward [modern] civilization. . . . They imported Disbelievers' legislation, be they oriental or western, and implemented them instead of the Islamic law, implying that Muslims who ask for Allah's law do it out of prejudice, a reactionary attitude, and barbarity! . . . They expressed doubt about the Traditions of the Prophet and vilified their records and the scholars who served their tradition and passed them on to us. . . . They supported the new godless people who promote nationality in the life of Muslims, like the nationalist calls of the Turks and Arabs and Hindus, etc. Muslim societies have been depraved by educational means and the spread of the intellectual war through the media and global systems.[26]

Giving up Jihad, Muslims have ended up substituting human-made law, this apogee of godlessness, to Allah's commandments.

Many aspects of the Muslims' decline, mentioned by Qahtani, are political and legal, but some are cultural. The "intellectual war" is close to the "cultural aggression" (*tahajom farhangi*) by Iranian Shi'ite Islamists. From this perspective, the Muslim world is being threatened not only from outside but also from within—by nationalism, its legislation, its lack of belief in Islam, its traditions, and the lure of Western culture. All these aspects are mentioned and extensively dealt with by Shi'ite radicals as well. Within the framework of Jihadism, the two major Islamic groups, Sunnis and Shi'ites, are in accord with each other, in spite of their deep mutual hostility.

Qahtani presents Loyalty and Disavowal as being merely the consequence of Allah's uniqueness:

> In order to discuss the Loyalty and the Disavowal (*Al Wala' wal Bara'*) in genuine Islamic thought, we should deliberate on three matters:
>   1. The truth of Islam as represented by the word *Tawhid* and the consequences of this word and its conditions.
>   2. Loyalty and the Disavowal as the necessary consequences of *Tawhid*.
>   3. Associationism [*shirk*, that is sharing Allah's privileges with another principle, like people's rule through their own legislation], disbelief (*kufr*), internal strife caused by fake Muslims (*nifaq*), and apostasy (*riddah*) as being opposed to Islam. . . .
>   Loyalty and Disavowal are part of the faith, and discussing them implies deliberation on the foundations of this faith, which is the word *Tawhid* [uniqueness of Allah]. In order to define the faith in a genuine manner, the Muslim has to abide by Loyalty and Disavowal. It is impossible to have a genuine faith without accomplishing Loyalty and Disavowal according to the religious law.[27]

This definition of Islam promotes a new hierarchy of faith. For Jihadists, Muslims performing religious rituals without engaging in Jihad are fake Muslims, not genuine ones. An authentic Muslim has to be unafraid of death, steadfast and confident in his lot as preordained by Allah.

A psychology of Islamic heroism is developed that mainly focuses on death. The attitude toward death distinguishes genuine Muslims from disbelievers, who fear their death:

> Master Mawdudi[28] in his precious book *Principles of Islam* mentions seven consequences of the word *Tawhid* as follows:
>   *Tawhid* encourages man and fills his heart with fortitude. Two things make a man a coward and weaken his will: love of himself, of wealth, and of the kinsfolk or his belief that someone else than Allah kills the man. Faith in "There is no god but Allah" [the first Islamic pillar] uproots from the heart both of these causes. . . .
>   There isn't in the world one more courageous and bolder than he who believes in Allah: he does not hide; he shows steadfastness in the face of marching armies, drawn swords, raining bullets, and bombings. Since he takes the lead in Jihad in the path of Allah, he is determined, and his force is multiplied by ten. Is this the case of Disbelievers and Heretics?

Faith in "There is no god but Allah" elevates the value of man and develops in him pride and contentment; he is happy with little goods, and his heart is clean of greed, voracity, envy, meanness, wickedness, and other ugly features.

The most important thing is that the faith in "There is no god but Allah" makes man responsible to the law of Allah, His protector. A genuine Muslim believes that Allah is aware of everything and is closer to him than his jugular vein and that he is able to vanquish whoever is an oppressor but is not able to vanquish Allah the Almighty.[29]

The prerequisite for Jihadism is this philosophy of heroic fearlessness that the Muslim espouses, leaning exclusively on Allah in his fight against the enemy, having no regard for human frailty, and, above all, rejecting compromise and tolerance. The whole edifice is based on the centrality of death and fearlessness toward it, which is strongly emphasized by contemporary Jihadists.

By "de-centering" the believer's ego, Jihadism makes death at the service of the holy war easier, supporting it through a complex system of religious symbols and references within a renewed psychological framework related to a martyr's state of mind and his willingness to sacrifice himself. In this Manichean vision Islam either dominates or is dominated—no other alternative exists within this mental framework.

Jihadism is triumphalist in its propaganda, but at the root of its approach there is a deep pessimism and the feeling of being dispossessed and estranged from what is the most precious part of the Muslim identity, the Islamic faith. This feeling of estrangement is shared by Fundamentalists, but many Muslims do not subscribe to it, leading their religious life without any major anguish. At a time of deep political and cultural crisis (which is the case within the Muslim world), however, apocalyptic ideologies become more attractive than those without a promise of a deep rupture in the world.

The novelty of the current situation does not escape Qahtani: "The system of life and the actual legal system was the law of Allah and its commandments [during the Islamic history], and the same was true for Jihad against Disbelievers. [Because of that] Islam was expanding in the world. Rejecting Islamic law by negligence [under the pretext that] it is a reactionary attitude and not adjusted to the developments of our time did not happen until Colonialism consolidated its grip on Muslims. They forgot themselves after they forgot Allah."[30] For Jihadists as well as major trends within Muslim Fundamentalists, Islam, in its essence, is about ruling and government. This statement is identical with Khomeini's *Velayat Faqih* (the rule by the Islamic Jurist) and the beliefs of Shi'ite radicals.

Islam is, in this sense, political even before being a set of religious rituals, since it aims at ruling humankind and organizing the world according to its commandments: "The Holy Koran and the Pure Traditions declare through clear texts about the problem of ruling (*hukm*) [Koran, Sura Ma'idah, 44]: Those who do not rule by what Allah has sent [Koran] are Disbelievers."[31] What is new is that Allah's law is to be applied not only in the legal system but also in the political realm. Islam is personal piety and monopoly on the juridical sphere (as in the dominant Islamic tradition), and it is governing and ruling according to the law of Allah. Thus, Islam encompasses the political realm that escaped it throughout most of its history. The word *hukm* is ambivalent: it can be juridical, but it can also be political. Traditional Islam usually settled for the right to mete out judgment in the legal sphere. The legislative sphere did not exist as such, and the executive was usually dominated by "barbaric" rulers who became committed to Islam without giving up their domination based on violence and fear rather than any theological asset. This was accepted by the ulama under the motto that "an unjust government is better than dissension among Muslims (*fitna*) in the absence of any government."

Political Islam gives an exclusive privilege to Jihad. Hassan al Banna (1906–1949), the founder of the Muslim Brotherhood in Egypt, made holy war a major obligation in Islam. He closely associated Jihad and martyrdom, arguing that Allah rewards those who engage in Jihad and punishes those who shun it:

> Jihad is an obligation from Allah on every Muslim and cannot be ignored or evaded. Allah has ascribed great importance to jihad and has made the reward of the martyrs and the fighters in His path a splendid one. Only those who have acted similarly and who have modeled themselves upon the martyrs in their performance of jihad can join the others in this reward. Furthermore, Allah has specifically honored the Mujahideen [those who wage jihad] with certain exceptional qualities, both spiritual and practical, to benefit them in this world and the other. Their pure blood is a symbol of victory in this world and the mark of success and felicity in the world to come. Those who can only find excuses, however, have been warned of extremely dreadful punishments, and Allah has described them with the most unfortunate of names. He has reprimanded them for their cowardice and lack of spirit, and castigated them for their weakness and truancy. In this world, dishonor will befall on them, and in the next a fire from which they shall not escape will engulf

them although they may possess much wealth. The weaknesses of abstention and evasion of jihad are regarded by Allah as one of the major sins, and one of the seven sins that guarantee failure.[32]

So as to pave the way for Jihad, radical Muslims begin by throwing out the multiple meanings the word yields in Islam. One of the major distinctions is based on the Greater Jihad (*jihad akbar*), which is the spiritual fight against one's own penchant for passions and lust that Muslim mystics value much more than the Smaller Jihad (*Jihad asqar*), which is the violent one, or holy war.[33] Abdullah Azzam rejects the former as being false and based on fake sayings of the Prophet: "The sentence 'We have returned from the small Jihad [the combat] to the great jihad [of the soul]' is forged, without [religious] foundation."[34]

The Gnawing Problem of Unity

Democracy in traditional Islamic culture encounters a major stumbling block: the Uniqueness of Allah (*Tawhid*) and the unity within the Islamic community (the Umma), traditionally interpreted as being organically related to each other. Since Allah is unique, the ideal Umma (community of the Islamic believers) should be united politically, culturally, and mentally.[35] Up to now, it has been extremely difficult, even for Reformists, to bypass this major problem within Islamic theology.

Tawhid has been reinterpreted by Jihadists in a militant version in accordance with the principle of "Loyalty and Disavowal," which declares war on every non-Islamic government in the world. For radical Muslims, Allah's uniqueness means that society should be ruled according to it, excluding any diversity in the political field. Allah's singleness means that His community (the Umma) should be "unique" as well, that is, preserving its organic unity and its ideological unanimity as well as its spiritual cohesiveness. The history of Islam is replete with deviant groups and sects that fought each other and refused to recognize the other's legitimacy. The Islamic community, just after the death of the Prophet, was divided into many groups that contested each other's religious legitimacy, among whom Sunnis and Shi'ites are the two major subdivisions. In spite of this real diversity, the obsession of Unity has been deeply entrenched in the Islamic world. The result has been that each group considers the other illegitimate and denounces it, this attitude being reciprocated by the others—for example, Shi'ite versus Sunni, but even among Shi'ite subgroups like Ismailis against Shi'ites and Sunnis.

Religious tolerance has always been fragile in the Muslim world because of this denial of the legitimacy of others' views, mainly induced by the cult of Unity, an ideological theme as well as a deep-rooted notion about the ideal Muslim community that should reproduce Allah's uniqueness through the organic ties of its members. This theological tenet was used by different political factions within the Muslim world to deny legitimacy to their adversaries. Obsession with Unity prevented the recognition and acceptance of diversity as a fact of religious life, unlike in the history of Protestantism, particularly in America. Substantive unity means that any diversity in the understanding of Islam has to be viewed as division and divisiveness. Almost all strands of Islam include differences in grasping the laws of Allah. But this does not lead to mutual tolerance; instead, it creates a protracted intolerance at best. The diversity in Islamic faith has never been conducive to reasoned and institutionalized tolerance, apart from small groups of philosophers and theologians. Anathematization was the result of *de facto* diversity. The Mu'tazilite school intended to promote some tolerance in the ninth century under the Abbasid caliphs but was repressed later on, and, since then, tolerance has not been officially accepted within the Muslim faith. The new reformism, dating back to the late nineteenth century but developing mainly in the twentieth and twenty-first centuries, which calls into question many tenets of religious intolerance, has been systematically denounced by Fundamentalists and Jihadists within a public sphere dominated by conservative religious institutions. Political autocracies in the Muslim world favor intolerance, for fear of a change in the balance of power, that is, a more open public sphere that would question their political supremacy. In this respect, there is an alliance between the conservative Islamic authorities and authoritarian rulers in the Muslim world, the roots of intolerance being not only social but also political in this respect.

Still, in spite of intolerance and aside from the Jihadists, many Muslims do not believe that differences in the interpretation of the faith should lead to the exclusion of deviant Muslims as heretics (*takfir*: Islamic excommunication; literally, treating someone as *kafir*, heretic). In Islamic history, with the exception of the Kharijites in the first Islamic century and some Islamic scholars during the Mongol domination of the thirteenth to fifteenth centuries, Muslims did not declare other Muslims infidels, even if they were sinful. Jihadism has renewed the tradition of exclusion from Islam by declaring disbelievers all those Muslims who do not match their highly restrictive definition of Islam. Contrary to such a view, most Muslims see licentious Muslims as negligent or misled but not infidels—that is, outside the Umma.

Jihadists, like Kharijites in early Islam, see every difference of opinion as divisiveness within the Umma and susceptible to *takfir (declaring infidel)* if publicized. Disunity can be fomented either by non-Muslims (everyone who is not a Muslim is for Jihadists a *kafir*, a heretic) for the sake of weakening Islam or by inauthentic Muslims who are hypocrites (*munafiq*, those who under the guise of Islam hypocritically introduce dissension into the Umma) and who, under the mask of Unity, break the unanimity within the Muslim community.

All those people who reject Islamic radicalism or preach the renewal of the Islamic faith and perception so as to embrace political tolerance (such as Mohammad Arkoun in France and North Africa and Hassan Hanafi in Egypt, among many others) or are in favor of a secular society (the Egyptian Naqib Mahfuz) are thus denounced as *Zindiq* (Manichaeist and, by extension, heretic) and can be put to death according to this radical view. Unity means rejecting any liberal interpretation of Islam. This anti-modern, anti-democratic version of religion leads to endless violence not only against the West, but also against all those Muslims (and they are numerous) who would like to reconcile their faith with the conditions of modern life in open societies or, more modestly, those who are attached to their faith and would spread it to the rest of the world without using violence, just by persuasion, education, publicity, and proselytizing (moderate Fundamentalists).

Nostalgia for lost unity is shared by all societies to different degrees. What distinguishes the Muslim world is the fact that for many believers, to restore Unity in this world in all realms of life (social, political, economic, and cultural) is still within reach in a foreseeable future, by establishing a purified world society that would embrace once more Allah's genuine religion. Islamic Unity is also a utopia for many Jihadists who are anguished by the opening up of Muslim societies to two major facts of modernity: promiscuity of men and women in the public sphere and lack of modesty for women, who take off their veils and question their traditional roles restricted to the family or to menial jobs (in rural or tribal areas). This cultural dimension of Jihadism can be found not only in the Middle East but also in the West, within the tiny Jihadist circles in the Muslim diaspora. Many Islamic radicals in French prisons insist on this aspect. One of them, jailed for his involvement in the plot to blow up the American Embassy in Paris, said, "I feel deeply humiliated by this lively pornography that is the society in the West."[36]

Others said the same about Muslim societies where depravity grows under the influence of Western mores and corrupt governments. Ahsen, an Algerian Jihadist jailed in France, said,

[What is shocking to me is] to begin with, homosexuality. In an interview, a homosexual said: "Do not put an end to homosexuality but use condom!"

Homosexuality should be forbidden [in the Muslim world]. It is an illness. One should find a medicine. One should explain to them that it is a sin, and a mortal sin (*kabira*). In the same way, alcohol [should be forbidden]. The Prophet forbade its consumption. It has to be forbidden, and one should explain to these people that it is bad, not only for Muslims, but also for everyone, without exception. Commandments of Allah are not for a particular group, but for all humanity. Moreover, not only in the West people drink, but it has been extended to the Muslim world. They have degenerated the Muslims who begin to drink for the sake of looking like the Westerners and feel "modern." Our problem is not only that the West does what it wants at home, but that in the Muslim world as well the West does the same as at home. One can say that Muslims have no home anymore. Jihad means conquering anew our home, but also to make so that also in the West they apply the Islamic rule, because the source of the ill is here [in the West], it is here that new forms of depravation are invented. They import them afterwards to the Muslim land. You don't need anymore an army to impose imperialism on Muslims; you make them imitate what are called cultural models, models of Western consumerism. The fight against the evil cannot anymore be restricted to the *dar al islam* [Muslim lands]; hitherto it includes the West. On this plane, Bin Laden is not wrong: it is at the heart of America that one should wage the war to save Islam.[37]

What is noteworthy is the way Ahsen interprets Jihadism: the West is corrupting Muslims within the Islamic world through its depraved mores and culture. The fight against evil cannot be restricted to Muslim lands anymore; it has to be extended to the West to become meaningful. Bin Laden, in this perspective, fights to preserve Muslim lands from the cultural depravation of the West, at least as much for political as for military reasons. Islamic unity is being endangered by a world culture in which homosexuality, consumption of alcohol, and sexual promiscuity are the norm. The Umma cannot preserve its unity unless it wages an all-out war against the West, a total Jihad.

Ahsen mentions as well the way Islamic values are jeopardized by women's emancipation and by importing the Western way of life, the wrongdoing of Jewish conspiracy looming behind all these misdeeds:

What I hate most in the West is particularly their way of life. All of this leads them to self-destruction. They want to create a human being [genetically]. They want to submit their body to deep-freeze [to be regenerated after death]. They want to clone human beings. The result is mad cow disease. They surely pervert Muslims at the same time; they import their lifestyle into the Muslim land. You have also the Jews (*yhudis*). The Jews rule over the world; the Jewish lobby led Mitterand [François Mitterand, president of France from 1981 to 1995]. [Madeleine] Albright, the minister of Clinton [from 1997 to 2001], was a Jew. Jews don't want to follow the Straight Path, "*sirat al mustaqim.*" They saw the miracle of Allah but did not want to submit to it. The solution to all of this is the divine law. You also have women who kindle the desires of men by showing themselves naked. . . . You see, those women who make pornographic movies in the West, who show their sex. All of this is slavery. The woman who shows her body to everyone, that is slavery. Islam is against it. Slavery in Islam is better than freedom in the West.[38]

Most of these criticisms of the West are identical to those made by conservative Christians about modern life, but the major difference is that massive violence through an all-out war is presented as the only credible solution. The Unity of the Umma is in deep danger because of the devilish culture of the West that has contaminated the Muslim world through consumerism and enticement promoted by the Jews. To save the unity of the Umma, Muslims have to declare holy war on the West.

The question of sexuality is at the heart of the malaise of the Umma among Jihadists, as explains Mohammad, another radical Muslim in a French jail:

Here, the modesty (*hojb*) and the sense of sexual honor (*qayra*) do not exist anymore. We are in a rotten world. Immorality cannot be stopped any more: pedophilia, aggressions. They speak of the freedom of women, but everywhere you see their buttocks displayed. They don't tolerate the veil, even a simple scarf, but women are encouraged to be in the buff; the TV shows all day long almost naked women and girls hugging men. It is exhibitionism, an illness: Why should one kiss in public when it can be done at home? Why do women wear high heels and miniskirts that excite men and push them to rape and violence against them? Modesty seems not to exist here. People talk about chastity as if it belonged to the past. Our *ird* [sense of honor preserved by the chastity of

women and their exclusive sexual relations with their husbands]
has something good: it protects women and preserves their chastity and prevents men from raping them. Here [in the West], you
have the permanent sexual excitement, you feel the desire to go
to bed with all the women you meet, and you are pushed toward
zina [illegitimate sexual intercourse with a woman to whom one
is not married]. . . . The drama is that even in the Muslim world,
under the influence of the West, people begin to act like here. By
choosing the Western way of life, Muslims are helping the heretics
(*kuffar*). . . . Family is sacred. They destroy it here [in the West].
And in the Muslim world, they follow the West. Family, morality,
chastity, and relations between men and women, all these have
been put into question.[39]

Most of the studies on Jihadism underestimate the cultural factors.
A major component of Jihadists' total war against the West is their
feelings of insecurity related to the endangering of the Umma and its
major principle, called Unity in Jihadist and Fundamentalist jargon,
which results from the influence of the Western way of life.

Historically speaking, the obsessive urge for Unity is related to
the fact that Muslim societies were, from the beginning, "covered
societies" based on the segregation of men and women and the
covering up of women.[40] Many other civilizations shared the same
characteristics. The peculiar nature of Islam is that this identity has
been associated with specific important social actors for whom these
characteristics define the essence of the "Islamic way of life," namely
the religious authorities, the conservative merchant groups, and, above
all, the authoritarian governments that find it easier to compromise
with conservatives on issues of mores and customs than to reform and
open up the political and cultural system.

Shi'ites as Fake Muslims

From the Jihadists' point of view, Shi'ites sow discord among Muslims, break up the Unity of the Islamic community, and should be
rejected—and the most radical ones, even put to death.

According to Bashar, a minor Jihadist intellectual, Allah's religion
is based on His uniqueness and the unity of His community (the
Umma). Unity excludes division.[41] Shi'ites sow divisiveness in the
Umma. Among the causes of the downfall of the Muslims he enumerates: "Division and dissidence among them and their friendliness
toward hypocrites [*munafiq*, Shi'ites among others] and Heretics and
not rejecting them. This caused the failure of the Abbasid [dynasty]

against the Tatars, due to the treason of a Shi'ite (*rafidhi*) minister.[42] The demons as hypocrites infiltrated the ranks of the Muslims, and the latter were unable to distinguish them from genuine Muslims."[43] Shi'ites, in this sense, are the icons of divisiveness and dissension. According to most of the Jihadists, they are a bane to the Muslim community. Abu Mus'ab al Zarqawi, a second-rate intellectual but a major Jihadist fighter in Iraq (he was killed in 2006 by American forces), characterizes Shi'ism as follows:

> Shi'ism is an imminent plague and a real challenge. Shi'ism is a religion that has nothing to do with Islam more than Christians and Jews under the name of the "People of the Book." . . . It is a proven idolatry: worship of the tombs (of their Imams) and the rite of walking around them, the fact of considering the companions of the Prophet as impious [the first three caliphs are considered as usurpers of Ali's caliphate by Shi'ites], insulting the wives of the Prophet [mainly Aïcha, because of her dispute with Ali, the first Shi'ite Imam] and the best Muslims [Omar, the second caliph, is considered impious by Shi'ites], modifying the letter of the Koran as a logical system in order to sow doubts about the works of those who know it [some Shi'ites believe that the original Koran was modified by Sunnis], their affirmation of the faultless nature of the Imams [Shi'ites believe that the Imams, descendants of the Prophet's family, received divine revelation and could not sin, were infallible]. . . . Shi'ites cannot forget the historical rancor against the "Nawasib" [the Sunnis, as they are named pejoratively by some Shi'ites]. . . . In the history of Islam, Shi'ites built up a deceptive and treacherous sect.[44]

In al Zarqawi's view, Shi'ites, who make up around 10 percent of the Muslim community worldwide, and all the others are fake believers. Muslims should fight them and put them to death. Thus Unity becomes deeply repressive, not only anti-democratic but also totalitarian.

Islamic tradition rejects many theological viewpoints to disqualify those suspected of deviant religious behavior. These notions are revisited and readapted by Jihadists to combat secularists and Reformist Muslims or simply those opposed to Jihadism. One major viewpoint was held by the Zindiq, or Dualists, whose origin goes back to the Persian religion of light and darkness (Manichaeism). Infidels, new Muslims, and secularists have been characterized as Zindiq in this way by other Muslims: "Zindiq were related to the Persian people who tried to overthrow the Umayyad dynasty and give power to the Abbasid. Persians and affluent people were involved with the Zindiq. The second-century H. [Hegira—the beginning of the Islamic calendar is the year of the migration of the Prophet from Mecca to Medina in 622] was a time of depravity and corruption in Islam, and Zindiq and communists (*sho'ubiyah*) thrived at that time. They had poets and literary men. . . . New Zindiq [of our time] are Taha Husein [1889–1973, the famous Egyptian secular writer], Naqib Mahfuz [1911–2006, secular Egyptian Nobel literature laureate], Mohammad Arkoun [b. 1928, Algerian philosopher, professor at Sorbonne in Paris, critic of the Islamic traditionalism], Adonis [b. 1930, Syrian poet of world renown], and Hasan Hanafi [b. 1935, Egyptian philosopher, working on the reform of Islam]."[45]

For Jihadists, Shi'ism plays a major role in the decay of Islam. Some Fundamentalist Sunni and Shi'ite intellectuals and ulama (like Qaradhaoui on the side of the Sunnis, Khomeini on the Shi'ite side) try to bridge the gap between the two major branches of Islam. Unlike them, Sunni Jihadists as a rule are hostile to Shi'ites. Some just denounce them; others believe that they are worse than godless people because they harm Allah's religion under the guise of Islam. For Bashar, the Shi'ites brought Islam to its knees: "Muslims lost the wars in Syria in the fourth century of Hegira because they were governed by Shi'ites [*rafidhun*, a derogatory word for Shi'ites]."

The "treacherous" nature of the Shi'ites is extensively narrated by Jihadist intellectuals like Sheikh Abu Hamza, who recounts their treason from the first centuries of Islam up to their present betrayal in Iraq, in connivance with American imperialists:

> We grasp therefore the greed of the Rafidhah, these apostates [who played a major role] in the overthrowing of the Abbasid Empire and the profanation of the Muslim land (*dar al islam*) and Baghdad, the capital of Islam. Sar ibn al Alqami was the spy of Tatars[46] against the Islamic government and the caliphate of Muslims. The history of Rafidhah is abashed by the repetition [of the same treason] up to now, when the community of Rafidhah and their supporters conspire with American Disbelievers worldwide. They appear to the Sunni people as the major threat to the existence of the Muslims. Between them and us there is no other solution than an incisive war. We also understand the reality of the contemporary apostate governments that adopt the apocryphal religion of democracy in order to put in jail and kill the propagators of truth and Jihad.[47]

For Abu Qatada, Shi'ites are heretical people; they are not Muslims. He quotes the famous medieval Islamic jurist Ibn Taymiyah (1263–1328):

> Shi'ites can be categorized in three groups:
> 1. Those whose wrongdoing is the worst: they grant Ali [the fourth caliph and the first Shi'ite imam] a godly nature or attribute to him the status of the Prophet, and this is disbelief for all the Muslims who know Islam. Their disbelief is of the kind of the Jews or the Christians in that respect, and they resemble the Jews in the last matter.
> 2. The second degree: they are the well-known Rafidhah, the Imamite, and the like. They believe that after the Prophet, Ali is the highest according to the public or hidden text and that his right was wronged, and they hate Abu Bakr and Omar [the first and second caliphs after the Prophet], and they insult them.
> 3. The third degree: the Yazidi and the like who prefer Ali to Abu Bakr and Omar but believe in the latter's spiritual direction and their justice, still turning away from them. This is wrong but only among some groups of Islamic jurists (*fiqh*) and devout. They are closer to the Sunnis than to the Rafidhah [Shi'ites of the second type].[48]

According to Abu Qatada, one of the major causes of the Muslims' past defeat by Christians is the political domination by the Shi'ites, these heretics in the guise of Muslims: "Deviation in faith is historically substantiated through the advent of the Shi'ite governments (*râfidhiya*) in the east of Saudi Arabia, Bahrain, Persia, Iraq, Syria, and the Ismailis in Egypt. . . . Only a small part of the Muslim lands escaped the Shi'ites (*rafidhi*). With the appearance of these heretic [Shi'ite] governments, Christians began to conquer some of the countries of the Muslims and committed innumerable crimes."[49] Shi'ites, according to Jihadists, broke the Unity of the Muslim community (Umma) and, through internal dissension, weakened it, becoming thus the root cause of Western domination of Islam. Shi'ism is a treacherous, fake religion whose intent and purpose is to destroy Allah's religion from within, according to the Jihadists and some Sunni Fundamentalists. The historical depth of this phenomenon and the reciprocal hatred between Shi'ites and Sunnis partially explain the merciless fight of some of the most radical Sunni groups in Iraq. But this mutual distrust, except for critical times, did not end up in systematic reciprocal killings. Today, in addition to ideology one finds political and economic causes that inflame passions in Iraq and result in massive killings on both sides.

MARTYRDOM AND JIHAD

The major difference between Jihadists and many other terrorists is that the latter intend to act violently against others without being killed themselves, whereas large parts of Jihadists engage in violence against their enemies and are willing (and, in many cases, desire) to die themselves in the course of action.[50]

Martyrdom in monotheism has a long history. In the Bible, Samson can be identified as the first martyr to have accepted death by shaking the pillars of the Philistines' temple. Again, in 66, at the beginning of the First Jewish-Roman War against the Roman Empire, a group of Jews called the Sicarii took Masada from the Roman garrison. They committed mass suicide when besieged by the Romans. In the Roman Empire, many Christians chose death to testify to the legitimacy of their religion.[51] They accepted death without killing their enemies, unlike Muslims, who, right from the beginning, defined martyrdom as dying in the path of Allah by actively fighting the enemy in order to neutralize it. The death of the Christian occurred while he shunned acting violently against the adversary, whereas the death of the Muslim as a martyr would be the unintended consequence of his fight against the infidels, his intent being to neutralize and, if necessary, maim or kill them.

The history of Muslim martyrdom and sacred death is related to the origins of Islam. Its history is replete with battles and wars, first within the Arabian Peninsula during the lifetime of the Prophet and then under the four Well-Guided (caliphs), who conquered the Persian Empire and parts of the Christian world. From the beginning, the "ability to die" was closely associated with genuine faith. Khaled bin Walid, the Arab general who conquered Persia and the Roman Syria in three years (633–636), wrote to the chief of the town of Hira: "Accept our religion, or pay a tribute [tax paid by non-Muslims to Muslims, *jiziyah*] or prepare for war. Because the men who are with me like war and death as much as you like pleasures and life."[52]

The subjective dimension of a readiness to die for the sake of Allah is deeply inscribed in the history of Islam, beginning with its origins. But this concept was taken at its face value only in the first generations of Muslims. After the establishment of the Muslim empire, Jihad became a remote ideal, and the new generations distanced themselves from it, with the exception of the Mongol era and the nineteenth-century reaction against Western colonialism. The renewal of martyrdom with the Islamic Revolution of 1979 in Iran and then its extension to the Palestinians and Lebanese marked a new era: the transnational Jihadists took it over in intensity and breadth never heard of before. The original Muslims, unlike suicide bombers, never thought of killing themselves but accepted being killed by enemies as a risk inherent in war. They cared for women, children, elderly people, and noncombatants, whereas the new Jihadists usually do not take them into account as they fight against "the enemy," which encompasses the entire society and at times almost the whole world.

The internal division in Islam between Sunnis and Shi'ites made the fate of Jihad different in each case. Sunnis, as the majority and the dominant elite, put martyrdom at the service of Jihad, whereas Shi'ites, as a persecuted minority (they were generally considered heretics by ruling Sunni elites), developed an attitude toward martyrdom that was dissociated from Jihad in many respects. They developed a grief-stricken attitude toward life and a religious attitude based on fatalism and pessimism, including in the pantheon of their imams those who were, according to the believers, mostly martyred by Sunni rulers. Besides short periods of turmoil, in the history of Islam, Shi'ites were basically quietists, believing that only at the end-time, with the advent of the "Hidden Imam" (the Shi'ite Messiah), would it be possible to wage Jihad. In contrast, Sunnis directly connected Jihad and martyrdom: one becomes a martyr when taking part in Jihad, dying at the hands of the enemy. This dichotomy did not resist the modernization of Muslims. During the 1979 Islamic Revolution in Iran, Jihadist ideology in connection to martyrdom was renewed as the last resort in the fight against the heretical government of Saddam Hussein, during the long war with Iraq (1980–1988). Ayatollah Khomeini never issued any fatwa (religious order) to wage Jihad against Saddam Hussein's army, but on the streets of Iran the masses chanted, "Beware [of the day] when Khomeini orders me to wage Jihad!" The modernization of Shi'ism has wiped out the traditional attitude of quietism within its dominant strands.

Martyrdom Departs from Jihad: The Death Show

Among Shi'ite ideologues, Shariati plays a paramount role in suffusing martyrdom with a revolutionary content. He distinguishes two types of martyrdom. The first is the model of Hamzah, the uncle of the Prophet, who died as a martyr against the disbelievers at the battle of Uhud in 625. This type of martyr dies in the battlefield to combat the enemies of Islam, aiming to achieve victory over them.

The second type of martyrdom is based on the paradigm of Imam Hussein, the third Shi'ite imam, who was killed by the army of the Umayyad caliph Yazid in 680 in Iraq: "Hamzah who was killed in the battle of Uhud received the title of the Prince of Martyrs (*seyyed ol shuhada*), but Shi'ism, after the day of Ashura [the day of the killing of Hussein] awarded this title to Hussein. . . . Both are members of the Prophet's family who attained martyrdom: Hamzah in the battlefield of Jihad, Hussein among the martyrs of martyrdom."[53]

In comparison, Hussein is far superior to Hamzah:

> Hamzah is a hero; he is a Mujaheed [he who wages Jihad] who engaged to defeat the enemy. He failed and died as a martyr. But he is an individual martyr. . . . Hussein is of another type. He didn't come to overcome the enemy by sword for the sake of achieving victory. . . . Although he could have stayed quietly at home and remained alive, he rose up and went to encounter death in total lucidity. At that time he chose death and annihilation, and he bore the danger before the eyes of the entire world. . . . Hamzah and the others came to achieve victory at the risk of dying, their aim being to vanquish the enemy. But the martyrdom of Hussein aimed at self-denial in a sacred path that was under the threat of perdition. Here, the holy war (*jihad*) and martyrdom get separated completely.[54]

The major difference between Hamzah and Hussein was that the first did not want to die but looked to defeat the enemy, whereas Hussein knew perfectly well that he was going to be defeated and killed in an unequal battle where the tragic issue of his death was a foregone conclusion. Shariati imparts this conscious death a religious meaning far superior to the first case. Here death is a premeditated one, more lucid because the chance of victory is totally absent. For Shariati, "the philosophy of the revolt of the Mujaheed is not identical to that of the martyr [of the second type]. . . . Martyrdom in the strict sense of the word is a religious duty after [the setback of] Jihad, and the martyr enters the scene when the Mujaheed has failed [to achieve victory over the enemies of Islam]."[55]

Shariati makes two major innovations: the first is the description of a desperate, death-centered martyrdom. The martyr does not die without his foreknowledge, just through the hazards of the battle. He has prepared himself for death; even more, he aspires to die, having broken off his ties with this worldly life. Through his sacred death he intends to spread his message worldwide. In this respect he is different from the Islamic mystics like Hallaj, who did everything to be put to death by the authorities in 922 just to display his love of Allah and prove his sincerity to himself, without any explicit social motive. The social martyr described by Shariati knows full well that he won't achieve victory in the battle, contrary to the Sunni martyr (who believes he might win the war). The Shi'ite martyr dies defeated in the battle with his fully conscious desire to do so, in a defeat that is fully accepted for the sake of testimony to a sacred cause, in spite of his incapacity to win over a much more powerful enemy in a hopeless battle.

Shariati's second major novelty is that the martyr refers to the world stage; he speaks to the world conceived as scenery surrounding him as he plays a tragic role, that of a messenger who makes his own death part of a cosmic show. Shariati only allusively (though unmistakably) suggests the "theatrical" dimension of this type of martyrdom. Martyrdom is not a singular deed; it is the self-conscious death of someone who is watched in a spectacular way by the entire world. In this respect, the martyr is the "heart of history," says Shariati. For many desperate young men in Muslim societies, the feeling of playing a central role on the world stage is at the heart of their martyrdom: not to achieve Jihad (it has failed; it is impossible to win against a much more powerful Western enemy), not to promote a cause positively (the world's domination is too crushing), but to become famous, the central figure in a universal drama unfolding in the world, which is the stage of a cosmic theater, centered around the media. The only thing that remains is to put on the show of one's death and to display with it the message of death as a heroic act that is self-sufficient in a noble yet exhibitionist way. The desperate message conveyed to the world is mere, pure heroism cautioned by a sacred cause that becomes meaningful only if accomplished through death as a tragic spectacle.

Death in this way becomes transitive, administered to the other or the self, succumbing to it one way or another. This annihilation becomes sacred in a theatrical fashion, before the eyes of the media; thus the martyr becomes a glamorous star for a short span of time on the world stage. The precariousness of fame in this world is offset by its eternity in the afterlife, within the gaze of Allah, His angels, and the beautiful virgin women, the Houris, welcoming the martyr at the gates of paradise. The transitive nature of death finds its apogee in a death-fascinated religious feeling that is closer to Shi'ism but becomes a source of inspiration for many young Sunni men within Jihadist movements, who believe that life is meaningless unless crowned by a glorious death, exhibited worldwide by the globalized media. The image of the world as an immense stage, where the starring role is given to those who are unimportant but once they embrace martyrdom become famous here and joyful in the hereafter, is part of a new vision that motivates many young Muslims, devoid of any hope in this world. Mostly jobless or having menial jobs or at best from the lower middle classes, without any vocation and filled with resentment toward the world as their major enemy, they fulfill both wishes: to die as "somebody" in this world and become part of the elite in the next, close to Allah in the gardens of paradise, where they are surrounded by lush nature and innumerable eternal beauties, the Houris. Among these potential martyrs, even those who belong to higher social groups are beset by resentment and a deep sentiment of injustice. The more modernized they are, the less satisfied they become with their lot in their daily life within a Muslim world where the political and cultural scene is often deadlocked.

Shariati, Khomeini, and Sunni Jihadists have instinctively understood a major fact of late modernity: the world is unified as an immense platform, and they occupy, for some time, center stage, leaving a message addressed to humankind through the media, who display them for the spectators even if they oppose the Jihadist mission. For modernized young Muslims living in an inhospitable world, dying before the cameras becomes a sacred and yet voyeuristic feat. Through their martyrdom they represent the entire Umma. A violent and sacred death is a vocation that provides solace as the modernized yet disaffected youth becomes the self-appointed representative of the entire Muslim community. A new global vision is at work, and it is dependent on the world media for its identity.

In the past, the Islamic world and non-Islamic societies (Christian and Chinese among others) were largely autonomous of each other, even ignored each other, aside from war and commercial interaction. Modernization has significantly changed the situation. The polarization of the world makes the enticements of the West much more available to the new generations of Muslims, and at the same time, the feeling of this affluence being out of reach is even more painful to them. Repression at home is attributed to the West, mainly through the popularization of leftist ideologies and the shortsighted policies of the United States toward the Muslim world. Too close in terms of shared dreams of modernity (consumerism, political participation, and willingness to endorse the dignity of the individual) and too far in terms of daily life (political repression, economic stalemate if not regression, permanent burdens left by a discredited tradition), the contradiction is solved through death as participation on a worldwide stage. Thus the domination of the West is symbolically inverted through recourse to death and killing.

The Delight of Martyrdom

In the Koran, many verses mention Jihad as "dying in the way of Allah" and encourage Muslims to choose this path for the sake of Islam:

"And if you are killed or die in the Way of Allah, forgiveness and mercy from Allah are far better than all that they amass [of worldly wealth etc.]. And whether you die, or are killed, verily, unto Allah you shall be gathered" (Sura al-Imran, verses 156–58).

The most common expression for martyrdom in the Koran is "dying in the path of Allah," with some variations. "Fighting" is implied in martyrdom: "Let those [believers] who sell the life of this world for the Hereafter fight in the cause of Allah, and whosoever fights in the cause of Allah, and is killed or is victorious, We shall bestow on him a great reward" (Sura the Women 4, verse 74). Being killed by the enemy on the battle field or killing him is rewarded by Allah: "Verily, Allah has purchased of the believers their lives and their wealth; for the price that theirs shall be Paradise. They fight in Allah's Cause, so they kill [others] and are killed. It is a promise in truth that is binding on Him in the Torah and the Gospel and the Koran. And who is truer to his covenant than Allah? Then rejoice in the bargain that you have concluded. That is the supreme success" (Sura the Repentance, verse 111). In Christianity the word "martyr" (*shahid* in Islam), of Greek origin, means testimony and dying in the path of God. Muslims may have borrowed it during the Crusades, preserving both meanings, testimony and dying in the path of Allah in Arabic (*shahid*). Scholars point to the fact that the word *shahid* in the Koran in most cases does not mean martyrdom but simply testimony, the usual word for martyr meaning "those who kill and die in the path of Allah."[56]

Jihadists ask for abnegation and readiness to die as a duty for the Muslim, one that is greatly rewarded by Allah, who elevates martyrdom to the highest rank. Azzam writes, "In a genuine Saying of the Prophet reported by Ahmad and Tirmidhi, the Prophet said: these are the seven favors awarded to the martyr: his sins are forgiven right from the moment his first drop of blood is spilled, he sees his place in paradise, he is dressed in the outfit of faith, he marries 62 Houris, he does not submit to the torments of the tomb, he is not submitted to the great terror, he is crowned a scepter of dignity in precious stones worthier than the world and its troves and he can intercede for 60 persons of his families."[57] Martyrdom as such is central to Shi'ites and its cult of the family of the Prophet, whose descendants, according to them, were mostly martyred by Sunni rulers. In the Sunni world martyrdom never wore the symbolic significance it has in Shi'ism. A few major martyrs existed at the dawn of Islam, like the Ethiopian slave Bilal, who was tortured by Meccans for his conversion to Islam but did not die; a slave woman named Sumaya bint Khayyat who was killed; and Hamza, the uncle of the Prophet, who was killed in the battle of Uhud in 625.

Jihadists aim to revive martyrdom in order to encourage people to choose its path and accept the holy death not only as their fate but as an ideal to which every Muslim should aspire, referring to martyrs as "lofty representatives." For Shi'ites and Sunnis alike, martyrs don't actually die; they live and benefit from many aspects of divine bounty, according to the tradition. As Azzam writes, "Ibn Chumayl says: 'The martyr means the living; they are called in this way because they remain alive, close to their Lord. . . . It is said: there is a witness to his death, namely his blood, because he'll resurrect and his blood will spurt. . . . It is said: his soul will see the paradise whereas the others don't see it until the Day of Judgment. . . . The four schools [in Sunnism] agree that the martyr should not be washed. . . . One should not make the mortuary prayers for the martyr because he is alive. . . . The martyr intercedes for 60 members of his family.'"[58]

The imaginary dialogue of a martyr with a pious Muslim who would like to choose the path of Jihad, written by a woman who claims to belong to Jihadist circles and reproduced in one of the Jihadist sites in French, is useful for understanding the underlying feelings and beliefs among would-be martyrs. The story is intended for a European audience, especially the young French Muslims who form the most numerous Islamic community in Europe (around five million), to spur them toward Jihad. Many traditional aspects of martyrdom are integrated into the text, to inform and also to lure Muslims who ignore these traditional dimensions of martyrdom. The dialogue serves as a vivid encyclopedia of martyrdom as well as an initiation into it. All the enticements are there to encourage young Muslims in French-speaking Europe (France, Belgium, Switzerland, as well as North Africa) to join Jihadist circles and to accept death for the sake of holy war. In the following excerpt the questioner is a pious Muslim considering Jihad, and the answering voice is the martyr:[59]

> Question: How are you, my brother?
> Answer: The pious go to paradise, in the gardens with rivers, among the best of humans. We are alive and well cared for.
> Q: And how was the passing to death? Because the worst thing I fear is the moment of transition from this life to the other.
> A: Like a sleeper who wakes up!
> Q: By Allah! Don't you feel the pains caused by the wounds of war? And what about the death throes just before the death?
> A: Not at all: not more than the sting of an insect on one of us.

Q: How do you endure the ordeals of the tomb? Have you been interrogated [by the angel of death who makes human beings suffer]?

A: Haven't you read the Saying of the Prophet: the reflection of the wound caused on top of his head will be his evidence [of piety]. What ordeals are you talking about, what interrogation, what balms [for the wounds]? No, there is nothing of that kind [for us martyrs].

Q: How happy you seem to be! For Allah's sake, after your departure [martyrdom] we are living a life of pain and malaise!

A: Do not despair of Allah's mercy because He is the most gracious among the gracious!

Q: Allah protects you from despair but here [in this world] Hypocrites [the fake Muslims] are more and more numerous as well as those who are discouraged. This is frustrating! On top of it, there is little means of assistance [to Jihadist Muslims]. . . .

A: Ah! If you knew all the marks of honor and prestige that martyrs receive at the moment of their martyrdom! The demonstration of the angels who are there to greet them, the Houris, these women of paradise, who announce them the good news! The martyr catches sight of the palaces that are waiting for him. I cannot describe you the great joy and the tremendous bliss of the martyr.

Q: What is your opinion about us?

A: Poor you! You are exposed to trials, temptations, pains, illnesses, humiliations, frustrations, and none of you knows what his end will be like.

Q: Do you know a way for Allah to grant me martyrdom?

A: Wage the Jihad in the path of Allah. Because the Jihad is a market opened by Him to those who accept the deal, until the Day of Judgment.

Q: But will Allah choose me [for martyrdom]?

A: Show him your merchandise [readiness to die for Him]. Have good thoughts about Him, and you won't be disappointed, if Allah is willing (*incha'allah*), because Allah is the most generous of all.

Q: How should I embellish my merchandise so that Allah accepts it?

A: By being sincere and disinterested. By being persevering and patient with your grief.

Q: Show me something that would help me toward this goal.
A: Lighten your burden; do not hang too much to this life or to the residents, particularly the family. Think a lot about Paradise and all that Allah has prepared for those who take the path of Jihad (*Mujahideen*): palaces, rivers, Houris. They will live there in peace

and security, close to the Most Generous among the generous. And remember Hell as well, by asking Allah to spare you. . . . Make your prayers of the night [a noncompulsory prayer that increases one's merits in the other world], because the prayers are the provisions of the people who take the path of Jihad.

Q: More!

A: The Jihad, the Jihad. Because those who take up this road (*Mujahideen*) are really men and heroes of all times and places.

Q: To what group should I adhere?

A: To the Mujahideen [those who take up the path of Jihad], the Mujahideen.

All the enticements are drawn together to push the European youth to Jihad, leading to martyrdom. To begin with, there is no tribulation for the martyr to pass from the state of life to that of death. In traditional Islam, the first night in the tomb is the most dreadful: the asking of questions by the angel of death entails the anguish of those who do not know whether they will spend the time between their death and the Day of Reckoning in a *Barsakh* (the equivalent of Christian purgatory) and its aftermath. Even the wounds inflicted by the enemy that result in death are described as being painless for the martyrs, like the "sting of an insect." Injuries are a passport to Heaven. The pious Muslim who holds a dialogue with the martyr envies his position near to Allah and asks how to attain it. The martyr describes his situation after death as so enviable as to be able to die another time without any remorse, were he to come back to life. The life after martyrdom with its joys and blessings is opposed to the miserable stay in this world with all its pains and frustrations: unending abundance and wealth, material and spiritual, opposed to the meanness of this worldly existence. To attain ultimate happiness, one has to cut off one's ties with earthly life and accept death for Jihad. This is the last recommendation of the martyr to the pious Muslim who is irresolute to make his way toward martyrdom.

Controversy around the Suicide Bombers

Suicide bombers have the approval of many radical ulama, who call them martyrs. One of these supportive ulama is Maqdisi, who from his prison in Jordan exchanged letters with one of his disciples over the legitimacy of suicide bombing according to Islam.[60] Maqdisi rejects the fatwa (religious recommendation) by the official Saudi religious authority (*mufti*), which dismissed suicide bombers as martyrs. He instead believes that the bombings are heroic acts, far from suicide in their intention. They bring solace to the hearts of Muslims. Since they act in the path of Allah in their intentions, suicide bombers qualify as martyrs. Maqdisi analyzes the notion of "shield" (*tars*), dating back to the times of Ibn Taymiyah (1263–1328), one of the major references in these matters: if other Muslims are used as shields by the heretics (as the Mongols in the thirteenth century did in their battles against Muslim rulers, the Westerners in modern times) so as to prevent Muslims from waging Jihad, the killings are authorized, and the fighters strive to minimize their casualties.[61] In the same way, if the people engaged in martyrdom operations (suicide bombers) unintentionally kill other Muslims, they have no choice, and if their operations were not performed, any fight against the invaders (Israelis occupying Palestine, for instance) would become impossible. He summarizes: "The heroic Jihad operations [another word for suicide bombers, avoiding the word "suicide"] are admitted under the conditions already mentioned [reducing to the minimum the number of casualties among Muslims and innocent people]. They terrify the enemies of Allah and occasion damages to them. The combatant in Jihad (*mujahidun*) needs these operations for fear that Jihad will be stopped, particularly under the conditions of peace and the decisions of the United Nations of Heretics that compel the end of fighting, make Jihad a criminal offense, prohibit terrorism and stipulate the cooperation of security organizations and conspiracy between all the governments against Jihad and combatants of Jihad."[62]

Many traditional theologians oppose suicide bombings as either un-Islamic or simply reprehensible. Even some Jihadist thinkers denounce this type of death as not being martyrdom but a disguised suicide and therefore forbidden by Allah and, even more, a major sin. The reasons put forward are the following:

- By killing oneself before killing the others, the bomber commits suicide, a mortal sin according to Islam. Only Allah can take one's life. By acting in this way, the suicide bomber usurps the place of Allah.
- By killing in an indiscriminate way innocent people, including women, the elderly, and children, the suicide bomber goes beyond what is allowed by the Koran and the Tradition of the Prophet (*Sunna*), which stipulate saving the lives of noncombatants.
- Among the victims there might be some Muslims, and Allah formally forbids killing of the latter through the verses of the Koran and the Sayings of the Prophet.

A major Jihadist thinker, Tartusi, rejects suicide bombing on the following basis:

> These operations are closer to suicide than to seeking martyrdom from my point of view and therefore, they are forbidden by religion (*haram*). They are not allowed for the following reasons: . . .
>
> The most important one is that they mean necessarily the killing of the person himself by himself, and this is against many religious solid texts in their arguments and proofs that declare it religiously forbidden for men to kill themselves by themselves whatever the causes inducing this act.
>
> Allah says: "O you who believe . . . do not kill yourselves. . . . And whoever commits that through aggression and injustice, We shall cast him into Fire, and that is easy for Allah" (Sura The Women, verses 29–30).
>
> Again, Allah says: "And spend in the Cause of Allah and do not throw yourselves into destruction, and do well" (Sura The Cow, verse 195).[63]

Tartusi quotes many Sayings of the Prophet in a classic argument used by Islamic ulama, condemning "the killing of oneself by oneself." Among these Sayings, according to Abul-Hussain 'Asakiruddin Muslim, a very important ninth-century compiler of the Sayings of the Prophet, is this one: "The Prophet says: he who kills himself for some reason in this world will endure the sufferings [of Hell] the Day of Judgment." He quotes some other Sayings stating the same punishments. Tartusi enumerates the reasons put forward by suicide bombers in their fight against the enemy. He rejects them as being irrelevant to the "killing of oneself by oneself." To condemn the killing of innocent Muslims through these operations, he quotes again many Sayings of the Prophet: "It is forbidden to the Muslim to shed the blood of another Muslim, to take hold of his goods and attack his sexual honor." He quotes another saying of the Prophet: "Killing a Muslim is toward Allah worse than the annihilation of the entire world!" Again, according to the Prophet: "Allah does not accept the repentance of someone who has killed a Muslim."

Concerning the killing of innocent Christians or Jews (the People of the Book), he quotes the Prophet: "Someone who kills the People of the Dhimma [those Christians or Jews who pay Islamic taxes to the Muslims or participate in a peace treaty with them] will not smell the scent of paradise, and its scent will be far from his way for seventy years [of travel]!" Again: "He who kills someone that is in peace within a treaty in a non-authorized manner, Allah forbids him Paradise, and he won't smell its scent."

Tartusi firmly believes that these Sayings do not allow suicide bombings under any circumstances. He further analyzes suicide bombings and finds fault with them not only on religious grounds but also from a military and strategic standpoint: the actor of Jihad reduces all his chances to a single combat without any opportunity left for a second. This type of operation puts an end to the lives of many young people who could fight for the cause of Jihad in the future. This attitude endangers the life, safety, and security of Jihadist people and is not acceptable from his point of view. The arguments of Tartusi against suicide bombings also have a moral component: among those killed there might be Muslims or Christians and Jews who are protected by Islam. He does not reject violent Jihad, but he condemns this specific type of violence that transgresses Islamic law.

Abu Qatada makes many restrictions on suicide bombings. In his article he analyzes the reasons why Islam forbids suicide.[64] The fact that one is exposed to tribulations and even physical pain does not justify putting an end to one's life because, according to the Sayings of the Prophet, Allah will not pardon suicide, and those who commit it will be sent to Hell. Allah, he claims, is putting pious Muslims to the test, and their pains in this world redeem them in the other. Some afflictions, he believes, are also due to the fact that people do not behave in a righteous way and Allah punishes them. But whatever the causes of the distress or pain, nobody is allowed to take his own life. He thinks that suicide is mainly founded on impatience: instead of endurance, people become impatient, and out of lack of forbearance they put an end to their lives. Impatience itself is the lack of confidence in Allah and a weakness in faith.

When it comes to operations against the enemies of Islam that might result in one's death, Abu Qatada quotes authorized sources (Muslim, Ibn Taymiyah) who distinguish many cases, among them that which involves one's death as beneficial to the cause of the Muslims, which is therefore authorized. If the Muslim wishes to engage in a military operation for personal reasons, for instance out of boldness, knowing full well that he will be killed, he is not allowed to act in this way. Self-glorification is rejected, and only the interests of the Muslims as an Umma can authorize martyrdom.

Abu Qatada devotes a long chapter to the contemporary situation. The major difference with the past is that modern suicide bombers bear explosives that kill themselves and the others at the same time.

It is not the enemy who kills them but they themselves, and this is a feature that distinguishes them from martyrs in the past. Is one allowed to kill oneself for the sake of killing or weakening the enemy? If one is killed at the hand of the enemy, this is equated with martyrdom by the Islamic commandments. A new factor is added by the new technologies that allow the actor to blow himself up, causing the deaths of those who surround him. Abu Qatada rejects this type of martyrdom because it is self-murder and Islam, he contends, forbids suicide. That is why, concludes Abu Qatada, Jihadists should not practice this type of operation. And what if Jihadists engage in a fight against the enemy and kill some Muslims? Here Abu Qatada puts forward Ibn Taymiyah's argument of the "shield," as already mentioned, which authorizes the killing of other Muslims in case of emergency.

As for the killing of innocent people in suicide bombings, it is justified by many Jihadists in two distinct ways. The first is that the intent of the Muslim who kills them is not to do so, but it is the unfortunate result of the war, in the same fashion as the matter is justified in the West as "collateral damage." The second, more radical point of view is that these innocent people are in many cases indirectly taking part in the war against Muslims. Women in Israel are enrolled in the army in the same way as the reservists; in the West, normal citizens vote for the rulers; therefore, the war against Muslims is waged with their tacit or explicit approval. Therefore, they are not innocent victims but soldiers, and their deaths are legitimate in Jihad. In this respect, democracy in the West is taken into account as a major variable, since citizens are accomplices of governments for which they have voted, and therefore the fight against the latter is the same as against the former. Another argument justifying the killing of nonsoldiers in suicide attacks consists in "quantifying" the dead and wounded. Compared to the massacres by Americans, Russians, and Israelis in Muslim lands, where they kill thousands of innocent people, the number of victims of suicide bombings is insignificant. In this case, the reciprocity argument, rather than a theological one, is put forward. At any rate, the arguments advanced by many Jihadists vindicate suicide bombing as martyrdom within Islam.

More generally, Jihadist intellectuals, like many leftists in the 1970s, do not necessarily agree with each other on major themes. They have a family resemblance among themselves and share many major ideas, but they progressively become litigious concerning the legitimacy and expediency of violence in absolute terms against infidels and other Muslims.[65]

Notes

1. Even today, within the Muslim world, those who intend to reject their adversaries' Islamic legitimacy characterize them as "Kharijites." See Jeffrey T. Kenney, *Muslim Rebels: Kharijites and the Politics of Extremism in Egypt* (Oxford: Oxford University Press, 2006).

2. These four were chosen because they are among the most prominent and are good examples of the major Jihadist intellectuals. Abdullah Azzam was killed in a blast in Pakistan, and he did not have the opportunity to extensively develop his ideas about Islam in the age of globalization.

3. For a provisional biography, see the Wikipedia entry for Abu Muhammad Asem al-Maqdisi, http://en.wikipedia.org/wiki/Abu_Muhammad_Asem_al-Maqdisi, and William McCants, ed., *Militant Ideology Atlas*, Research Compendium, Combating Terrorism Center, West Point, New York, November 2006.

4. See Murad Batal al-Shishani, "Abu Mus'ab al-Suri and the Third Generation of Salafi-Jihadists," *Terrorism Monitor* 3, no. 16 (August 11, 2005).

5. "It is my contention that a new generation of Jihadists is born today after the September 11 events where Iraq is occupied and the Palestinian uprising has reached its apogee, thus leaving it at a crossroads." See al Suri, *Da'wat al muqawama al alamiya* (Call for a Worldwide Islamic Resistance), *Minbar al Tawhid wal jihad.*

6. For a translation of various examples of Jihadist literature in English, see McCants, ed., *Militant Ideology Atlas*; G. Kepel and J. P. Millelli, ed., *Al Qaeda dans le texte* (Al Qaeda in Their Own Words) (Paris: PUF, 2005).

7. The typical Arabic words used for "infidel" are *Kafir, Mushrik, Mulhid,* and *Murtadd* (apostate) and could also be translated as "disbeliever," "associationist" (one who believes that Allah has associates), "unbeliever," "godless," "apostate," etc.

8. "Loyalty and Disavowal" was first theorized by Sulayman Ibn Abdallah, grandson of Abd al Wahhab, in 1818. Shariati used the dual aspects of the Shahadah (the first pillar of Islam, "There is no Allah but Allah") in the 1970s to suggest that the negative aspect (the denial of idolatry) meant revolution in the name of Islam against class society, imperialism, and colonialism: in them the idols are Gold, Violence, and Duplicity. This notion has been further explicitly developed by Maqdisi in his 1984 work, *Abraham's Community.* He makes it the heart of Islamic belief. Since then, almost all the Jihadists refer to it as the touchstone of the faith that justifies Jihad.

9. See, for instance, Muhammad Ismail Ibrahim, *Al jihad, rukn al islam al sadis* (Jihad, the Sixth Pillar of Islam) (Ramallah: Dar al Fikr al Arabi, 1964). These theologians are not necessarily Jihadist; they can simply be fundamentalist, seeking the return to the Salaf, the forefathers of Islam.

10. If we compare Islam's first pillar, namely "There is no god but Allah" to the Ten Commandments (Decalogue), we see an inversion. In the Decalogue, the first assertion is positive and the second, against idolatry, negative (denial of idols). See Exodus 20:2–17; Deuteronomy 5:6–21, "I am

the Lord your God, who brought you out of the land of Egypt, out of the house of slavery. Do not have any other gods before me"; or Deuteronomy 5:6–21, "I am the Lord your God, who brought you out of the land of Egypt, out of the house of slavery; you shall have no other gods before me." In Islam, the negative sentence is placed before the positive one, contrary to the biblical tradition. This has had heavy consequences among Islamic radicals, at least in terms of giving vent to interpretations authorized by the precedence of negative over positive assertions.

11. The Jihadists are almost all Sunnis, encompassing around 90 percent of the Muslims in the world. Some of these radical tendencies appear in Shi'ism, whose followers make up about 10 percent of Muslims. The Shi'ite radical thinker Ali Shariati wrote a long interpretation of the *Tawhid* in the 1960s. He stated that Islam denies all idols, namely the idol of wealth (*zar*, gold), the idol of oppression and violence (*zur*), and the idol of duplicity (*tazwir*). Since Islam is the denial of these idols, its aim is the establishment of Allah's unitary rule, denying the legitimacy to any class society (where wealth is the decisive factor) and imperialism (based on the fact that people are reduced to the situation of subservience through alienation, *istihmar*, literally, being forced to become "stupid" like asses, *himar*). In the 1970s, Shariati based his anti-imperialist interpretation of Islam on the two sets of meanings implied by the first pillar of Islamic faith, without explicitly mentioning the concepts of Al Wala wal Bara'. See Ali Shariati, *Eslam shenasi* (Islamology) (Tehran: Qalam Publishers, 1380 [2001]), first published in the 1970s.

12. Seyed Qutb, *Ma'alim fil tariq* (The Signs of the Road), *Minbar al Tawhid wal Jihad*.

13. In the first centuries of Islam, when Muslim armies conquered non-Muslim land, this "defensive" interpretation of Jihad was certainly not legitimate. See David Cook, *Understanding Jihad* (Berkeley: University of California Press, 2005).

14. Qutb, *Ma'alim*.

15. Qutb, *Ma'alim*.

16. Qutb, *Ma'alim*.

17. Qutb, *Ma'alim*.

18. Abdallah Azzam, *Join the Caravan!* www.al-haqq.org.

19. Abdallah Azzam, "Customs and Jurisprudence of Jihad," *Minbar al Tawhid wal Jihad*.

20. Ayman al Zawahiri, *Aqidah manqulah wa waqi'ah mafqudah* (The Transmitted Faith and the Lost Reality), *Minbar al Tawhid wal Jihad*.

21. Al Zawahiri, *The Transmitted Faith*.

22. Al Zawahiri, *The Transmitted Faith*.

23. Abdolrazzaq Afifi, foreword to Mohammad ibn Saeed Qahtani, *Al wala' wal bara' fil islam*, *Minbar al Tawhid wal Jihad*.

24. Qahtani, *Al wala' wal bara' fil islam*.

25. Qahtani, *Al wala' wal bara' fil islam*.

26. Qahtani, *Al wala' wal bara' fil islam*.

27. Qahtani, *Al wala' wal bara' fil islam*.

28. Abul Ala Mawdudi (1903–1972) was a prominent figure of Islamic fundamentalism in Pakistan. He founded the Jamaat e Islami, a political party and through his writings spread the new version of theocratic Islam in which the *hakimiyah* (the government) should be according to Allah's rule. He is, along with Seyed Qutb, one of the modern forefathers of Islamic radicalism.

29. Qahtani, *Al wala' wal bara' fil islam.*

30. Qahtani, *Al wala' wal bara' fil islam.*

31. Qahtani, *Al wala' wal bara' fil islam.*

32. Hassan al Banna, *Jihad,* www.youngmuslims.ca/online_library/ books/jihad/.

33. In Islamic history the notion of Jihad has been, by far, predominantly the violent Jihad rather than the spiritual, although the latter became important, as a minority phenomenon, among the Islamic mystics (sufis). The historical fact is that even among the latter, some became militant Muslims, violent Jihad being integrated into the framework of the spiritual and mystical Jihad. Still, mainly from the late nineteenth century onwards, new waves of Islamic Reformists insist on the "spiritual Jihad" (Greater Jihad) as opposed to the "violent Jihad" (Lesser Jihad). This opposition did not exist as such among many Islamic mystics before the advent of modernity, although some of the mystics, like Mansur al Hallaj (858–922), were absorbed by the Love of Allah to the exclusion of any other act. Nowadays, opposing the spiritual Jihad to the violent Jihad has become one of the common features of the Islamic Reformists, within the Muslim world as well as in the West. See for example, Sheila Mussaj, "A Spiritual Jihad against Terrorism," www .theamericanmuslim.org/tam.php/features/articles/a_spiritual_jihad-against-terrorism/. See among a large body of literature, John L. Esposito, *Islam: The Straight Path* (New York: Oxford University Press, 2005); Richard Bonney, *Jihad: From Qu'ran to Bin Laden* (New York: Palgrave Macmillan, 2004).

34. Azzam, *Join the Caravan!*

35. The idea of Unity is deeply entrenched in Islam. In the Koran, the stress on unity and the identification of the enemies from without (non-Muslims at war with Muslims) or from within (*Munafiq,* he who under the guise of Islam spreads dissension within the Umma and breaks up its unity) is paramount. The suras Al Tawba (Repentance) and Al Anfal (The Spoils of War) are full of references to these people who spread dissension among Muslims.

36. Farhad Khosrokhavar, *Quand Al Qaeda parle: Témoignage derrière les barreaux* (Paris: Grasset, 2006), quoted on the title page. All translations from *Quand Al Qaeda parle* are mine.

37. Ahsen quoted in Khosrokhavar, *Quand Al Qaeda parle,* 72.

38. Ahsen quoted in Khosrokhavar, *Quand Al Qaeda parle,* 77.

39. Mohammad quoted in Khosrokhavar, *Quand Al Qaeda parle,* 109.

40. There were exceptions in the tribal areas in many parts of the Muslim world, where the veil was much looser because of women's work and

their frequent moves. See Farhad Khosrokhavar and Chahlâ Chafiq, *Sous le voile islamique* (Paris: Editions du Félin, 1995).

41. Democracy means that no opinion within the public sphere should be considered as absolute or unsusceptible to questioning on its legitimacy. Substantive unity is incompatible with democratization and political pluralism. That is why part of the Islamic Reformists' effort is devoted to questioning the rigid unity of thought within the framework of faith (*Tawhid*). The Jihadists, on the contrary, overstress the unity of thought and behavior of the Islamic community, vindicating their opinions' absolute legitimacy and labeling their opponents' views totally illegitimate. See chapter 4 (on democracy).

42. The Abbasid rule was ended by the Mongol Hulagu Khan in 1258. Since the Mongols feared that spilling the blood of the last Abbasid caliph might cause the Apocalypse, a Shi'ite minister proposed to kill him not by spilling his blood but by wrapping him in a carpet and having horses trod him to death. Since then, this event has been brandished by the Sunnis as one of the signs of the Shi'ites' treacherous nature.

43. Bashar ibn Fahd al Bashar, *Asbâb al nasr val hazima fil tarikh al islami* (Causes of victory and failure in the Islamic history), *Minbar al Tawhid wal Jihad.*

44. Abu Mus'ab al Zarqawi, *Letter to Bin Laden and Zawahiri, Minbar al Tawhid wal Jihad.*

45. Hâni al Sabahi, "The Zindiq [*zanâdiqa*] in Education and Thought: Lecture in the History of the Ancient and New Zindiq" (*Zanâdiqa al adab wal kifr: Qara'a fi tarikh al zandiqa qadiman va hadisan*), *Minbar al Tawhid wal Jihad.*

46. In 1258 the Mongols under Hulagu Khan utterly wiped out Baghdad, a shattering blow to the then thriving eastern part of the Islamic world.

47. Sheikh Abu Hamzah al Baqdadi, member of Hey'at Shar'iya li Tanzim al Qaeda fi Bilad al Rafidayn (Iraq), *Limadha nuqatil wa nuqatil man?* (Why Do We Fight and Whom Do We Fight?), *Minbar al Tawhid wal Jihad.*

48. See Abu Qatada, *Hal al dimuqratiyun kuffar bila mathnawiyah?* (Are Democrats Godless [*kuffar*] without Exception?), *Minbar al Tawhid wal Jihad.*

49. Bashar ibn Fahd al Bashar, "Causes of Victory."

50. Of course, many other radical, nationalist groups accept death as well, like the Tamil Tigers, who have had one of the highest numbers of secular "martyrs" among their fighters. See Robert Pape, *Dying to Win: The Strategic Logic of Suicide Terrorism* (New York: Random House, 2005).

51. For a more extensive discussion of this theme, see Farhad Khosrokhavar, *Suicide Bombers: Allah's New Martyrs* (London: Pluto Press, 2005).

52. See Abu Ja'far Mohammed ben Jarir Tabari, *La Chronique, Volume II: Les Quatre Premiers Califes* (Paris: Actes Sud-Sindbad, 1983).

53. See Ali Shariati, "Shahadat," in *Hussein vares e adam* (Hussein the Heir to Adam), *Collected Works*, vol. 19, 2nd ed. (Tehran: Qalam Publishers, 1982), 187.

54. Shariati, "Shahadat," 218.

55. Shariati, "Shahadat," 189.

56. "Verily, Allah has purchased from the believers their lives and their properties for (the price) that theirs shall be Paradise. They fight in Allah's Cause, so they kill (others) (*yaqtoluna*) and are killed (*yoqteluna*)" (The Surat Repentance, 111).

57. Azzam, *Join the Caravan!*

58. Abdullah Azzam, "The Origin of the Word Martyr," *Minbar al Tawhid wal Jihad.*

59. See Oum Nossayba, "Dialogue avec un Chahid," June 26, 2004, http://www.assabyle.com/; note that this site is no longer active.

60. See Abu Mohammad Maqdisi, *Howle fitwa mufti al saudiya bi sha'n il amaliyat al istishhadiyah* (About the Fatwa of the Saudi Religious Authority Concerning the Martyrdom Operations), *Minbar al Tawhid wal Jihad.*

61. After the Mongol invasion of the Muslim world in the thirteenth century and their conquest of Muslim lands, they hired Muslims to fight in their armies. Fighting in the Mongol's armies implied fighting and killing other Muslims. Ibn Taymiyah justified this in reference to the defense of Islam. Some of the Mongols embraced Islam, but their religion was a fake one, and therefore Ibn Taymiya considered the fight against them as a personal duty. He gave a specific definition for the notion of *takfir*: there are Muslims who are in reality heretics, *kafir*. He identified the Shi'ites and the Ismailis as well as the Mongol rulers as heretics. See A. Morabia, *Le Jihad dans l'islam mediéval* (Paris: Albin Michel, 1993).

62. Maqdisi, "About the Fatwa."

63. Abu Basir al Tartusi, *Mahadhir al amaliyat al istishhadiyah ow al intihariya* (Warnings Against the Operations Aiming at Martyrdom [*istishhadiya*] or Suicidal Ones), *Minbar al Tawhid wal Jihad.*

64. Abu Qatada al Falastini, *Jawaz amaliyat al istishhadiya wa innaha laysat bi qatl nafs*, (Authorization for the Martyrdom Operation and the Fact That It Is Not to Kill Oneself), *Minbar al Tawhid wal Jihad.*

65. The case of Dr. Fadl is emblematic of the dissensions among Jihadist intellectuals. Born Sayyid Imam al-Sharif, former head of the Egyptian Jihadist group Al Jihad, he became a prominent member of Al Qaeda. He is now in Tora Prison in Egypt. He sent a fax to the Arabic newspaper published in London, *Aharq al Awsat*, to reject Al Qaeda's violence publicly. See Lawrence Wright, "The Rebellion Within: An Al Qaeda Mastermind Questions Terrorism," *New Yorker*, June 2, 2008.

3

Jihadism: A Culture of Violence Turned into a Culture of Death

Jihadism is fascinated by violence. Jihadists believe that Islam is under attack and the only way to defend it is through violence, which is legitimate because it returns the violence perpetrated against it by infidels (mainly Western civilization and particularly America, but also almost all Muslim governors who are the lackeys of the West). But the relation with violence is much deeper than mere defense against those who impose their domination on Muslims. In the back of the minds of many Jihadists rests the fundamental idea that Islam, as the only legitimate religion in the world, has to conquer the earth and impose its own imprint on it—and Jihad is the only means to achieve this goal. In a world dominated by the West, the duty of Muslims is not only to fight a just war against the occupying Western armies but beyond that, to spread the religion of Allah all over the world and subdue non-Muslims.

Of course, most Muslims are unconcerned with this viewpoint, and that is why Jihadists view them as unreliable and sometimes as spurious Muslims (*munafiq*, Hypocrites). Still, violence is not simply the means but also a way of life that many Jihadists find compelling, beyond the mere realm of religion. The reasons are local, regional, national, and global. At the root of the violence is a holistic view of the Self and the Other that makes violence both a means to achieve the desired ends and a self-contained goal. In the contemporary world Jihadism is a response to situations that Jihadists feel call for violence:

the predicament of Palestinians in the face of the overwhelming military superiority of the Israeli army, which Arabs know not only through the media worldwide but also from Palestinian intellectuals and the Palestinian diaspora spread all over the Arab world and the West; the Chechens and their plight, although for lack of an appropriate intelligentsia in the West and their being non-Arabs and marginal in the Muslim world, their suffering, inflicted by the Russian army, radicalizes few (the Chechen group that intended to blow up the Russian Embassy in Paris in 2002 being one of the few examples at the international level); the suffering of the people of Kashmir in their fight against the Indian army; and the situation in Iraq, Afghanistan, and Muslim countries where pro-Western governments rule oppressively (Egypt, Saudi Arabia, Jordan, North African countries, etc.). All these vindicate the grievances of the Jihadists in the eyes of many Muslims, who are frustrated by the West, mainly because of American support of pro-Western Arab governments and of Israel.

Beyond these particular international situations, the culture of violence is deeply ingrained in Jihadists' minds. A hypothetical peace in Palestine, Iraq, Afghanistan, Chechnya, and other countries will marginalize them within the Muslim world but won't put an end to their existence. They are advocates of a merciless war not only against Western imperialism or the Western way of life, but also what they call all "human-made" (*wadh'i*) legal, political, legislative, and economic systems. That term encompasses all political systems that do not accept the Jihadist version of Islam as the cornerstone of the world's political and social system. Opposition to "human-made" political systems in a complex world where social, political, and cultural relationships cannot be exclusively based on a "thin" legal system inherited from religious traditions creates global violence that cannot be solved at the local level. The worldview of hard-core Jihadists is based on the ideology of perpetual war not only against non-Muslims but also against those Muslims who do not follow their path. In this sense, Jihadism is a culture of violence based on a specific view of the Self and the Other, the former being in perpetual war with the latter, violence being legitimized by a reading of the Koran and the Sunna that leaves no room for compromise or any peace other than a temporary reprieve (*hudna*) in preparation for the future war. The main bone of contention is not a specific grievance against the outside world but the fact that the legal, political, cultural, and economic systems are not set up according to the rule of Allah and therefore those within them are idol worshippers (*taqut*). Islam, according to the "Loyalty and Disavowal" principle, is dead set against idol worshippers. Waging

Jihad against them is a personal religious duty for true believers (Jihad-ists) until the time when non-Muslims and Muslims alike submit to their warrior version of Islam. In the case of Christians and Jews, as a specific brand of non-Muslims (People of the Book), they should accept the hegemony of the Jihadist brand of Islam by paying taxes of submission (*jizyah*) and adopting a posture of obedience. In the case of other religions or creeds, the situation is even worse: they should adopt Islam or be put to death because of the unrecognized status of their religions, which are treated as not only inferior by Jihadists (like Christianity and Judaism) but simply idolatry. This is the case of all the other creeds like Chinese religions or Hinduism, for instance. This principle makes any compromise with non-Jihadists, be they Muslims or not, impossible.

Jihadism is a religious ideology that spawns violence because of its fundamental relation to the Self, the Other, and the sacred values, independent of any outside conditions. It is riding high nowadays because of the American policy in the Middle East (Iraq has become a breeding ground for Jihadists), the acute crisis of the Muslim world, the inability of Arab and more generally Muslim secular nationalist ideologies to achieve open and dynamic societies, and the permanence of autocratic governments that manipulate public opinion in a populist manner. Islam is the only set of ideas and practices that is not discred-ited by the history of more than a century of failed modernization through secularization in most of the Muslim world.

Modern Forefathers of Jihadism

For the new brand of Jihadists, whose fathers are al Banna, Qutb, and Mawdudi in the Sunni world and Navvab Safavi, Ayatollah Khomeini, Ali Shariati, and the clergyman Morteza Motahhari in the Shi'ite world, Jihad's aim is to expand Islam worldwide. Hassan al Banna, founder of the Muslim Brotherhood, quotes the Koran to justify it:

> Islam allows jihad and permits war until the following Koranic verse is fulfilled:
> "We will show them Our signs in the universe, and in their own selves, until it becomes manifest to them that this [the Koran] is the truth." (Sura al-Fussilat, verse 53)
> Muslims at war had only one concern, and it was to make the name of Allah Supreme; there was no room at all for any other objective. The wish for glory and reputation was forbidden to

Muslims. Love of wealth, misappropriation of the benefits of war, and striving to conquer through unjust methods were all forbidden to the Muslim. Only one intention was possible, and that was the offering of sacrifice and the taking of pains for the guidance of mankind.[1]

With the domination of Western technology and imperialism in the Islamic world, long before the end of the Ottoman Empire in 1922, Muslim scholars asked themselves about the sources of their weakness and the causes of the strength of Christian unbelievers. With the subsequent failures in the Muslim world—particularly the unwillingness of the secularizing regimes to promote political and economic development in the lands of Islam; the defeat of Egypt, Syria, and Jordan by Israel in 1968; the invasion of Afghanistan by the Soviet Union in 1979; and in the 1990s the presence of the American army in the holy land of Saudi Arabia after the expulsion of Saddam Hussein from Kuwait in 1991—Islamic radicals gained in momentum and legitimacy throughout much of the Muslim world. This time the problem was not only to take revenge against Western oppressors, to humiliate those who humiliate Muslims, but also to return to the primary call of Islam, namely, imposing its faith worldwide, by word and by sword.

Jihadists vindicate violent Jihad, the love of fearlessness, and the warrior's mentality. They denounce "cowardice" and love of this world at the expense of Jihad. Their "conquering" attitude is related to the radicalization of many Muslims: to combat infidels worldwide, it is necessary not only to push the invaders off Muslim lands but also to return to Islam as an ecumenical religion that intends to spread its message throughout the world, by persuasion or by coercion. A tiny minority of Muslims espouses this attitude up to its last consequences, and the overwhelming majority simply ignores it. Fundamentalists agree with this message but reject the use of violence to achieve it, whereas Jihadists believe that violence should be the major means to fulfill the aim of universal Islam.

Jihadism has an ambivalent attitude toward weakness and strength. Muslims are in a weak position, militarily, economically, and politically. Still, this weakness is perceived as being potentially a genuine superiority. For Maqdisi, quoting the sources of Islamic traditions, Muslims are superior in intelligence, thought, and action to non-Muslims, because this is the verdict of Allah. For him, "it is necessary for the Muslim to learn from the religion of Allah what gives him weapons to face those devils. Therefore, there is no anguish and no sadness because 'The sly of the Devil is weak' and a stupid person among the [Muslim] believers dominates thousands of the Ulama of the unbelievers, as the Almighty says, 'Our army dominates them,' and the army of Allah is superior to them in arguments and in expression as they are superior through their sword and their spearhead." For Maqdisi truth (*haq*) is one, not multiple (*al haq wahid, lâ yata'addad*) in his quoting of the Koran: "Besides the Truth there isn't but evil (*zilal*)." He accepts differences of opinion on secondary religious matters (*foru'*) but not on religious principles among the Muslims, for instance the distinction between infidelity toward the faith and Islam (*Shirk/Tawhid*): "It is not allowed to anyone to accept or to decide or to use a pretext or an excuse to be on friendly terms with apostates and infidels or to help them or to support them."[2]

One source of endless violence among Jihadists is the rejection of other religions, even "religions of the Book," that is, Abrahamic faiths that Muslims are supposed to recognize, as Maqdisi asserts: "Allah establishes brotherhood, love and friendship (*wala*) and mutual assistance among genuine Muslims and forbids friendship with all the Infidels, Jews, Christians, Godless, the polytheists and the like. This is among the creeds upon which all Muslims are in agreement."[3] The major problem, still unresolved by Muslim societies, is that traditionally Christians and Jews were either under Islamic rule (and they paid taxes, the so-called *jiziyah*) or outside the realm of Islam and in the "House of War," although, during many centuries, Muslims came to recognize de facto the House of Treaty (*dar al ahd*) as well, based on mutual, peaceful agreement. In the twentieth century Islamic Reformists and even Fundamentalists developed ideas to cope with this new situation for Muslims living as minorities in Western societies and Muslims living in a world where they cannot dominate through the sword. The concept of the "*fiqh* of minority" (Islamic jurisdiction within non-Muslim societies where the legal system is "human-made" and is not of divine origin) is an attempt to cope with this new situation: Muslims have to accept the hegemony of non-Islamic laws in societies where they are a minority who can perform their religious rituals and duties freely. Reformists propose Islamic ways to promote tolerance toward other religions in reference to the Koranic saying "There is no coercion in religious matters."[4] But Jihadists reject this attitude and denounce it as a fake interpretation of the Koranic verse. For Jihadists either non-Muslims convert to Islam, or otherwise they must choose between two solutions: they pay tribute to Muslims (*jizyah*), or they are at war with them. There is no third way.

THE CENTRALITY OF DEATH IN JIHADISM

Death plays a central role in Jihadism. Qahtani believes that the love of this world (earthly life) and the fear of death are the main reasons for Islamic decay. He quotes one of the Sayings of the Prophet:

> The Prophet said: today you are numerous, but you are like foam in a flooding, and Allah will wipe out of the heart of your enemies the fear from you and send in your heart debility and languor.
> He [a disciple] asked: What is debility, Prophet of Allah?
> He answered: It is the love for the world and the hatred toward death.[5]

In his booklet on Jihad, Hassan al Banna denounces cowardice as the vice of unbelievers, not genuine Muslims. He quotes the Koran to justify death for Allah's sake: "And if you are killed or die in the Way of Allah, forgiveness and mercy from Allah are far better than all that they amass [of worldly wealth]. And whether you die, or are killed, verily, unto Allah you shall be gathered" (Sura al-Imran, verses 156–58). Notice how 'forgiveness' and 'mercy' are associated with slaying and death in Allah's way in the first verse, and how the second verse does not refer to this because it is devoid of the idea of jihad. In this verse, there is an indication of the fact that cowardice is one of the characteristics of Unbelievers, not Believers."[6]

The forefathers of Jihadism were for universal Jihad, but they still bore in mind mercy toward noncombatants and forbid aggression against them. This was true for al Banna, who belonged to the generation of the 1960s and not that of the new Jihadists, who are by far more intolerant than their forefathers: "It is forbidden to slay women, children, and old people, to kill the wounded, or to disturb monks, hermits, and peaceful people who oppose no resistance. Contrast this mercy with the murderous warfare of the 'civilized' [Western] people and their terrible atrocities! Compare their international law alongside this all-embracing, divinely ordained justice!"[7] Today Jihadism is much more radical in practice than in theory.

The centrality of death can be analyzed in two complementary ways, toward the self and toward the other. In the first case, a "death culture" is focused on the martyr. The Jihadist believer literally needs to die to prove to himself and the others that he is elected. He does not look primarily for a "victory" against the enemies, all his intent and purpose being to embrace death in the path of Allah. The Bassij model in the Islamic Revolution in Iran is a case in point.[8] But violence can be as well diverted from the self toward the other. Jihad means in this case putting to death "spurious Muslims" in a fight that extends the limits of Jihad to Muslims themselves, far beyond the unbelievers. Martyrdom is praised, but the major intent is to kill "bad Muslims." Algerian Jihadism is an example of this view.

Both Shi'ism and Sunnism, in different ways, have developed a subculture of death within the framework of the traditional subculture of violence that has always existed, as a minority phenomenon, in Islam. "Perverse modernization" has induced the transformation of the subculture of violence into a subculture of death. The latter has four main components (analyzed in the following chapters): first, the only way to surpass the West is to let it see that Muslims not only die voluntarily but also aspire to die; second, the values of life are monopolized by the enemy (the West or the Muslim governments at large), and therefore only the values of death are available, superior to those of life; third, death is not only a second-best solution in dire situations requiring the ultimate sacrifice but the ideal to be achieved through violence; fourth, death is the realization of the self as an individual, in total contempt for reality and its requirements. All these ingredients are incorporated by Jihadists in their vision of life. Still, Sunnism and Shi'ism develop different styles pertaining to the subculture of death among their radical sympathizers.

The Iranian Case: The Violence Turned against the Self

The Islamic Revolution opened up new vistas to the generation of young Muslims who sincerely believed that the Islamic government would restore justice, social bonds, and the mythical harmony within the Umma in the so-called Golden Age of Islam.[9] The revolutionary chaos, the long war with Iraq (1980–1988), and the flight of more than a million professionals and middle-class people from Iran all contributed to a situation of shortage, inflation, and revolutionary intolerance within a deeply divided society. The Islamic unity of hearts and minds based on the uniqueness of Allah (*Tawhid*) disappeared, and in its place opposition between rival factions and social chaos created disillusionment and bitterness among many social groups that supported the Islamic Revolution from its beginnings. The theocratic government, *Vilayat Faqih* (government of the Islamic jurist), which was elaborated by Ayatollah Khomeini, was implemented. It is the equivalent of the Hakimiya, conceived by Mawdudi and then Qutb in the Sunni world. In both cases, political power was declared to belong to Allah, whose representative would rule in his name, in reference to the Koran and the Sunna. The main difference was that the Iranian type of theocracy was created within the Shi'ite world but failed to materialize among Sunnis.

The revolutionary youth mainly gathered within an organization called Bassij that sent young volunteers to the front lines during the war with Iraq. For a minority of the young Bassijis, the failure of the Islamic Revolution in creating a paradise on earth was the result of the sin of Muslims as well as the conspiracy of Western powers.

A deep sense of guilt, encouraged by the government, was built up in accordance with the traditional Shi'ite mournful culture, based on the remembrance of the sufferings of the third imam, Hussein, killed as a martyr with his close companions in an unequal battle with the Umayyad caliph Yazid in 680 in the desert of Kerbala, in today's Iraq. Every year, for forty days, Shi'ites mourn the martyrdom of Hussein and vent their guilt for having failed to help Hussein in his legitimate fight against the devilish Yazid. Ceremonies commemorating the event give free rein to emotional outpourings, public crying, flogging, and sometimes self-inflicted wounds. These ingredients of Shi'ite "mournful" culture were integrated into the guilt-ridden Bassiji culture.

Among the four hundred thousand Bassijis, a small group of a few thousand became famous for their longing for death and was more and more involved in a death-centered subculture: they longed to die for the sake of paying for their sins. They developed a "martyropath" vision of themselves and the others. They aspired to martyrdom for its own sake, and they saw nondying a martyr's death on the front as a sign of nonelection by Allah. Their major conviction was that instead of living for the thriving of Islam—the revolutionary experience proved that life in the service of Islam simply does not contribute to its flourishing— they had to die, first to redeem their faults and second to prove their sincerity to themselves and others. Dying as martyrs became not only a means to defend the religion of Allah through Jihad, but also their deepest longing, their most ardent desire so as to make amends and to overcome their sentiments of failing toward Islam.

Martyropaths intended to die first and foremost because they felt that the shortcomings of the Islamic Revolution were their fault. If the revolution failed to create an Islamic paradise in Iran, it was due to the defects of Muslims who did not act with abnegation and selflessness. In the same fashion as the inhabitants of the town of Kufa (the city that promised to help the Third Imam, Hussein, in his fight against the impious caliph Yazid) failed to act according to their pledge toward Hussein, the Iranian people failed to live up to their promises to Khomeini. The broken promise to the leader of the Islamic Revolution gave birth to a pang of conscience among the members of this subgroup within Bassij. For them, to defeat the impious army of Saddam Hussein, supported by Western unbelievers, was almost secondary, contrary to the majority of the Bassijis, who combined Islam and nationalism to push back the intrusive Iraqi army from Iranian territory.

This subgroup of Bassijis aspired to die to wash away their sins. This theme is constant in their testaments. Hamid Enayat, a young martyr, notes, "I am bending under the burden of sin. I am going to do a miniscule service to Islam my religion by spilling my blood and for the sake of relieving myself of this burden."[10] Another martyr, Charbiani, expresses the same guilt, being overwhelmed by the heavy burden of his sins: "My God! I have so much sloshed in sin and depravation that I do not have the courage to take the pen and write down my last will. . . . I feel pain, my heart is broken, my soul is burning from the pains I feel and I keep alive the hope of offering to Islam, with Your assistance, my unworthy life, although this is not enough to buy back my sins. Perhaps in this way will I be able to redeem my sins, and You will accept my remorse."[11] Fighting the Iraqi army is thus not the main aim; dying as a martyr so as not to be a sinful Muslim is their major concern. Bassijis use sufi (mystical Islamic) themes like the "Annihilation of the Self in the Beloved" to justify their attitude, but the mystics mostly had a deeply personal motive, without any explicit social aim. Bassijis aspiring to martyrdom believe that there is no other bliss than to pass away through the holy form of death (martyrdom), in order to escape Hell.

For Ghanbari, to die as a martyr opens up new vistas, since the gaping wound out of which his blood spills is the messenger of a possible redemption after death: "My God, only martyrdom can wash away all my sins. Isn't that true that the first drop of the martyr's blood that is spilled washes all his sins? . . . O! My blood, if the way of Kerbala [where Hussein was slain by Yazid's army in 680] is not opened up through your spilling [to overthrow Saddam Hussein] and if your spilling throws out of me all my sins, then I don't want to hold you fraudulently—spill out of my body!"[12] Another martyr, Kazemi, is convinced that the goal of existence is not to live but to die. Therefore, it is better to leave this world as a martyr so as to compensate for the sins in this world: "You people! You should know that you are created for the other world, not this one, for Void, not for Being, for death, not for life. You should beware of being surprised by death, being jammed with sin!"[13] The idiom of Islamic mystics (Sufism) is used to express the love for death in a situation of deep failure, where living on earth becomes meaningless and despair cannot be overcome but through longing for sacred death. Whereas most Sufis used death metaphorically to depict their torments (with the exception of Hallaj and Sufi soldiers[14]), martyrs apply it concretely, literally. Death is achieved not allegorically but in reality.[15]

The Beloved (Allah) cannot be joined otherwise than through martyrdom, according to Shateri:

> My only desire in my sullied sinful life is to be at last pure and without soiling, so as to yield the force of taking flight toward the Beloved for whom life is the emanation of His love, a Beloved looked for by the dear martyrs of the Pasdaran Army. . . . And I, poor dead loss, I dare follow the same road! My only provision for the other world is my soiling, the baseness, and the sins, each of which have woven a thick veil around my benighted soul. My heavy sins have blinded my gaze that does not perceive anymore the reflections of love. . . . I am an erring man within darkness. Sometimes, I see a beam from afar. I run, with the burning desire of quenching my thirst by drinking from this pure spring, but my stubborn and sick Ego comes between the light and myself and commits, in this way, another sin.[16]

Oftentimes the fight against the enemy is mentioned as a cause for the longing toward martyrdom, but the enumeration of this enemy shows that it encompasses almost the entire world, since few people are free of depravation and they, paradoxically, cannot attain purity in another guise but through sacred death. Life is, from this perspective, only the lot of the sinners, and one cannot achieve ultimate bliss but through martyrdom:

> Every day, people face the diabolic monitoring of the world imperialism. For Heaven's sake, because of the presence of our dear Imam [Khomeini] and of our people who are present on the [political] scene and instructed by the [Islamic] doctrine, these conspiracies have been neutralized one after the other. One slave, lackey of the East and West, Saddam [Hussein], and the mercenary party, Ba'th, have imposed war on the Islamic Republic [of Iran], under the aegis of their master America. . . . And what to say about Hypocrites (*munafiq*) and our internal counter-revolutionaries who are spending their last efforts, full of hollow ideas! . . . Regarding you, counter-revolutionaries, do not say all the time: "What kind

of revolution is this! There is no meat, no oil, no rice etc.!" Our martyrs won't be satisfied with your statements![17]

True believers should fight a large cohort of sinning people: "Fight against those who spread rumors, the followers of the counter-revolution, those who are not in the path of [Islamic] Revolution, those who trample on the ideals of our martyrs and ignore their spilling their blood [for Islam]."[18] Inflexibility and intolerance toward those who think differently and deep pessimism toward the end goals of life in this world are the main features of the "martyropath" Bassijis, a minority, considered by other Bassijis as elite heralds of Islam.

The worldview of martyropaths is, on the whole, obsessed by the omnipresence of death within a subculture where dying as a martyr becomes the only dignified goal in life. Ya'ghoub-Zadeh's message to the others is nothing but painful death and endless sufferings before attaining the felicitous martyrdom. A death-centered subjectivity is the central element in this subculture:

> In remembrance of the moment the Prophet was in his death throes and was making his last will to Muslims. In remembrance of the moment when Ali [first Shi'ite imam], his forehead transfixed and bloodstained, said: "I take as witness the God of Ka'bah (Allah): I'll be happy in the next world!"
>
> In remembrance of the moment when Fatima [the daughter of the Prophet] hugged Hussein and Hassan [her sons] at the last moments of her life! In remembrance of the moment when Hassan called his sister Zeynab to him: the poison had devoured his immaculate liver, and from the mouth of the holy man came out blood and lumps of his liver! In remembrance of the moment when Aba Abdillah [Hussein] lay on the ground, the body transfixed, in the desert of Kerbala and waited, in the last moments of his life, for the visit of one of the members of Bani Hashim clan. At that moment he discovered the Shemr the Damned who was going to cut off his head, the sword drawn! In remembrance of the sons of Muslim who convulsed, the body beheaded! In remembrance of the martyr who, at the last moments of his life, discovers Imam Hussein at his side, close to his body, torn to pieces, and Imam Hussein embraces his body and commends him. In remembrance of the orphans who have lost their father [in the war] and each night ask to meet him. In remembrance of disconsolate mothers who groan on the tomb of their sons [martyred in the war] Friday nights! In remembrance of the moment when the bodies of the martyrs in love with God are laid down in the bosom of the earth, the earth

greets them and thousands of angels descend on the earth, spread out their wings, and convey to the martyr the blessing of God. How delicious is the coup de grace! This shot is the most agreeable feeling of the thirsty man drinking water in the arid desert![19]

Within Bassij, martyropaths as a small group did everything to carry out their own deaths, despising the most elementary precautions to preserve their lives in the battles against a much better armed enemy. They believed martyrdom was akin to marriage with Allah, a union with the Beloved in the mystical sense. Therefore, they thought that instead of crying, their families should express their joy; instead of regretting the deaths, they should make their own way toward martyrdom; instead of dying as cowards in their bed, they should choose the heroic and sacred death as martyrs in the path of Allah. They despised those who wanted to live, preferring the unworthy life to worthy martyrdom.

Historically, Shi'ism, as the religion of a mostly persecuted minority (mainly repressed by the Sunni rulers) found refuge in a culture of self-recrimination and quietism that could find solace only at the end of times, by the Islamic Messiah, the Twelfth Imam. This subculture of internalized violence was transformed, through the modernization of the twentieth century, into a culture of death in which dying as a martyr became of the utmost importance. At the same time, quietism was transformed into revolutionary activism. The Sunni culture of death is close to the Algerian case, in which killing the enemy of Islam is the aim, the death of the Muslim being subordinated to that goal. In Shi'ism, dying as a martyr is more important than inflicting death on the enemy, although achieving the latter through one's sacred death is the most desirable.

The body, for the young Bassijis, was the putrid flesh that should be purified through the spilling of its blood for the sake of martyrdom. They developed mortuary rituals that imitated the sacred martyrdom of Hussein, the third imam, aspiring before anything to join Hussein in the paradise of the martyrs by suffering the same woes as he and his companions did in the war against Yazid (indeed, Saddam Hussein, the Iraqi president, was called Saddam Yazid).

Deep remorse, sin, and guilt transformed death into a longing for many distressed Islamic revolutionaries,[20] who directed death toward others as well. Many thousands of leftist revolutionaries belonging to Marxist or Islamic-Marxist parties (Peykar, Fedais, Mujahedin Khalq, etc.) were executed after summary trials—more than thirty thousand, according to some accounts. In the prisons, as recounted by some witnesses, young girls belonging to the opponents of the Islamic Republic were raped before their execution, their virginity making them religiously inappropriate for the death sentence. In the same fashion, many Bassijis became power holders within the society, repressing the others in the name of their ideology and becoming imbued with a sense of superiority through government recognition and military power. Numerous people were executed in the first years of the Islamic Revolution through a summary Islamic justice that denied them the most elementary right to defend themselves. The self-inflicted subculture of death became, at the hands of the Islamic theocracy, an awesome instrument of inflicting death on others, in the name of the purity of the power holders, who thought that Islam needed to assert its potency against those whom they held to be inauthentic Muslims or Hypocrites (fake Muslims sowing the seeds of dissension in the Islamic community).

In other words, a subculture of death, even turned toward the self, easily becomes a gruesome instrument of death against others, once it is applied to them in the name of a transcendent principle by the Powers that Be.

The Algerian Case: Absolute Violence against the Other

In the 1990s Jihadists in Algeria killed more than a hundred thousand people in what became a civil war. Most of the victims were noncombatants, civilians from villages and towns.

One can add to them women, around two thousand, who were raped and tortured.[21] Many were reduced to the status of a slave by their kidnappers (*sabiya*). Some were forced to marry them, their fathers being coerced to give their approval. When pregnant, many of them were killed by their abductors. Sometimes the entire Jihadist group raped them. Oftentimes the women's heads were shaved, thus preventing them from escaping, in a society where honorable women should have their heads fully covered by a scarf or a veil. In some cases kidnappers introduced temporary marriage (*mut'a*), although it is forbidden by Sunnism (but allowed in Shi'ism).

Men were kidnapped and tortured, and sometimes their bodies were lacerated. Many victims had their throat slit and then were emasculated before being thrown in the street. Many had their nose cut. The Arabic word for nose is *neef*, which also means honor. Cutting the nose symbolically means dishonoring the person after killing him. Sometimes Jihadist groups raped women before the eyes of their families and then put them to death, both men and women without distinction. The same type of violence seems to have been practiced by government forces against presumed Jihadists after they were arrested.

To terrorize the population, Jihadists predominantly used a knife to cut the throats of their "enemies." Sometimes they used swords and even saws and axes. They ripped stomachs, beheaded people, and cut up the bodies of their victims[22] before exhibiting them publicly on the street. To recover the bodies cut to pieces, coffins were introduced (not normally used by Muslims). Sometimes torturers cut off the heads and sent them to the family or threw them over the wall into the house of the victims. Rape, collective massacres, and cutting the throats of children and babies were used as means to intimidate the population. Often travelers were arrested by armed men wearing military uniforms and then put to death. Army units were frequently attacked, and soldiers were put to death using shards of broken bottles, saws, or even chainsaws.

To justify their barbaric acts, Jihadists claimed that Algerian society was neither *Dar al Islam* (the land where Islamic law is applied) nor *Dar al Harb* (the non-Muslim land that does not pay a tribute to Muslims and therefore is at war with them) but the *Dar al Murakkaba* (the Mixed House), where Muslims and non-Muslims lived together. Therefore, there was a struggle within it between the Mujahideen and the nonbelievers.[23] The murder of impious Muslims, from this point of view, is as legitimate as the killing of infidels. The extreme ferocity of the killings and the public maiming and torturing were not only to intimidate society but also the consequence of the internal dynamic of a clandestine movement whose members use the most barbaric tortures to distinguish themselves from more moderate ones. These actions contradict the idea that terrorist acts are possible only when the perpetrator is unable to see the victim, namely when he succeeds in rendering the other invisible. According to the Jihadists, the Other must suffer because he is guilty of the most hideous crimes, namely not getting involved in Jihad.[24] The most striking feature is the dehumanization of the adversary, but the notion of "enemy" itself undergoes a notable change.

Be it among martyropath Bassijis in Iran during the war with Iraq in the 1980s or among Algerian Jihadists in the 1990s and the beginning of this century, the concept of enmity is distorted. It encompasses not only the immediate enemy or those who indirectly contribute to the continuation of the hostility, but also all those who do not act according to the protagonists' directives and norms. Dehumanization does not only include the enemy but also the self, since the mere definition of the foe broadens so much as to involve almost all humankind with the exception of an extremely small, self-proclaimed elite of Muslim Jihadists who fight the others as enemies of Allah.

Cruelty toward the others does not mean that the Mujahideen intended to preserve their lives and that they exerted violence and death only against their opponents. Many of them, trained in Afghanistan, used to treat their own bodies as dead or simply ready to die: they smeared themselves with henna (normally performed by the family after the death of the Muslim), mortuary ablutions being part of their preparation for combat. At the same time, many future martyrs believed that they were invincible; they would not actually die because martyrs are alive and receive Allah's rewards in paradise.

The Algerian case is perhaps one of the most violent in the history of cruelty. Of course, there is nothing exclusively Islamic about it. Consider the killing of more than seven thousand Muslim men and boys by Serbian security forces in the Bosnian town of Srebrenica in 1995, the Rwandan genocide of many hundred thousands of people in 1994, and other cases showing the extremes of human cruelty in situations of war or acute crisis. In the Algerian case, some studies have pointed to the complicity of the government security forces with the emirs of Jihad, part of the cruelty being thus promoted by the Algerian government in order to discredit Jihadists. But what is at stake here is to see how Jihadism can become as radical as any other extremist ideology and how it can inflict the worst types of tortures and degrading pains on the victims, who are first dehumanized and then put to death in the name of a radicalized version of the religion. Jihad becomes a machinery that kills indiscriminately all those who are not part of it.

VIOLENCE IN THE JIHADIST NARRATIVE

Jihadist discourse is full of polemical, dichotomist, Manichean, incriminating, agonistic, warmongering, and resentment-laden words. Jihad is waged against the Shi'ites, quietist Muslims, the West, and all Muslim rulers. The fight against the disbelievers and the "fake Muslims" obsesses Jihadist discourse. Those who are called Hypocrites (*munafiq*) are only Muslims by name; their major crime is to disagree with Jihadists on the necessity of holy war. Their obsession makes the Jihadist version of Islam almost entirely devoted to violence and its justification. Other dimensions of Islamic culture are rejected in three interconnected ways: either as reprehensible innovation (*bid'a*) or as depravation (*fisad*) or as condemnable dissension (*fitna*). Within these three categories the Jihadists place other Islamic tendencies. They treat new Reformist intellectuals, like Nasr Hamid Abu Zayd or Hassan Hanafi,[25] as false Muslims (*Zindiq*) or simply as apostates (*murtadd*); major Islamic thinkers of the past (Avicenna, but also the major figures of the Mu'tazila philosophy of the ninth and tenth centuries who professed some form of tolerance) are stigmatized as perverting Islam. Sufis (Islamic mystics), like Ibn al Arabi, who have opened up Islam to a world of spirituality are treated as heretics.

Jihadist ideology is not in fact traditional. In many respects Islamic traditions are more tolerant and pragmatic than the Jihadist conception. A few concepts summarize the Jihadist tendency: de-modernization, de-secularization, political regression into a mythologized virtuous Islamic leadership (called interchangeably imam, caliph, or emir), and violence against the so-called enemies of Islam. In all these ways, Jihadists hold the reactionary attitude of those who would fight against a manifold enemy: to begin with, the world of Islam that is secularizing in spite of the acute crisis it faces; more generally, the world at large, which is becoming more hedonistic, changing in different directions without any single tendency, and within which Muslims are looking for their place, mostly in disarray.

The discursive violence of the Jihadists is expressed in the occurrences of the words they use to dismiss others.[26] The frequency of words related to battle, be it simple combat or holy war (Jihad), is unusually high in the four books of the four major Jihadist ideologues, Maqdisi, Tartusi, Abu Qatada, and al Suri.[27] Incriminating their opponents as *mushrik* (associationist, godless, disbeliever, unbeliever) or *kafir* (unbeliever) is common. In a single book, Maqdisi uses the two words or their derivatives 1,548 times; Tartusi, 1,544 times; Abu Qatada, 602 times; and al Suri, 3,012 times. In proportion to the total number of words of their respective books, for Maqdisi one word out of every 28 is a form of *mushrik* or *kafir*, for Tartusi one out of 55, for Abu Qatada one out of 53, and for al Suri one out of 213. (The proportion is much lower in the last book because of its sociological nature and the fact that it is more descriptive, inducing fewer occasions for condemnation.)

In the same fashion, *Jihad, qital* (combat), *harb* (war), and *a'da'* (enemies) have very high occurrences (respectively 323, 640, 393, and 10,931 times). Religious feeling is defined not as a peaceful, spiritual, self-centered aspiration to salvation (as is the case with many Islamic Reformists, mystics, Sufis, or Urafa) but a defying and confrontational attitude toward others, in order to assert one's own righteousness. References to injustice and oppression are numerous (75, 110, 21, and 611 times). Religion is exclusively related to the social, political, cultural, and economic environment and not to the person's spiritual needs or to one's intimate relation to the Creator or even to rituals.

The main recipients of the Jihadist discourse are the new generations, the young people. They are often addressed (respectively 26, 12,

57, and 424 times). The objective is to win them over to the Jihadist conception of Islam and to enroll them in holy war. The purpose is twofold: to win the war of conviction (the defense of the Jihadist version of Islam against the Reformist or even Fundamentalist versions) and to push the youth to join the Jihadist ranks so as to wage a total war against the enemies. Jihadist discourse is Manichean. It is based on accusing others of not being true Muslims, as being apostates or unbelievers (*takfir*, whose legal punishment is death). The total number of appearances of the notion of godlessness or unbelief is respectively 1,733, 1,732, 797, and 3,822 times (including the words *riddah, shirk, kufr,* and *takfir* or their derivatives).

Jihadist discourse is resentment-laden. Muslims are from the Jihadist point of view suffering deep humiliation under the yoke of the enemies of Islam from within (inauthentic Muslim governments) and without (Western governments, in particular the United States). The number of occurrences for the word "humiliation" (*dhill*) and its derivatives is respectively: 555, 621, 166, and 4,149 times. In proportion to the total number of the words of each text, one word out of every 80 by Maqdisi is a form of *dhill,* one out of 140 by Tartusi, one of 190 by Abu Qatada, and one out of 150 by al Suri. Feelings of oppression, humiliation, frustration, and unease are common Jihadist traits. This reflects in part the situation of Muslims in their relation toward the United States, Israel, Russia (Chechnya), and the modern world in general. But the major difference between Jihadists and other Muslims is that this humiliation is only part of the latter's world perspective, whereas in the Jihadist discourse, it excludes all other aspects of life, creating an all-encompassing view that swallows up other considerations altogether and does not leave any possibility for openness and flexibility. Jihadism makes a restrictive, exclusive Muslim viewpoint the only base upon which to build up an Islamic identity. It makes violent Jihad (not the spiritual form, the Greater Jihad, *jihad al akbar,* promoted by the Reformists since the end of the nineteenth century) the central pillar of the religion, giving it a significance and a magnitude that go far beyond many Muslims' sentiments.

Another major Jihadist position is their opposition to "lukewarm" Muslims and those Muslims who do not share their vision. These are qualified as "Hypocrites" (18, 99, zero, and 491 times). In the same fashion, the depravation of the world and especially Muslim countries is their obsession (respectively 54, 128, 39, and 522 times; one word out of 800 by Maqdisi, one out of 660 by Tartusi, one out of 820 by Abu Qatada, and one out of 1,230 by al Suri). Al Suri perceives the culture dominating the world as corrupt, non-Islamic, devoid of sacred values, and centered on non-Islamic rules. Moreover, the Muslim world dominated by deviant rulers faces internal dissension (*fitna*) that can endanger the faith (76, 46, 12, and 198 times respectively).

As for the use of all the words signifying unbelievers or spurious Muslims and the fight against them or by them (Jihad, combat, fight) as a result of their depravation, reprehensible dissension, or "hypocrisy," the number of occurrences are 3,236 by Maqdisi, 3,723 by Tartusi, 1,522 by Abu Qatada, and 21,254 by al Suri—that is, respectively one word out of 13, one out of 22, one out of 21, and one out of 30. In these totals not all pejorative words are taken into account (like *Jahmiyah*, *Irja'*, *talbis*, etc.—words denoting nongenuine Muslims). Thus the Jihadist universe is obsessed with the war against the enemy, its values are dualistic, its vision rejects those who don't share its belief system, and its actions are directed toward violence against those who disagree with its understanding of Islam.

In the Koran, Jihadists usually choose those verses that denote antagonism, war, and damnation toward the impious, the miscreant, the Hypocrite (inauthentic Muslims who spread dissent within the Muslim community), and the disbeliever. These are mostly verses belonging to the Medina period, when the Muslim community was exiled from Mecca and felt under siege by its opponents.[28] The sura usually referred to are from the Repentance, the Cow, the Family of Imran, the Women, and the Table Spread with Food, but also some from the Mecca period, like The Cattle, the Heights of the Wall with Elevations, and so forth. In the four books from which the statistics mentioned above were collected, many suras were quoted, mostly against democracy, passive Muslims, Jews, and Christians, urging Muslims to wage Jihad against them.

The verses most commonly quoted are from the sura the Repentance and among them those verses that are critical toward Jews and Christians: "They [The Jews and the Christians] took their rabbis and their monks besides Allah, and Messiah, son of Mary . . ." (verse 31). The verses that enjoin the faithful to fight against infidels are the most commonly quoted: "Fight against those who believe not in Allah, nor in the Last Day, nor forbid that which has been forbidden by Allah and His Messenger [Muhammad] and those who acknowledge not the religion of truth [Islam] among the people of the Scripture [Jews and Christians], until they pay *jizyah* (Islamic tax) with willing submission and feel themselves subdued." Jihadists apply this verse to the current situation, in which Christians do not submit to Muslims, making the fight against them necessary. Other verses of the Koran that treat Christians as sharing features with Muslims as "People of the Book [Scripture]" are simply ignored, and those related to the tense Medina period, when political litigations for hegemony prevailed with other communities of faith, are given absolute value and taken for granted for all times and situations.

The verse in the Repentance that pushes toward the fight even against fathers and sons if they do not abide by Allah's rule is willingly cited: "O you who believe! Take not as supporters and helpers your fathers and your brothers if they prefer Disbelief to Belief. And whoever of you does so, then he is one of the wrong-doers."

In order to condemn democracy and all "human-made" political regimes that rule and legislate through sovereign bodies and institutions, Jihadists mention the sura Yusuf (Joseph), which says that no law but that of Allah should be applied to His community: "The command [or judging] is for none but Allah" (verse 40). Or: "Everything will perish except His Face. His is the Decision [judgment, ruling], and to Him you shall be returned" (The Narration, 88). To condemn the majority rule within democracy, they quote verse 103 of the sura Yusuf: "And most of [the majority of] mankind will not believe even if you desire it eagerly." Or: "Nay, most of them [the majority of the people] have no sense" (The Spider, verse 63).

Democracy supposes equality between citizens, independently of their being believers or not. The following verse (18) of the sura Prostration is quoted to confound Muslims who look for a pluralist polity: "Is then he who is a believer like him who is a disbeliever and disobedient to Allah? Not equal are they." Or again: "Is he who is obedient to Allah . . . [like he who disbelieves]? Say: are those who know equal to those who know not?" (The Groups, verse 9). Again: "Truly, Allah is full of bounty to mankind; yet, most of [the majority of] mankind gives no thanks" (The Forgiver, 61). Democracy is based on society being ruled by the people themselves in an autonomous way, without reference to Allah, which makes it a fake religion, because whenever judgment among the people is implied, the laws according to which the sentence is made should be Allah's: "And in whatsoever you differ, the decision thereof is with Allah" (The Consultation, 10).

Martyrdom and Jihad are praised and those who fear death or would not accept death in the way of Allah are condemned without appeal. The following sura is often quoted to persuade youth to accept dying for Allah's sake: "Say [O Mohammad] to these Hypocrites who ask your permission to run away [from the battle]: Flight will not avail, or if you flee from death or killing, then you will enjoy no more than a little while!" (The Confederates, 16).

In the ideological battle against Muslim governments that treat them as disbelievers, Jihadists oppose their faith and quote the Koran to support their claim against those who reverse the truth: "Shall We treat those who believe in the Oneness of Allah and do righteous good deeds as unbelievers who commit crimes on earth? Or shall we treat the pious as the Disbelievers and the wicked?" (Sad, 28).

Those suras in the Koran that can be interpreted in a liberal way are also construed in a radical fashion. This is the case of the famous sura The Consultation, in which it is said: "Those who answer the call of their Lord . . . [conduct] their affairs by mutual consultation" (The Consultation, 38). For Islamic Reformists this verse is an encouragement to pluralism and democracy, since "consultation" means sharing the others' views. For Jihadists the verse means that the rulers should only consult the pious (that is, those who share Jihadists' views), although the last decision is theirs. Democracy, for them, is irrelevant here.

In the same fashion, the sura The Disbelievers interpreted by Islamic Reformists as implying tolerance is read as meaning a provisional reprieve before the general attack rather than any recognition of the others' religion: "Say [O Muhammad] to these Disbelievers: I worship not that which you worship, nor will you worship that which I worship, and I shall not worship that which you are worshipping, nor will you worship that which I worship. To you be your religion, and to me my religion" (verses 1 to 6).

The major problem in Muslim societies is the lack of influential Reformist ulama who could oppose the Jihadist interpretation through lectures on the Koran. Of course, many reform-minded intellectuals exist in the Muslim world, but they are by far outnumbered by Fundamentalists and Jihadists, and they do not yield the same influence and do not have powerful networks within religious institutions. The Reformists' view of Islam is at best marginal, compared to that of Fundamentalist and Jihadist thinkers. Violence is vindicated by the Jihadists' exegesis of the Koran, many of the verses they quote being unacceptable to the modern mind and in dire need of reinterpretation in the same fashion as biblical interpretation was developed by Protestants beginning in the sixteenth century. The advantage of Jihadists over Reformists in the interpretation of the Koran is that in many respects, religious institutions, mainly dominated by conservatives, are in agreement with them regarding the principles of exegesis but not in their application to social reality. Most Islamic Fundamentalists, influenced by Wahhabism and financially sustained by its proponents, share the intolerance of the Jihadists, but they propose peaceful ways to achieve their goals rather than violence.

Reformist theologians in the Sunni and Shi'ite world propose a pluralist reading of the Koran and the Sunna, but they are intimidated, rejected, repressed, or simply marginalized. Sometimes they are forced to migrate to the West, for fear of being assassinated by fanatical Muslims, like Nasr Abu Zeyd, the Egyptian theologian who was condemned as an apostate and was forced to leave his country for the Netherlands in 1995, for fear of being assassinated. Religious institutions in the Muslim world, mostly dominated by conservative or Fundamentalist Muslims, are not prone to open up to Reformist intellectuals. The latter are usually marginal in institutional terms and have no say within the large body of Islamic theology throughout the Muslim world.

THE JIHADIST VIEW OF HISTORY: THE WEST'S PERMANENT FIGHT AGAINST ISLAM

The history of the Muslim world is that of a great civilization and great empires up to the eighteenth century. In it, relations with the West are interspersed with periods of peace and war, mutual exchange of goods and ideas, and reciprocal rejection. In their writing of history, the West and the Muslim world gave prominence to different sets of ideas and facts. For instance, for the Europeans, the defeat of the Muslims in Poitiers in France in 732 was a significant historical event, the prelude to a long history of reciprocal wars that ended up with the expulsion of the Arabs from Spain in 1492. For the Arabs, the specific battle of Poitiers was barely mentioned.[29] It was one of the numerous "incursions" into the Christian lands for booty and eventual conquest. Historical events are thus approached differently in light of each of the protagonists' interests and worldview.

Relations between Muslims and Christians have been marked by wars (the Crusades and then the Ottoman wars in Eastern Europe before the colonial wars) but also long periods of peace. Jihadists do not see the peace but only preparation for war and do not believe in any peaceful coexistence but under the rule of Islam. For them, almost from the beginning infidels, mainly Christians, threatened Islam. From the Jihadists' point of view, there is a deep-rooted enmity of Christians toward Islam, not only because of territorial disputes or for the sake of political hegemony or European imperialism, but because Christians are fake believers in Christ, distorting Christ's message, which announced the advent of Islam and the obligation, for Christians, to embrace Allah's religion. As deviant disciples of Christ, they will not accept Islam as the only legitimate religion. The Christian world also rejected Islam up to the eighteenth century. The West's view of the major characteristics of Islam was constituted in the Middle Ages, according to the historian Norman Daniel. It developed a stereotype of Islam as having as its main features extreme violence and unbridled sexuality. Even today, he contends, prejudices about Muslims are built up around these themes.[30] Today, secularized Western societies by and large do not actively attempt to fight Allah's religion to destroy it, in the way depicted by Jihadists. Still, many reciprocal prejudices block the way to a mutual understanding between Muslims and Westerners.[31]

For many Jihadists, the failures of Islam are due to the misdeeds of Christians but also to the treacherous or guilty neglect of Muslims, among which Shi'ites play a major role. A large body of Jihadist literature on the history of the West addresses its successes and failures as well as its relations to the world of Islam. For Qahtani, the deviations in the history of the Muslim world begin with the making of the Islamic empires: "And once we glance through the pages of the Islamic history to look for deviations in the religious thought we find that it began at the era of the Umayyad [the first dynasty after the four Well-Guided Caliphs] in an extensive way but attained its height at the time of the Abbasid in the translation of Greek, Hindu, and Persian sciences into Arabic. With the expansion of the Islamic conquest and the extension of the Islamic faith, many people entered Islam outwardly, but inwardly they concealed their fake religion. Deviant Muslims (*zandaqa*) resulted from the blending of these translations. There is no difference between the Good and the Evil in these foreign sciences."[32] The root of the Muslim decay lies precisely in what Western historiography identifies as the apogee of Islamic civilization: the opening up of the Muslim world to Greek science.

The major contribution of Greek science is what Qahtani calls "the intellectual self-indulgence" (*taraf al aqli*): "They imported the scum of the Greek godless thought (*Jahiliya*), and this was called by these misled people Philosophy. They were dazzled by this import filled up with grammatical mistakes and complications, playing with words and arguments. They dressed their dazzle in Islamic garb, which was alien to it and a mask covered its true nature, alien to the Islamic land and its people. The gist of the matter is that there is a profound incompatibility between this philosophical conception and the conception of religion [Islam], between the philosophical method and the religious one, and between Islamic truth and those mean, obnoxious, passive attempts that are warranted by philosophies and human discussions on the existence."[33]

Qahtani's stance is not noticeably different from that of conservative Christians, who regard philosophical ideas and their intrusion into the religious sphere as obnoxious. He continues to ask why Greek philosophy, deeply anti-Islamic in nature, could have had such a large success in the Muslim world:

> It would be convenient to ask ourselves about the secret of the attempt at the harmonization between the human philosophy of godlessness (*jahiliya*), which grew up and blossomed out in an atmosphere of idolatry and godlessness, and the well-spoken religion of Allah, Islam. Is this the consequence of blind imitation and the effort beyond any ranting? Or is it the result of the forsaking of Jihad and renouncing to spread Islamic faith all over the world? Or is it intellectual self-indulgence and the adversity of the people, debating in their own style? Or beyond this is there the cunning of Islam's enemies in their attempt at disfiguring the purity of this faith and blending it with Western imperfection?
>
> It seems—although Allah knows better—that these causes have played together their role, in proportion to their importance. But through the enterprise of the translation from the beginning it appears that the cunning of the enemies of the [Islamic] religion has been in accordance with the inclination of some Muslims, in particular some of the governors in the Abbasid period like Ma'mun [the Caliph]. This induced what happened with the translation of the books on the subjects of the discussions of Greek Sophists and the others. This is [historically a] true [fact]: Ma'mun [the Caliph] asked the Sicilian Christian governor to send him the library of Sicily, rich in philosophical books. The governor was hesitant to do it, but the global correspondence of his government and their consultative opinions on this subject signal the fact that the Archbishop told him: My God, all these sciences will bring only depravation to their community! The governor obeyed to this opinion and acted accordingly. . . . Most of the translators were Christians. They put in their translations into Arabic what they believed in. How can one trust a Christian who believes in Trinity and who translates for Muslims those books that teach them and their sons . . . ?

This long passage depicts how staunch Fundamentalists perceive their history: a conspiracy based on the cunning of the Christians and the carelessness of the Muslims (here the Abbasid caliph Ma'mun). Qahtani mentions the conspiracy of which the archbishop of Sicily was the kingpin. Greek science translated by Christians, who were by definition against Islam, was the major tool for the deviation of the Muslims from the right path.

Jihadist intellectuals' rewriting of history stresses, right from the beginning, the diabolic nature of Christians opposed to Islam and their attempt to destroy what made it strong: Muslims' faith in Allah and in the Umma. Greek philosophy with its complicated questionings and its perverse nature was used to weaken Allah's religion. One of its major figures is Socrates: "He who follows the faith in Allah [Islam], it gives him a strong power over all his beliefs, contrary to the [Greek] philosophy and Kalam [Islamic philosophy]. Their reasoning is based on the recognition of their ignorance and one of them, Socrates, said: what I still know seriously is that I don't know anything."[34] He quotes other differences between Islamic faith and the belief in deviant Islamic philosophy. Contrary to philosophical gabble, pure faith spreads over all levels of human life without the slightest doubt. Genuine Islam to the contrary, complicated philosophical expressions lead to doubts and suspicions. The Islamic way is based on following the Koran, the Prophet, and his immediate disciples. Everything else is wrong.

The same model that explained the origins of Muslims' deviation can be applied to the present times and the Western attempt at destroying Islam from within by cultural means, with the complicity of Islamic leaders. Mohammad Qutb, the brother of the famous Seyed Qutb, refers to Christian civilization and its two major roots, Greek and Roman heritage, which are both against the right path: "The truth is that contemporary *Jahiliya* (godlessness) encompasses many principles and various influences, a mixture of Right and Wrong but most of which is evil at the bottom because of their disaffection of Allah and their refusal to believe that everything has its origin in the divine revelation."[35]

The major problem is faith: the fight against the Christian world is not primarily political, economic, or cultural; it is theological with deep historical roots. The West strove to destroy Islam from its inception, and Islam, as the religion of Truth, endeavored to dominate the world. This issue goes back to the Middle Ages and two major events: the fall of Muslim Spain and the Crusades. Islam lost Spain, and particularly Andalusia, after seven centuries of rule. But it succeeded in throwing out Christians from Jerusalem during the Crusades from the eleventh up to the beginning of the thirteenth century. One failure and one success—both have marked the history of the West and of the Muslim world up to the present.

The idea of the Crusades, while not intensely present at the core of Muslim societies with their social, political and economic problems, is much more tangible in the mind of Fundamentalist Islamic thinkers and theologians. Its revitalization has taken three distinct paths. One that is close to Marxism and claims that Islam is the religion of the oppressed (*mustadh'afin*) is represented by Ali Shariati and Ayatollah Khomeini, mainly in the Shi'ite world, but also within the Sunni

Hamas (Palestine). A second insists on the political and military domination by the West and advocates the return to the purity of Islam's origins in order to conquer the world anew. The third points to the moral depravation of the West and its attempts at corrupting Muslim civilization from within by its deviant culture, spreading alcohol consumption, prohibited sexual relations, women's emancipation, and the like in the name of modernity. These three tendencies are present within Jihadist movements to different degrees.

Mohammad Qutb denounces Greek philosophy as alien to Islam and its influence as deeply harmful to Muslims. He describes how the Middle Ages in Europe were the age of darkness because of the deviation of the Church from true Christianity and how Islam awakened Europeans. He keeps on repeating the same sentence in different forms: "What awakened them [Europe] was Islam!" How did Islam awaken Europe? "Whatever their contacts with Muslims, there was the peaceful one in Andalusia and the warlike one in the Crusades. It is the last contact that made them conscious of the darkness in which they were and incited them to recover the will to live after they had taken refuge in a torpor that looked like death." Islam awakened the West and gave it back the "will to live." Mohammad Qutb further insists: "The gist of what Europe gained from Islam was the will to live."[36]

Christianity, misinterpreted by the Church, pushed toward renunciation of this world for the sake of the other, but Islam brought Europe back to life. The Church stopped Europe's progress and blocked the opening of Europe to the Muslim world by depicting Islam in a hideous way, as a barbaric, savage, bloodthirsty, and sultry religion, distorting the image of the Prophet of Islam and his disciples, giving an inaccurate picture of its history. This pushed Europe onto the wrong path, away from Islam: "And Europe falls in a historical deadlock. . . . Europe hates the Church because it trespassed its limits, blocked the thought and prevented people from living and reforming the world. It barred the way to the religion of Truth [Islam], its writers distorting the image [of Islam] among their people. . . . And the refuge the Europeans found to overcome this historical impasse was to reject the religious thought entirely and to return to the heritage of idolatry, resorting to the Greek and Roman godlessness (*jahiliya*), attempting at building up the Renaissance upon this heritage."[37]

According to this view, Europe would have embraced Islam had the Church not distorted its image. Europeans rejected the Church by returning to their nonreligious heritage, initiating the Renaissance. Secular trends in the Western world are thus the result of European hatred toward the Church, which prevented them, among others, from embracing Islam, the only religion of Truth. Since then, the West has moved in the wrong direction. Jihadists infer from this view that Islam is irreconcilable with a perverted West and at perpetual war with it. Fundamentalists choose to bring back the lost sheep into the right path by peacefully converting Christians to Islam; for example, that is what Hizbu Tahrir intends to do in Britain and, more generally, Europe.

Many Jihadists believe that the contemporary world is more seriously damaging to Islam than ever before. Qahtani sketches a brief history of Islam:

> Since its onset by the Prophet, Muslim society began to abide by Islamic law, and this continued with the four Well-Guided Caliphs. Then, Umayyad caliphs continued this although they somehow deviated, but the law under which they governed was Allah's. They acted under its protection and respected its wisdom and justice. Then came the Abbasid rule, and Islamic law was again the source of the judiciary in spite of the existence of some strong rifts. Then came the Tatar and Hulagu and their law (*yaseq*). . . . But what is perilous in the Muslims' existence for the first time in their history is the marginalization of the Islamic law in the commandment and its being considered as reactionary and a deviation. This does not accompany cultural headway and a period of development. Instead, it is the new apostasy in the life of the Muslims. The problem cannot be summarized in these valueless pretensions; it is nothing but the exclusion of the Islamic law from the life of the Muslims and its substitution by something that is lower. French, English, American or godless communist laws or the like have taken its place in this system of Disbelief and Godlessness (*Jahiliya*).[38]

In the history of the Muslim world, it is the first time that Allah's law is being systematically set aside. Even at the time of the Tatars (the fourteenth-century Mongols who invaded Muslim countries and ruled over them) the situation was not so perilous as it is now. Islam succeeded in converting Mongol rulers, and they adopted the more advanced Islamic civilization, whereas now we are in a new era of generalized godlessness (*jahiliya*) that is by its nature more dangerous than ever before, threatening the very foundations of Islam. Godlessness is twofold: non-Muslims are by definition godless, be they Christians or Jews, according to the Jihadists, while Muslims themselves have become godless because they have abandoned the major principle of Islam, Jihad, this "neglected duty,"[39] adopting instead an attitude of meekness and passivity toward the enemy.

Jihadist intellectuals extensively describe the causes of the victories and downfall of Islam. Their explanation emphasizes faith, orthodoxy, and deviation from it. For Bashar, beyond any contingent historical situation, "Allah promised the final victory of Islam. At the end Islam will prevail."[40] He enumerates the causes of the victories of Islam:

- sincere faith and straightforward action based on the sincere worship of Allah, without any deviation, performance of daily prayers, payment of Islamic taxes and submission to the Prophet's commandments, acceptance of what is prescribed by religion, and refusing to act against the Islamic laws
- leaning on Allah, having confidence in Him, asking for His help, and imploring His support
- being patient and constant, patience being necessary to endure pain and catastrophe
- repeating the name of Allah many times a day

Further, according to him, Muslims should do the following to achieve victory against the West: bring to completion their unity within the Umma, provide a strong and pious leadership within the Umma, and prepare the people for the struggle by taking into account the causes of victory. Disbelievers were militarily always stronger than Muslims, but Muslims were stronger in their faith. This situation leads to many required tasks: preparing the army of pious people and leaders, providing munitions and the financial means to the army of the pious, and preparing Muslims to know their enemies and their strength.

Among all the causes just mentioned, faith—that is, the stringent daily practice of the rituals and submission to religious prescriptions—plays a major role. It is much more by faith than by other means that Muslims won the wars in which the godless were stronger. Strong belief is paramount although material, financial, and military preparations are important as well. Bashar insists on faith as the major cause of victory for Muslims, and he breaks it down into the following components:

- Confidence in Allah Almighty and in His promise [of victory] . . .
- The knowledge, by the Muslims, of the level of their strength, so as not to grow frustrated and desperate . . .
- Jihad for Allah's commandments, promotion of what is religiously allowed, and prohibition of what is religiously forbidden (*amr be ma 'ruf and nahy an al munkir*)

He finally concludes: "Jihad is the cause of Muslims' greatness."[41]

In analyzing the causes of Muslim defeats, Bashar takes up the concrete case of Andalusia in Spain, where Muslims ruled for seven centuries and which definitively fell into the hands of Christians in 1492: "Imam al Qordhabi [from Cordoba], who lived at that time, identified the causes of decay: shunning combat, not letting their blood being spilled, refusal to put their belongings at stake [for Jihad], preference for quietude and enjoyment in this world, and devotion to home and country. All this is a curse. It pushes toward meanness and lack of respect for the honor and sexual dignity (*irdh*) of the Muslims by the others, and the domination of the Heretics (*Kuffar*) upon them."[42]

Fearing for one's life is a curse, and a genuine Muslim should not be frightened of death. Clinging to worldly values like enjoyment of goods and leisure is the opposite of the heroic Islamic values, praised by the Jihadists. The major cause for the decay of the Muslims is their bent on this-world values and their giving up the original Islamic virtues that brought them victory in the path of Allah. Besides this major deviation, there are others, divided into two categories: "The most important cause of powerlessness and failure is deviation from the right path: this could be a deviation in faith or a deviation in one's action. Deviation in faith is embracing religions like communism, nationalism, and secularism. The stories of the People of Saba and Sabt, the drowning of the people of Noah, the annihilation of the people of Ad and Samud and Lot, and the fate of the people of Moses are in point: in all these cases the cause [of decay] has been sin."[43]

Modern fake religions, such as nationalism or communism, have caused havoc among the Muslims: "In the same fashion, the failure against Israel is related to Arab nationalism and communism."[44] Jihadists and Islamic Fundamentalists are convinced that the Western world has a deep hatred of Islam. A somewhat obscure Islamic Fundamentalist who does not share Jihadists' vision of killing nonbelievers, Jalal al Alam, wrote his book *Leaders of the West Say: Destroy Islam, Kill Its Followers* in the 1970s, before the critical events that shook the world (the Islamic Revolution of 1979, the build-up of the Algerian terrorist group Groupe islamique armé [GIA] in the 1990s, the September 11 attacks, etc.). In it he states, "Those who follow the history of the relationships between the West and the Islamic people note a constant rancor that fills up the bosom of the West, up to the degree of madness. This rancor goes hand in hand with a deep fear of Islam to the furthest point of the European soul. . . . In the West and the Western civilization in all its nationalist brands and its political colorings the position toward Islam hasn't changed: they try to destroy Islam and stamp out its people without mercy. They attempted to destroy Islam in the dreadful Crusades, but their armies that attacked Islamic land by millions failed in their mission. Then, they made new plans to stand up again with the help of new armies and new thoughts. And their aim is the destruction of Islam."[45]

According to Al Alam, violence is the main feature of the West's relationship to Islam, and the West aims to annihilate Allah's religion. He describes the case of Andalusia, in southern Spain, in which Muslims ruled for seven centuries and then were expelled after the Reconquista in 1492; those who remained in Andalusia were forced to convert to Christianity or leave the country. Then the invading Christians undertook the torture and killing of Muslims and the destruction of mosques: "The Inquisition liquidated the entire Muslim community, destroyed the mosques or transformed them into churches, then burned down mosques, and then set afire Muslims themselves."[46] Al Alam believes that millions of Muslims (greatly exaggerating the actual number) thus disappeared from Spain. The Arab language and Arabic names were forbidden, and those who did not comply were put to death by burning after having undergone atrocious torture by the Inquisition. Later on, the horrendous crimes committed by the Inquisition were revealed to the world. Their henchmen tortured, maimed, and killed countless Muslims in caves, hidden from the outsiders' view.

Many Jihadists base their arguments about the West's goal of destroying Islam on the Inquisition's torture of the Muslims and the suppression of Islam in Spain. They believe that this was not simply a historical episode but a premeditated policy that is in continuity with Western policies today. It is true that for centuries Inquisition tribunals repressed and tortured Muslims and even those Muslims and Jews who had converted but allegedly did not have the "purity of the blood" (*limpieza de sangre*) of true Christians. After many centuries the events in Andalusia had been lost to the past, but the modernization of Muslims led to their return to history and a quest to understand what had happened. The Inquisition's torture chambers were discovered by the French military during Napoleon's war in Spain (1807–1814), and since then the new Muslim intellectuals have used them as an example of the West's cruelty and inhumanity toward Islam. Jihadists and Fundamentalists insatiably repeat the story of the French discovering the torture chambers—subterranean rooms under churches, where lay the skeletons of thousands of Muslims (a number of whom, it is alleged, were buried alive). Some Jihadists refer to "Muslim genocide" occurring at that time.[47] The remembrance of the past serves here not so much as pedagogy to prevent future misdeeds but to prove that the West's attitude toward Muslims has always been marked by cruelty and savagery. For Jihadists, as for many Muslims all over the world, the Guantanamo Bay prison in Cuba, the Abu Ghraib prison in Iraq, and the killing of innocent Muslims in American air strikes in Iraq and Afghanistan in recent years are reminiscent of the West's constant ferocity toward Muslims.

For Al Alam, Inquisitorial tribunals have been transferred to modern times, under the rule of oppressive Muslim governments that are themselves under the aegis of the West, organizing torture under the leadership of Jews and Nazi Germans. In the past as in the present, the dominance of Western governments has been possible because of treacherous Muslim rulers. The examples provided are, among others, the misdeeds of Ethiopia against the Muslim Eritrea with the approval of the French and the English under Haile Selassie (1930–1974), who ordered the closure of Muslim schools and the forced enrollment of Muslim pupils into Christian schools with an eye to converting them to Christianity. All this was done with the approval of the US Congress, according to Al Alam.

He then describes how in Bangladesh, the Indian army under the leadership of a Jew killed tens of thousands of Muslims after its victory over the Pakistani army in 1971, executing a hundred thousand students from Islamic institutes and civil servants, imprisoning fifty thousand of the Ulama and university teachers, murdering a quarter of a million Indian Muslims who had migrated from India to Pakistan before the war, and so forth. In his opinion, one can take numerous examples from all over the Islamic world today to prove that the West aims at decimating Islam. He then asks, "Are the stances of the West and their followers merely emotional and exceptional? No. These are the stable stances that have their roots in the thought of the West and the mind of their leaders. Westerners and their followers practiced them through conscious decision and by conscious will, and wittingly."[48]

Al Alam sincerely believes that the West, intent on killing Muslims and wiping out Islamic civilization and its people, not only is putting its views into practice today but has always done so through its entire history, since the beginnings of Islam. This idea is deeply ingrained among both the Jihadists and many Fundamentalist intellectuals, who regard the West as engaged in obliterating Islam: "The West built up its relations with us on the basis of the continuation of the Crusades and their perpetuation between them and us, and the American politics toward us is conceived upon this principle. . . . The war broke out between Christianity and Islam since the Middle Ages and is going on up to this moment in different ways. And since a century and a half Islam has submitted to the West, and the Islamic heritage has surrendered to the Christian heritage. . . . The aim is to destroy the Islamic civilization, and Israel's emergence is part of this project, and this is nothing but the continuation of the Crusades."[49]

History, from this point of view, is nothing but the constant attempt by the West to wipe Islam off the face of the earth. Why this hatred? Because the only obstacle to the total domination of the world by the West is Islam: "According to Lawrence Brown, Islam is the only wall against European colonialism. And Gladstone, the previous British prime minister, said: 'As long as the Koran keeps on living in the hands of the Muslims, Europe won't be able to dominate the East.' And the French governor in Algeria said at the anniversary of a hundred years of French colonial rule over Algeria: 'We won't be able to dominate the Algerians as long as they read the Koran and speak Arabic. We should stamp out the Koran from their heart and remove Arabic as their tongue.'"[50] The West is fighting Muslims not only through the occasional organization built up during the Crusades but also, continuously, because the only obstacle to its hegemony in the world is Islam. This view gives prominence to Allah's religion as anti-imperialist and anti-colonialist, a view that brings it close to leftist ideologies.

Al Alam describes the Western attempt at eliminating Islam as having ten different strategies. The first was to put an end to Islamic rule as it was embodied in the Ottoman Empire. Although the latter was only Islamic in its form, the West feared its evolution toward a real Islamic caliphate. The "golden opportunity" came during the First World War, when the West imposed on Turkey a secular government under the auspices of Kamal Atatürk (1923–1938). He put an end to the Islamic government, suppressed any movement by the proponents of the caliphate, broke Turkey's ties with Islam, and established a legal constitution replacing the Islamic system.

The second strategy was the war against the Koran and the attempt at eliminating its legitimacy. The Western powers knew that the Koran is the fundamental principle behind the Muslims' strength and their relying on it would lead to the renewal of their strength and their civilization. A missionary once said, "Not before the Koran and the city of Mecca disappear from the Arab countries can we see the Arabs head toward the Western civilization away from the Prophet Mohammad and his book."[51] To do this Westerners publicized the idea that "what is right in the Koran is not modern and what is modern in it is not right!"

The third strategy was to destroy the Muslims' morals, their reason, and their ties with Allah and to unleash their base instincts (*shahavat*) in order to impose colonial rule. A Muslim who begins to love ease and relaxation does not take care of important matters concerning Jihad. He will simply look for ways to satisfy his base instincts: how to become rich and indulge in indolence until these become his aim in life. Then comes the conversion of Muslims to Christianity, which leads to their support of Western civilization against their own community.

The fourth strategy was the war against Muslims' unity. As a priest named Simon apparently said, "Islamic unity musters the aspirations of the Islamic people and helps them escape European domination. Proselytizing for Christianity is an important factor to break off the dignity of this movement. Through missionary acts we should move Muslims away from their Islamic unity."[52]

The fifth strategy was to sow seeds of doubt within Muslims' minds about their faith. According to al Alam, a book of the gathering of the Christian missionaries among the Muslims states, "'Muslims pretend that Islam answers to all the social needs of mankind. We missionaries should resist Islam through the weapons of thought and spirit.' Putting this into practice, in the books of the Oriental-ists that set traps against Islam, one finds nothing but insults against it and doubts about its principles and contempt against its prophet Muhammad."[53]

The sixth strategy was to put Arabs in a state of chronic weakness: "The Westerners believe that the Arabs are the key to the Islamic community (Umma). In his book *The Arab World* Moreau Birjer said: 'It is a historical fact that the strength of the Arabs means the strength of Islam. If we destroy the Arabs, we destroy Islam.'"

The seventh strategy was to set up political dictatorships in the Muslim world: "The American Orientalist W. K. Smith, who is an expert on Pakistan, says: 'When Muslims are given the freedom in the Muslim world and if they live under democratic rule, Islam wins over in these countries. It is possible to separate Muslim people from their religion only through dictatorship.' In his book *Travel through Asia*, the editor in chief of *Time* counsels the American government to spread military dictatorships in the Islamic countries to deflect Islam's rule on the Muslim Community and its victory over the West, its civilization, and its colonial rule."

The eighth strategy was to keep Muslims from acquiring industries and attempt to force them to be consumers of Western commodities.

The ninth strategy was the West's constant effort to prevent strong Islamic leaders from ruling Islamic countries, since they might resort to the Islamic commandments. Al Alam writes, "In 1968, the

British Orientalist Montgomery Watt said in the *Times* of London: 'If an appropriate leader is found who speaks the appropriate language about Islam, it is possible that this religion becomes the unique major political power in the world for another time.'"[54]

Finally, the tenth strategy was to spread the depravation among women and promote their sexual deviation:

> The missionary Ann Milligan says: "We should gather all the young girls in Cairo who are the daughters of the Pashas and the Bays [in Christian schools]. There is no other place where one can gather so many Muslim girls under the influence of the West and there is no better way to demolish the fortress of Islam than through the school."
>
> What do they mean by that? The exit of Muslim women from their religion entails the exit of the generation they will educate and with it, the exit of their husbands and brothers. That is the means to destroy all the values of the Muslim community, which they [the Westerners] intend to destroy, thus stamping out the role of Islam as a civilization in the world.
>
> The leader of the Gaza Strip recounts: the Zionist government summons the Arab Youth in their constant campaign to mix up with the Jewish women, particularly in the seaside areas. He encourages Jewish women to invite those young men to have non-marital sexual intercourse with them (*zina*). The Jewish government accuses those young boys who refuse these invitations of being members of the Fedai movements. They let inside the West Bank only immoral erotic movies . . . to corrupt the morality of the youth and warrant their not joining the resistance movements in the occupied territories.[55]

Historical facts are mixed up with fictions and rumors to give a hateful picture of the West. The Israelis are identified with the West, and their government is supposed to push Arab youth to enter sexual relations with Palestinian men, aiming at destroying their Islamic morality. On the other hand, missionaries aim at sullying the honor of Muslim girls. Jews and Christians jointly work to stamp out Islam as a religion and Muslims as representatives of the only genuine resistance to Western domination. This paranoid vision is not only the Jihadists'. Many Fundamentalist Muslims share its major components. This deep-seated hostility toward the West, partially related to American and Israeli actions in recent times but also rooted in the history of the Muslim world, is strongly influenced by an intolerant ideology that has developed since the Wahhabis spread their closed

view of Islam all over the Sunni world in the nineteenth and twentieth centuries. The Jihadists simply reignite the hatred and bring it
to violent fruition.

Still, the roots of Jihadism are much deeper than Westerners and
even many secular people in the Muslim world might imagine. The
movement is not only a campaign or a mere social movement. It is
an ideological movement with historical credentials that go back to
the beginnings of Muslims' relations with the West. The same type
of attitude prevailed in the West up to the dawn of modern times.
Change occurred through secularization and political and military
domination that washed away resentment and the hateful image of
Muslims, replacing it with the nineteenth-century stereotype of the
passive, quietist, fatalist, and backward Muslim. Since September
11, another image has replaced the old, characterizing the Muslim as
a menacing terrorist—lurid, violent, and irrational. In the extreme
right movements of the Western world, Islam is threatening the West
from within and without. Both these images are partially rooted in
historical realities, but they shape those historical truths in such a
way as to make confrontation easier and mutual understanding more
improbable.

The major difference between Western and Muslim stereotypes
is that the image of the "ugly Westerner," domineering and moved
by a deep aspiration to destroy Islam, is much more widely shared in
the Muslim world, because of its historical roots, than the equivalent
image of Muslims is held in the West, where, since September 11,
Muslims are globally viewed not as destroyers of Christianity but as
terror-mongering, primitive fanatics. Secularization in the West makes
religion much less central in people's minds than in the Muslim world,
where many people from all walks of life are still attached one way or
another to Islam as a religion, way of life, and set of values or ethics.

In the 1990s Jalal al Alam added a final section to his work first
written in the 1970s:

> Woe to our foes for the dirty task they perform! They impose on
> us to bear a grudge against them during the time they dance on
> our corpses after having torn them down and reduced them to dust
> and having thrown them as food to the dogs! The Prophet said
> to the leaders of his enemies in Mecca, after having conquered it,
> "Go away, you are free!" and they were the very same people who
> killed his family and followers. And Saladin left the Crusaders in
> Jerusalem after having conquered it, without killing them, although
> they had killed his followers and brothers. Therefore we question:
> taking into account the rancor of these people and what they did

to the people of Islam by killing them, should we be kind toward them another time, once we win? And we have to win because Allah can achieve this and accomplish it. Then, should we exchange rancor for rancor, killing for killing and blood for blood? Allah permit us! But it is said: those who pardon and make peace, Allah will reward them. We cannot but tell them at that date: you are free to go since you are under the protection of the Community of Allah's justice![56]

There is an unshakable belief on the part of some Fundamentalists that in spite of their significant military and economic inferiority, Muslims will prevail over the West. This is not seen as happening at the end-time but in the foreseeable future. The major difference between al Alam and the Al Qaeda Jihadists is that the author still believes in Islamic munificence and does not pitch murder and killing as the only sign of Allah's glory.

CULTURAL AND POLITICAL DOMINATION BY THE WEST

Jihadists wage war on the West not only because of its political, economic, and military domination of the Muslim world. The opposition goes much deeper into the Muslim world and, in particular, among Jihadists themselves. Culture is the major bone of contention between Jihadists and the West, more generally between the former and the modern world. What Jihadists feel they suffer from is the dominance of the West in almost every sphere of social life in the Muslim world. In this, Fundamentalists agree with them, even though many of them are Westernized. What distinguishes Jihadists, however, is their deep belief that no other remedy to this domination can be found besides an endless war, the Jihad.

One of the major fields in which the fight is its most bitter is education. Jihadists believe that through education and its components, the new Western-inspired secular culture is inexorably destroying the very foundations of Islamic belief. Maqdisi, a major Jihadist intellectual, is among those who denounce both Western civilization and the Muslim authorities who admire it: "They praise their Western authorities, their rotten civilization, and their different organizations, and they describe these systems as being based on fraternity and friendship. They pass on their depravity, their falsehood, and their corrupt culture through their lies by means of their system."[57]

One of the items of concern is musical education. According to Maqdisi, Islam forbids music if it arouses the senses, as contemporary music does. But this view is totally rejected by educational authorities in the Muslim world, whose references are Greek philosophers or the like, instead of Islamic authorities:

> They proclaim their exclusive preoccupation with the West and its music from their chairs, for the purpose of influencing the opinion of the youth [and they quote Aristotle, who says]:
> "Music purifies the manners and since we are convinced of it, we should teach it to the youth as a compulsory matter . . ." [They also mention Beethoven]:
> "Music is the word of love and peace; it is the word of the highest wisdom and the deepest philosophy." (Beethoven) . . .
> For these people what is religiously compulsory, indifferent, preferable to avoid or forbidden in Islam[58] is what Aristotle or deadly philosophers like him have determined, and music is one of these necessities.[59]

According to Maqdisi, in the Muslim world government authorities are totally imbued with the anti-Islamic culture and politics of the West, of which they are staunch defenders: "These people do not merely settle for these systems from the beginning to the end in order to dominate the education of the generations and make them love idolatries, their government, and their laws. They also don't settle merely for the manifold depravity that attracts them to their Western godless (*kufrah*) chiefs through the praise of TV, music, theatre, stars, singing, man-made laws, legislative parliaments, and their [sexual] promiscuity, their adornment and their identification with the West and its culture, flags, intellectuals, books, philosophers, poets, superstitions, [sexual] abnormality, and the like."[60] Characteristically, Maqdisi puts together many different factors to signify the cultural depravity of the West: its political structure (human-made instead of God-made laws), its art (music, theater, movies, stars, singing, etc.), and its poets and intellectuals. For him there is no difference between these dimensions. All share the same features: *Jahiliya* (deliberate ignorance of Allah) and domination of the world by the godless West, extending to Muslim lands. It is religiously compulsory to reject the system as a whole, not just one of its aspects.

Jihad is the holistic means of fighting against a world system based on godlessness. Opposition to the secular world encompassing the West but also most of the Muslim world is not merely political but global, total: no compromise (political or other) is possible, and the only solution is Jihad. Holy war (or, according to some, a just war) does not solely aim at the political hegemony of the West but also purports to impose Islam in its radicalized version on the entire world so as to escape degeneration. Islam as a whole is threatened by the secular, spurious, and perversely "religious" culture of the West. No peaceful solution can be found because the stakes are not only territory or a specific grievance. The conflict is total. What is needed is an all-out war in order to salvage Islam from its annihilation at the hands of Westerners and their Muslim henchmen.

Saving Islam means also fighting against the findings of the so-called sciences that attribute the origin of humans to the apes (the theory of evolution) or postulate that the Earth emerged without a Creator in a process that contradicts the Koran's story of the Creation, close to the Bible's Book of Genesis. It is also necessary to combat the perverted effects of Western civilization like consumption of alcohol, nakedness of women, and the like:

> They do not content themselves with the man-made laws and legislative parliaments, they make the praise of idolatrous religions and call them civilization. . . . They also insult the veil and the [Islamic] cover and praise alcoholic beverages, chanting their praise. . . . They praise those philosophers like Avicenna and the like and Greek philosophers like Aristotle, and they refer to the words of the Greek philosophers like Plato and their like, Al Kindi[61] and Farabi.[62] . . . They teach deviant ideas that are corrupt and depraved like the evolutionary theory of Darwin and the origin [of human beings attributed to] monkeys. . . . And [they teach] geology and biology and the sciences of the origin of the earth that posit that the earth did come into being without a Creator through the development of different factors that lasted millions of years! And in the same manner, in geology and geography the theory of the fixity of the Sun and the statement that space is infinite, which means that there is no sky for them after a journey of 500 years as is stated in our religion; (and they state) that there is no Throne beyond the skies and no Allah for them.

This attitude is akin to the creationist Christians who dispute the Darwinian theory of evolution and strictly hold to a literalist interpretation of the Bible. The difference is that Jihadists are waging a double war: against the godless West and against secularized parts of Muslim societies that are deeply influenced by Western mores, to the detriment of the Islamic way of life. In this battle, imperialism, crusade, and cultural attempts at breaking Muslims' ties to Islam are considered the main characteristics of the West. Everything is seen as a unified, monitored, and preconceived strategy against Islam.

Another aspect of the rotten culture of the West is its questioning of women's place within society. Quoting an Islamic scholar whom he entirely supports in his anti-modern views, Maqdisi describes the extent of the Muslims' plight in a world besieged by a heretical culture, explaining that the emancipation of women is a curse that shatters the entire edifice of traditional Islam by allowing them to take part in public life: "Sheikh Abdullah Suleiman ibn Hamid [talks about] the depravation of teachers and female students and the corruption that ensues by teaching women geometry, geography, and the like sciences that are not useful to them, neither in this world nor in the other. This is the large program of the West to take women out of their home and make them participate with men in the offices, factories, and schools."[63] Maqdisi also quotes Mohammad Qutb: "Sheikh Mohammad Qutb says: 'From the schools comes out the generation of Westernized people (*mostaqrab*), their neck bowing toward Europe and hateful toward Islam. During the lectures in these schools, poisoned principles are taught that are conceived by the Crusading colonialism, aiming at attracting Muslims away from Islam.'"[64]

The war against the West is thus not only military but also cultural, ideological, political—in one word, total. The same all-out war, according to the Jihadists, is waged against the Muslim world, where secularization and women's liberation are making headway.

The West as the Perverse Culture
of Humankind's Fight against Allah

According to the Egyptian Mohammad Qutb, Western civilization is marked by the undue privilege granted to the material sciences and technology and ignorance of spiritual values that are necessary for the blossoming of human beings.[65]

Godless Western civilization has a dual heritage, Greek and Roman. The first worships reason and the body and harbors an idolatrous sense of existence. Its distinctive feature is the incontrovertible conflict between humans and gods. Whereas the gods wish to destroy humans, humans want to prove their identity by transgressing upon the gods' commandments.

From the Roman culture, godless as well, the West inherited the worship of the body in the form of physical desires, the urge to enhance life through the enjoyment of the senses brought to an extreme, and the endeavor to build up the material world accordingly. From both of these heritages, Qutb contends, the West inherited the will to colonize and enslave members of other cultures in service to its desire to dominate, on the one hand, and as a result of the excesses of the activities of the senses, on the other hand.[66]

For Qutb, Prometheus is the essential icon of Western civilization. He stole fire from Zeus and offered it to humankind. Zeus condemned him to perpetual torture through an eagle eating his liver, which regenerated each time. For Qutb this myth symbolizes the relationship between the West and Allah based upon reciprocal animosity between humans and their Creator. This is related to Greek culture based on godlessness (*Jahiliya*): humans realize their nature through sinning against the gods! These ideas destroy the human mind, contends Mohammad Qutb. This point marks the essential difference between the godly principles of Islam and those of godless systems (*jahiliya*). All godless systems, particularly the contemporary versions, are based upon a lack of faith in Allah and Resurrection. The Islamic conception, on the contrary, is that humankind has been created to be afflicted. But affliction is not only by Evil. It can be the revenge of Allah against the beings He created, after they tasted the blessings Allah awarded them without being grateful.

For Islam, worldly life, contrary to the Greek system of godlessness, is not the entire story and is not even the most important part of human existence. Humans do not hate Allah, but their aim should be to express their gratitude to Him for all His graciousness toward them. For Western civilization, the only way for humans to realize their essence is to violate the rules set up by God, and He punishes them as a consequence! This, according to Qutb, is a sick conception, against the Islamic vision based on the acceptance of Allah's rules by humans in gratitude for His grace. In the West, the history of the Church and its illegitimate domination over the people resulted in the hatred of the latter toward it and their rejection of the pope. The revolt against the Church is in accord with the primal essence of the Western person, defined by revolt against God. The consequence of this perverse civilization based on a wrong definition of the human is the depravity spreading throughout it: moral corruption, sexual disorder, debauchery, and the like. These are not accidental problems; they are deeply ingrained in this civilization of turpitude, as its essence. In its modern version, this civilization is fond of material goods and consumption, without any limitation on sexual drives and their enjoyment.

Qutb's depiction of the West points to secularization, perversity, and depravity as its major characteristics, with deviation from Allah's path inducing desire for the goods of this world and a sensual delight in dominating others. Since there is no world but this one in which one has to live intensely, in an egoistic manner, subjugating others becomes the goal of life.[67] In his book he does not refer to the successes of the West and its domination over the Muslim world as a result of the punishment of Muslims who strayed away from the path of Allah. Certainly, Muslims have not been faithful to the message of Allah, but Westerners are not seen as the scourge of God to punish them, as other Islamic radicals interpret Western supremacy. Instead, Qutb insists on the fact that material success is worthless in the eyes of Allah, and Muslims will have the final say against the West.

Qutb's unified portrayal of the West, based on the initial depravity of ancient Greek culture, gives an utterly negative view of it, without any possibility of its improvement. The West is damned irreversibly, indelibly stigmatized by its rejection of God. The only way to redeem it is to return to Allah through Islam in its radical version, which wages an all-out war against Western turpitude.

NOTES

1. Hassan al Banna, *Jihad,* www.youngmuslims.ca/online_library/books/jihad/.
2. Maqdisi, "Uncovering the Fallacies of Those Who Discuss the Subject of the Soldiers of Infidelity and the Defenders of Law," *Minbar al Tawhid wal Jihad.*
3. Maqdisi, "Uncovering."
4. Many Reformists favor a tolerant reading of the Koran. Among them is the Tunisian Mohamed Talbi, who believes that Islam is to be understood rationally and that the adhesion to it should be voluntary and critical. Therefore any compulsion in this matter would be against the spirit of Islam, which promotes "no coercion in religion." Otherwise, according to the Sura 10:99, if Allah wanted it, He would have coerced people to embrace His religion. See Mohamed Talbi, *Plaidoyer pour un Islam moderne* (Paris: L'aube, 2004). In the United States see Abdullahi An-Na'im, *Islam and the Secular State: Negotiating the Future of the Shari'a* (Cambridge: Harvard University Press, 2008. In this book An-Na'im defends the idea that a secular state provides Islam with the best opportunities for its development.
5. Mohammad ibn Saeed Qahtani, *Al wala' wal bara' fil islam, Minbar al Tawhid wal Jihad.*
6. Hassan al Banna, *Jihad.*
7. Hassan al Banna, *Jihad.*
8. Bassij is an organization of voluntary recruits, founded in 1979, just after the Islamic Revolution, to fight against the remnants of the Shah's regime. In the war against Iraq (1980–1988) Bassij provided the human wave attacks against the much better-armed Iraqi army. Since then it has become a popular army whose task is to repress the opposition to the Islamic regime.

9. For the Shi'ites, the Golden Age is the time of the First Imam and the Fourth Caliph after the death of the Prophet, Ali, who reigned from 656 to 661. For the Sunnis the Golden Age is the time of the Prophet's rule in Medina from 622 to 630, when he was the religious and political ruler simultaneously.

10. Testament of the martyr Hamid Enayati, quoted in Farhad Khosrokhavar, *L'Islamisme et la Mort : Le martyre révolutionnaire en Iran* (Paris: L'Harmattan, 1995), 140.

11. Testament of the martyr A. Charbiani, quoted in Khosrokhavar, *L'Islamisme*, 126.

12. Testament of the martyr Ayyub Qanbari, quoted in Khosrokhavar, *L'Islamisme*, 230.

13. Testament of the martyr Kazem Kazemi, quoted in Khosrokhavar, *L'Islamisme*, 126.

14. In the history of Islam, Sufis' attitudes in regard to Greater (spiritual) and Lesser (violent) Jihad were complex. The two did not exclude each other the way they do in modern Sufism since the twentieth century. One can characterize Sufis in at least three different ways:
(1) Those who made up dynasties of warriors and mystics (Safavid dynasty in Iran (1501–1722); in North Africa the revivalist al Murabitun movement transformed into a dynasty (1091–1145).
(2) Those who were warriors and mystics individually (Abdallah ibn al Mubarak or Abu Mu'awiya al-Aswad in the eighth century).
(3) Those who did not reject Lesser Jihad but still inclined toward the spiritual or Greater Jihad, like Al-Ghazali and Ibn al-Arqabi (thirteenth century). See the *Journal d'Histoire du Soufisme,* with five volumes already published, edited by Thierry Zarcone, Ekrem Isin, and Arthur Buehler, in 2001, 2005, and 2007.

15. It is true that the Hadith collections contain reports praising the longing for death and martyrdom. But these were exceptional cases and meant to be so, whereas in Bassij, thousands of young people were exposed to the propaganda machine of the theocratic state, manipulating their emotions and their religious sentiments in this direction. See Keith Lewinstein, "The Revaluation of Martyrdom in Early Islam," in *Sacrificing the Self: Perspectives on Martyrdom and Religion,* ed. Margaret Cormack (Oxford: Oxford University Press, 2002).

16. Testament of the martyr Fereydoun Meysam, quoted in Khosrokhavar, *L'Islamisme*, 104.

17. Testament of the martyr Abolfazl Shateri, quoted in Khosrokhavar, *L'Islamisme*, p. 118–19.

18. Testament of the martyr Sa'adat-Khah, quoted in Khosrokhavar, *L'Islamisme*, 119.

19. Testament of the martyr Hojatollah Ya'ghoub-Zadeh, quoted in Khosrokhavar, *L'Islamisme*, 363.

20. The Sufis who praised death (the great Persian and Arab poets and mystics) usually did it in a metaphoric sense, with the exception of Al-

Hallaj in 922 and a few others. Other mystics engaged in the Jihad to spread Islam, but their intention was not to spread death but to die themselves. For a description of them see David Cook, *Martyrdom in Islam* (Cambridge: Cambridge University Press, 2007).

21. See Abderrahmane Moussaoui, *De la violence en Algérie: Les lois du chaos* (Paris: Editions Actes Sud/MMSH, 2006).

22. Moussaoui, *De la violence*, 137.

23. Djamel Zitouni (the GIA's Emir), "Guidelines of the Lord of the Two Worlds in Clarifying the Origins of the Salafi and the Obligations of the Mujahidin to Enroll" (*Hidayat rabb il alamayn fi tabyin usul as salafiyin wa ma yajib min al ahdi ala al mujahidin*), photocopied and distributed in 1998.

24. See Randy Borum, *Psychology of Terrorism* (Tampa: University of South Florida, 2004).

25. See Abu Qatada, "Lectures and Confrontation with Hasan Hanafi, a Religious Leftist Zindiq" (*Qara'at wa muwajiha Hasan Hanafi, zindiqa al yasar al dini*), *Minbar al Tawhid wal Jihad*. Abu Qatada criticizes Hanafi for his rationalism and his attempt to free Islam from the cult of the Salaf (the companions of the Prophet) and his belief that human beings can understand religion without relinquishing their reason.

26. I chose four books by major Jihadist intellectuals: Abu Maqdisi's *The Clear-Sightedness of Intelligent People about the Ambiguities of the Fake Tolerant Muslims concerning the Commandment in Islam* (*Tabsir al Uqala bi talbisati ahl il tajahum wal irja' al hukm al islam*); Tartusi's *The Verdict of Islam on Democracy* (*Hukm al islam fil dimuqratiya*); Abu Qatada's *Between the Two Methods* (*Bayn manhajayn*); and Abu Mus'ab al Suri's *Call for a Worldwide Islamic Resistance* (*Da'wa al muqawama al alamiya*), a major Jihadist book on the sociology and theology of contemporary Islamic movements around the world.

27. The project of counting the number of occurrences of Jihadist words was coordinated in collaboration with my PhD student Mohammad Al Zubai.

28. The Koranic Sura are for the most part divided into the Meccan and the Medinan (a few are unidentified by scholars). The first are usually more peaceful; the second were based on the Prophet's inspirations after the forced migration to Medina. He and his followers felt they were under threat by the Meccan tribes, pagans, Christians, and Jews.

29. See Bernard Lewis, *The Muslim Discovery of Europe* (New York: Norton, 1982).

30. See Norman Daniel, *Islam and the West: The Making of an Image* (Edinburgh: Edinburgh University Press, 1960).

31. See the comprehensive picture offered by C. Liauzu, *Empire du Mal contre Grand Satan* (The Evil Empire against the Grand Satan) (Paris: Armand Colin, 2005).

32. Qahtani, *Al wala'*.

33. Qahtani, *Al wala'*.

34. Qahtani, *Al wala'*.

35. Mohammad Qutb, *Ro'ya islamiya li ahwal al alam al mo'asir* (An Islamic View of the Situation of the Contemporary World), *Minbar al Tawhid wal Jihad.*

36. Qutb, *Ro'ya islamiya.*

37. Qutb, *Ro'ya islamiya.*

38. See Qahtani, *Al wala'.*

39. This is the title of a major Jihadist book by Abdel salam Farag, *Al faridha al gha'iba* (The Neglected Duty; 1981). He was executed in Egypt for his participation in the assassination of President Sadat in 1981.

40. Bashar ibn Fahd al Bashar, *Asbâb al nasr val hazima fil tarikh al islami* (Causes of Victory and Failure in Islamic History), *Minbar al Tawhid wal Jihad.*

41. Bashar, *Asbâb al nasr.*

42. Bashar, *Asbâb al nasr.*

43. Bashar, *Asbâb al nasr.*

44. Bashar, *Asbâb al nasr.*

45. Jalal al Alam*, Qadah al qarb yaqulun: Dammaru al islam abidu ahlihu* (Leaders of the West Say: Destroy Islam, Kill Its Followers), seventh edition with important additions, 1978, *Minbar al Tawhid wal Jihad.*

46. Al Alam, *Qadah.*

47. Among the sites with a description of the Inquisition's torture chambers is http://www.kavkazcenter.com/eng/content/2007/03/20/7784.shtml, where a long article, "Inquisitions and Muslim Genocide in Andalusia," by Feras Nour Al-halk, was published on March 20, 2007.

48. Al Alam, *Qadah.*

49. Al Alam, *Qadah.*

50. Al Alam, *Qadah.*

51. Quoted in al Alam, *Qadah.*

52. Al Alam, *Qadah.*

53. Al Alam, *Qadah.*

54. Al Alam, *Qadah.*

55. Al Alam, *Qadah.*

56. Al Alam, *Qadah.*

57. Abu Mohammad al Maqdisi, "Preparation of the Knightly Leadership in Order to Put an End to Depravity in the Schools," *Minbar al Tawhid wal Jihad.*

58. Within Islam, acts are divided into different categories: those which are necessary (the daily prayers, for instance), those which are forbidden (consumption of alcohol), and, in between, those which are indifferent, better to perform, or preferable not to perform. Both performing when it would have been better not to perform and not performing when it would be better to perform are not sinful acts

59. Maqdisi, "Preparation."

60. Maqdisi, "Preparation."

61. Al Kindi (801–873) is one of the first Arab thinkers to introduce Aristotle's philosophy into Islamic thought. He was called "Alkindius" in the Middle Ages in Europe.

62. Farabi (872–951) is one of the greatest Muslim Neoplatonist thinkers; he was influenced by Greek philosophy and called "Alpharabius" by medieval Christian theologians.

63. Maqdisi, "Preparation."

64. Maqdisi, "Preparation."

65. See Mohammad Qutb, *Ro'ya islamiya li ahwal il alam al mu'asir, thalithan, khasa'iss il jahiliya al mu'asira* (The Islamic Picture of the Situation in the Contemporary World: The Third Chapter: The Characteristics of Contemporary Ignorance), *Minbar al Tawhid wal Jihad.*

66. The will to dominate is the equivalent of the Nietzchean will to power. This generation of Islamist intellectuals as well as the secular ones has been in general influenced by German philosophies of will with an utterly anti-democratic bent.

67. Qutb, *The Islamic Picture.*

The Jihadist View
of Democracy

THE NEGATIVE CONTEXT OF DEMOCRACY
IN THE MUSLIM WORLD

Most of the Muslim world has never had any concrete experience of democracy. In the twentieth century, Muslim countries have undergone timid political openings only at the time of a state crisis.

Iran is a case in point. Political modernization began with the advent of Reza Shah, whose reign began in 1925 and who imposed a centralized, Jacobin, and autocratic government on Iran, building up a subservient bureaucracy and an army totally dependent on the monarch. All manifestations of dissent were repressed through military violence. The yoke of the centralized state did not loosen until the time of his abdication in 1944, after the occupation of Iran by the Allied armies in the Second World War. At the shaky beginning of the reign of Mohammad Reza Shah, Iran had some free press and a few political parties. In the first half of the 1950s, under the nationalist government of Mossadeq, the country witnessed some measures of democratization. A military coup supported by the United States and Great Britain put an end to them in 1953. In the beginning of the 1960s the Shah implemented agrarian reform. During that time, some liberalization gave leeway to the government in its fight against large landowners. But once the goal of reform was achieved and the political clout of the large landowners was annihilated, the state banned all political parties and tightened its grip on society through repression. At the dawn of the Islamic Revolution of 1979, again the crisis of the state induced some openings before the theocratic government shut down free press, closed political parties and gatherings, repressed the opposition, and put an end to the opening of the political system. The latest case of provisional political opening was the Reformist movement (1997–2005) under the aegis of President Khatami, with limited cultural and political freedom. The advent of the Conservatives in 2005 put an end to the political opening process once more.

The same model can be extended to Egypt, Syria, and most Muslim countries with minor differences. In most of the Muslim world (with the exception of Turkey) "democratization" is the sign of a crisis in the political system and the state rather than the expression of its evolution toward a pluralist regime. The consequence is extremism by those who try to exploit the weakness of the system rather than building up a more diverse political scene. Once the government overcomes the crisis, the democratization process ends and a new repression halts the provisional reform for some time, until the next crisis. Extreme anarchy and extreme repression go hand in hand. This model of transitional democratization and stabilized autocracy is the general feature of most of the Muslim world, particularly those oil-rich rentier states where the "black gold" gives the government leeway in repressing citizens.

In the last few decades, new factors have been added to this picture without fundamentally altering it. One factor is the privatization and liberalization processes within the economy. In many parts of the world this has been synonymous with the constitution of a class of independent entrepreneurs who become proponents of a more open government. This has not happened in the overwhelming majority of Muslim countries. Privatization policies have resulted in enriching the clientele of the state, the military, or other segments of the ruling elite, which have used it to become more affluent by taking advantage of corruption and trafficking influences within the state apparatus or at its margin. Lower classes have been dispossessed of the economic protection provided by the state through subsidized prices for essential consumer goods (bread, sugar, meat, etc.) and rent control. They have endured the economic hardships of transformation without, in most cases, benefiting from its positive side effects: job creation and constitution of a new elite diversifying the political system and giving them the opportunity to express their social aspirations in the political arena. Political closure has been contemporaneous with privatization and "liberalization" of the economy (Syria, Egypt, post-Khomeini Iran, Algeria, Tunisia, and so forth). Having lost the state-controlled system that provided them with some measure of social and economic protection, the majority has not won in the political or economic sector. The new lower middle classes emerging in society (students, educated women, the new class of engineers, the new small entrepreneurs) are deeply frustrated by the social and economic changes that have not entailed the opening up of the political system. New Muslim states are more insidiously repressive within rejuvenated and better-educated societies, in which opportunities are even scarcer than before, when the state apparatus provided a large strata of lower and lower middle classes jobs and other benefits.

An underlying frustration and a feeling of being "cheated" are found in most of the Muslim world. This does not provide automatic support for Jihadism, but it atomizes society and gives vent to a hostile attitude toward the government, providing the background for Jihadist activism. In the 1950s and 1960s Islamists would not have been able to find large support among Muslims because of the new message of modernity and hope provided by socialist and nationalist governments, which brought some measure of social justice to the masses and gave many people from the modernized strata the partly illusory sentiment of having a brighter future. The combination of socialism and nationalism put Islamists on the defensive, repression playing its role as well. At the beginning of the twenty-first century, most of the Arab and even Muslim world is in the doldrums: the ideals of secular modernization have subsided, and no other vision has replaced them. Instead, a strong sense of bitterness and an enduring feeling of humiliation by the government and the West, in almost every respect, have replaced the feeling of dignity and national self-assertion of the postindependence regimes. Muslim societies earned some pride from their opposition to the West (Nasser's Egypt [1956–1970] nationalized the Suez Canal, Syria's Hafez Assad [1971–2000] asserted Syrian nationalism, etc.) and their victorious fight against old colonial powers (Algeria, Tunisia, Morocco). Disenchantment is now total. The feeling of being dispossessed of one's present and future is intense among the masses.

In this context, "democracy" has come to signify deception by a dual deceit: on the one hand, by Muslim governments that conceal their autocracy in the garb of fake pluralism; on the other hand, by the American government, which disguises its imposture through the support of unpopular regimes that are its "stooges." The sense of victimization is so strong as to deny these governments any degree of autonomy from the United States, the most powerful representative of Western domination in the region. The latest cases (Hamas's democratic elections and victory in January 2006 in Palestine,

Hezbollah's winning of 10.9 percent of parliamentary seats in the general election of 2005) and the opposition of the US government to both corroborated the idea of American hypocrisy in relation to the ideology it publicly supports as being suitable to the Muslim world: namely, democracy. Paramount here are the victimization sentiment; the economic, political, and social embitterment of lost modernization opportunities; and the discredit of the idea of modernity as either unattainable or simply a hypocritical means of domination by the West. In this context, Jihadist ideology finds a favorable environment for its development. Most Muslims do not identify with it as a realistic way of tackling genuine social and political problems (only the Jihadist minority does), but they see it as a symbolic revenge against the West and particularly the United States.[1]

Muslim societies criticize democracy or even reject it in part not because of concrete experiences but because of its signifying duplicity and disguised Western domination in a predicament of deep mistrust toward corrupt national governments and venal political elites. Deep victimization does not allow most people to look for realistic and pragmatic ways of coping with problems. They take refuge in a holistic vision of the self and the other in which the only way of saving one's honor and overcoming humiliation is denial or a self-imposed confinement in the imaginary world of revenge at the global level. The holistic, global, and mythological ideology of Jihadism becomes a way of life for a tiny minority, whereas it functions as an imaginary escape for large groups of people, who just dream about it as retaliation against an all too powerful enemy: the United States. Alienated Muslims find a symbolic gratification to their resentment against a world within which, they believe, they have no say. Global Jihad is a mythical solution to a global malaise of disempowerment in an unjust world where Muslims believe that they are denied dignity and honor.

In the past, a warrior's ideology and a merchant's outlook combined with a mysticism deeply rooted in Islamic culture, besides the legal orthodoxy, provided diversified ways of building up Muslims' self-esteem in the world. Conquest, commerce (in Indonesia, for instance, between the thirteenth and sixteenth centuries), and Sufism (in Central Asia but also in Africa), as alternatives to formal Islamic orthodoxy and legalism, strongly influenced Islamic societies. All these ways of building up identity are in deep crisis, and the thrust toward modernity by nationalism and socialism after independence also aborted in the Middle East and Pakistan in the second half of the twentieth century. In Muslim society there is a profound loss of self-confidence and a deep sense of disillusionment with the world as it is, with the exception of Turkey and, to a lesser extent, Indonesia and Malaysia. The Jihadist worldview brings a glimmer of hope as a global utopia opposed to the current economic and political system that denies Muslims any honorable place in the concert of nations. Its death-centered culture and its inflexible combatant view, which rejects others in the name of a repressive version of the religion, appeal to many who seek refuge in victimization and see their identity as a hopeless attempt at leading a dignified life. An honorable death becomes a substitute for an undignified life—and even more than that, as holy death is a promise of eternal happiness in the afterlife.

Criticism of democracy is also influenced by a radical view of reactionaries and fascists in the West. The idea of the tyranny of the majority put forward by Western reactionary intellectuals is replaced by the idolatry of the majority within Jihadist circles. Democracy as "massification" of culture and morals and the alienation of the people is replaced by democracy as alienating Muslims from their religion. The idea of the "irrationality" of democracy implies that masses need the Islamic elite, namely the Jihadist Ulama and thinkers, to lead them on the right path. Democratic oppression against minorities such as ethnic groups and feminists in the 1960s is turned into the notion of democracy as an oppressive rule directed against the minority of devout Muslims by a brutish majority. Democracy as the apogee of secularization is synonymous with godlessness.

The societal context within Muslim countries gives an utterly negative meaning to democracy, with few exceptions.[2] For many people in the Muslim world democracy means a disguised domination orchestrated by the West through corrupt Muslim governments against Muslim societies. Muslims are hostages and cannot be freed but through legitimate violence embodied in Jihad. Democracy is also denounced as an alien culture that serves as a pretext for destroying Islamic culture and way of life in the name of a heretical modernity. Formal aspects of democracy as mask for class domination or imperialism in communist doctrine have been transformed into an Islamic rejection of pluralism, embodied in the domination of Muslims by secular, Zionist, or Crusader elites. The fact that Israel is a democracy is viewed as a negative symbol in the Middle East: a regime that oppresses Muslims cannot be a legitimate one. The invasion of Afghanistan and Iraq by the United States and its Western allies and their claim to spread democracy there are brandished again as the clear domination of Muslims by Americans in the guise of political pluralism. Laden with victimization and a deep resentment, part of the Muslim world accepts these loose assertions as strong evidence against democracy. In this context, the theological critique of democracy as Western, secular, Crusaders', or Zionists' oppression against Islam finds sympathetic ears among many Muslims, who do not concretely know anything about it besides their experiences of failure and oppression by repressive regimes and of cultural and political domination by arrogant Western powers.

In the Muslim world, the political scene is also in a deep crisis. Three types of political parties emerged in the last fifty years: the secular nationalist, the Islamic Fundamentalist, and the radical Islamist that was repressed and from time to time subjugated and tolerated by the state in its less extremist fringes. Secular politics was the outcome of independence movements in North Africa or the modernization of the state through the renewal of power elites of military origin (Nasser in Egypt, Qadhafi in Libya, Saddam Hussein in Iraq, etc.) or the establishment of fascist-type political parties (Ba'th in both Iraq and Syria). Fundamentalist parties emerged to defend Islamic values against the background of secular modernization, the major model in the Muslim world being the Muslim Brotherhood in Egypt. Radical Islamist parties are more recent, and their birth is due to the failure of Fundamentalist parties to dislodge secular autocracies from power. Fundamentalist parties play an ambivalent role: they agree with Jihadists on cultural and political issues, namely the rejection of Westernization within the family, and more generally, in the civil sphere, on the desire to establish an Islamic political system and the return to religion as the basic source of inspiration in politics, society, culture, and economy. They believe they can attain this goal through peaceful means and participation in the political process, whereas Jihadists are convinced that it cannot be achieved except through holy war. Fundamentalist parties like the Muslim Brotherhood (Egypt), Hizbu Tahrir (Syria), and Justice and Development (Morocco) therefore play an ambivalent role in Muslim societies: they contest the monopoly of power by the old and discredited postindependence elites and accept playing the "democratic" role through elections, but their goal is to put an end, in a distant future, to the secular political system that is the indispensable means of preserving political pluralism. Jihadists seek the end of political parties and a return to Islamic rule by the emirs and the constitution of a caliphate in which a Muslim Ulama of Jihadist leaning will rule society instead of the "ignorant" people, who constitute the majority of the population.

Fundamentalist parties in the Muslim world can open up the political scene, but they can also become an obstacle to democratization if they become the ruling elite. They are a bulwark against the monopoly of power by ruling castes, as long as they are a minority within the opposition. If they accede to power, their pattern of conduct is not predictable in advance. They might adopt the Taliban model (repressive and regressive) or the Turkish one (respectful toward democracy), the outcome being dependent on the cultural, historical, and political context. In Turkey, the military are the bulwark against the absolute domination of religious parties. In Afghanistan and some other Muslim countries with a more recent history of modernization, the countervailing power does not necessarily exist. The Fundamentalists have an ambivalent position in relation to political pluralism, and the Islamic radicals can outflank them, once they hold power.

Jihadism feeds on three major Muslim countries, all of them US allies: Egypt, Saudi Arabia, and Pakistan. In all three the premises set out above are verified: lack of democratic government, absence of democratic experience, and a cultural and social environment in which democracy is laden with a negative symbolic content. A closed political scene characterizes all of these countries, where frustration and discontent can find no political solutions. All have deep political and cultural problems, and their governments propose no viable economic solutions for the future. The political structure is a bulwark against any real opening, and the only solution consists in co-opting some Islamic Fundamentalists, tamed in the process of their integration within the political system, becoming thus part of the establishment (like in Morocco, Algeria) or finding a subservient role in the legislature (like Egypt). Jihadism reinvigorates this situation. In some countries segments of the state apparatus (usually part of the intelligence services or the army or both) collaborate with Jihadist circles. A segment of the intelligence services—in Pakistan the Inter-Services Intelligence (ISI), in Algeria the Département du Renseignement et de la Sécurité (DRS), and in Saudi Arabia, part of the Saudi Intelligence Service[3]—is more or less cooperating with Jihadists to vent their resentment against the political system. The continuing fight against Jihadists gives political legitimacy to the regimes in the West as being the only bulwark against radical Islam. The war against Islamic terrorism justifies the closure of the political system and the indefinite postponement of a more open political regime. In this situation, victimized and deeply suspicious Muslims find new reasons to denounce American duplicity. The picture is completed as well by American incoherence and biases and by a lack of continuity in US foreign policy.

DEMOCRACY AS THE NEW FALSE WESTERN RELIGION IMPORTED INTO THE LAND OF ISLAM

The attitude toward democracy is mainly divided among three major Islamic groups: the Reformists, the Fundamentalists, and the

Jihadists. Reformists assert that there is no incompatibility between political pluralism and Allah's religion. Many fundamental principles of democracy are found in the Koran and in the Prophetic traditions, according to them.[4]

For the Fundamentalists, democracy in Muslim countries can be a blessing. Muslims can gain access to parliaments and take hold of part of the political power that would be otherwise denied to them under autocratic regimes. The Muslim Brotherhood in Egypt and their offshoots in other Arab countries accept playing the parliamentarian game to gain a political foothold and spread the Islamic faith, working against secular political tendencies. In the West, common sense proves that democracy cannot be put into question and that Muslims cannot accede to power without accepting democratic premises. Therefore, many Islamic groups subscribe to democracy so as to spread Islam peacefully and, in the future, give Muslims a say in the political system. In the Muslim world they seek a compromise with the authoritarian regimes that would otherwise rule against them.

Unlike Fundamentalists, Jihadists are opposed to the parliamentary system—and, more generally, to democracy—because it is, from their point of view, a new idolatry frontally opposed to Islam. Their attitude toward democracy is even more antagonistic than toward autocratic regimes because they perceive in the former a major threat to Islam, whereas despotic regimes in the Muslim world present no ideological alternative to Allah's religion. Democracy is a formidable enemy, endowed with an autonomous ideology of its own, universal, pretending to be the best political and social system and having therefore a hegemonic vista that makes it, from the Jihadists' perspective, a new religion. This "faith" promises equality before the law, equal opportunity for all, the end of discrimination and unjustified privileges, and a political system to which every citizen can equally participate, his or her voice being equal to the others, independently of their religion. These tenets are contrary to traditional Islam (but also traditional Catholicism, Judaism, and even Protestant Christianity) because they disregard religious belonging and the importance of faith, and, more generally, they do not take into account religion as the pillar of the political order.

Jihadists devote a large body of literature to combat democracy. They consider this new "faith" a terrifying enemy. For Abu Qatada,

> There is no doubt that democracy is a religion and in its principle it is a religion that is set against the religion of Allah in all respects. Democracy introduces dissension among all faiths, be they celestial

or earthly. . . . The closest to it is the religion of Sufism: Sufism . . . is based on unity of existence and divergence with Islamic law with respect to hunger [fasting] and religious retreat. . . . Those who believe in the Sufi faith are Heretics. . . . The same holds true for democracy and the democrats. Democratic belief is the sovereignty of the people in legislative, executive, and judicial matters. This supersedes Allah's sovereignty even if He speaks on those matters in the Book [Koran] and the Prophetic tradition. Someone who acts that way is a heretic, and there is no doubt about his disbelief. Those who do not condemn him religiously are Heretics like him, unless they are ignorant people.[5]

Abu Qatada compares democracy with Sufism, Shi'ism, and Jahmiyah.[6] For him this type of disbelief is not new and only adds to the long list of heretics. Democracy is a religion not in a metaphorical sense but in a literal one, and therefore the war against it is a religious war. Just as Jews and Christians, whom he groups with the worst kind of Shi'ites, should be fought by Jihad, so should adherents of democracy. The only way to deal with them is to subdue or kill them.

Maqdisi's attitude toward democracy is not fundamentally different from Abu Qatada's:

> Those who desire democracy as a religion in substitution to Allah's religion become heretical (*yakferun*). . . . Democracy is a religion invented in Greece. Obviously it is not Allah's religion and therefore it cannot be the Truth (*haq*). . . . Democracy and Islam cannot be compatible since Allah does not accept anything but Islam and Islam is the exclusive Allah's religion that stipulates legislation and the commandment of Allah alone. Democracy is a heretical and unfaithful religion that stipulates commandments and laws according to the people, not to Allah, and Allah the Graceful does not accept that people mix up heresy and Islam or the disbelief and the Unity [of Allah]. . . . Likewise, as it is forbidden in Islam to be at the same time a Muslim and a Christian or a Muslim and a Jew, Allah does not accept from someone to be a Muslim and a partisan of democracy because Islam is Allah's religion and Democracy is a heretical religion. According to the Koran, if someone desires a religion other than Islam, it won't be accepted from him, and he will be among the losers in the day of Resurrection.[7]

Democracy is not merely a political organization; it is a system of belief that encompasses the relation to the Absolute. Its keystone is the recognition that human beings can legislate in an autonomous manner. This is in contradiction to the Holy Koran, which has brought to the world Allah's legislation, which is perfect and absolute. Believing that human beings are able to propose and apply human-made laws is an arrogant and unbearable blasphemy toward Allah and has to be rejected as pure disbelief. This attitude is not unlike that of the reactionary defenders of the Catholic Church and the Old Regime after the French Revolution: democracy is against God's will to rule the world according to His laws.[8]

Democracy means putting Allah on a par with humans, and this is nothing but disbelief. Any political system that encroaches upon Allah's privilege to rule over humankind is heretical. In this respect, democracy, autocracy, and dictatorship are alike; they are all against the rule of Allah. In a way, Jihadists are blind to the differences between democracy and despotism. They implicitly believe that democracy is more dangerous than autocracy because of its seductive ideology and its foreign, Western origin, which makes it glamorous.

Democracy is closely associated with the modern international system (e.g., the United Nations) and modern media: "Those rulers who recognize the United Nations and their rulings are infidels for this reason. In the same way, the affairs of idolatrous Arabs and those of idolatrous Westerners and Easterners, among them Christians, Buddhists, communists, Hindus and the like, are hidden only to blind eyes. . . . Those who flout Allah's religion are Infidels. The same holds for those who allow it through the radio or TV or else through the unfaithful licentious news agencies that protect them with their laws and armies."[9] Democracy sets freedom of faith and the supremacy of human-made law over Allah's law: "They believe in a religion which they put higher than Allah and His commandments . . . and their laws impose on them the freedom of belief and the right to live in spite of the fact that these are apostates in the religion of Allah."[10]

In another book Maqdisi develops his ideas in a more polemical way:

> Democracy is a heretical religion with reprehensible innovations. Its worshippers put legislators as gods and their followers, as believers. . . . This dirty word is Greek and not Arabic, and it is the incorporation of two words, *demos* signifying people and *kratos* the government or the domination or the legislation, and the meaning of this by the verbal translation is the government of the people, or the domination of the people, or the legislation of the people. And this is the most significant meaning of democracy by its pro-

ponents, and they make its praise to you, the People who believe in the Unity of Allah! This is, at the same time, one of the most prominent features of Unbelief (*kufr*) and Heresy (*shirk*) and the Wrong (*batil*) that contradicts Islam and the religion of the Unity of Allah at most. . . . In its reality, democracy is domination of the multitude or the majority of the people, the highest protectors of democracy being secularists and affiliates of this religion. . . . But what remains in reality today is: the public government of the elites and their gangs who are close to them with family ties or the most powerful businessmen and the richest who are at the top of the wealth and dominate the media. Through them, they are able to get in touch or connect to the parliament (the place of democracy) whenever they like, in the same way as their head (the king or the governor) can dismiss the parliament or get in touch with it whenever he wants and as he wants.[11]

Borrowing a simplified version of the Marxist critique of democracy, Maqdisi believes that wealthy businessmen, mafia chiefs, and media power holders are the actual rulers, not those elected by the parliamentary system. For him, and the rule of the majority is nothing but a figurehead that covers up the real power: the majority is the victim of the rule of a tiny minority of unscrupulous mighty people who hide their power under the guise of pluralism. In this way, democracy is doubly illegitimate: it is against Allah's system and untruthful to its very principles (the rule of the majority).

Maqdisi summarizes his critique of democracy by treating it as an illegitimate offshoot of secularism, which, in his view, is nothing but a fake religion: "Democracy is the fruit of mischievous secularism (*ilmaniya*) and is its bastard because secularism is a heretical religion that intends to separate religion and life or disjoin religion from the government and the judiciary."[12] Democratic freedom, in this respect, is nothing positive: it is trespassing on one's limits and infringing on the limits set by Allah for creatures: "This is democratic freedom: freedom from the religion of Allah and its laws and trespassing its boundaries by . . . their stinking democracy (*demoqratihum al afina*)!"[13]

The advocates of democracy within Muslim circles refer to many events within Islamic history to prove its legitimacy. Maqdisi enumerates them one after the other and rejects them successively. One argument put forward by the Muslim democrats is the so-called attitude of Yusif toward the Pharaoh. Another one is the conduct of the Prophet toward the king of Ethiopia (Najashi). The third is the claim that democracy is nothing but Islamic counseling (*Shura*), as is mentioned in the Koran. But all these arguments are, according to Maqdisi, mere fallacy. He enumerates them in detail:

> The first fallacy [put forward by the followers of Democracy]: The conduct of Yusif toward the King of Egypt. Didn't Yusif take up the position of a minister toward the heretical King who did not govern according to what Allah had sent [the Koran]? Therefore it is permitted to take part in the heretical governments and even enter parliaments and houses of representatives and their likes.
>
> [Answer:] The reference to this misinterpretation for entering the legislative parliaments and its justification is wrong because these heretical parliaments are based on a religion that is other than the religion of Allah (whereas at Yusif's time there was no such religion as yet) . . .
>
> The second fallacy: they say that Najashi [King of Ethiopia] did not rule according to the Word of Allah. After he converted to Islam, he remained the same, up to his death, and nevertheless the Prophet called him a good Muslim, and after his death he made a prayer before his corpse and ordered his disciples to do the same. (The answer is that Al Najashi died before the Koran was completely revealed.)

Maqdisi is quick to quote from the Koran those verses that denounce godless, unbelieving, ungrateful, and heretical majorities. Contrary to extreme-left ideologies, according to which the masses are alienated only because of the prevailing social system (capitalism, exploitation, etc.), Islamic radicals believe that majorities are wrong in principle and unable to find the right path without a religious leader. In traditional Islam this entailed the promotion of the "caliph." Nowadays, this means nothing other than an autocratic or oligarchic system in which the leader is right against the masses: "The law of Allah and His religion indicate the depravation of the majority and their corruption and therefore, Allah rules: 'The commandment accrues only to Allah.'"[14]

To sustain his argument against democracy, Maqdisi embarks upon the genealogy of democracy and its historical background:

> Democracy in its form and content grew up in the land of Heretics and Infidels and flourished at the source of godlessness and depravity in Europe when they separated religion from life. This word takes root in that environment which bears all those poisons and depravations. In its roots, it has no relation to the lands of Faith [Islamic countries], and there is not a shred of belief or benevolence in it.

It could not assure its permanent existence in the West otherwise than after the separation of religion and government there. It did authorize homosexuality, fornication [sexual relationship without marriage], and alcohol and the promiscuity of the kinship members and besides this, other prostitutions, obvious or hidden. Therefore there is no way of putting it as equal to Islamic Council (*Shura*) unless for two reasons, excluding a third one: either the democrat is a godless man or a stupid and ignorant one.[15]

Political heresy and deviant mores are closely intertwined: democracy is a corrupt political system that is rooted in a depraved society of the Sodom and Gomorrah type, where morality and religious interdictions are simply ignored. The association of democracy with sexual and social depravation are constant among Jihadists, and their deep belief is that one is the consequence of the other: godlessness breeds a heretical political system that, in turn, encourages depravity in sexual relations, destroying the foundations of family.

Maqdisi vigorously denounces the two other fallacies as advanced by some Muslims (the Muslim Brotherhood and others) to justify their participation in the parliamentary system in the name of Islam:

> The fourth fallacy is the reference to the cooperation of the Prophet with the group of Fodhul [a group Mohammad founded at the age of twenty-five, to help the downtrodden, before having his Revelation of Prophethood]: Some of these idiots [who equate democracy with Islam] reason about the participation of the Prophet in the alliance of Fodhul before being elected by Allah as Prophet, so as to justify their cooperation with heretical legislative parliaments.
>
> [Allah says in the Koran]: "Do you believe you are left without obligation toward Allah? (Resurrection, 36); "Do you think that We created you in vain?" (Al Mu'minun, 110)
>
> Still, in the democratic religion and its community there is no place for these solid verses because the human being is himself the legislator. They say: yes, man is left without obligation, and he has the absolute liberty to choose and decide and leave and impose what he wants to religion, through legislation. And it is not important whether the legislation he invented is in agreement with the Book of Allah or in contradiction to it. . . .
>
> The fifth misinterpretation is [based on the fact that they play the democratic game] for the benefit of calling the others to Islam (*masliha al da'wa*). They say: to enter the parliament presents

many advantages, it is a recorded advantage (*masliha morsila*), and they quote: the invitation to follow Allah and pronounce the word of Allah [in the parliaments]; and they say: [through their participation in the parliament they intend to] change some of those things that are religiously forbidden (*munkirat*) and lessen the pressure on calling the others [through legislation] . . . and quote: one should not leave these places and the parliaments to Christians or Communists and the like.[16]

Against those Muslims who quote obscure verses from the Koran to vindicate their democratic tenets, Maqdisi quotes this Koranic verse, which is the pillar of his attitude, rejecting Islamic democracy:

> Allah says: He has sent to you the Book. In it there are verses without equivocation that are the basis of the Book and those verses that can be interpreted in different manners. Those people, who have in their heart a disposition toward depravation, emphasize the verses with equivocation, looking for dissension by trying to find an interpretation for them while no one knows their meaning besides Allah. But those who are well versed in science say: We believe: everything in the Book is from our Lord! . . . (Al Imran, 7)
> Allah shows that in regard to religion people are of two kinds: Those of science and solid faith and those of depravation and false-hood who follow what is ambiguous in the Book [Koran], look for it and enjoy it only out of inclination to promote deep dissension among Muslims (*fitna*).[17]

This verse is important to Jihadists to justify their rejection of any allegoric or metaphorical interpretation of those Koranic suras that may imply political pluralism. According to them, to interpret ambiguous Koranic sentences so as to justify democracy is trespassing upon the rules imposed by this verse that prohibit the exegesis of those ambivalent suras. One should leave the task of grasping them to Allah alone rather than looking for their clarification. This attitude is akin to that of the Catholic Church when it prohibited the reading of the sacred texts that might spread depravity among the faithful through a potentially lax (unorthodox) interpretation.

Jihadist intellectuals disparage democracy not only because of its godless content, but also as a result of its egalitarian view of Muslims and non-Muslims and of men and women, as well as its support for equal rights among nations, believers and disbelievers alike. Maqdisi summarizes his criticisms as follows:

The heretical character [of the legislative bodies] is based on legislating parity with Allah, vouchsafing equal rights to men and women without any distinction, abiding by the stipulations of the international treaties and laws, honoring the laws asserting the equality and peaceful coexistence with the heretical people and their various governments, be they Christians, Buddhists, Jews, Communists, Zoroastrians, Idol-worshippers, Hindus or other, observing the religion of the Charter [of the United Nations] and its heretical articles, granting the same rights to other religions [which should have inferior rights compared to Islam], acknowledging the domination and the politics of the governments of Idolatry (*taqut*), dismissing Jihad against the Heretics and their various people, and declining any kind of Jihad and fight against them and commitment to help and cooperate with this heretical assembly [the United Nations?] and the International Idolatry (*taqut al dawli*).[18]

Maqdisi denounces secular Arab regimes not so much because of their autocratic nature as for their being secular, subservient to the West, forbidding polygamy, and authorizing the consumption of alcohol: "The acceptance of communist ideas, democratic ideas and [in general] secular ones by the Alawis [an Islamic sect in Syria, rejected by the others as being deviant] and the Ba'th [Syria's and Iraq's political parties under the Asad (Hafiz and his son Bashir) and Saddam Hussein, respectively], the acceptance of the leadership of America, Britain, and Russia, the authorization [of the consumption of] alcohol, and the prohibition of polygamy [are clear signs of godlessness]."[19] He combines political and cultural features almost constantly, much like other Jihadist intellectuals.

Maqdisi denounces the Murji'a—those Muslims who were tolerant and believed that faith is a matter between a person and God—as well as those who believed in predestination (*jahmiya*) and the extremists (Kharijites):

The Murji'a's belief was that one couldn't treat the other as heretic but only through the internal faith. The Jahmiya [who believed that there is no free will and one acts due to constraints, *jabr*], or the Kharijites [extremists in their treating other Muslims as godless, *takfir*]. . . . The Murji'a of our time (*murji'a al asr*) forgive the Taqut (non-Islamic governments), the Zindiq (fake Muslims), and the Apostates: they believe that reprehensible action cannot be subject to *takfir* [public denunciation as contrary to Islam] but can only be related to the intention of rejecting Islam [that cannot be proven].

The distinction between Muslims and Heretics, between the people of [Allah's] graciousness and those of the Devil is blurred as well as the commandments condemning the Heretics (*takfir*) are neglected by Idolatrous Ulama [who behave like the Murji'a].[20]

In the Jihadist enterprise, the task is to Islamize what modernity has at least partially taken away from religious rules, allowing diversity in the mores and secularization of political systems. This legitimizes "human-made laws." Maqdisi and the other Jihadists treat as *Taqut* (idol worshippers) those who put forward the supremacy of human law against god-sent legislation. By Islamizing modernity they are not adapting it to "indigenous" cultures as do the Islamic Reformists or Fundamentalists; on the contrary, they "de-secularize" Islam and break off its ties to modernity, thus building up a regressive and repressive worldview that is against the tide of social change. Even in the Muslim world, sizeable minorities, particularly in the large cities and urban centers, are secularized or in favor of a nonrigid interpretation of Islam.

Abu Mus'ab al Suri enumerates the principles of democracy:

The democratic system is based on the following essential principles: equality between the people in the society in regard to their political rights as being elected or electing in total disregard of religion and faith, ethnic, race and color, language, science or ignorance, gender or any other difference; the absolute personal freedom in regard to belief, interpretation, or activity within the framework of the Constitution or the law that is the foundation of this freedom; the pursuance of the political domination by the people through the elections and the commandment of the majority to institute the legislation and the laws and the organization of the three types of power (that is, legislative, judicial, and executive); the alternation in holding power between political groups and the parties, based on elections and the dominance of the majority.

In spite of all this, the democratic process in the West is relative and a comedy to the extreme degree. Real politics are shaped by the Lobbies who press the parliament and the political parties and are in most cases dominated by the Jews or the members of the Jewish organizations like the Masons, the members of the Christian radical organizations like the Tricontinental and the other pressure groups made of the most important political media men, wealthy people, capitalists and contemporary criminal mafias who adapt the electoral campaigns to their general policies. The electoral process remains indispensable for them [to give it a popular legitimacy].

Bribes and those assets that finance the political campaigns play a major role to purchase the conscience and the mind of the people and dominate them during the elections. The prominence of the candidates through the capitalist system follows in general the market economy or the free economy, and the society in general puts the Christian identity at the base of the immense popularity founded on Unbelief (*ilhad*). From Christianity nothing else remains, besides religious fanaticism, booze, pork, and something from the religious liturgy.[21]

Like Maqdisi, al Suri summarizes the principles of democracy in theory and in practice. Like many Western extremists he believes in the conspiracy of the minorities (Jewish lobbies, Christian radicals, prominent media men, rich capital holders, etc.) to dominate the political system in the name of the majority. In his view, democracy is based on godlessness in its principles, immorality, and illegitimate domination by the few. He adopts as well some of the radical leftist criticisms of democracy in terms of the alienation of the masses through consumerism and the duplicity of the political and economic elites who manipulate the people: "And the reality [of democracy] is the sovereignty (*siyadah*) of the political and capitalist elites who dominate the fate of the people and acquire tremendous might out of the vain freedom and the licentiousness (*ibahiya*) that benefits [the masses] for a life of consumerism. They are well off compared to the others, and they leave their bridle to those players who rule over their destiny and mock them in the guise of democracy."[22]

Contrary to Maqdisi, who hasn't lived in the West, al Suri has spent more than a decade in Europe, including France, England, and Spain. His critique of democratic regimes contains an existential note: "I acquainted myself with numerous examples and live cases of the false democratic pretensions during my stay in Europe for more than fourteen years, three years in France, three in Britain, and the rest in Spain."[23] Such a long stay in Europe can result in two types of consequences, diametrically opposed. The person can get acquainted with Western culture, become secular, and internalize the same types of attitudes toward social and political problems as mainstream Westerners.[24] Or he can get radicalized: some degree of Islamophobia within the Western world, Western racism, individualism (interpreted as utter selfishness), and a feeling of rootlessness can antagonize him against the West and make him adopt an extremist view of the West as a "totality," at war against the Muslims and Islam. In Europe, the colonial past, the establishment of large Muslim diasporas, and the spread of Islamic radicalism through new intellectuals and the crisis of the Muslim world with its sequels (the Bosnian, Palestinian, Iraqi, Afghan, and Chechnya problems among others) induce a feeling of antagonism toward the West and the United States in particular. Al Suri is convinced that democracy, besides being a godless product of the West that is incompatible with Islam, is concocted by Western intelligence services to subdue Muslims: "But the worst type of democracy is the one reproduced by misbegotten demons in the Intelligence services of the West and their colonial configuration of our countries for the sake of imposing it on our dominated people, who would therefore follow their orders willingly, mocking their weary minds by [giving them the impression of] fighting the dictatorial regimes, the autocratic kings and inherited republics that are the last reprehensible innovations of the feeble-minded Arab regimes."[25]

Al Suri's major target among the Muslims is what he calls "democratic Muslims" (or Muslim democrats), that is, those who believe that democracy and Islam are compatible and one can live in a Muslim land ruled by a democratic system without being a sinner. He divides them into five categories:

> 1. Democratic Muslims believe, according to their declarations and books, that democracy is not opposed to Islam. And one group says that democracy increases our possibilities and the other group, that democracy is the compulsory *Shura* [Islamic consultation, as mentioned in the Koran].
>
> 2. Democratic Muslims propose an Islamic conception of democracy and say that they try to choose from the latter those parts that do not contradict Islam. It is possible [from their view] to develop a parliamentary Islamic jurisprudence (*fiqh barlemani*) that configures the idea of an Islamic democracy through specific rules. They see no wrong in adhering to legislative power through democracy and do not consider it as incompatible with Islam because they do not accept what the religious law forbids (as it is the opinion of "parliamentary Muslims" in Jordan). And among them, people see no ill to be in charge of the ministries in the executive branch, pretending that Joseph [Yusuf] was in charge of a ministry under the rule of the Pharaoh! . . .
>
> 3. The third type declares that democracy, in its essence, certainly contradicts Islam and still, there is no Islamic prohibition to fight it within the Parliament. They do not allow themselves to get into the executive power, since it is the field that was forbidden by Allah, based on the prevailing laws in the Muslim countries. They believe that the Islamic law allows the democratic practice

within the parliamentary mandate so as to dissent within it!

4. The fourth group clearly declares that democracy is denial of Allah's legitimacy (*kufr billah*) and that its principles lead to disbelief (*kufr*). And out of powerlessness (*istidh'af*) they indulge in it in order to accomplish the Islamic Awakening (*Sahwah*). They do not enter the Parliament other than as a majority in order to start building up a government that rules by the religious laws and abrogates democratic action in the Western sense. The Front Islamique de Salut in Algeria practiced this model, particularly through the declarations of its religious leader Ali Bilhaj. And this is the least deviant type of democracy [in regard to Islam] and the most rare.

5. The last type does not aim to hold the power, [believing that] there is no hope [to impose Allah's rule through democracy], taking into accounts the situation of the countries and the cooperation within the parliamentary mandate in order to attain the Right through that means.

Al Suri's analysis owes much to social and political sciences. His aim is to prove that the Muslim democrats cannot succeed. In many cases, from Algeria to Egypt and elsewhere, they have been unable to shape the political landscape according to Islam. For him, the first two of the five groups he enumerates are not authentic Muslims, the last two being moved by a genuine concern for Islam but unable to achieve their goals within the godless political system. He extends his criticism to democracy much in the same way as Maqdisi does, underscoring the incompatibility between political pluralism and Islam:

> Muslim Democrats have to comply with an elective constitution and electoral laws and the following items:
>
> 1. The recognition of the system's legitimacy and the legitimacy of its leaders—they may be presidents, kings, or emirs.
>
> 2. The recognition of the [non-Islamic] Constitution that is applied in the country and the oath of allegiance to its supremacy and to acting according to it.
>
> 3. The recognition of its fundamental principles for governing within the prevailing system and the foundations of its creation as such.
>
> 4. The recognition of people's equality in their political rights in regard to the right of candidacy and election and vote within the parliament, setting aside their religion, sex, belief, or any other factor.
>
> 5. The recognition of the alternation of power and the right of all to compete and to be candidates in the elections.

6. The recognition of the principle of acceptance of the majority decisions and their coming into effect in a lawful manner, setting aside the specific position of the person during the vote and its value for the Umma after its becoming operational.

7. The recognition and subscription to the electoral law in force in all its aspects according to which power is granted [to those who have the majority] according to the results [of the vote].[26]

In addition, parliaments cannot resist the dictates of the rulers, and in many cases secular constitutions exclude any real action within the legislative body in favor of Islam:

> Reference is made to the Constitution and the official tribunals concerning the prevailing laws in case of litigation between legislative, executive, or judicial powers or within each of these powers and the right of the President or the King to dismiss the parliament and to suspend the Constitution in most cases. There are also other conditions to which those who take part in the elective operations submit in special cases in specific countries, as the ban on political parties based on religion as in most of the Arab and Islamic countries like Egypt, nowadays. The secular nature of the power in its principle and setup is constitutionally recognized in countries like Turkey as well as the direct occupation [of Muslim lands by unbelievers] like Palestine and Iraq nowadays.[27]

Al Suri's main argument is that without Jihad the political arena will be dominated by godless political systems under the aegis of the West. To bring genuine Islam to Muslim lands necessitates the recourse to legitimate violence through Jihad. Democratic Muslims are prisoners of a political system whose legitimacy they are forced to recognize by playing parliamentary games and whose power structure precludes any significant initiative for the sake of Islam.

Tartusi identifies democracy and idolatry (*taqut*) much in the same manner as Al Suri and Maqdisi. For him, the history of Western democracy is not the emancipation from the yoke of despotic regimes; it is rather the deployment of a fake theocracy. The latter usurps the right of Allah and attributes it to humans by deifying the human being, legitimizing the domination of another type of pope over the people, namely the legislative assembly:

> Democracy acted to uproot the political domination of the popes of the (Catholic) Church so as to give it to the [new] popes of

representative assemblies, setting the principle of power in people, as well as the domination of Man (Creature) over Man and the divinity of Man over Man.[28]

Democracy is the separation of religion and State, ruling and life (*hukm wal hayat*), brandishing the famous slogan: give to Caesar his due and to God, His.

To God belong prayers in some corners of the temple and monastery, and otherwise, whatever belongs to the realms of political, economic, social, and legal life and other domains of it are not the attributes of God but the attributes of Caesar. . . .

They say: God doesn't exist, and life is only matter. . . . And to those who believe in the Creator of the world, Democracy says: this belief is yours, but you don't have the right to impose it on others or force them to adhere to it, even if they oppose you in that belief, because this is based on the freedom of belief.[29]

Freedom of belief, from this viewpoint, is the denial of Allah and therefore unacceptable. Democracy allows all those acts that are forbidden by Allah, like indulging in games, exploiting the weak, monopolizing economic activities, and satisfying one's sexual drives outside any institution, all within a secular rule:

And those who want to exploit the others, to monopolize or to gamble, it is their right, and no one can under democracy deny them these because this is based on economic freedom, freedom of property, acquisition, and profit-making.

Democracy is the large garment people dress in because it allows them to escape from all the ties that limit their whims, their sensual pleasures, and their reprehensible passions. It enables all groups to head toward their sexual drives and their wishes, be they heretical communities who do not believe in Allah or those who believe in Allah but are secular (*almani*); or be they nationalist or ethnically based. We even find many low-level or high-level Muslims who believe in democracy and ask for it to rule the country.[30]

Democracy is seen not as a political system but as a holistic culture, encompassing society and economics, all outside the realm of divine rights. As such, the fight against democracy is directed not only toward a political system but toward a global, depraved civilization with its illegitimate religious creed, its bestial sexual drives, its reprehensible "passions," and its corrupt economic rules. Jihad is not meant to be simply defensive (to recuperate Muslim land, as in the

traditional view) but global and offensive, against generalized godlessness. It encompasses all aspects of life and in this way is a total war
against unbelief and secularism.

From the perspective of the Jihadists, democracy and secular
dictatorships are of the same stuff: denial of Allah's rule on earth. As
Tartusi writes, "Seyed Qutb—Allah bless his soul—said: people in all
[political] regimes on the earth hold one another for god and exclude
Allah. Be that the highest democracy or the lowest dictatorship, it
is the same."[31] Freedom of belief is in reality nothing but apostasy:
"Democracy is based on freedom of religion and belief. People can
believe in what they want under the shadow of democracy and choose
the religion they want. But this is apostasy, or resulting in apostasy,
directed against the religion of Allah, ending up in heresy and the
worship of someone else than Allah."[32]

Reference to Ibn Taymiyah, the major hardliner medieval theologian, is one of the common denominators among Jihadists in their
fight against modern freedom and political pluralism: "Ibn Taymiyah
says: religion is obedience, and some people obey Allah, and some others don't. The combat is necessary until the only religion is Allah's."[33]
Proponents of materialism are heretics, and according to Islam they
should be eliminated from the face of the earth: "Islam determines
its rulings toward the People of the Book including Zoroastrians as is
predominant [in the traditions] in three ways: either [conversion to]
Islam—and Islam makes it necessary to follow what was said—or the
religious tax (*jiziyah*), and they are therefore abased [*saqirun*: slavish,
lowly] or [besides the two mentioned alternatives,] killing and fighting. Those Heretics who say: there is no god but the life of the matter,
they worship idols, and they can be Arabs or others. In Allah's religion
there is no other way to treat them than to kill and to fight them. Allah
says: Fight them until sedition (*fitna*) ends up and there is no religion
other than Allah's (Anfal, 39)."[34] The idea of mutual understanding
and peaceful coexistence, although historically a rule between Muslim
and non-Muslim lands for centuries (with ups and downs), has no
legitimacy from the Jihadists' point of view. Besides their conversion
to Islam, there are two ways to cope with non-Muslims, either humiliating them (through paying a tax) or killing them.

Democratic freedom is not only a political choice irrespective
of faith but also freedom in depravity, obscenity, and lewdness, and
it tramples all the moral values that ensure the permanence of the
patriarchal family: "They say: democracy does not enter the problems related to the personal freedom. One can be an apostate and
he is free; one decides to have a girlfriend or a mistress, he is free; a

woman decides to betray her husband [by taking a lover], she is free, and the husband should not complain!"[35] In this respect, Jihadists share the convictions of religious conservatives in the West and many anti-modern individuals who fear contemporary threats to traditional moral values, irrespective of their religion.

Another aspect of democracy that is unbearable to Jihadists is freedom of speech, which allows desecrating and insulting Islam (Allah, the Prophet, and the Holy Koran among others):

> Democracy is based on the principle of the freedom of interpretation and expression, whatever it is, even if it insults and reviles the very essence of Allah, His books, and His Prophets. There is nothing sacred in Democracy that would be forbidden to insult or to attack through abominable words. Putting into question this principle means putting into question the democratic regime of freedom in totality, and this means undermining the holy freedoms from the viewpoint of Democracy and the Democrats!
>
> What Democracy in this respect treats as sacred is from the Islamic viewpoint disbelief and heresy because there is no freedom in Islam for mean and false words, words that create dissent among the Believers about their religion and prevent the victory of Truth, words that propagate divergence instead of unity, words that disseminate debauchery and what is forbidden.[36]

The secular political system separating religion and the state is seen by Tartusi as another democratic feature to be rejected in the name of Islam. Although for centuries Muslim lands were ruled by non-Muslims (like the Mongols) or rulers that were not totally respectful toward religious prohibitions (the consumption of wine in the Umayyad and Abbasid caliphates), Tartusi joins the minority of inflexible Muslims who declare war against moderate Muslims and those whom they treat as heretics.

Repeating the Jihadist creed about democracy as worship of idols and a fake religion, al Suri underscores the incompatibility between Islam and political pluralism:

> Democracy is based on the belief that people are the unique commanders for the solution of conflicts and hostilities. If there is any conflict between the governor and the governed or between the leadership and the others, both threaten to consult people, and it is the right of the people to solve their conflicts. This contradicts the principle of the Uniqueness of Allah, which specifies that the ultimate

reference in conflicts is uniquely Allah Almighty [represented by the Koran and the Prophetic tradition, Sunna] and no one else.[37]

Excluding religion from the realm of politics is ignoring the Creator's right over the Creature and the subservience of the latter toward the former, Allah's commandments determining man's politics: "Democracy is based on the principle of the separation of religion and State, of politics and life: what belongs to Allah is His and . . . people are like Caesar in Democracy. . . . This is Heresy in Islam's commandment stipulating that Islam is religion of State, Politics, rule and legislation and is much wider in scope than restricted only to rituals or to the walls of temples and there is no doubt that the former is Heresy to Islam."[38]

Democratic freedom is totally different from Islamic freedom. The latter implies that one accepts Allah's prohibitions and willingly submits to them, those restrictions extending to the most elementary acts in daily life:

> Democracy is based on personal freedom, and under Democracy one can do what they want and practice what they want if it is not opposed to the man-made law of the country. This word is obviously wrong and corrupt, and to warrant it means to declare allowed what Allah has forbidden to Creatures. Freedom to act as one wishes and desires is among the mortal sins in religion.
>
> From the Islamic perspective man's freedom is borrowed from Islam and is restricted to the limits of religious law and what is imposed through the necessities and obligations and religious traditions, and it is not in the Muslim's realm—in case he wants to remain within Islam and its customs and rules—to be free in order to violate Islamic restrictions, its customs and rules and to commit what is forbidden. . . . [In Islamic traditions] we find that the duties of the religion are imposed upon the Muslim, and they are part of those strict rules in man's life. They restrict man's life in how he eats, how he drinks, how he dresses, how he sleeps and even how he defecates, how he enters the WC at home and how he exits, in relation to the important matters that wield general rules and the general interest for which Islam leaves no room for the desires and opinions of the people.[39]

Another aspect of democracy that is in total disagreement with Islam is the freedom of political parties, irrespective of their religious tenet: "Democracy puts at its foundation the freedom of organizing political parties and groups, whatever the religious faith or the ideas or morals of these parties and groups! This foundation is wrong for the following reasons: . . . They have the right to exist in order to disseminate their false ideas, their depravity and heresy in the country and among the people and this is in contradiction with the commandments and texts of the religious law. . . . According to Ibn Taymiyah, any group of people who publicly refuse to abide by the Law of Allah (*Shari'ah*) recurrently bring upon themselves Jihad, until the religion of Allah is applied by them with the consensus of the Ulama."[40] Muslims and non-Muslims are fundamentally unequal from the orthodox Islamic view. Giving the latter the same rights by their votes as the former is declaring war on Islam: "Political pluralism within democracy—equality between Muslims and non Muslims—is against absolute arguments that forbid Muslims to follow non-Muslims according to the verse: 'Allah won't give Heretics the opportunity to lead Muslims.' . . . Pluralism leads to disunity, and dissension is the cause of Allah's punishment. . . . Political elections in the democratic fashion are forbidden by Islam because they aren't conditional on the religious stance of the elector and the elected, according to general or specific commandments of Islam."[41]

Democracy is based on individualism, and traditional Islam rejects individualism in the name of the Umma and its welfare. Fear of individualism is embodied in orthodox Islam and is being revitalized by Jihadist intellectuals in terms of waging holy war to save the Islamic community from the havoc of democratic egocentrism. Al Suri expresses his views by mentioning two Sayings (Hadith) of the Prophet:

> A Hadith of the Prophet says: in a ship those who were at the bottom received the water resulting from the waves. They said to themselves: if we make a hole in the ship we'll get rid of the water flowing from above us. They did it, and they sank the ship. Those at the lowest level in our time stand for the propagandists of democracy, who would like to dig a hole in the ship by their doubts, their desires, and their false deeds.
>
> The Umran in Koran, 103 says: "Cling together to Allah's string and do not scatter."
>
> A trustworthy Saying of the Prophet (*hadith sahih*) says: "You should be together, beware of breaking up because the Devil is with he who is alone. Satan already moves away when two persons are together and if people wish the prosperity of paradise, they should be together.[42]

From al Suri's point of view, the togetherness warranted by Islam is against the principles of democracy. In it, the individual decides in a sovereign manner on every matter of concern. Multiplicity of political parties wreaks havoc on the consensus within the Umma and severs the organic ties within it: "There are many commandments and texts that order the community to preserve the unity of the minds. . . .The constitution of numerous political parties is nothing but the scattering and the dispersal of the Muslims, and, in this respect, it is Heresy."[43]

Another feature of democracy is the rule of the majority, and this is in total contradiction with Allah's religion: "Democracy is based on the validity of the majority's stance even if they agree on what is religiously wrong and ungodly, Truth being what the majority decides and nothing else!"[44] This principle is wrong: "If their majority does not believe in Allah, they are heretical" (Sura Joseph, 106). "A Saying of the Prophet states: 'Islam began as a lonely stranger (*qarib*) and will be as it began, as a lonely stranger and the bliss is with lonely strangers. . . . The Prophet said: 'Upright people are a minority, whereas disloyal people are numerous and those who sin are more numerous than those who obey Allah.' In a trustworthy Saying, the Prophet says: People are like a hundred camels. Among them only one can endure the hardships and the sufferings of the journey that is the religion, and this is the reason for the lonely and the stranger nature (*qurbah*) of the vanguards of Islam, who endured sufferings and took them on themselves to lead the way for this religion."[45]

The anti-majority and anti-democratic features of traditionalist religion are blended with modern radical ideology: the majority is alienated, and the revolutionary vanguard's duty is to awaken them by their action. "Revolutionary vanguard" is conflated with the traditional perception of "Men of Allah" as a minority of "lonely strangers." This combination makes it possible to bring together those who are dissatisfied with modernity and those who are merely traditional, although the two groups are distinct and in many ways opposed to each other.

Al Suri insists that the majority's view is generally wrong and that a tiny minority of genuine Muslims is right: "Many texts and works underscore that the majority is in most cases heretical and wrong, depraved and untrue, and that people of truth are scanty, wrongdoers are numerous, and those who sin are more numerous than those who obey Allah. The right standard for the knowledge of truth is according to the absolute Truth written down in the Book and the Traditions of the Prophet and what its [genuine] followers and disciples say.

Anything else is wrong and perverse, even if most of the inhabitants of the Earth approve it."[46]

The idea that the majority is right is offensive to the ears of traditional Muslims (it used to be the same for traditional Catholics in the eighteenth and nineteenth centuries). It is, at the same time, offensive to the ears of those who suffer from the consequences of modernization. It is also offensive to the ears of those for whom Western domination is carried out under the guise of democracy and democratization. This makes the alliance of many different people possible under the banner of radical Islam. It explains as well the success of radical Islam after the collapse of communism as the only alternative ideology to liberalism in the Muslim world, bringing under the same banner reactionaries, leftists, and all those who are anti-modern for different reasons.

Democracy is "dissension" (*fitna*: a dissension from within that tends to destroy the unity of the Muslim community) because of its endless quarrel and quibble among those who propose different interpretations of freedom and right and wrong as well as constitutional rights and duties. For Jihadist intellectuals the Koran and the traditions are transparent, unequivocal, and entirely clear at their core. There is no other valid interpretation than theirs, and it is within the reach of humans to have a true and unquestionable interpretation of the sacred text as proposed by them. The Koranic sura that contradict their tenets are qualified as "ambiguous" in the sense that they are beyond the reach of human understanding and therefore should not be referred to, as we have already seen. This attitude denies any pluralism in the interpretation of the sacred text. Against democratic uncertainty and endless doubts, Jihadism presents a set of clear-cut ideas that can be mottoes for action. This is a solace to many, tormented by infinite discourses on what is good and what is bad, what is right and what is wrong, without any certainty to cling to.

Another major feature of democracy that makes it abominable to Jihadists is the equality of rights among citizens, irrespective of their faith. All Jihadists (Maqdisi as already mentioned, al Suri and Tartusi as well) agree on this issue: "Democracy is based on the principle of equality of the rights and duties between all religions and people in society, aside from their religious belonging and belief, their way of life and their moral values. In Democracy, the most heretical, depraved, and ignorant people are equal to the most pious, righteous, and cognizant ones in voting for the ruler of the country and people as well as their rights and duties! This equality undoubtedly confirms their depravity and their falsehood and expresses their opposition and their incompatibility to so many solid texts of the [Islamic] religion. . . . Those who do not differentiate between Jews, Christians, and other Heretics on the one hand, Muslims on the other . . . are Heretics themselves."[47]

Islamic tradition is by its very nature nonegalitarian in matters involving Muslims and non-Muslims. Reformists (and in their own way, Fundamentalists) seek to question inequality between Muslims and non-Muslims by reinterpreting Islamic commandments. Jihadists opt for a much more radical attitude, becoming even more inflexible than traditional Islam in matters related to politics and culture. For Tartusi, political pluralism is set against Allah's rule and is the worst enemy of Islam: "Allah does not allow secular parties and their liberties, and they are neither recognized [by Him] nor legitimate. Those who attribute this absolute Untruth [equality of all citizens] to the religion of Allah and to what Allah revealed to His Prophet and ordered him to do commit a greater crime and express a more obvious lie than those who give the authorization to prostitution in the name of Allah's religion and His commandment (according to verse 28 of the Sura Al A'raf)."[48]

Political parties are like a cursed dissension (*fitna*) among Muslims. They jeopardize the Unity of the Islamic community, which should be the reflection of Allah's uniqueness:

> These political parties and, in particular, secular ones, intensify the dissension within the Umma, jeopardize its Unity and multiply its allegiance to different factions and parties that are antagonistic, adversarial and cause hatred among Muslims about what Allah sent to them as evidence of His religion. This is against Allah's commandment about the unity (*wahdat*) and the collective clinging of Muslims to His rope [alluding to: "Cling to the Rope of Allah and do not disseminate," Sura Imran, 103], which rejects dissension and division, mutual hatred and antagonism. . . . A confirmed Saying of the Prophet (*hadith sahih*) states: you have to be together and don't be in factions because the Devil is with lonely people and strays away from two persons together; those who desire the pleasures of paradise should stay together.[49]

The stress on unity, even the obsession with it, as already mentioned, is one of the main characteristics of Jihadists. They don't accept the complexity of modern life, and they present as a solution to the ills of modernity the return to Allah's religion in its most uncompromising form. But their view of Islam is also an "interpretation," based on an inflexible attitude toward modernity, the nostalgia of lost unity in the Muslim world, and the cult of heroism embodied in the original Muslims. Unity without dissension is the opposite of democratic diversity and its management of dissension within the institutional bounds provided by human-made constitutions.

For Tartusi, democratic diversity is dissent among Muslims and their weakening. The only way to restore the past glory and the power of Islam is to return to its organic unity: "In unity lies power and in factions, weakness. . . . Islam is the religion of unity in everything, and it is the religion of healthy hearts and their purity and righteous fraternity and sincere cooperation among all the people in virtue of the united Umma and united people. It does not agree with political parties and does not accept it!"[50] What he proposes is a unique political party, akin to the fascist system, that would be the image of Umma's unity: "There is no way other than dismissing all political parties and assemble Umma's forces in a single party (*hizb wâhid*) that would act to achieve its independence and freedom and establish the principles of the general internal reform (*islah*). Then it would trace the lines of action to the people by organizing them according to the unity required by Islam."[51]

In a world beset by uncertainty, dismemberment of traditional societies, and the breaking of their organic bonds and organizations, the obsession with Unity becomes a potent utopia to eliminate all those traumatizing aspects of modern life, in particular in the Islamic world, dominated by secular despotic powers or by corrupt religious rulers:

> Islam is the religion of Unity in everything: Allah is unique in His names and attributes, His acts and His characteristics, and there is no partner to Him, no one similar to Him. And the Prophet who compels the unity of his followers, and there is no prophet after him, and the Qibla that requires to make the unique daily prayers in its direction, and the Community of the redeemed and victorious [Muslim community] that demands its multiplication as a single [unique] entity that does not become multiple, whatever the distance between its members in different regions, and the Truth (*haq*) that requires that its followers be unified and not divided. In all these cases besides this [the Unity] there is nothing but perdition: "Therefore, besides Truth there is nothing but perdition" (Sura Yunes, 32).[52] Political parties oppose god-ordained Unity: "Religious law orders unity and togetherness, commanding that one should cling collectively to the noose of Allah [reference

to the Koranic verse Al Umran, verse 103] and to be Creatures of Allah as loving brothers. Dispersion [because of political parties] breaks us as much as difference [of opinion], tension, rancor, and opposition. The former [Unity] is impossible to realize under the laws of [political] parties."[53]

What is disturbing to Jihadist intellectuals is that political parties mark the end of the myth of a unified Muslim society. Modern Muslim countries are bleak pictures of what the caliphate used to be at the time of its splendor. They impute present weakness and disorganization within Muslim societies to their inability to achieve organic unity. They share this feeling with many critics of modernity, according to whom modernity puts an end to the "harmonious" original life of humanity. According to Jihadists, political parties carry with them sentiments and emotions that are non-Islamic, even anti-Islamic in their deep layers, like vying, envying, "hating" (competing), all of them considered as legitimate by them: "It does not escape anyone seeking the Truth that political parties in their famous shape, their contradictory programs, their obvious aspirations to power and the pursuit of power and domination, are destined to spread dissension among the Muslims, break their unity, abase their dignity, and divide their sense of belonging. Their division within parties and groups far from each other results in their hating each other, their heritage being hatred and jealousy, rupture and mutual rebuttal and, on top of it, social illnesses that cause depravity and other ills that no one measures up besides Allah."[54]

Political parties introduce the individualization of politics in the shape of personal ambitions and individual choices, and this endangers the sense of Unity within the Umma and is dreaded by Jihadists. In their modern form, Jihadists are themselves at least in part the result of the individualization and failed modernization of Muslim societies, but they point to individualization as a curse against Islam, promoted by the West in a conscious manner to destroy Allah's religion.

One of the few Jihadist intellectuals who do not frontally reject the concept of the political party is Abu Qatada. He shares much criticism of democracy with other Jihadists but introduces some nuances in regard to political parties. He distinguishes between the corporatist attachment to parties (*al asabiyat al hizbiyah*) that is deeply negative and divisive and the system of political parties (*hizbiyah wa tahazzub*) that is a way of organizing society.[55] For him, contrary to other Jihadists, there is no organic nexus between the two. The ills attributed to political parties have their roots in the individualism (*fardiyah zatiya*) that engenders divisions and illegitimate groups (*firaq*), not every political party. He inverts Jihadist arguments by asking the question "Is it better to see the Umma gathering in a thousand organizations and a primary political party or each one, according to their whims and passions, having thousands of people? If there aren't political parties, won't they create within themselves new parties and numerous organizations?"[56] For him, according to the Prophet, "every Muslim is to another Muslim like a part of a unique body, and therefore, when an organ of the body suffers, the other parts become vigilant and support it."[57]

He recognizes some Muslims reject political parties and others join them, without knowing which attitude is legitimate from a religious viewpoint. His stance is based on the assumption that a unique political party is legitimate in Islam. He justifies his claim with a Saying of the Prophet that refers to a small group of people among the Muslim community who continue to fight up to the Day of Judgment, called the "assisted group" (*ta'ifah mansurah*). This group will be the leader of the Muslim community in situations in which the majority has given up Jihad. It will lead the only political party that is allowed in Islam (the party of Allah, Hizballah), against all the others. This unique political party made of "virtuous" people gives Abu Qatada the opportunity to legitimize it because it has no "corporatist" (*asabiya*) bias and can lead Muslims to victory through holy war. This Jihadist political party is very close to the Communist or Fascist Party, called to lead the rest (the proletariat or the Volk) to final victory.

Another aspect of democracy that arouses the wrath of the Jihadists is economic freedom. People can earn and spend as they wish, without having to pay Islamic taxes. This makes their financial dealings unlawful from the Islamic perspective. Moreover, interest rates (*riba'*, usury) are illicit, as much as is refusing to pay Islamic alms and taxes (*zakat*): "Democracy is based on the principle that the real owner of the goods is the Human being and therefore, it is up to him to earn it the way he wishes, in the same way as it is up to him to choose how to spend it as he desires and wishes, even if this is prohibited and banned by the religion of Allah. That is what they call economic freedom and free capitalism! This is against the Islamic rule. Allah is the actual owner of goods and Human being is only His delegate and is responsible for them before Allah: how he earns them, how he spends them. . . . And the Human being in Islam is not free to earn his living in forbidden manners (*haram*) and in non-authorized ways like usury, bribe, and other prohibited ways."[58] In financial matters, Islamic radicals and Muslim Fundamentalists are in agreement on the principles. What distinguishes them is the way they intend to deal with it. For Jihadists violence and Jihad are the sole meaningful way of dealing with the phenomenon worldwide, whereas most Islamic Fundamentalists seek alternative ways of supervising economic activities, opening up "halal banking" and "Islamic finances" within the prevailing international banking system.

For Jihadists, Muslims are in a deep crisis in their confrontation against the West. The unique solution is renewed faith in Allah: "The crisis affects Muslims in their confrontation with the victorious and triumphant West that dominates Muslim countries. [We can win] if we are confident in ourselves as being uplifted by our Faith, as Allah explained it to us: 'Don't feel weak and don't be sad because you'll be the highest if you are a believer.'"[59] Against internal and external ills that besiege Islam, the proposed remedy is "subjective": rejecting the feeling of weakness (*wahn*) and sadness and being uplifted by Islam. There is a deep voluntarism in this perception of faith, which is interpreted in two different ways, modern and traditional at the same time, without major conflict. In modern fashion, the will overcomes all the shortcomings in reference to Allah, by multiplying its energy and power. In traditional fashion, Allah sustains the will and saves the believer in a miraculous way. The subjectivism of the Jihadists satisfies therefore two distinct, yet often opposed categories of believers: traditionalists (reference to miracles) and modernized (reference to voluntarism of the faith and the individual belief of the Muslim).

For Jihadists, democracy is close to the Arabic word *Ibahiyah*, whose meaning is "licentiousness" and accomplishment of what has been forbidden by Allah. In this sense democracy is the reign of bestiality: "A Muslim is not allowed by religion to use the word democracy in his discussions in a positive way. . . . The synonym to democracy in Arabic is *Ibahiya* [licentiousness, license, libertinism, dissoluteness]. *Ibahiyah* proceeds in its principle from the authorization of what is prohibited by religion like the banning of nakedness and adultery, sodomy (*liwat*), drinking alcoholic beverages, marriage with those who aren't allowed to get married to (sisters, mother . . .), forbidding of apostasy and ruling according to other norms than those of Allah. All that is forbidden by religion. They avoid nothing but what their passions and desires ban from them or what their influential idols (*tawaqit*) agree to ban!"[60]

Political parties are based on the thirst for power and greed, and this is against the true Islamic ruler who should follow Allah, be disinterested, and accept power without any greed: "Political parties—it is clear from their action and ethics—look for domination, even through mutual killing and fight, so as to get power and leadership. This attitude is their maximum motivation and they cover it up by their [supposed] intentions of reformation and the love for counseling (*Shura*). This . . . does not satisfy Allah the Great."[61]

Democracy squares with the desires of "lowly people" and their unhealthy passions rather than of those "who know." This is the typical attitude of reactionary elites all over the world toward pluralism. In this respect, Islamic radicalism is synonymous with reactionary traditionalism: "The parties, through their publications and their specific means, spread the politics of bad examples and expand baseness and depravity in the public. They push people to listen to their actions. . . . Their action . . . is in accordance with the passions of the lowly people."[62]

Political parties, at best, waver between Islam and godlessness; at worst, they create a dual allegiance (to the caliph and to the head of the party) that results in hypocrisy (*munafiqun*: those who, under the guise of Islam, spread dissension and distrust toward Allah). "Political parties under the Islamic government educate Muslims toward duality, hypocrisy, fickleness, dishonesty, and disunity. On the one hand, they offer their commitment and their fealty to the Muslim ruler and on the other hand, to the party and its leader! And this is peculiar to the people of Hypocrisy and to those who waver in a dishonest way as says Allah the Almighty (The Women 143)."[63] This double allegiance is punished in Islam by the execution of those who spread it: "Paying allegiance to the leader of the political party—when the real Imam of the Muslims exists—and obeying him in what stimulates or repels is what Islam forbids to the utmost degree. It orders the murder of he who asks people for allegiance for his own sake after the general allegiance to the Muslim Caliph."[64] The Muslim caliph is here the equivalent of the Platonic virtuous "philosopher king." The major problem Jihadists face is that the caliph does not exist under the present circumstances. They present solutions to that as well (see below). Still, the virtuous caliph, under modern conditions, turns out to be an autocratic ruler rather than a disinterested, righteous governor.

Al Suri puts forward another reason for his rejection of political parties in reference to the notion of "reprehensible innovation" (*bid'a*). Traditional societies do not like change in an explicit manner. Change is perceived as utterly negative, contrary to modern societies, where it is considered positive, unless the contrary is proven. In reference to the frame of mind of traditional Islam (and this can be extended to many other religions as well), political parties are a reprehensible innovation (*bid'a*): "These political parties in their present shape innovate reprehensibly in matters that were unknown to the forefathers of the Umma (*salaf al umma*), and every reprehensible innovation is perdition, and every perdition merits the fire of Hell."[65]

Contrary to the Jihadist trend, Islamic Reformists treat political parties as the equivalent of the *Shura* (Islamic counseling) or *Hizballah* (the Koranic term for the "party of Allah") or as equivalent to the diversity of the Islamic juridical schools (there are four official schools in the Sunni world—the Hanafi, the Hanbali, the Shafi'i, and the Maliki—which tolerate each other in their minor differences) and therefore totally dissimilar from reprehensible innovation. The crisis of Muslim societies pushes many people to positively credit the Jihadist interpretation rather than the Reformist.

Jihadists contend that political parties tend to be a safe haven for those politicians who have been discredited: "The existence of the multitude of political parties whose program and aims are against a unified community (*mojtama' wahid*)—even though called Islamic—prepares a fertile ground for the action of the Hypocrites (*munafiqin*) and besides them, deviant Muslims (*zanadiqeh*) with their sick mind and their dangerous aims. They find in these parties the cover up for their destructive actions and a secure sanctuary for their persons once their situation worsens and their true nature is exposed to the public. Political parties, as is obvious, intend to defend their members, particularly if they are their leaders when their treason is discovered."[66]

Jews, Masons, and other godless groups manipulate political parties. They threaten the security of Muslim societies because they might be spies in the service of foreign powers: "By following the history of many contemporary political parties, one finds many dangerous personalities, Jews, Masons and people following security organizations of godless regimes (*tawaqit*) who infiltrate them, using the antagonism between the parties to attain high positions within their hierarchies and straighten out danger for the security and the peace of the group and even perhaps, the Muslim community as a whole."[67]

Al Suri summarizes his rejection of political parties in seven points:

> The purpose of political parties is, as they say, the alternation of power through peaceful means for each period, and it is limited between the parties for about five years, more or less! This line of thought is unacceptable [for Islam] for many reasons. First of all, this is a modern thought, a stranger to the politics in religion and Islamic law (*fiqh*), and those who innovate within our religion without its being in accordance with Islam should be rejected.

Second, this thought is from the fabrication of the contemporary Godlessness (*jahiliya mu'asera*), and Islam commands us to differentiate from it, to distance oneself from it, and not to imitate it in its opinions and principles. Third, this thought is incompatible with that which is founded by the Islamic law and politics, grasped from the Book and the Prophetic tradition, based on the fact that the Muslim Sultan or the Muslim Caliph cannot be dismissed otherwise than for religious reasons that require his removal from office [and not through periodic elections]. The desires of the political parties and their aspirations out of their love for domination and their claim to be superior to the religious law in governing cannot find justification in religion. . . . Fourth, this thought ends up with the lack of political, economic, and social stability and the like . . . and when the new arrives, it destroys the old that was built before, and this is obvious in the loftiest contemporary democracies! Fifth, this thought is the clear opportunity for the deviant and reprehensibly innovating Islamic political parties to adopt queer ideas and guidelines, which are religiously unfounded (with weak religious justifications) and far from the Prophetic Tradition. . . . Sixth, this idea signifies competition between different Islamic tendencies in order to rule through sectarian groups, causing resentment and animosity among the Muslims. Seventh, Sayings of the Prophet necessitate the killing of those who compete with the Caliph or the top Muslim ruler and contest his rule, and this completely denies legitimacy to this kind of foreign idea that pollutes many of the contemporary propagandas [namely, the periodic change in leadership through elections].

In summary: there is no freedom for political parties under the Islamic government, whatever the idea and the identity of these parties and their names. Muslims are not allowed to constitute political parties under the Islamic government.[68]

This powerful pleading against political parties in particular and the democratic regime in general is one of the most potent ones in the Islamic world. Like many other Jihadist intellectuals, al Suri presents a strong case in his critique of the democratic system. He underlines the weaknesses of democracy in minute detail. Since the Marxist critique of "bourgeois democracy," this is one of the most comprehensive (this time in the name of a conservative, even reactionary) and still revolutionary conception of religion. It operates for many Muslims, Jihadists or not, as a counterculture to the official propaganda machines of autocratic regimes in the Muslim world, be they secular or religious, discredited by their inability to improve the lot of Muslims and open up to them new vistas of hope. Jihadism operates against the background of despair and bitterness within the Muslim world.

Against the multiplicity of the political parties al Suri brandishes the unique figure of the caliph or the imam: "In the Islamic government Islam is cherished in its commandment. In their government, Muslims cherish their own magnificence and their own Imam who concentrates in himself all of them and gives unity to their words. They seek protection in him and combat behind him [the enemies]; the community stands firm, and those who deviate from it opt for Hell, and those who distance themselves a span from it die as adherents of Godlessness (*Jahiliya*)."[69]

In the name of the cherished unity of the Muslims and their ruler, al Suri puts forward the imam, the unique ruler who knows better than the others the interests of Muslims and behaves accordingly. This is the despotic "philosopher king" or its modern equivalent, the dictator who heads the military or political apparatus of the state. Islamic dictatorship is the result of this conception, not the unification of the Umma under the banner of a just ruler. This conception is much closer to Fascism than to traditional Islam, which idealized the Times of the Prophet but, at the same time, underlined its exceptional nature and its inaccessibility to mortals.[70] Here, the model is supposed to be realizable, and the unity of the Muslim community and its unified leadership under the imam are taken for granted.

Tartusi, like many other Jihadists, sincerely believes that the ruler obeyed by Muslims (*Amir muta'*) is the only salvation for them. He can inspire awe and fear in the powerful idol worshippers (Western governments), contrary to the diluted rule within political parties, which are a safe haven for treacherous spies and other mischievous leaders whom the Western powers do not fear at all: "I know there is nothing that the illegitimate governments [*Tawaqit*, plural of *Taqut*] fear from the Muslims more than their concerted action with prescribed aims, because they know that this is the type of action that can succeed. The Taqut knows that if a Muslim acts for his religion in an individual and egoistic manner, they can scoff at him and humiliate him. . . . And when the same Muslim, on the contrary, acts for the sake of his religion through his community, collectively and orderly, the Ruler whom he obeys (*Amir muta'*) elevates him, and they fear him [Western governments] and open up for him thousands of accounts!"[71] According to Tartusi, Islam cannot be dissociated from a ruler with the characteristics already mentioned: "There is no religion without a Community [of believers], no Community without a religious ruler [imam] and no religious ruler without obeying [of the Faithful], and these three are indissociable."[72] Still, what is to be done if the imam is lacking? The answer is common to all Jihadists: this does not stop Jihad. "The absence of the Imam of all Muslims, who brings together their words and gathers them, should not stop from the march toward Jihad in the path of Allah."[73]

How to act in the absence of Imam? Al Suri, like other Jihadist intellectuals, refers to the notion of *isabah al mu'minah*, namely, a group of devout Muslims who keep on waging Jihad at those times when the situation might seem hopeless to many. This group strangely looks like the "revolutionary vanguard," as seen by Maqdisi: "A Hadith with high credentials (*hadith sahih*) from [the scholar] Muslim declares: there continues to exist a group (*isâbah*) of my Umma who fight for Allah's commandments and who are unforgiving to their enemies and for whom it is not a bad thing to oppose their opponents until comes the Hour [Day of Judgment] and they endeavor in that sense. The Hadith mentions that this group of fighting devout Muslims exists in our time and in all the times until arrives the Hour. This group fights, of necessity, in the path of Allah."[74] More generally, the praise of the absolute ruler in the name of Islam is common to Jihadist Sunnism as well as radical Shi'ism. The notion of the *Vali Faqih* developed by Ayatollah Khomeini is akin to that of the "Imam (or the Caliph) of the Muslims."[75] The two radical traditions, although antagonistic to each other in terms of their respective claim on Islamic legitimacy, are remarkably convergent in their denunciation of democracy and political pluralism.

One of the items to which al Suri devotes a long chapter is the claim by Islamic Reformists that democracy is legitimate since Allah has approved the *Shura* (Islamic council). Al Suri vehemently rejects this identification: "To spread democracy among people, they lie to make them believe that Counseling in Islam is democracy and that there is no difference between them and no contradiction."[76] He enumerates nine major differences between democracy and Islamic council (*Shura*):

1. *Shura* is an Arabic word, mentioned by the Holy Koran that orders to abide by it in the majority of its quotes, whereas democracy is Western and devilish, according to its birth place and origin and has no roots and does not exist in the Arabic language, and neither in the religion of Allah.

2. *Shura* is the commandment of Allah, whereas democracy is the commandment of the people and Idolatry (*taqut*).

3. *Shura* imposes the rule of Allah alone, whereas Democracy imposes the rule of the people.

4. *Shura* is based on the position of religious competence (*ijhihad*) when there is no textual reference to it, whereas democracy refers to everything and rules over everything, whatever the religious commandments about them. There isn't from the democratic viewpoint anything sacred that cannot be put into question and abased by the vote and the choice [of people].

5. *Shura* obeys the Ulama, specialized and competent people in religious matters, whereas Democracy obeys all the classes and corporations, Heretics and pious alike, ignorant and cognizant, depraved and righteous—and there is no difference between them in what is the ruling and the [political] decision-making!

6. *Shura* cares through its assessments about what is the closest to the truth and the right, even if it is contrary to the majority and the opinion of people. Democracy cares about the quantity and the trivial and works with the majority even though the result might be against the Truth and favorable to the Falsehood!

7. *Shura* is a consultative parliament whose duty is to express the ideas closest to the truth according to the rulings of religion, whereas Democracy proceeds from the legislative parliament that has the right of declaring what is allowed and what is forbidden and to enact laws different from those of Allah.

8. *Shura* derives from the religion of Allah. To believe in it is necessary, and to reject it is apostasy and exit from religion, whereas Democracy is the religion of idolatry, belief in it is Heresy, and its rejection is faithfulness to Allah.

9. *Shura*'s ruling is necessary but not compulsory, whereas Democracy's ruling is compulsory through the votes of the people, whatever its characteristics and its proximity or disaffection toward the Truth.[77]

Suri rejects historical particularity or relativity to any part of the Koran. His statements about *Shura* underscore his counter-modern attitude, his attempt at "de-secularizing" religion. In reaction to the Islamic reformists and Fundamentalists who endeavor to secularize Islam, the Jihadists reinstate religious laws and reject any adaptation to modern society. Ideologically, this is an important trend in today's Islam, the more so as Muslim societies have been deeply shaken by political as well as cultural change in the last century, without finding plausible solutions to the crisis, unlike many other societies—for example, South Korea, India, and some South American countries,

Turkey being the major exception within Muslim societies, Malaysia and Indonesia being in between.

Democracy does not only mean rejection of Allah's legislation; its concept also encompasses all thoughts and deeds condemned by the law of Allah. Maqdisi and al Suri both excoriate political pluralism as a symptom of a much deeper disbelief where "prostitute parliaments" (*majalis al fahsha'*), mixed associations and universities, and morally corrupt (*fasida*) foundations and schools go hand in hand. Democracy is a political system, but it is, as well, a perverted, deviant, immoral, and destructive culture and way of life—indeed, a perverse religion. Maqdisi calls the democratic assemblies "parliaments of godlessness, depravation and revolt against Allah" (*majalis al shirk wal fusuq wal usyan*).

Jihadists reject the idea that Democracy corresponds, at least in part, to the aspirations of the new generations. Even in the Muslim world, part of the new generations in the large cities long for a more open political system and a more participatory society. This major internal tendency within most Muslim societies is seen by Jihadists as an external conspiracy by the West to impose its laws on the Muslim world so as to extend its domination to all aspects of life. Having failed to convert Muslims to Christianity, the Occident now attempts to lure Muslims through another religion, namely secular democracy, so as to subvert the Islamic faith and prepare the way for the total submission of Muslims. Democracy is a Crusade set down in a new idiom, so as to deceive the followers of Allah: "The crusading democratic West does not stop asking Muslims—in the same fashion as Missionaries did before them—to adopt Christian religion. This objective is difficult to achieve for them, and therefore, they ask them to adopt the new religion that is the democratic one."[78]

Democracy is reprehensible in principle, but in practice it does not even apply the very same lofty values that violate the rule of Allah. In fact, according to al Suri as well as other major Jihadist intellectuals who adopt the Marxist notion of alienation, democracy is the illegitimate domination of the few over the alienated masses:

> In democratic elections enter into account many external factors that are illegal and immoral, the result being unbalanced and imprecise, not representing the real desire of the majority of the people, as they pretend it: the factor of wealth intervenes in the electoral campaign, the factor of ethnicity and family ties, the media factor, the intervention of the elites and powerful people for the success of a person against another one, or a party against another

party. Democratic elections allow as well international Unbelievers' powers to interfere in the country's politics. What precedes points out that in the democratic system, even in the US and the Western countries, people are not free. They are prisoners of many external factors that force them to take a way that is not the one they would like to take.[79]

In its essence, democracy is depravation and turning away from the right path. It ends up in destruction: "Democracy in its nature leads the way to destruction and to follow it, one has to be a crook and deviate from the [right] path."[80] There aren't only isolated intellectuals and clerics who reject democracy in the name of Allah, but also groups of clerics who sign statements together and whose signatures bear prestige and weight because of their involvement in the fight against the autocracy of Muslim regimes. The mere fact of their opposition to the prevailing political systems regarded as illegitimate by most of the population gives them credit. A group of Ulama and activists in Egypt called *Jama'at al Jihad* (community of Jihad) has signed a document, "Jihad Against Idol Worshippers: Prophetic Traditions Do Not Change," which summarizes the main objections to democracy from the Fundamentalist point of view. It begins by pointing out the classical radical view that in Islam the Testimony to Allah (the first pillar) begins by denying the existence of any other god—which means war on all the idols, including democracy (this is what the radical Muslims call Loyalty and Disavowal, as discussed in chapter 2). From this perspective, holy war against idols and idol worshippers is a founding principle of Islam. The meaning of the Testimony to Allah's uniqueness cannot be fully attested but through Jihad against the heretics. On the situation in Egypt, they summarize their view:

> The situation in Egypt can be summarized in four points:
> (1) The government is godless; (2) a group of apostates are ruling over it; (3) people are lost; (4) Muslim youth is in disarray.
> The first point is due to the lack of ruling according to the laws of Allah, and the existence of mixed laws [partially Islamic, partially human-made] attached to them. . . . (2) The mocking of the Islamic law is the worst because it postpones it or gives precedence to non-Islamic laws over it. . . . (3) Ruling through democracy was called by Mawdudi the republican ruling, and it is the deification of man. It is well-known that democracy is in contradiction to Islam in many respects.[81]

They enumerate what we have seen other Jihadists utter recurrently. The relevant point here is the concrete cases they describe, in which Islamic law and "human-made law" contradict each other:

> If a man buys a bottle of wine from somewhere, and a young Muslim tries to apply the Islamic law "Ordering what is lawful and preventing what is unlawful" (*amr bil ma'ruf wa nahy an al munkir*), he breaks the bottle. They go to the police. Who is wrong from the point of view of the man-made law and from the point of view of the Islamic law? From the Islamic view the Muslim youth [who broke the bottle] is totally innocent, and he who carried it is to be condemned under the divine law, deserving punishment. From the perspective of the man-made law, the courageous Muslim is guilty for having trespassed on the rights of a citizen to carry a bottle [of wine], who is innocent because the text of the law stipulates it.
>
> Have you seen that heretical diabolic text of the law . . . ? And if a citizen goes to a cheap place and drinks two glasses of wine, how should one treat him? What he has done is a sin according to the Islamic law but legally speaking, he is innocent and there is no punishment according to the text of the law. . . . The man-made law does not forbid the consumption of alcohol and therefore, what is forbidden [by Islam] is allowed [by the man-made law].
>
> If a man has sexual relations (*zina*) with a non-married woman with her consent, the debauchery outside the couple is not allowed, and what is its treatment through the Islamic law? This is a sin; fornication is a mortal sin, implying the criminal punishment. But according to the text of the man-made law, the woman is innocent because the law does not prohibit sexual relationship outside the marriage for an adult woman if she is acquiescent. . . .
>
> If a man changes his religion from Islam to socialism or secularism or any religion that does not comply with Islam or contradicts the religion of Allah, or someone mocks it or insults the Prophet or accuses him of cowardice, what is the sentence by the Islamic law? He is an apostate, and he deserves execution. Legally speaking (according to man-made law), there is nothing against him because he is free in his speech, and therefore, there is no punishment.[82]

The problem raised is not Western domination or the corruption and subservience of the Islamic rulers or the necessity to defend any Islamic group (Palestinians, Afghans, or anyone else) but the defense of Allah's law against human-made law, which is, for many Muslim Fundamentalists, the essence of democracy. The text of the Ulama goes on in the same fashion, mentioning what is happening on a daily basis in Muslim countries like Kuwait, Egypt, and elsewhere: "This [apostasy] happened in the country of Kuwait when a professor of sociology, Ahmad al Baghdadi, claimed that the Prophet fell back on fighting and violence after he failed in his call to the Heretics in Mecca for their conversion to Islam! There was no juridical sentence against him under the pretext of encouraging the freedom in voicing religious legal opinions (*fatwa*). If a woman appears on the stage of a theatre and sings, dances, or is dressed in a dancing costume according to the rules of the artistic corporations, what is her religious case? It is a mortal sin that deserves Islamic legal punishment, but what does the man-made law stipulate? She is an artist, free and innocent!"[83] These religious cultural issues related to Islamic traditions offend Muslim traditionalists and Fundamentalists as well as the Jihadists: women's "nakedness" in the public sphere (that is, in most cases, their not covering up their face and head with a veil, *hijab*), consumption of alcohol in public, defiance against the religion, insults against the Prophet, and so forth. All these facts publicized by the media destabilize many devout Muslims, who feel that Islam is trampled on by the new culture, mainly imported from the West.

Economic problems come into play as well. The banking system, based on loans with interest rates, is viewed by the Ulama as authorizing "usury" (*riba*), which is formally condemned by Islam. Impoverished people in Muslim cities, where traditional community assistance does not work properly anymore, feel that their economic life has deteriorated as a result of the secularization that breaks down Islamic philanthropy and mutual aid, the only one known by many Muslims. Secular governments are targets of the incriminations, including the accusation of breaking Islamic law at the service of foreign, heretical powers.

Added to these motivations related to the religious shaping of public life and its being called into question by new generations and by new secularizing trends within the Muslim world are political factors, related to the critical situation of Muslim societies and in particular, Israel's military supremacy over the Palestinians. The situation in Israel is perceived as the general model through which the United States imposes its hegemony on Muslims by humiliating them on a daily basis. In this matter, Muslim governments are accomplices of America:

> What do you say about Israel? According to the man-made law, the appropriate action is the consultation against it and the approval of the parliament against it. . . . But according to the Islamic law,

even if there are thousands of consultations against it, they are wrong because Palestine is a Muslim land, wrested by force and there is no legality in the heretical Jewish government's claim on it and therefore the [Egyptian] parliament legalizes what Islamic law forbids.

And what about Camp David that declared the end of the war against Israel . . . ? In the law of Allah and His Prophet, this is absolutely wrong because this attitude negates the proven religious duty of Jihad in the path of Allah (*fi sabil illah*). It is obvious by the consensus of the Ulama that Jihad in Palestine is a personal duty [*fardh al ayn*, each one's individual responsibility, and not a loose duty, as when Muslims attack a non-Muslim lands, *fardh al kifa*] for every Muslim.[84]

Religious malaise combines with political frustration related to Israel and the political mayhem in other Muslim lands to mobilize those Muslims who suffer from the internal evolution of society (tolerance for alcohol, women's new behavior patterns, relaxing the religious laws governing the public sphere) and those who are mainly concerned with the question of the Palestinian nation and more generally, Arab identity.

The condemnation of this situation is total and categorical, and democracy is seen as the main culprit: "Democracy is sin against Allah because it grants the right to legislate to people."[85] What is ironic is that most of the malaise related to the prevailing situation in the Muslim world is due to the lack of democracy, parliaments not being elected democratically in most Muslim countries and authoritarianism being the general rule. Still, democracy is stigmatized and condemned for its secular nature, calling into question the law of Allah. Democracy is "trash," according to Tartusi.[86] What many Muslims condemn under the heading of democracy is the new despotic rule with a mock form of democracy in Arab countries; otherwise there is no concrete experience of democracy in most of the Muslim world that would have led to disappointment and rejection. It is true that some of the major figures of Jihad lived part of their lives in the West, and they grew deeply disillusioned by their experience of democratic rule. The major object of their critique is secularization in the West, as they witnessed it in their daily life (Tartusi, al Suri, and Abu Qatada have lived long periods of their life in the West).

The critique of democracy is made not only by major Jihadist figures but also by a swarm of middle-range intellectuals or clerics who echo these critics by amplifying them through their personal links and group affiliation and by popularizing what the major intellectuals say in a more sophisticated way. Hassan Mohamed Qa'ed is one of these popularizers.[87] He begins by giving a sociological explanation of the enticements of democracy in the Muslim world, referring to despotism and the desire to achieve through democracy some of the social goals that are impeded by Arab autocracies. This is an illusion, from his point of view. Democracy is incompatible with Islam in the following cases that are akin to those raised by the Egyptian *Jama'at al Jihad*: loyalty to Islam means the rejection and disavowal of other political systems; the Islamic injunction to spread what is religiously approved and actively forbid what is banned by Allah's religion (one should, for instance, therefore act personally against those who publicly drink alcoholic beverages) is contrary to the democratic rule of law prohibiting such acts; Islamic ruling on apostasy (the execution of the apostate) contradicts democracy and its freedom of belief; the Islamic commandment toward other religious communities stipulating that they pay religious taxes (*jiziyah*) contradicts the democratic equality of citizens, irrespective of their religion; and finally, Islamic Jihad against the enemies of Islam cannot find any justification within democracy. Qa'ed does not have any original ideas of his own, but he serves as an amplifier for major Jihadist intellectuals and clerics by echoing their voices in the Muslim world.

In Islamic countries governments that have monopolized power under the heading of modern mottoes (democracy, nationalism, socialism, etc.) have done tremendous harm to the cause of democracy by turning Muslims against it. The antagonistic attitude of the United States toward the issue of democracy in Palestine (Hamas's democratic elections were rejected) and Lebanon (Hizballah characterized as a terrorist organization, although it acquired 10 percent of the seats in the Lebanese Parliament) and the American portrayal of Israel as the paragon of Western democracy have turned parts of the Muslim world against pluralism. Still, democracy is seen as the culprit even where it does not exist, like most of the Muslim world: it is the symbol of Western self-righteousness.

One major problem with democracy is the advent of complex political systems. Traditional Islam did not distinguish between legislative and juridical spheres. The former was the privilege of the ruler, based on the violence of those who dominated Muslim societies. With the advent of nationalism in the twentieth century, parliamentarism became part and parcel of Muslim political systems. But instead of contributing to its democratization, it promoted different types of oligarchies, which were disrespectful of people's votes, their members finding their place in parliaments through rigged elections and clientelism. For these reasons, parliamentarism in the Muslim world has a bad reputation. Islamic radicals manipulate this feeling of illegitimacy of the parliaments, adding to it their own inability to cope with the diversification of political systems and the necessity to adapt religious laws to new social contexts. Instead, they innovate by applying Islamic rule to the entire political system, denying freedom of action even in those spheres where Islamic tradition was rather tolerant. In fact, traditionally every situation that did not contradict Islam but did not wield a juridical commandment was usually treated as "customary" (*urf*) and more or less recognized as harmless. For Islamic radicals, politics should be subordinated to the rule of Allah, particularly in the legislative sphere. This new domain, where human society needs codifying new rules in order to cope with situations that were not anticipated by Islamic jurisprudence, is thus annexed to radical Islam, which solves the problem by recourse to fascistic solutions.

In its new form, parliamentarism puts into question traditional Islamic tenets because it promulgates "human-made laws" that are also applied to the judicial realm, with secular constitutions claiming to be the foundation of the law. This is why the hostility of many Jihadist jurists toward political pluralism is much deeper than toward dictatorships, under which people are "victims" and therefore do not have to give their approval to the social system as such. In democracies, people themselves are supposed to be the source of legislation, and this scandalizes Jihadists. Reformists and Fundamentalists try hard to find religious justifications for parliamentary systems, but radicals refuse to do so, declaring the entire system presumptuous and against Allah's privilege to legislate and rule. For them, turning away from the law of Allah and adhering to "human-made laws" are the cause of Muslims' decay: "The servility in which Muslims live in the world is nothing but the consequence of their leaving the Law of Allah."[88] Human-made law is lowly and based on an unbearable arrogance: "The rules (*ahkam*) of the creatures [opposed to the Creator] are rubbish of the mind and litter of the thought."[89]

NOTES

1. Pew Foundation statistics show that in general support for Al Qaeda is not unconditional, and in many cases, especially after Al Qaeda attacks against Muslim countries (Egypt and Jordan among others), there is outright rejection. In general, Al Qaeda embodies the "Robin Hood" syndrome in Muslim lands against an arrogant West and repressive Muslim governments. See *The Great Divide: How Westerners and Muslims View Each Other*, June 22, 2006, http://pewglobal.org/reports/display.php?ReportID=253.

2. This is the case of Turkey and, partially, Iran, where civil society movements strive to promote Islamic pluralism. Kuwait is as well the theater for a new civil society, which is in its inception.

3. "Al Qaeda," says William Wechsler, the task force director of the CIA's Illicit Transactions Group, was "a constant fundraising machine." And where did it raise most of those funds? The evidence was indisputable: Saudi Arabia. America's longtime ally and the world's largest oil producer had somehow become, as a senior Treasury Department official put it, "the epicenter" of terrorist financing. This didn't come entirely as a surprise to intelligence specialists. But until the attacks of Sept. 11, 2001, U.S. officials did painfully little to confront the Saudis not only on financing terror but on backing fundamentalists and jihadists overseas.

Charities were also instrumental in sending money to different fundamentalist groups, without any serious checking:

> The charities were part of an extraordinary $70 billion Saudi campaign to spread their fundamentalist Wahabi sect worldwide. The money helped lay the foundation for hundreds of radical mosques, schools, and Islamic centers that have acted as support networks for the jihad movement, officials say.
>
> U.S. intelligence officials knew about Saudi Arabia's role in funding terrorism by 1996, yet for years Washington did almost nothing to stop it. Examining the Saudi role in terrorism, a senior intelligence analyst says, was "virtually taboo."

David E. Kaplan, "The Saudi Connection: How Billions in Oil Money Spawned a Global Terror Network," December 7, 2003, *U.S. News and World Report.* Since 2003, when Al Qaeda began direct attacks against Saudi Arabia, the fight against it by the Saudi security and military has become much more uncompromising.

4. Reformists are the outcome of modernization within the realm of Islam. In the past groups of philosophers (*mu'tazila*), mystics (some Sufis), or poets (like Hafiz) or schools (Jahmiyah, Murji'a—see below) proclaimed different types of tolerance. But this was limited, mostly within the realm of Islam, and not legally or politically based. At the end of the nineteenth century a new type of Islamic exegesis emerged that tried to reconcile the rule of law, the pluralist political system, and democracy with Islam. Reformists revisited the tradition by reinterpreting and updating it. Today they are still a minority, mostly powerless, within the Islamic ulama and among Muslim intellectuals.

5. Abu Qatada, "Are Democrats Godless [*kuffar*] without Exception?" *Minbar al Tawhid wal Jihad.*

6. Jahmiyah and Murji'a were two Islamic groups that believed that no one should be excluded from Islam because of his deeds (or misdeeds) because religion is something internal and spiritual and God alone is able to

judge or punish people. They were rejected by orthodox Muslims for their tolerance. These expressions have gained a negative meaning in orthodox Islam, in the same way as the beliefs of the Kharijites, who were among the most intolerant.

7. Maqdisi (al sheikh Abi Mohammad), "Uncovering the Fallacies of Those Who Discuss the Subject of the Soldiers of Infidelity and the Defenders of Law," *Minbar al Tawhid wal Jihad.*

8. For example, Joseph Le Maistre, Louis De Bonald, Lamennais, Ferdinand d'Eckstein. For Le Maistre, the monarchy should be reinstated because of its divine origin, contrary to the political order inspired by the French Revolution, which is of human origin and flawed.

9. Maqdisi, "Uncovering."

10. Maqdisi, "Uncovering."

11. Maqdisi, *Al dimoqratiya din* (Democracy as a Religion), *Minbar al Tawhid wal Jihad.*

12. Maqdisi, *Al dimoqratiya.*

13. Maqdisi, *Al dimoqratiya.*

14. Maqdisi, *Al dimoqratiya.*

15. Maqdisi, *Al dimoqratiya.*

16. Maqdisi, *Al dimoqratiya.*

17. Maqdisi, *Al dimoqratiya.*

18. Maqdisi, "Uncovering the Obvious Heresy of the Saudi Government," *Minbar al Tawhid wal Jihad.*

19. Maqdisi, "Uncovering the Obvious Heresy."

20. Maqdisi, "Uncovering the Obvious Heresy."

21. Abu Mus'ab al Suri, *Da'wat al muqawama al alamiya* (Call for a Worldwide Islamic Resistance), *Minbar al Tawhid wal Jihad.*

22. Al Suri, *Da'wat.*

23. Al Suri, *Da'wat.*

24. This is at least partially the case of a former radical Islamic ideologue, the Tunisian Rashid al Ghannushi, who has lived in England since the early '90s. His view has changed over time, and he advocates a minimal state whose role is to deter violence against Muslims, change within society taking precedence over that in the government. He is nowadays very close to the Islamic Fundamentalists who reject the use of violence against others in the name of Islam, a view defended by the Jihadists. See Rashid al Ghannushi, "A Government of God?" *Al-Ahram Weekly,* December 24–30, 1998.

25. Al Suri, *Da'wat.*

26. Al Suri, *Da'wat.*

27. Al Suri, *Da'wat.*

28. Abu Basir al Tartusi, *Al Taqut* (Idolatry), *Minbar al Tawhid wal Jihad.*

29. Tartusi, *Al Taqut.*

30. Tartusi, *Al Taqut.*

31. Tartusi, *Al Taqut.*

32. Tartusi, *Al Taqut.*

150   *Chapter 4*

33. Tartusi, *Al Taqut.*
34. Tartusi, *Al Taqut.*
35. Tartusi, *Al Taqut.*
36. Tartusi, *Al Taqut.*
37. Al Suri, *Da'wat.*
38. Al Suri, *Da'wat.*
39. Tartusi, *Al Taqut.*
40. Tartusi, *Al Taqut.*
41. Tartusi, *Al Taqut.*
42. Al Suri, *Da'wat.*
43. Al Suri, *Da'wat.*
44. Al Suri, *Da'wat.*
45. Al Suri, *Da'wat.*
46. Al Suri, *Da'wat.*
47. Tartusi, *Al Taqut.*
48. Tartusi, *Al Taqut.*
49. Tartusi, *Al Taqut.*
50. Tartusi, *Al Taqut.*
51. Tartusi, *Al Taqut.*
52. Tartusi, *Al Taqut.*
53. Tartusi, *Al Taqut.*
54. Tartusi, *Al Taqut.*
55. See Abu Qatada al Falastini, *Bayn manhajayn* (Between the Two Methods), *Minbar al Tawhid wal Jihad.*
56. Qatada, *Bayn.*
57. Qatada, *Bayn.*
58. Qatada, *Bayn.*
59. Qatada, *Bayn.*
60. Qatada, *Bayn.*
61. Tartusi, *Al Taqut.*
62. Tartusi, *Al Taqut.*
63. Tartusi, *Al Taqut.*
64. Tartusi, *Al Taqut.*
65. Al Suri, *Da'wat.*
66. Al Suri, *Da'wat.*
67. Al Suri, *Da'wat.*
68. Al Suri, *Da'wat.*
69. Al Suri, *Da'wat.*
70. See Olivier Carré, *L'Islam laïque ou Le retour à la Grande Tradition* (Paris: Armand Colin, 1993), who shows Islamic realism encouraged a new path, distinct from that of the Prophet at Medina, simply because the Times of the Origin were unattainable.
71. Tartusi, *Al Taqut.*
72. Tartusi, *Al Taqut.*
73. Tartusi, *Al Taqut.*
74. Al Suri, *Da'wat.*

75. See Ayatollah Khomeini, *Velayat Faqih* (The Government of the Islamic Jurist), also published under *Hokumat-e Islami: Velayat-e faqih* (Islamic Government: Government of the Islamic Jurist), first published in 1970 in Persian, with many variants published later. English version: Ayatollah Ruhollah Khomeini, *Islamic Government*, trans. Joint Publications Research Service (New York: Manor House, 1979).

76. Al Suri, *Da'wat.*

77. Al Suri, *Da'wat.*

78. Tartusi, *Al Taqut.*

79. Tartusi, *Al Taqut.*

80. Tartusi, *Al Taqut.*

81. Jama'at al Jihad, "Jihad against the Idol Worshippers: Prophetic Traditions Do Not Change," *Minbar al Tawhid wal Jihad.*

82. Jama'at al Jihad, "Jihad."

83. Jama'at al Jihad, "Jihad."

84. Jama'at al Jihad, "Jihad."

85. Jama'at al Jihad, "Jihad."

86. See Abu Basir al Tartusi, *Al dimuqratiya al qadhira* (Democracy Is Trash), *Minbar al Tawhid wal Jihad.*

87. See Hasan Mohamed Qa'ed, *Dimoqratiyah, al sanam al asri* (Democracy: The Contemporary Idol), *Minbar al Tawhid wal Jihad.*

88. Mohammad ibn Saeed Qahtani, *Al wala' wal bara' fil islam, Minbar al Tawhid wal Jihad.*

89. Qahtani, *Al wala'.*

5

Fundamentalism in Islam

Islamic and Christian Fundamentalism have major characteristics in common as well as significant differences. Both reject secular views of religion and society; both oppose autonomy for human beings and the ideology of Enlightenment that promotes it; both are dichotomous in their worldview (one true, orthodox religion versus a diluted and marginalized version of it); both refer to a golden age and reject the accretion of traditions, promoting the notion of *sola scriptura*, which means in Christian Fundamentalism a reliance on a so-called literal reading of the Bible as the ultimate religious authority and in Islam, the privilege accorded to the Koran and the example of the Pious Forefathers (usually the Prophet and the Four Well-Guided Caliphs for the Sunnites; the Prophet, the Fourth Caliph Ali, and the Twelve Imams for the major Shiite groups); both have a theocentric view of the world; both favor conspiracy theories, believing in the existence of hidden groups plotting against them; both stress a morality with patriarchal[1] and sexual values that go against modern social trends.[2]

One major difference that distinguishes Christian and Muslim Fundamentalisms is their relation to politics. Mainstream Fundamentalism in the Christian world, with some notable exceptions like the so-called Reconstructionists, is much more independent of politics than Islam. Christian Fundamentalists generally accept democracy and intend to change society from within, asking for a minimal state and a moral society rather than challenging the government or the rule of law. In the Muslim world, Fundamentalism is directly translated into the political realm, at least since Wahhabism in the eighteenth century, with some minor exceptions like the transnational pietistic

152

association Tabliq wal Da'wa. Nowadays most major forms of Islamic Fundamentalism cannot be disconnected from politics, at least since the founding of the Muslim Brotherhood in Egypt and its offshoots in the Sunni world. In the Shi'ite world, since the Islamic Revolution of 1979, Fundamentalism has also been politicized; only traditionalist Shi'ites avoid politics.

Another feature that distinguishes Muslim Fundamentalism from its Christian counterpart is its relation to violence. Minority currents in Christian Fundamentalism become more or less violent, in particular in regard to issues like abortion. Still, recourse to physical violence is avoided in its major Fundamentalist trends, whereas in Islam, the relation to it is at best ambivalent. Islamic hyper-Fundamentalist currents are prone to violence, the most violent tendency being Jihadism, which can be identified as the radicalization of Islamic Hyper-Fundamentalist tendencies.

Finally, Christian Fundamentalism considers itself to be opposed to the secular world, whereas major Islamic Fundamentalism sects (particularly Hyper-Fundamentalists and Jihadists) view their fight not only against secularism but also against "false" (or fake) religions, among which secularism is but one of the numerous enemies: fake Muslim rulers, spurious Muslims, Crusaders and Zionists, secularism and nationalism. For them we are in a war of religions rather than battling against a nonreligious world, and secularism is a fake religion just like democracy and other major modern movements.

THREE BRANCHES OF FUNDAMENTALISM

The notion of Fundamentalism is too broad to explain the complexity of the Islamic phenomenon. A three-pronged division gives a better indication of its complexity. The first level is mainstream Fundamentalism. Many Fundamentalist groups in the Muslim world strongly believe in the literalist interpretation of the Koran and the Prophetic tradition, but they are open to participation in the pluralist parliamentary system and the right of the majority to rule. These groups have a religious understanding of Islam that is contradictory to their practice. But they live with this contradiction, accepting the verdict of the ballot and believing that in the long run people themselves will accept Islamic rule. In this scenario, imposition of their version of faith through violence or coercion is excluded on principle. These Fundamentalists, for opportunistic and sometimes ideological reasons, reject violence in their dealings with the West and dominant political powers in Muslim societies.

The second group is hyper-Fundamentalist. It accepts playing the democratic game as long as it is in the minority position, but it is not sure that it will abide by the majority rule if it holds the reins of power through democratic elections. Its basic tenet is that Islam should rule over society, but it refuses to use violence as a means to achieve that end. In reality, this group can help radical Islamists indirectly or financially, but they refuse to engage in direct fighting through violence. The FIS in Algeria was hyper-Fundamentalist. GIA, its offshoot, became Jihadist, after the military coup that ousted the FIS from the parliament in 1991.

The third group is Jihadists. Their views are close to those of hyper-Fundamentalists, but they strongly believe that the parliamentary game or peaceful attempts at imposing Allah's rule are doomed to failure and only sacred violence warranted by Jihad can overcome the obstacles.

The three groups have a common denominator, namely the aspiration to build up an Islamic theocracy in Muslim countries and, beyond that, the world. Still, the commonalities between them do not prevent them from fighting each other or even using violence against each other.[3] Fundamentalism, hyper-Fundamentalism, and Jihadism maintain ambivalent relations with each other. Unlike Judaism and Christianity, Islam has not undergone a long process of secularization. Islamic Fundamentalism is not only a means of living a pure faith within the closed circle of a self-proclaimed elite but also a movement that intends to conquer the world, peacefully for the major groups within it, through violence in the case of Jihadists. Islamic Fundamentalism can be pushed toward hyper-Fundamentalism, and the latter can become Jihadist through many mechanisms. Fundamentalist converts and born-again Muslims indicate that in some cases Fundamentalists become Jihadists (for more on converts and born-again Muslims, see chapter 6). The utopia of the unified and worldwide Umma has to be realized in this world, not the other, and there is projection not toward an "undetermined" future but toward a future to be construed in real terms, for Islamic Fundamentalists and hyper-Fundamentalists alike.

Secularization has a long way to go in Islam in order to renounce the accomplishment of religious utopia here and now or in the near future, mainly through violence. Islamic hyper-Fundamentalism is ideologically close to Jihadism, although strategically it is far from it. Another feature that distinguishes Fundamentalism from Jihadism (and hyper-Fundamentalism is closer to Jihadism in this respect) is that personal involvement for Jihad is not on the mainstream Fundamentalist agenda, whereas Jihadists are ready to engage individually in violent action, to accomplish the City of Allah (here, *madinat an nabi*, the City of the Prophet, the Golden Age of the rule of the Prophet in Medina) on earth.[4]

Another characteristic of the Muslim hyper-Fundamentalists is that they are anti-modern in a much more active way than Christian fundamentalists. The "nudity" of women (that is, their taking off the veil) and women's involvement in public life are much more "painful" than in the West, where feminist movements have exerted a deep influence. Other faiths have a similar anti-modern stance among their Fundamentalist believers (Hindus and even some Christian sects, for example), but they do not have the same type of unified ideology, with intellectuals and religious institutions that would enable them to mobilize, as in Islam. It is essential to understand the role of cultural factors, especially the extent to which they contribute to the strength of Fundamentalism in Islam. The breakdown of barriers between the public and private spheres, women's entry into the public sphere, and the influence of Western mores on Muslim societies (like the consumption of alcohol, homosexuality in the public sphere, and the entire industry of movies that promote exhibitionism as a new "faith")—all these are much more deeply wounding to the Islamic identity than other forces like Chinese culture or Hinduism.

Islamic Fundamentalism in general (encompassing hyper-Fundamentalism) and Jihadism share many roots. One is the Kharijite tradition. One of their members, Ibn Muljam, killed the Fourth Caliph, Ali (600–661), because the Kharijites believed that he had not acted properly to promote the Islamic ethos: he had not violently fought the dissenters.

The second source of Fundamentalism is Wahhabism. Ideologically, Jihadism is at least partially the offshoot of Wahhabism, a brand of Islam that from the eighteenth century onward pushed toward an intolerant, closed, and literalist system of interpretation of the Koran. Its understanding of Islam excluded Sufism and other Islamic tendencies like Shi'ism in the name of the purity of the faith. In the course of the nineteenth and twentieth centuries, Wahhabism supplanted Islamic traditionalism and imposed itself, through Saudi Arabia, as the major Islamic tradition. Jihadists denounce the Saudi regime, but their religious orientation is imbued with Wahhabism and its exclusivist view of Islam.[5] They simply push it to its extreme consequences, and their strategy is based on violence, whereas Wahhabism, as the official ideology of the Saudi government, advocates *da'wa* (proselytizing for the sake of Islam) as its main line of conduct. Still, opposition to all "human-made" political and legal systems is their common denominator. For this reason, Wahhabi hyper-Fundamentalism and Jihadism

engage in a close relationship ideologically and a deep hostility strategically, unlike Christian Fundamentalism, which, for the most part,
rejects violence.

The third source of Fundamentalism is Islamic Reformism,
which began as an intellectual movement in the Muslim world in the
late nineteenth century with people like the Egyptians Muhammad
Abduh (1849–1905) and Rashid Ridha (1865–1935), the Persian
Jamal addin al Afghani (1839–1897), the Indian Sir Ahmed Khan
(1817–1898), the Indian Mohammad Iqbal (1877–1938), and political figures from North Africa and Turkey. They intended to find out
the original meaning of Islam (therefore the reference to the *Salaf,*
the close followers of the Prophet) and adapt it to modernity. Their
attitude was based on the adoption of Western rationalism to promote
Muslim societies. They did not refer to revolution but to Awakening
or Renaissance (*Nahda*), and their main aim was to let Islam catch
up with the West. Their enemy was Islamic traditionalism, whose
main characteristics were quietism, scripturalism, authoritarianism, and conservatism. This was their common denominator with
Wahhabism. To promote their rationalist approach they referred to
the Origin of Islam, purged from superstition and traditionalism.[6]
Nahda failed as an intellectual movement in the Muslim world and,
paradoxically, helped Islamic Fundamentalism through its references
to the Islamic Golden Age and to the pious Salaf and their rejection
of mysticism.

In the course of the twentieth century, Salafism radicalized and
embraced Egypt, mainly through the Muslim Brotherhood. This organization constitutes the fourth source of Fundamentalism. It is an
ideological movement that began with its founder, Hassan al Banna
(1906–1949) and attained its zenith in the 1950s under the aegis of
Seyed Qutb (1906–1966) in Egypt (and in Pakistan, with Mawdudi
[1903–1979]). This movement was also called Salafist, in reference
to the direct disciples of the Prophet, the so-called *Salaf as Saleheen*
(the pious ancestors). Salafism pitched Jihad as the prominent way
of achieving Islamic goals. It ended with the killing of the Egyptian
president Anwar Sadat in 1981 by Lieutenant Khaled Islambuli, a
member of the Jihadist group Takfir wal Hijra (Excommunication
and Exodus), a breakaway group from the Muslim Brotherhood.

Saudi Arabia imported the Egyptian brand of Salafism in the
1960s by giving wide coverage to the writings of its protagonists al
Banna and Qutb, among others, and by providing job opportunities
to many of its intellectuals, like Abdullah Azzam (1941–1989); Omar
Abd al-Rahman (born in 1938 in Egypt), the leader of Gama'a al
Islamiya, considered a terrorist organization, and serving a life sen-

tence in the United States; and Muhammad Qutb—the influential brother of Seyed Qutb—who as of 2006 still lived in Saudi Arabia. They served as academics in the Saudi kingdom, which is dominated by the ideology of Wahhabism: "In terms of their respective formation, Wahhabism and Salafism were quite distinct. Wahhabism was a pared-down Islam that rejected modern influences, while Egyptian Salafism sought to reconcile Islam with modernism. What they had in common is that both rejected traditional teachings on Islam in favor of direct, 'fundamentalist' reinterpretation."[7] The combination of Saudi Wahhabism and Egyptian Salafism produced a new type of Fundamentalism to which Jihadism owes many of its major ideas.

ISLAMIC FUNDAMENTALISM AND HERMENEUTICS

Jihadism, in its intellectual and theological trends, is rooted in the Fundamentalist hermeneutics of the Koran and the Prophetic tradition (Sunna), mainly based on the Sayings of the Prophet (*hadith*). Unlike Protestantism, which opened up the reading of the Holy Scriptures in the Christian world, in Islam a conjunction of historical, institutional, and cultural factors has ended up in "locking" the Koran into a rigid straitjacket. Many Islamic Reformists who have attempted to propose new interpretive frameworks for the understanding of the Sacred Book have been either executed like Mahmoud Taha (1909–1985) or forced to flee for fear of being executed as apostates (the Egyptian Nasr Abu Zeyd was condemned as an apostate for his interpretation of the Koran and escaped to Holland in 1995).

The hermeneutics of the Koran, sealed through conservative traditionalism, favors Jihadists and Fundamentalists alike, to the detriment of Reformists. Traditional procedures are based on a few more or less established principles with some divergence of views on marginal issues. The major determining factor is the historical date of the verses. If two verses contradict each other and one verse is historically later than another, the more recent is privileged over the older, because it has come later on and in that respect it "abrogates" the other. This is called the "abrogating and abrogated" (*nasikh/man-sukh*). Other considerations, like the generality or specificity of the verses, the degree of their determination by circumstances or their universality, and their being commandments or statements of fact (imperative versus indicative), also enter into account. Since the so-called Medina verses came after the Meccan verses, the former are systematically privileged over the latter. The Medina verses are, as a rule, much more focused on the war (in Medina Muslims feared the attack by the Meccan tribes) than the Meccan. Therefore, they are seen as superseding the latter, when the verses are in conflict in terms of exegesis. The rules governing the "abrogating/abrogated" verses shed light on the monopolization of hermeneutics by the conservative ulama. Around two hundred Koranic verses were the object of this rule in the high-medieval period. Their number decreased to twenty in late-medieval times and has been reduced to some seven in modern studies.[8] This is partially due to Islamic scholarship on the Koran, but it is also due to the closure of interpretation and locking of the understanding of the Koran, mainly by traditionalist ulama who refuse to open it to modernity.

Since the rule of "abrogation" applies in its traditionalist garb, Jihadists refer to the late Medina sura Repentance, which was revealed to Mohammad under circumstances of war in Medina, as abrogating other verses that preach tolerance and peaceful coexistence among the People of the Book (mainly Christians and Jews) and which were revealed before the Repentance. This verse (9:29) is among the harshest in the Koran: "Fight those who believe not in Allah nor the Last Day, nor hold that forbidden which had been forbidden by Allah and his Messenger, nor acknowledge the Religion of Truth, from among People of the Book, until they pay the *Jiziya* [Islamic tax for non-Muslims under the protection of Muslims] with willing submission and feel themselves subdued [humiliated]." This verse is used by Jihadists to declare war on Christians and Jews, since they refuse to pay the so-called tax (*jiziya*). There are 12 verses enjoining Muslims' peaceful conduct toward other groups and between 124 and 130 that preach tolerance and peace in the Koran (respectively, according to authorized interpreters Hibat Allah, Nahhas, and Ibn al Jawzi), but they all are abrogated according to the tradition by the verse 9:29 that declares war on non-Muslims, because this verse was revealed to the Prophet later than the others.

The limitations placed on Koranic exegesis thus helps extremists in their fight against non-Muslims and reform-minded Muslims as well. Since Conservatives and Traditionalists all over the Muslim world overwhelmingly dominate theological universities or schools and official religious institutions of learning, the situation is favorable to Fundamentalists and Jihadists in regard to the legitimacy of their view. What has to be changed is this factual monopoly of the conservatives over the interpretation of the Koran and the Prophetic tradition. In theory, the power of interpretation is free in Islam and not dependent on an institutional authority, but in practice Traditionalists who monopolize it and unwittingly give an enormous advantage to radical Muslims lock it up. Reformists find themselves in a predicament of structural marginality; their voices are not heard at the grassroots because the conservative ulama have seized power since long ago.

As we can see, ideologically and socially, Jihadism is a movement deeply embedded in the radical version of Islam. It is not only a social movement but also, and more importantly, an ideological one. Its stance on social change and history is directed against modernity and secularization, but it cannot be simply reduced to a movement "against" modernity. Its project for society is repressive, but it fascinates many Muslims, and its complexity makes it paradoxically suitable not only for the Muslim world as such but also for Europe as one of its major theaters. Without understanding Jihadism in its depth and creativity, one underestimates its scope and reach. Even without the present crisis within the Muslim world, it would survive, although it wouldn't thrive as it does now. If we call a social movement a collective action resulting from the prevailing social situation and closely dependent on it, an ideological movement is much more profound in the sense that it has its cultural protagonists in continuity with the past, its own representation of social issues through intellectuals, and social roots that are much more autonomous vis-à-vis the social setting than a mere social movement. An ideological movement is grounded in history and is inspired by its roots in the past. Jihadist movement is of this kind in Muslim societies. It enjoys the support not only of intellectuals and soldiers, but also of the hyper-Fundamentalist Muslims and even some mainstream Fundamentalists who are deeply committed to its ideas, independent of circumstances. The predicament of the Muslim world swells the ranks of Jihadists and brings to it sympathizers that do not become violent themselves but are able to give it financial and political leverage within the Umma. Jihadism renews a sense of dignity within the Muslim world that has been dangerously eroded by European imperialism and contemporary American policies as well as the crisis and decline of Muslim societies.

Islam is the only monotheistic religion with a single sacred book dictated by Allah to a single person, the Prophet Mohammad, in two decades, with the professed aim of expanding worldwide through deeds and words. It finds itself in the humiliating position of being dominated by Christian and Jewish powers in the places that used to be part of its very sphere of influence. While Judaism and Christianity have had their sacred books compiled through the ages, the dominant trend in Islamic theology is the belief that the Koran has remained unchanged from its inception, is the direct word of Allah and not the human expression of a divinely inspired revelation to the

Prophet Mohammad (the Mu'tazila in the Middle Ages and the Islamic Reformists nowadays question this tenet, which remains dominant in the Muslim world). The belief that the Koran remained unchanged from its revelation to Mohammad up to now is historically inaccurate, but most believers strongly endorse it. But the Koranic text was collected in a relatively short span of time, under the reign of First Caliph Abubakr and the Second, Omar, in comparison to the Old and New Testaments, which were compiled during a much longer span of time (the Gospels were put in a definitive form decades after the death of Christ).

The symbolic value of the Koran to Islam is by far superior to that of the Old Testament (a set of books) or even the Gospels to Christianity. The Koran as the direct word of Allah makes the issue of its interpretation (Islamic hermeneutics) a very sensitive one. Christian theology interjects between the holy text and the social world a hierarchic set of interpretations (some of the texts are to be understood metaphorically, some others are historically determined, some are more important than the others, some are allegoric or symbolic, etc.). By contrast, Islamic hermeneutics is still by and large dominated by the idea that interpreting the Koran in metaphoric ways means desecrating and violating the Word of Allah. Today, the overwhelming majority of Reformist thinkers in Islam are not from the traditional ulama, and their utterances against the traditional interpretation of the Koranic texts meet with stiff resistance from the ulama, who still dominate major Islamic institutions in the Muslim world (the Al Azhar in Egypt, the major religious institutions in Saudi Arabia, the Zeituna in Tunisia, the Qom and Najaf religious schools in the Shi'ite world, and so forth).

MODERNIZATION AND THE MUSLIM WORLD

In the Muslim world, the rift between Fundamentalists and part of society has widened as well. In major cities in the Muslim world, a sizeable minority of the population leads a secular life, and this is the very same minority that is middle class (rather well-off) and Westernized. Fundamentalists, many of them from the lower middle classes, resent this separation between religion and the emerging modernized people, seeing it as the West's treachery against Islam. The rift in terms of secular people and Fundamentalists exists elsewhere, but in Muslim societies by and large, because the modernization process was so late (mainly the second half of the nineteenth century, except for Turkey, which began at the eighteenth century), there is a deep sense of ambivalence toward modernization and secularization. Muslims, who have institutions of learning, religious schools, and a tradition of juridical Islam, are usually able to mobilize these groups to combat secularism and Westernization.

Historically, secular movements leading to independence (in Algeria among others), the rejection of Western imperialism (Nasser in Egypt), or an end to direct Western influence (Reza Shah in Iran) failed to open up Muslim societies from below. Their real nature was secular and modern rule minus democracy. Their failure helped Fundamentalists, who had an easy task to identify modernity with crisis, not with major progress. Modernizing regimes in the Muslim world have been mostly authoritarian, despotic, and Jacobin, concentrating politics in the hands of a single person (Nasser in Egypt, the Shah in Iran, Bourguiba in Tunisia, Boumedienne in Algeria, etc.). They failed to modernize Muslim societies other than by infusing in them a sense of hatred for democracy (perceived as a Western fallacy because the very same dictators were usually supported by the West, like the Shah or even Saddam Hussein before attacking Kuwait in 1990). Unlike them, traditional autocratic regimes before modernization referred to Islamic rules in general and found compromises with the Muslim communities' hierarchies, expressing themselves in an idiom that could be understood by people or their religious elites. Modernizing regimes became autocratic through their reference to one of two Western models, capitalism or communism, and both led to dismal results as a consequence of their meager achievements and their destruction of the community tissue.

As a world system, communism, until the Soviet invasion of Afghanistan in 1979, was a bulwark against the expansion of Islamic radicalism because it protected against the American-Israeli alliance and in some countries like Algeria its industrialization model was seen as an alternative to capitalism. Communism competed with Muslim Fundamentalists, and part of the Muslim world was influenced by it, to the detriment of the Fundamentalists. The end of communism gave the latter a monopoly over opposition to the corrupt and autocratic regimes in the Muslim world as well as over the critique of the West. Where the political regime was less autocratic and more open to society, Islamic Fundamentalism would be much less violent and more prone to compromise than elsewhere (e.g., Turkey).

Islamic Fundamentalists and, in particular, Jihadists are convinced that they are fighting against another religion, a fake one. They believe that secularism is epitomized by democracy, parliamentarism, hedonism, and individualism. For them, the major battle is not against a nonreligious world, but against one that is religious in its own perverse way. They are certainly fighting this world of secular values to the utmost of their capacity, but they identify secularism as another faith and not as nonreligious. From their perspective, they are fighting within a religious universe where the religion of truth (their version of Islam) is at war with religions of Untruth (secularism, Christianity, Islamic reformism, and Judaism, among others).

The Jihadist Critique of the Fundamentalist Ulama

The critique of democracy (see chapter 4) goes hand in hand with the critique of those Ulama (Islamic jurists) who promote Reformist ideas and those Fundamentalists who try to find compromises between their religious views and modern trends toward political participation (like elections, political parties, etc.). Among the latter, Qaradhawi, close to the Muslim Brotherhood, is one of the most prominent figures. Jihadist Ulama and intellectuals cross swords with him as they did with Bin Baz, the Saudi religious authority, before his death in 1999. One of the main concerns of Fundamentalist Ulama is to avoid useless bloodshed in the name of Islam. On the contrary, Jihadists believe that violence is unavoidable and that Islam cannot thrive without recourse to Jihad, defined in terms of combat (*qital*) or killing and subduing infidels.

Tartusi, a major Jihadist intellectual, believes that Truth cannot be established unless there is violence and bloodshed: "How is it possible to promote Jihad without spilling a single drop of blood? [He then quotes the Sura Repentance, verse 111]. . . . Do you want the domination of this religion without sacrificing a single drop [of blood] in the path of Allah (*fi sabil illah*)? This is a stingy attitude beyond any measure! Do you see, Doctor [Qaradhawi] the defense of the Right against the Wrong without spilling blood?"[9]

From the Jihadists' point of view, violence is the major means to achieve Allah's purpose on earth. There is a ruthless war between right and wrong that cannot be escaped if the Muslim community wants to maintain its dignity and honor: "If the Umma wishes dignity and life, it should engage in Jihad for the sake of Allah, and there is no alternative to it than Jihad. Be happy or unhappy whoever is concerned, this is what hundreds of religious texts say from the Koran and the Traditions of the Prophet, which assert the war between Right and Wrong."[10]

Any compromise with modern life is rejected in the name of the purity of the faith and loyalty toward the Word of Allah and the Prophetic tradition:

The Sheikh and Doctor [Qaradhawi] says that the principle in Islamic ruling is based on satisfying people and their desires and their free choice and so on! According to this idea, should we respect the wishes, the choices, and the desires of people if they choose another religion than Islam . . . ? Should we break religious texts that compel us to fight against apostates everywhere on earth, without respecting the desires and the wishes of people in that sense? From this point of view Abu Bakr [the First Caliph after the Prophet] and all the companions in arms (*sahabah*) of the Prophet were wrong to fight against Musaylamah the liar [he pretended to be the Prophet] and those with him among the apostates, since they opposed the wishes and desires of those people.[11]

Qaradhawi, a prominent member of the Muslim Brotherhood, is not a reformist Islamic thinker. His positions are brandished in the West as radical, inimical to it. Still, Jihadists stigmatize him and other members of the Muslim Brotherhood as not being genuine Muslims, for lack of engagement in violent Jihad. They are, according to Jihadists, at best spurious Muslims, sustaining their interpretation through the Sayings of the Prophet: "The Prophet said: Will come out of my Umma a group of people who read the Koran although their reading is not valid and their rituals and their fastings are the same [as the others]; they read the Koran and believe it is theirs, but in reality it is against them and this [reading] does not go beyond their vocal cords [throat]. They have left Islam in the same way as the arrow leaves the bow."[12]

The obsession with unity in all aspects of Muslim life is in contradiction with major trends in modernity, where diversification and multiplicity of choices are fundamental aspects of individualism as well as complex social organizations. Jihadists are dead set against the cultural and social consequences of modernization, and they refer to the Origins of Islam, this Golden Age where all hearts beat at the same pace, to vindicate their fight to the death against these major trends, namely secularization, individualization, and a non-Manichean world. The myth of unity wipes out all these dimensions of modern life in which Muslim societies are inevitably involved: "If we return to the Beginnings of Islam, we find nothing but a unique community under a unique leadership, the Islamic community under the unique Imam, the Prophet and after him, under the leadership of the Well-Guided Caliphs [the first four caliphs]."[13]

To give legitimacy to their stance, they make a polemical distinction between the Ulama of the Islamic awakening (*Ulama al sahwah*) and the Ulama of the illegitimate kings and rulers (*Ulama al Salatin*). The latter are complicit with illegitimate rulers who work hand in hand with Western idol worshippers (*taqut*).[14] This distinction, made by many Jihadist intellectuals, has the same features in Shi'ite radicalism: Khomeini distinguished between the Ulama of "purely Mohammedan Islam" and those of "American Islam."[15] Shi'ite and Sunni radicalism are very close to each other, in spite of their mutual hatred and rejection.

The Ulama of the illegitimate rulers are accomplices of the "evil Trinity" (*salus al khabis*): Jews, Crusaders, and Apostates. Contrary to Reformist Islam, which treats Christians and Jews as "People of the Book" and therefore of the same Abrahamic roots, and unlike Islamic Fundamentalists who endeavor to find compromises with the two other Abrahamic religions in terms of pacific coexistence, Jihadists reject them in sometimes insulting ways, qualifying Christians and Jews as "Brethren of monkeys and swine" and fundamentalist Ulama as the people of apostasy and perversity (*zalalah*), betrayers of Islam and the heritage of the Prophet.[16]

What is the aim of the illegitimate Ulama, those who are subservient to the idolatrous kings and rulers (*the Ulama of the Salatin*)? Within the "Alliance of the Evil," with the Unfaithful (*Kuffar*), the Apostates (*murtaddin*), and the Hypocrites (*munafiqin*), they intend:

> to prove the religious legitimacy of [illegitimate] governments who should be followed necessarily [by Muslims]; to prove the religious legitimacy of Western occupation and their economic and military colonial institutions in [Muslim] countries under the pretext that they are "protected" (*mustamin*) by Muslim governments, being their guests; to prove the religious legitimacy of the Zionist Israeli occupation in the three worshipping places [of Islam] and the first of the sacred places, Jerusalem and its surroundings and the recognition of the religious legitimacy of the People of monkeys and swine; to prove that all those who put into question this evil trinity [Jews/Crusaders/Muslim Apostates] are spreading depravity on the face of the earth (*mufsid fil ardh*), being Kharijites and having nothing to do with Islam; [to pretend that] those who want to call for Islam can do it peacefully through the elections into the Idolatrous Parliaments (*birlimanat al tawaqit*) and their participation in the government in ways that are [from the genuine Islamic view] not accepted by the word of Allah.[17]

The denunciation of non-Jihadist Ulama is not confined to the theological and intellectual realm but extends to the symbolic sphere. Thus al Suri finds fault with Bin Baz (1909–1999), the former official religious authority (Grand Mufti) in Saudi Arabia, for having endorsed the Saudi king's reception of insignia in the shape of a cross from a foreign government: "Whilst the King [of Saudi Arabia] hung the Cross [the medal] on his chest and appeared with it before the world with joy and pleasure, you [Sheikh Bin Baz], justified and interpreted this in a ghastly manner, in spite of the evidence of its being a heretical act."[18] Likewise, supporting the American government in its war to recover Kuwait from Saddam's occupation in 1991 is seen as collusion with infidels and Saudi Arabia's sin, contrary to Bin Baz's approval: "When Crusaders and Jewish forces fought in the Gulf War [1990–1991], in collusion with [the Saudi] system—occupation of the countries in the name of the liberation of Kuwait—you [Bin Baz] justified this through a repressive fatwa which legitimized this horrible act that insulted the dignity of the Umma, sullied its honor, and defiled its sacred values, giving as a pretext the notion of 'seeking the help' (*isti'anah*) of the Heretics at times of emergency, neglecting the restrictions imposed on this notion and the necessary religious conditions of its application."[19]

For Jihadist thinkers, there is an ongoing battle between arrogant Westerners and Muslims worldwide, and those who delay or hinder it in any manner are to be fought against. Ayman al Zawahiri, the main ideologue of Al Qaeda, expresses this Jihadist creed in a transparent way: "This decade of Muslim community's history witnesses a huge conflict between the forces of Heresy and Revolt against Allah and domination and arrogance (*istikbar*) on the one hand, and Muslim communities and their jihadist vanguard, on the other. This conflict reaches its apogee in the fortunate attacks against New York and Washington [September 11] and as a consequence, the declaration by Bush of a new Crusaders' war against Islam and what he called the war on Terror."[20]

In the contemporary world, many Muslims experience humiliation, a lack of confidence in the future, and a feeling of despondency. Modernity, which has been for many societies a promise of better life and material and intellectual progress, has been for most of the Muslim world an age of decadence, historical regression, despotism in both its religious and its secular forms, and economic and cultural crisis. From a past of glory, Muslims have been thrown into an age of decline: once a world power, Islamic lands have been subject to colonial rule and then dictatorships (the nationalist dictatorship of Nasser in Egypt, the fascist dictatorship of the Ba'th party in Syria and Iraq, the autocratic rule of the Shah in Iran and subsequently the Islamic Republic's theocracy, the military rule in Pakistan, etc.) No Islamic country besides Turkey has had an open political system, and in Turkey this has been achieved at the cost of some religious freedom through the laïcité system imported from the French version of secularism. Moreover, the creation of Israel has been a traumatic experience in the Muslim world, where the majority of the population refuses to recognize its reality other than being an excrescence of Western (and particularly American) imperialism. American politics in the Middle East has also played a role in polarizing Muslim societies against democratic values.

Islamic countries' management of modernization has been a failure in the overwhelming majority of cases (with some exceptions, like Malaysia). Everything "modern" is therefore seen as a threat to personal as well as national and religious identity by many embittered Muslims. The success of radical ideologies in Islam is not so much due to the lack of reformist ideas within Allah's religion (there are many reform-minded Islamic intellectuals over almost all the Muslim world) but to the fact that modernity is deemed as a menace to the Muslim way of life as well as Muslims' dignity and self-respect among large stratas of the population. The situations in Bosnia, Afghanistan, Iraq, Palestine, and Lebanon are one factor; furthermore, many Muslims experience humiliation through television coverage by Al Jazeera as well as national media throughout the worldwide Islamic community undergoing defeat and abasement. These are the reasons that push many Muslims to favor radical and pessimistic ideas over those laden with hope and openness to the world. Jihadist intellectuals propose an understanding of the prevailing predicament and a mythical solution to it that, in times of deep crisis, are met with a feeling of relief by mainstream Muslim society.

Mohammad Qutb is one of those who propose a gloomy interpretation of present times and an explanation as to how a godless society can be superior to god-abiding Muslims. He defines Western society as "Promethean," that is, a community that defies God: "Modern Prometheus, according to Julian Huxley, represents contemporary Europe. He defies God Almighty and succeeds in doing it! From another point of view, some people are amazed at European successes in spite of their being godless (*kafir*) and ask themselves: Is it the permission of Allah's Providence that also promises Godless people destruction and annihilation?"[21] Why are unbelievers thriving and Muslims aren't? The answer is that prosperity on earth is not related to any specific belief: "Allah destines man for his residence and enjoyment on earth in the time, and He does it for all men, believer and disbeliever alike."[22] For Allah, prosperity in this world is worthless. Only otherworldly merits are of significance: "Allah the Almighty did not offer Disbelievers benefits of earthly existence at the beginning but did it to both, Believers and Disbelievers alike. It has to be said that the world is not even worth the wing of a mosquito, and He offers it to the Disbeliever out of contempt for him, but Resurrection will only benefit Believers."[23]

There is an indifference toward life in this world that makes success equally accessible to the believer and the godless, contrary to the other world, in which only believers have access to paradise: "The Prophet says: Allah offers this world to those whom He likes and those whom He dislikes but offers the Other World only to those whom He likes [The Saying of the Prophet, quoted by Ahmad, the Hadith compiler]."[24] Destruction of disbelievers follows their earthly success: "The first fact is that Allah offers Disbelievers earthly goods before destroying them. . . . The second fact is that welfare to Disbelievers that includes their taking possession of the Earth and opening them the doors to all things for a longer or shorter time, implies their being deprived of otherworldly merits and their ending up in Hell."[25]

Allah lets people act on earth, but He can intervene sometimes against natural causes in a miraculous way, contradicting causal links between events. Qutb proposes a few cases, implying that Muslims could get the upper hand since they are those who will inherit the Earth, in spite of the fact that they are not the most powerful: they become leaders in an supernatural way that cannot be accounted for through a cause-and-effect chain of events:

> Natural causes do not act by themselves but through the will of Allah. A few examples:
> Hitler took all that human beings can do to vanquish the Allies and challenged through it the power of Allah. And he said that his army would take hold of Russia as easily as the knife cuts a piece of cheese! He said that he would not commit the same mistakes as Napoleon and would not let it last up to the time of freeze that killed Napoleon's army. Allah's will imposed what was not Hitler's will, and Russians made it last up to the time of freeze that destroyed his army as it did Napoleon's!
> [Another set of events is the fact that] Russians entered Afghanistan and they were sure of their victory and thought that it would not take more than a few months (to pacify that country), taking into account their overwhelming superiority in numbers and military preparation. But they did not take into account Allah's will, and they don't believe in Allah at all; they only believe in material causes, and taking them into account, there was no common measure between what they possessed and what Afghans

possessed [in military might]! But again, Allah's will was different from that of Russians, and Afghans succeeded in fighting for ten complete years, and Russians were forced to leave Afghanistan at the end![26]

Disbelievers are under the illusion that their successes will lead them to their victory over Islam, but Allah will at some indefinite time reverse the trend and condemn them to annihilation: "Allah lets Disbelievers know that He had destined this religion [Islam] to take hold of the Earth and that Disbelievers won't be able to destroy it on earth as they wish in the innermost of their conscience. . . . They should be taught that causes do not lead to effects by their own existence if it is not with Allah's will. But Allah brings Disbelievers gradually closer to the incentives they take—as a punishment for their disbelief and their cold shoulder [toward Allah]—until their incentives put them to death at the end!"[27] How is this possible? By luring them. Allah deceives Disbelievers into an earthly success that is a prelude to their death:

> The strengthening of contemporary Jahiliya and their disposing of power and their opening of all doors continue according to godly Traditions without opposition. We should still know that there is a difference—and even differences—between the strengthening [enablement] through Allah's consent by which Allah helps Believers and the strengthening by luring that Allah offers to Disbelievers for their wish of this world and for their spending much effort to achieve it. Allah offers them rewards in this world and opens them up all the doors that belong to this type of strengthening.
>
> Contrary to godless people, who are enabled by Allah's luring, genuine Muslims are strengthened by Allah's consent. The latter substantially differ from the former in their duration.
>
> The first difference is that strengthening by luring is a temporary one, whatever its duration. It always ends up in destruction, whereas strengthening by Allah's consent is permanent, even if something in people's mind changes and they are brushed aside and are moved away from it. But they don't change their mind in reaching to this type of enablement (*tamkin*). . . . The second difference is that opening all doors to Disbelievers when they delve into sin is the enablement into the material world only. Two doors never open to Disbelievers because Allah forbids them to Disbelievers: the door of *baraka* (blessing, happiness) and the door of *toma'ninah* (quietude, peace of mind, confidence). These two doors are exclusively open to Muslims.

Disbelievers are denied eternity and happiness in its major components, even in this world. They have material ease and affluence, but
they lack quietude and blessing. It is a comfort to see that, in spite of
their economic and military might, arrogant Westerners are denied
happiness, whereas Muslims, even in a situation of despondency and
material inferiority, are enabled by Allah to accept the benefits of His
blessing. These felicitous ingredients of a fulfilled life are denied to
those who do not embrace Allah's religion:

> The word *Baraka* does not signify only material welfare; it is more
> inclusive and vaster in meaning. We might even say that it is not
> mainly material, although it implies it. It is something in the life
> of people that makes them felicitous, pure, transparent, spiritual,
> and clean so as to light up the mind. . . . Regarding the *Toma'ninah*,
> people who are anxious, worried, insecure, anguished and those who
> undergo nervous breakdown from anxiety, dread, and bad premoni-
> tion look for it. They look for *Toma'ninah*! And Allah shows them
> the door that leads to it: Only through the remembrance of Allah
> the heart is filled with quietude (Sura Ra'd, verse 28).

Modern godlessness (*Jahiliya*) can achieve whatever success in
technological and military fields it wants; it is devoid of the subjective
component of happiness that Allah provides only for His devoted
followers. A feeling of emptiness chases people in the Western civilization of disbelief:

> We don't need to say that contemporary *Jahiliya*, in spite of all
> the means of enablement that is at its disposal from the military,
> political, material, economic, and scientific power, lacks happiness,
> lacks the felicity that man looks for in his life. Booze, narcotics,
> and crimes are only signs of the lack of happiness and quietude, by
> dint of anxiety, suicide, madness, and mental and nervous illnesses.
> Booze like narcotics are attempts at escaping from reality. And why
> should people try to escape from reality if they were happy!! . . .
> And why crimes extend and their proportions increase?
>   But the mad glee in which contemporary *Jahiliya* indulges in
> moments of evasion in nightclubs, casinos, and nightspots is not
> a sign of bliss but much more a sign of its lack and an attempt at
> artificial compensation for the psychological vacuum induced by
> this lack.
>   And this is the stern picture of contemporary *Jahiliya* that fails
> to disguise huge factories, immense material production, and sky-
> rockets reaching the moon or the planet Mars!

The process of destruction has set in; illnesses like AIDS and cancer and scourges like the thinning of the ozone layer are there to prove it. The scenario is that of Noah: "The ill omen of Allah does not cease to reach Disbelievers until their ultimate destruction promised by Allah to them and to arrogant people (*mostakbarin*). . . . AIDS [illness] is enough to awaken the heart of ignorant people and open up their eyes. . . . It is vibrating with all that bears the word in meanings. It spreads, and they are anguished about it and are powerless to stop its expansion. . . . And it is enough to mention the hideous spread of different cancers. . . . And it is enough to mention what threatens the ozone layer and what threatens through it [climate] change and the tempest like Noah's."[28] The quickening pace of destruction is perceived even by some of *Jahiliya* intellectuals: "Before a decade or two people will be convinced that it is possible for this *Jahiliya* to collapse! . . . And a group of *Jahiliya* thinkers are beginning to see the signs of destruction. Although destruction might be slow because *Jahiliya* put in lots of efforts to save it, it is nevertheless sure."[29]

Mohammad Qutb insists on Allah's intervention in the destruction of heretics, Muslims' efforts being of lesser import than Allah's action. His brother Seyed Qutb and many other Jihadist intellectuals insist more on human intervention and Jihad to achieve the very same goals. The two sides fulfill complementary roles: whereas activist Jihadists insist on Muslims' mobilization, "naturalist" Jihadists stress the coming Apocalypse that will cause the destruction of the arrogant West through Allah's will. This brings solace to those who deeply resent their marginal role in the world, in a sharp difference with the past, when Muslims were feared and respected for their military and material achievements.

For other Jihadists, Muslims' situation is related to their own lack of faith. Fahd al Bashar sees avoidance of Jihad as the cause of Muslims' decay: "Jihad is the cause of Muslims' greatness. The fall of Andalusia [in 1492] can help us understand the mechanisms of [Muslims'] defeat. Imam al Qordhabi [from Cordoba], who lived at that time, identified the causes of decay: they shunned the combat, refused to let their blood being spilled, refused to put their belongings at stake [for Jihad], preferred peace and enjoyment in this world, were devoted to home and country [instead of Islam]. All this is a curse and pushes toward meanness, lack of respect by the others for Muslims, their honor and sexual dignity (*irdh*), and the domination by the *Kuffar* (Disbelievers) upon them."[30] Nowadays, lack of dignity and loss of honor are paramount among Muslims. Many feel humiliated by Americans, Israelis, Russians, and others and are oppressed by them. The plight of the Palestinians, Iraqi suffering, Chechen humiliation—all adds up to a sad picture. Jihadists exploit this deep malaise.

There is a merciless war between disbelievers and Muslims, and any peace between them illusory, the former looking for the annihilation of Muslims by every means: "Every reasonable person knows that the *Kuffar* [Godless, Heretics] do not leave Muslims in peace if Muslims leave them in peace, and this religious truth and godly tradition is mentioned in the Koran. They will fight Muslims through cultural war, intellectual war, through women and propaganda. They will fight Muslims to destroy their religion and to hit their faith. Muslims should beware of the *Kuffar*."[31]

SHI'ITE HYPER-FUNDAMENTALISTS AND THEIR REJECTION OF DEMOCRACY

In Shi'ism, the same tendencies are visible among Fundamentalist and hyper-Fundamentalist Ulama and intellectuals.[32] The main Shi'ite revolutionary intellectuals and Ulama were Ali Shariati (1933–1977), Morteza Motahhari (1920–1979), Ayatollah Khomeini (1902–1989), the first president of the Islamic Republic, Abolhassan Bani Sadr (b. 1933), and Ayatollah Taleqani (1910–1979). These were mostly revolutionary and reactionary (Motahhari, Khomeini) or messianic and revolutionary (Shariati). Second-generation thinkers appeared in the 1990s, and they are mostly Reformists, questioning the foundations of Shi'ite theocracy, *Velayat Faqih*, through another interpretation of Islam that endeavors to reconcile Allah's religion and political pluralism. They include Abdolkarim Soroush (b. 1945), Mojtahed Shabestari (b. 1936), Mohsen Kadivar (b. 1959), and Youssefi Eshkavari (b. 1958), Mostafa Malekian (b. 1956), among others.

But Fundamentalist thought was renewed, as well, by a new generation of clergymen and intellectuals who are not popular and are working as "organic intellectuals" within the new Shi'ite theocracy. In the younger generations of these fundamentalist Ulama, Ahmad Beheshti is a significant figure. For him, human beings must be under the salutary burden of religion so as to accept their duties (*taklif*). The language of rights (*haq*, mainly used by Islamic Reformists)—instead of duties—is not adequate to put a check on humans' egoistic tendencies.[33] Religious duties have to be internalized; the eternal damnation of Hell must be present in their minds to educate genuine Muslims. Secularism is against the religion of Allah and has to be rejected outright.

Another Shi'ite cleric, Hamid Parsa, is an ardent opponent of secularism who believes that the modern Islamic reform movement is a hidden way of introducing secularism in the guise of Islam. He views it as being totally incompatible with Islam.[34] For him, secularism is tightly bound to the emergence of Western civilization and cannot be applied to those societies that live according to the spiritual values of Islam. Islamic societies must reject the divide between religion and politics. The only legitimate way is the domination of the political sphere by Islam, owing to the latter's sacred mission. Those who entertain a privileged relation with Islam (Shi'ite clergy) have the right to benefit from this "power of the sacred" (*qowweye qodsiyeh*) and exercise the right to rule (*haqe hakemiyat*) over society. Secularism denies Islam its right to rule. Under secularism, these intellectuals understand not only that the legal and legislative sphere has autonomy from the religious one, but also that forces within the Islamic world seek to open up spheres of freedom in accordance with Islam, much in the same way as Protestantism did, in terms of freedom of conscience, against Catholicism. A major feature of secularism is democracy, a system in which the unstable laws made by humans reign supreme, with no sacred principle prevailing over them. Between Islam, based on stable divine laws, and democracy, based on unstable human laws, there is an insurmountable discrepancy.

Ali Akbar Reshad is another Shi'ite cleric who attacks secularism as a Western phenomenon borrowed by Islamic Reformists and irreconcilable with Islam.[35] Other neoconservative Shi'ite clerics, such as Asqar Ehtekari and Ali Akbar Kamali, denounce Western secularism by pointing out the fraudulent character of the scriptural bases of Judaism and Christianity.[36] Since both religions have deviated from their genuine origins—they were fated to forsake their faith to Islam—they have experienced throughout history the development of an internal self-denial through secularism. Their spuriousness is the main ground for their mutual cooperation against Islam, their cultural aggression against Allah's religion being based on three principles: imposing their values on Muslims, destroying the fundamentals of Islam, and coercing Allah's religion into renouncing its legitimate domination over society in the name of secular values.

The fight against Islamic values is an ambiguous phenomenon. On the one hand, it is directed against Islam; on the other hand, this struggle destroys the West from within, through nihilism. The latter is an avatar of secularism that postulates the resemblance of God to Human, which is, in turn, the philosophical linchpin of Western humanism. Therefore it is an imposture to talk about "Islamic humanism" as the Islamic Reformists do directly or indirectly. Islamic humanism is a creeping attempt at secularizing Islam, and deep down in its principles, it is based on the anti-Islamic tendencies prevailing in the Western world. At the root of deviant ideas like "freedom of expression" lies the attempt at combating Islam by denying legitimacy to its divine values and rejecting its role in politics.

Hasan Rahimpoor Azqodi is another hyper-Fundamentalist Shi'ite intellectual who defends Islamic theocracy and *Velayat Faqih* (the government of the Islamic Jurist) against those who would like to promote Islamic democracy. For him, Islamic theocracy is the only legitimate way of applying Islam to politics. Through it, Islam embraces even those domains of social life that were *mobah* (religiously indifferent) in traditional Muslim societies.[37] Islamic theocracy encompasses all the aspects of personal and social existence and therefore totally Islamizes society, away from secularizing undercurrents within the Muslim world. He attempts to de-secularize Muslim societies through Islamic theocracy. Even apparently neutral acts like talking, walking, or writing can be permissible or not, according to the rulings of Islam, depending on the intentions of the believer and their consequences for the Muslim community. Acts become illicit if they result, directly or indirectly, in the weakening of Islamic law. In this respect, every voluntary act has an Islamic prescription. *Velayat Faqih* is the cornerstone for the new Islamic society, where each act has to be measured up through the Islamic yardstick. Since Allah's religion is of divine inspiration, it cannot be exposed to the popular vote, which is the basis of democracy. The latter is anti-Islamic in its essence because it supposes the secularization of religion and the self-determination of human beings in society.

Sadeq Larijani, another clergyman and a member of an influential family in Iran, rejects democracy for the same reasons as Rahimpoor Azqodi. For him, democratic regimes are characterized by the prominence given to the arbitrary laws made by people. Islamic society, in sharp contrast to democratic ones, gives absolute precedence to the commandments of Allah. That is why Islam cannot accept the notion of civil society, defended by Islamic Reformists, because their philosophical foundations are irreconcilable:[38] "In the Islamic government, according to *Velayat Faqih*, the source of legitimacy is the authenticity of the duty and not the authenticity of the individual. Therefore, while all the pillars of the State, whatever their significance, are important for the efficiency of the system, they owe their legitimacy to their divine origins. . . . As for those who say that in the Islamic government Allah has given to the people the right to choose their ruler, that they can do so and so with their votes, and that they may give the reins of power to anyone, these people are referring to the liberal doctrine, which is not in accord with the concept of *Velayat Faqih*."[39] Pillars of democracy—namely, individual sovereignty, voting based on majority, and changing leadership according to popular vote—are rejected in the name of Islamic theocracy.

The major hyper-Fundamentalist ideologue of Shi'ite radicalism, close to Jihadism, is Ayatollah Mesbah Yazdi, who, among others, has built up a new group of "candidates for martyrdom" (*istishhadiyun*). According to him, Shi'ites did not develop a political theory in the past because they were a minority oppressed by Sunni rulers. In a situation of political oppression, their main concern was to conceal their religious tenets, perceived as deviant by Sunni caliphs. Thus they lacked a political theory until Ayatollah Khomeini broke the deadlock and conceived not only the possibility but also the necessity (from the religious point of view) of an Islamic state. Political authority in this Islamic state is vested in the Islamic ruler, *Vali faqih*, who must be obeyed by all, including the clergy, even if they are in disagreement with him. *Vali faqih* thus takes precedence over the Ulama, even those whose religious knowledge is superior to his.[40] Mesbah Yazdi believes that Islam is under an "all-out attack by Infidels and Arrogant forces (Imperialists)"; the believer's duty is to be active "in fighting the enemies of religion, taking Jihad to Unbelievers, foes, and assailants of Muslims' rights," so as "to establish the Just Islamic System all over the world."[41]

Ayatollah Khaz'ali has advanced similar ideas. For him, *Velayat Faqih* is not a human-made institution but one that is the gist of the rule of the Prophet and the imams, representing the rule of Allah on earth.[42] That is why *Velayat Faqih* is not subordinated to the vote of the people, his government being the representative of Allah. The people's vote is necessary to implement his commandments, not to contest his choices.

Ayatollah Mesbah Yazdi emphasizes the autocratic nature of the Islamic ruler; he underscores the fact that the leader, who happens to be the representative jurist (*Vali faqih*), is not elected by people but chosen by scholars of Islamic jurisprudence. Through Islamic theocracy, religion becomes the sole source of legal, cultural, economic, and political legitimacy in society, extending Islamic rule to all aspects of human life—unlike traditional Islam, in which many domains belonged to the realm of Customs (*urf*) and tolerated as such, when they did not directly contradict religious law. According to him, the government of the *Velayat Faqih* is, from a theological perspective, the absolute rule of the Islamic jurist (*velayate motlaqeye faqih*), entailing society's subservience to the rule of Allah embodied by the *Vali faqih*.

In the same vein, another cleric, Mohammad Hadi Ma'refat opposes religious society to civil society.[43] Islamic Reformists bring up the notion of civil society, sometimes by adding to it the qualifying attribute "religious," to point out that there is no incompatibility between Islam and civil society that is religious because people believe in Islam and not out of the coercive nature of the Islamic creed. For Ma'refat, the two are incompatible because civil society is based on human-made laws, whereas religious society is founded on sacred laws, grounded in divine Revelation. Religion leads to happiness by following its rules and not by submitting to the majority's commandments. Civil society's spirit of secular tolerance is also incompatible with Islam because it supposes indifference to religion or even its suppression in the public sphere. Islam, from his point of view, means society's submission to the rule of Allah, achieved through the absolute rule of the Islamic jurist (*velatyate motlaqeye faqih*).

It is obvious from this viewpoint that there shouldn't be respect for secular law. In the case of secular law, the basis for the obedience of the individual is the people, whereas in Islamic society it is Allah's laws approved by the absolute Islamic ruler. Western countries give absolute priority to secular law because the Church has been on the side of the rich and the powerful. In an Islamic society, the religious institution based on the theocratic rule of the Islamic jurist is on the side of the oppressed and downtrodden (*mostadh'afin*) and fights against the oppressors (*mostakberin*) and evildoers (*setam garan*). This makes it unnecessary and even impossible for people to look for an alternative to Islamic society in a secular one. For proponents of absolute Islamic theocracy, those who disagree with their version are not genuine Muslims. Opposition to Islamic Reformists comes close to declaring them heretics, as Sunni Jihadists do. The cleric Molla Hasani, who is the representative of the *Vali Faqih* in Urumiyah, a town in northwestern Iran, has said:

> Those who go to the universities to deceive students are worse than the United States, Israel, and the Hypocrites [fake Muslims, in particular, the dissident Mujahideen Khalq political group]. You, university members, if you want [Islamic] unity, why do you bring this person to the university who says that freedom is more important than Islam and the Koran? Death to this freedom! Ayatollah Khaz'ali said: "I'll shoot this person in the head and get rid of him with the coup de grace!" Imam Khomeini answered the question of some revolutionary tribunal heads who did not want to sentence people to death. [He said,] "Even if they are a million of them, I'll order the slaughter of them overnight by shooting them

collectively." You reformists! Since you know the commandments of Ali and Imam Khomeini, what are you doing? . . . Why are you deceiving yourself and people?[44]

In the same way that Sunni Jihadists attribute the ills of the universe to Shi'ism, some of the Shi'ite radicals see in the Sunnis the culprits in the ills assaulting Islam. For Ali Davani, the alliance of Western cultural aggression (*tahajome farhangi*), the conspiracy of Western powers, and Wahhabism (Islamic Fundamentalism, Saudi style) intend to undermine the Islamic Republic in Iran.[45]

Hussein Abadian and Musa Faqih Haqqani, two Iranian hyper-Fundamentalists, trace the cultural aggression of the West back to free masonry, which they see as having exposed Iranian Muslim intellectuals to dangerous ideas such as nationalism and tolerance. They undermine Islam and society. Such ideas tend to make secular intellectuals subservient to foreign interests, thus guilty of treason toward Islam and Iran.[46]

Critique of democracy and its ideas goes hand in hand with the denunciation of what fundamentalist Shi'ite ideologues call "liberalism." By this notion they mean a mixture of its European and American meanings (namely, unbridled capitalism and open society with free economics). For Fatemeh Rajabi, a woman who rejects Western freedom for women in the name of Islam, liberalism is depravity and moral corruption (*fasad*).[47] Liberalism in the West was a period of immorality that resulted in relinquishing spiritual and sacred values, with art becoming the focus of deviant sexual tendencies, particularly in sculpture, painting, and literature. Liberal freedom is based on sexual instincts, superstitions, reprehensible behavior, and misconceived freedom of thought, all cut off from religion. She discredits liberalism by denouncing its links with capitalism and hedonism. Looking for profit, the liberal attitude is marked by violence, egotism, ambition, the urge for wealth, and the propensity for religious disbelief. In order to earn more money, liberals do not hesitate to trample under foot all religious principles that prevent illicit earnings. Rajabi calls this attitude *ebahiyat*, or declaring licit and free from religion the immoral attitudes of capitalists. Fundamentalist Ulama and intellectuals use this term not only to denounce liberalism and Western-style capitalism, but also all those Islamic Reformists who, since the early 1990s, have defended the view that social and political relations are neutral from a religious perspective (and therefore open to the vote of people, the results being binding on everyone).

This liberal view—that religion is confined to personal aspects of life, not applicable to the management of society and its politics—promotes, according to Rajabi, social deviance, in the same way as did

Edmund Burke, who defended homosexuals, thereby justifying those vile acts that are condemned by a sane religious person. The wild liberty of liberalism frees the individual from religious constraints and is detrimental to the collective well-being. It gives birth to tolerance (*modara*), or the equivalents of it, like *tasamoh* or *tasahol* (terms used by Islamic Reformists to denote religious tolerance). According to such notions, state and society should not intervene or have any moral or doctrinal sensitivity toward the ideas and beliefs of people, even if they are wrong or immoral. By defending tolerance, liberal freedom promotes a godless human, devoid of moral sentiments and unhindered in his desires. Rajabi believes that the only way to oppose liberalism is through Islamic movements throughout the world. (Abu Mus'ab al Suri, the arch-enemy of Shi'ites, has identical views about Jihad as a worldwide movement.) According to Rajabi, Jihadist movements are the most appropriate way of promoting Islam all over the world. Had it not been for the Sunni characteristics of Al Qaeda that makes it abhorrent to Shi'ites, she would have approved its anti-Western, anti-democratic, and anti-liberal features in which Western sexual permissiveness and Islamic Reformism are denounced altogether.

Shi'ite Fundamentalism and hyper-Fundamentalism share many common features with their Sunni counterparts. Since a Shi'ite theocracy rules Iran, Shi'ite Fundamentalists don't have to oppose the government. Since Shi'ite radicals and Sunni Jihadists reject and hate each other, they cannot, as a rule, act jointly. But their ideologies are very close to each other, and their social action can become violent in specific circumstances like the group of *Istishhadiyun* (those who look for martyrdom) under the leadership of Ayatollah Mesbah Yazdi, who can be mobilized against those who are seen as enemies of the Shi'ite theocracy in the world, mainly the American government but also the Jihadist Sunnis. The two "enemy brothers" (Sunni and Shi'ite Jihadists) share at the core the same ideology, mercilessly opposing each other in the name of their monopoly over Islam.

The Weakness of Secular Tendencies in Islam

Historically, different groups and actors have carried out the secularization of Islam:

- Christian minorities (Armenians in the Ottoman Empire and Iran in the nineteenth century)
- colonial powers, particularly the French in Algeria and more extensively North Africa as well as the English in India and their colonial Muslim countries

- the new states and governments (Atatürk in Turkey, Reza Shah in Iran, postindependence regimes like Bourguiba's in Tunisia)
- theological movements within Islam inspired by the ninth-century Mu'tazila and by Nahda movements in the Sunni and Shi'ite world in the late nineteenth and the twentieth centuries and Reformist movements in the contemporary Muslim world
- cultural trends imported from the West and in particular the "cultural industry" in the second half of the twentieth century and the first decade of the twenty-first century, secularizing daily life through movies, TV shows, and the Internet and spreading the seduction of individualism and consumerism.

In the nineteenth century and the first half of the twentieth century, secularization resulted in new social groups, self-conscious and "strong" because of the weakness of the traditional and Fundamentalist trends and tendencies in Islam. In the second half of the twentieth century, Fundamentalists have become more modern, radical, and aware of their own strength. They are joined by new people with modern educational backgrounds (many of them graduates of scientific and engineering programs), frustrated by the evolution of the Muslim world and secular nationalism. They denounce the West and secular tendencies within Islam as corrupt and depraved, and above all they benefit from the support of two new groups generated by modernization.

One group is the so-called *Mustadh'afin* (the oppressed, the downtrodden), resulting from the urbanization and the migration of peasants to the cities and the inability of the new governments to deal with the social issue of these new marginal people who are economically fragile and culturally uprooted: the so-called *hittists* (those who stay by the wall because they are unemployed), the *trabendists* (those who engage in illegal commerce) in Algeria, the *mustadh'afin* in Iran, and so forth. Since these groups benefit more or less from the traditional forms of assistance through Islamic charity (the Islamic tax *zakat*, among others, and in Shi'ism, *khoms*), they are quick to denounce the new modernized middle classes as Westernized in a derogatory sense (*mostaqrab* in Arabic, *gharb-zadeh* in Persian) and the new governments as godless (*taqut, jahiliya*), in both the Shi'ite and the Sunni worlds.

A second group is the new technical, scientific professionals produced by the modern educational system. They have been marginalized by the autocratic systems in Muslim countries, and some of them become Fundamentalists as a result of their malaise within the new world, where the wrongdoings of modernization are tangible but its benefits are still imperceptible to the large majority. Their scientific mind-set does not easily accept the authoritarian rule of the new cliques, in the name of a modernity that is alien to most people. Their rising expectations do not cope with the derisory benefits of modernization amid the dislocation of old social bonds.

In many cases, a third group, traditionalist in its cultural outlook and conservative in its social tendencies, joins the other two in rejecting modernity, which is perceived as destroying the benefits of the tradition through the rule of selfishness and irreligion and promoting upstarts who hold the reins of power for the sake of profiteering and assisting their own clientele. Within Shi'ism this group consists of clergymen and within Sunnism of religious teachers and lawyers coming out of the Islamic schools. They are unable to see modernity as the construction of a new order in which justice would be preserved and violence would be contained.

In the Muslim world, the failure of democratization, secularization, and economic development have given rise to the rejection by many modernized groups (as well as the traditional, which goes without saying) of modernity. It is seen as a change for the worse. The origin of this change, the West, has become synonymous with utter violence, injustice, and illegitimate domination for a large strata of the population, who are vulnerable to change and unable to shield themselves through the positive sides of modernity (new job opportunities, participation in political life, and equality of all before the law). Among these groups that turn to Islamic Fundamentalism as a solution to the crisis of modernity, some find Jihadism as the best solution.[48] Many are upset by political events (the crises in Bosnia, Afghanistan, Iraq, Palestine, Chechnya), and these situations serve as triggers for their transition from Fundamentalism to Jihadism.

The secularization trend within Islam is three-pronged. First is the ambiguous Fundamentalist trend marked by timid openings toward the parliamentary system, without explicitly giving up the traditional religious tenets related to the setting up of an Islamic political system. Still, Fundamentalists like the Muslim Brotherhood in Egypt, refuse to have recourse to violence for the sake of establishing an Islamic political system and accept the parliamentary system even though they maintain an ambivalent posture toward democracy as such. While Fundamentalists are in a minority position, they contribute to the diversity of the political system, but if they accede to a majority position, it is not obvious that they will accept democratic rule. The political regimes in most of the Muslim world are themselves nondemocratic, and therefore their legitimacy is also open to question. The political deadlock in the Muslim world helps the anti-democratic forces to claim legitimacy in the name of Allah, opposing a "legitimate" nondemocratic religious vision to an "illegitimate" dominant, nondemocratic political system. Sometimes directly but more often indirectly, these groups strive to Islamize modernity by choosing those aspects that are not immediately opposed to Islam and by more or less accepting or rejecting in an ambivalent way other aspects of modernity (for instance, when it comes to the popular vote, they accept the result of the ballot box, without renouncing the "Islamic" view of politics, in which the pious and the religiously learned are superior to the others). This is true for the Muslim Brotherhood in Egypt, Hamas in Palestine, Hezbollah in Lebanon, and Hizbu Tahrir in England.

A second approach to secularization is taken by the hyper-Fundamentalists, who are ideologically close to Jihadists: rigid in their attitude toward the rituals, intolerant of issues related to women and freedom of expression, and anti-Western and anti-democratic. But they reject direct violence and do not get directly involved in Jihad. Their role in secularizing Islam is at best ambivalent. This is the case of some Wahhabi groups in Saudi Arabia and the legal branch of the FIS in Algeria, among others.

The third approach is the "neutral" and sometimes "pro-democratic" tendencies marked by mainstream modern values, defended by part of the new middle classes. But this occurs within Muslim societies where secular trends are still stigmatized, unless they reinvigorate the religious values (like the first trend) and strive to find a religious justification for their secularization. These groups intend to "modernize" Islam by translating democratic ideas into Islamic idioms (for instance, by claiming that democracy is, in its gist, the Shura or the Koranic consultation).

There are also groups that act to de-secularize Muslim societies. One can distinguish among them at least two groups. First are the traditional conservative groups, including conservative merchants, the Ulama and their clientele, and all those people who are destabilized by social change and seek refuge in mythic traditions. Second are the Jihadists who intend to break off ties with the changing world by waging war against democracy, the West, and those Muslims who do not follow their course of action.

The second group reacts to cultural modernization through non-religious values within the world of Islam. The modernizing groups who spearheaded secularization were intrinsically "illegitimate" in the second half of the twentieth century in the eyes of the Muslims in a Muslim world marked by the trauma of the creation of Israel, the failure of postindependence political regimes, the setbacks of secular populism (Nasser in Egypt), and, more globally, the breakdown or miscarriage of the secular regimes (the Shah in Iran). The advent of the Islamic Revolution in Iran in 1979 and the resurgence of Sunni hyper-Fundamentalism and radicalism in the Muslim world from the 1980s onward, in reaction to the invasion of Afghanistan by the Soviet Union, reinforced this tendency. Besides the few countries where secular groups have deep roots (in despotic Tunisia, in Turkey, and paradoxically in Iran), in most of the Muslim world the secular trends are fragile and perceived as "illegitimate" by large numbers of the hyper-Fundamentalists and Fundamentalists alike as well as the Jihadists, who violently reject them. For them, secularization has resulted in the downfall of Islamic values and the decline of the Muslim world.

FUNDAMENTALISM AND NEW SOCIAL GROUPS

For many Jihadists, the critique of democracy is made in conjunction with a cultural malaise resulting from women's treading on traditions of modesty and from national and social problems that authoritarian nationalism has been unable to cope with. The reaction to these failures now emerges under the guise of Islam because it is the only collective reference still untouched in its symbolic meaning by the corrosive discredit of ideologies within most Muslim societies, reinforcing Jihadist tendencies that have always existed in the Islamic world as a tiny minority phenomenon.

The transformation of Jihadism from a marginal and small minority's mind-set into a significant ideological movement is related to the global malaise of Muslim civilization. The failure of secular-autocratic governments to open up their societies politically and provide job opportunities to modernized and highly educated people is one of the causes of thriving Jihadism. Some of the most exposed groups—engineers and, more generally, professionals with a scientific background—are among the new generations of Jihadists. They have had access to higher education, mainly in technological fields, without real job opportunities for most of them. In much of the Muslim world, a high proportion of engineers are Jihadists.[49] In Europe, the picture does not hold, and people with less education get involved in Islamic radicalism because of their lack of opportunities in society. But one cannot reduce the phenomenon to a lack of opportunities, since many engineers are influenced by the new radical ideology as well as by their technological view of the society.

On the other hand, engineers and students of technological faculties in Iran are nowadays at the head of the movement for political pluralism (Sharif Technological University, Amir Kabir University, and science departments in Tehran University). In Turkey, engineers are active in nonviolent Islamic political parties. Where opportunities are seen as nonexistent, engineers and other professionals (doctors, scientists) might be quicker to radicalize because of their technicist frame of mind, which is accompanied by the sense of having a calling within society.

In Muslim societies where Jihadism is thriving, new modernized groups engage in the movement because they feel they lack a future otherwise and are now offered an opportunity to be the protagonists of Islamic revival as well as the discrediting of democracy as an anti-Islamic secularizing trend. Democracy is experienced not so much as the actual political participation of all society (this has almost never occurred) but as a secularizing trend resulting in the decline of the Muslim world. In those Muslim societies where a possibility, minimal as it may be, seems to be open for these groups to imprint change within society (like Turkey and Iran), modernized groups might engage with pluralism. The cases of Iran and Turkey tend to prove that the new social actors, like modernized women, students, engineers, and scientists in general, can be enrolled either in a plural-ist movement against the closure of the political scene or in radical movements to topple corrupt and autocratic elites that do not allow the opening of society. Mobilization can therefore operate in both ways, through membership in Fundamentalist or Jihadist groups and through engagement in groups fighting for pluralism. In both cases, these new social groups, resulting from the modernization process, become prone to social activism.

Notes

1. See Martin Riesebrodt, *Fundamentalismus als Patriarchalische Protestbewegung* (Tübingen: J. C. Mohr, 1990), where he develops the idea that Shi'ite Fundamentalism is "hierocratic" and clientelist, susceptible of becoming revolutionary through modernization, whereas Protestant Fundamentalism is democratically minded, individualistic, voluntaristic, and reformist in nature. According to Riesebrodt, Fundamentalism, in its deep nature, is a patriarchal moralism. It criticizes modern societies for their moral decline, with one of the major roles played by women and their emancipation.

2. See David Zeidan, *The Resurgence of Religion: A Comparative Study of Selected Themes in Christian and Islamic Fundamentalist Discourses*, Studies in the History of Religion 96 (Leiden: Brill, 2003); Rudiger Lohlker, "Islamismus und Globalisierung," in *Religioser Fundamentalismus, vom*

Kolonialismus zur Globalisierung, eds. Clemens Six, Martin Riesebrodt, and Siegried Haas (Innsbruck: Studien Verlag, 2005).

   3. Some Hyper-Fundamentalists (like members of the party FIS in Algeria in 1991, after the military rejection of the parliamentary elections in which FIS won the majority, and in the following decade, or Salafist groups in Morocco today) join Jihadists. Some of the members of Fundamentalist parties like the Muslim Brotherhood can be tempted by the same attitude, but they have to break off ties with the party or denounce its pacifism in the name of Islam (like members of the group Takfir wal Hijra in Egypt in the 1970s, who were inspired by the Muslim Brotherhood). In England the Hizb ul Tahrir has hyper-Fundamentalist tendencies. In France, the Union des Organisations Islamiques de France (UOIF), close to the Muslim Brotherhood, is Fundamentalist (it has relinquished violence and accepted the opportunity to gain power through party politics), whereas the so-called Salafi minorities are hyper-Fundamentalist (they do not act violently but are much closer to Jihadist ideology than UOIF).

   4. The obligation to act individually (*fardh al eyn*) and not loosely in a collective manner (*fardh al kifayah*) has been proclaimed by many major Jihadists, among them Bin Laden, who, in the February 23, 1998, fatwa, "Declaration of the World Islamic Front for *Jihad* against the Jew and Crusaders," proclaimed that the individual duty for each Muslim was to kill Americans and their allies, both civil and military.

   5. See Hamadi Redissi, *L'Exception Islamique* (Paris: Le Seuil, 2004).

   6. See Jan-Erik Lane and Hamadi Redissi, *Religion and Politics: Islam and Muslim Civilisation* (Burlington, VT: Ashgate, 2004).

   7. See Trevor Stanley, "Understanding the Origins of Wahhabism and Salafism," *Terrorism Monitor* 3, no. 14 (July 15, 2005), http://www.jamestown.org/terrorism/news/article.php?articleid=2369746.

   8. See John Burton, *The Sources of Islamic Law: Islamic Theories of Abrogation* (Edinburgh: Edinburgh University Press, 1990).

   9. Abu Basir al Tartusi, *Taqut*, (Idolatry), *Minbar al Tawhid wal Jihad*.

   10. Tartusi, *Taqut*.

   11. Tartusi, *Taqut*.

   12. Tartusi, *Taqut*.

   13. Tartusi, *Taqut*.

   14. See Abu Mus'ab al Suri, *Shahadah qadah al mujahideen wa ru'us al islah wal mu'aridhqh fi bilad al haramain ala ulama' al sultan fi biladihim al musammah saudiyah* (Testimony of the Leaders of Jihad and Reform and Dissent in the Country of the Two Sacred Mosques against the Ulama of the Kings in Their Country Called Sa'udi,) *Minbar al Tawhid wal Jihad*.

   15. See Daniel Brumberg, *Reinventing Khomeini: The Struggle for Reform in Iran* (Chicago: University of Chicago Press, 2001).

   16. Al Suri, *Shahadah*.

   17. Al Suri, *Shahadah*.

   18. Al Suri, *Shahadah*.

19. Al Suri, *Shahadah*.

20. Ayman al Zawahiri, *Aqidah manqulah wa waqi'ah mafqudah (The Transmitted Faith and the Lost Reality), Minbar al Tawhid wal Jihad*.

21. Mohammad Qutb, *Ro'ya al islamiya li ahwal al alam al mu'asir, rabi'an: Al sunan al rabbaniyah allati tahakkam owdha' al jahiliya al mu'asirah* (The Islamic Interpretation of the Situation of the Contemporary World: The Fourth Part: The Divine Providence that Rules the Jahiliya's Contemporary Situation)*, Minbar al Tawhid wal Jihad*.

22. Qutb, *Ro'ya*.

23. Qutb, *Ro'ya*.

24. Qutb, *Ro'ya*.

25. Qutb, *Ro'ya*.

26. Qutb, *Ro'ya*.

27. Qutb, *Ro'ya*.

28. Qutb, *Ro'ya*.

29. Qutb, *Ro'ya*.

30. Bashar ibn Fahd al Bashar, *Asbâb al nasr val hazima fil tarikh al islami* (Causes of Victory and Failure in Islamic History), *Minbar al Tawhid wal Jihad*.

31. Bashar, *Asbâb*.

32. See Farhad Khosrokhavar, "Neo-Conservative Intellectuals in Iran," *Critique: Journal for Critical Studies of the Middle East* 19 (2001).

33. See Ahmad Beheshti, "*Hagh va taklif*" (Right and Duty), *Ketab fiqh* 1 (Winter 1375/1996–97).

34. See Hamid Parsa, "*Mabaniye ma'refati va chehreye ejtema'iye secularism*" (The Gnostic Foundations and Social Features of Secularism), *Ketab fiqh* 1 (Winter 1375/1996–97).

35. See Ali Akbar Reshad, "*Dala'ile peyda'ee va paya'iye secularism*" (Grounds for the Appearance and Duration of Secularism), *Ketab fiqh* (Winter 1375/1996–97).

36. See Asqar Ehtekhari and Ali Akbar Kamali, *Ruykarde dini dar tahahome farhangi* (Religious Action toward Cultural Aggression), *Kitab fiqh* (Summer 1377/1999).

37. See Hasan Rahimpoor Azqodi, "*Urf va maslehat dar tarazuye hokumate eslami*" (Non-Religious Tradition in the Scale of the Islamic Government), *Ketab fiqh* (Winter 1375/1996–97).

38. See Sadeq Larijani, "*Nesbate din va jame'eye madani*" (The Relationship between Religion and Civil Society), *Andisheye Howzeh* 4, no. 2 (Autumn 1377/1999).

39. Larijani, "Relationship."

40. See the dialogue with Ayatollah Mohammad Taqi Mesbah Yazdi, "*Velayat faqih va eyniyat haye fiqhe eslami*" (*Vilayat faqih* and the Objectivity of the Islamic Law), *Ketab fiqh* (Winter 1375/1996–97).

41. Ayatollah Mohammad Taqi Mesbah Yazdi, "Towards a Comprehensive Defense of Islam and Islamic Culture," http://www.mesbahyazdi.org/english/index.htm.

42. Interview with Ayatollah Khaz'ali, "*Ta'amoli bar ehyaye tafakkore dini*" (An Attempt at Understanding the Revival of Religious Thought), in *The International Congress of Imam Khomeini and the Revival of Religion, 11–13 Khordad 1376/1997–98,* Tehran (Organization for the Arrangement and Publication of the Works of Imam Khomeini, 1376/1997–98).

43. See Mohammad Hadi Ma'refat, "*Jame'eye dini ya jame'eye madani?*" (Religious Society or Civil Society?), *Andisheh Howzeh* 4, no. 2 (Autumn 1377/1998).

44. See Hasani's "Collective Prayer" in the town of Orumiyeh, *Hayat Now*, 10.2.1379 (December 22, 2000).

45. See Ali Davani, "*Mabazeye olama dar barabare hojume farhange qarb be iran*" (Positions of the Ulama toward the Cultural Aggression of the West against Iran), *Ketabe Sorush* (Summer 1375/1996).

46. See Hussein Abadian "*Gharb va padideye monavvar ol fekri dar iran*" (The West and the Phenomenon of Intellectualism in Iran), and Musa Faqih Haqqani, "*Framasonori ba gostareshe farhange qarb dar irane mo'aser*" (Free Masonry and the Expansion of Western Culture in Contemporary Iran), *Ketabe Sorush* (Summer 1375/1996).

47. See Fatemeh Rajabi, *Liberalism* (Tehran: Ketab Sobh, 1375 [1996–97]). The book is said to be of a "series of political and social essays, concerning the religious belief of the younger generation."

48. For an alternative view, see Gilles Kepel, *Jihad: The Trail of Political Islam* (London: Tauris, 2004).

49. See Diego Gambetta and Steffen Hertog, "Engineers of Jihad," Sociology Working Papers, no. 2007-10, Department of Sociology, University of Oxford, www.sociology.ox.ac.uk/swp.htm/.

6

The Transmission of Jihad
to the West

In the West sophisticated Jihadist ideology has to be translated into a simpler language in order to be understood by Western Muslim extremists, who generally have a rudimentary knowledge of Islam. Most European Muslims have little education, and even Arab-speaking Muslims from North Africa (Algerians, Moroccans, and Tunisians) do not master literal Arabic (*fus'hah*), which is distinct from dialectal Arabic (a simplified and colloquial form of the language, spoken in most Arab countries). Their fathers and grandfathers, who migrated to Europe, were unskilled workers from rural backgrounds or poor districts in the cities. They spoke Arabic dialects, and many were illiterate. The transmission of the Jihadist message to their children and grandchildren happens through new types of associations, intellectuals, and the Internet, as well as Jihadist imams, who are more and more clandestine in Europe.

THE SOCIAL ORIGINS OF JIHADISTS IN THE WEST

The environment of Muslim diasporas in Europe makes any deep knowledge of Islam highly improbable for the overwhelming majority of Islamic youth, mainly because of a lack of economic and cultural resources. Most imams are non-Europeans, with little knowledge of the European national tongues, while most Muslim youth in Europe do not speak a language other than that taught at school, some rudimentary oral expression of their parents' idioms being their only cultural connection. When they do speak it, many handle the regional languages of their parents in a superficial manner but are in general utterly unable to read or write it. Arabic dialects are different from the written (*fus'hah*) Arabic of the Koran. On the whole, the gap between Middle Eastern religious leaders and European Muslim youth is deep, and the latter learn about Islam through means other than official mosques. This is not the case for self-proclaimed imams and charismatic leaders of small cultic groups that proclaim Jihad as the main goal of Islam.

Most European Muslims involved in Jihadism in the West have a rather rudimentary level of Islamic knowledge, unlike many of their counterparts in the Muslim world who know much more about Allah's religion. Jihadist people in the West are the more easily radicalized as their knowledge of Islam and its traditions are sketchy, even nonexistent. In French prisons most of the inmates (more than 80 percent) who claimed to be followers of Allah's religion were unable to recite daily prayers in Arabic or even to perform the rituals of purification (*wozou*) before the daily prayers (*salat*) according to the religious prescriptions. Their Islamic culture was almost nil. They had vague notions about the prohibitions against alcohol, premarital sex, and eating pork and religiously nonauthorized meat (*haram*) as well as about women's veiling and a few other topics related to Islam, but otherwise they knew little about it. Besides their limited religious knowledge, a deep resentment toward global society was their common denominator.

For those individuals from the poor suburbs or ghettoes of France and England, hatred toward society and ignorance of Islam make Jihadism, in an apparent paradox, easier: it is enough that a few exalted individuals brandish Jihad against infidels in order to find an attentive ear among them. "Infidel" equals Europeans (French, English, Dutch, etc.) who treat Muslims in arrogant, downgrading, stigmatizing, Islamophobic, and sometimes racist ways. Hyper-secular Europe has made religion (and in particular Islam) even less understandable to second- and third-generation Muslims who are for the most part culturally uprooted, even among part of the Muslim middle classes. Their parents or grandparents, whose religion was ritualistic, had no capacity to impart it to their offspring. For this reason, new generations receive very little Islamic education through the family and even less through the school system. They are left to themselves, full of rancor toward society and with little capacity to grasp Islamic culture or history in its religious and cultural diversity. They are gullible prey for the first comer who equates Islam with Jihad, taking revenge against a society where Muslims are despised or at best ignored and are mostly second-class citizens.

Even those European countries that once had a sense of religion (England, Italy, and Germany, for example) have been deeply secularized in the last two decades. New European generations are looking for a new sense of religion, but their mind-set is on the whole much more secular than that of Americans in general.[1] One major difference between European and American "white" Muslims is that Muslim Americans are mostly middle-class, while their European counterparts are typically from working-class backgrounds.[2]

In France, where the highest number of Muslims live in a single West European country (between four and five million) and where the proportion of Muslims to the global population is one of the highest (around 8 percent), the problem of religion is even more acute, because of the laïcité system. The rigid separation of church and state prevents the state from giving any direct help to Muslims (generally lower class or lower middle class). A hyper-secular public is opposed to the "visibility" of Islam in the public sphere; the Islamic scarf is considered an icon of Fundamentalism by a large majority of citizens. Moreover, the problem of poor suburbs (*banlieues*) makes "Arabs" (the French of North African origin) second-class citizens in those ghettoes.

Within these suburbs an underground economy takes shape that represents large financial assets: an estimated ninety billion euros a year, around 15 percent of the French GDP.[3] Organized networks within gangs operate in poor suburbs. The *caïds* ("big shots") in the suburbs of Paris, Lyon, Marseille, Toulouse, Bordeaux, and Strasbourg are the new figures of local mafias.[4] For menial jobs, many young men of the *banlieues* are hired, working not only with drugs but with all types of products, illegally imported mainly through the southern port of Marseille but also through many other border cities in France. As many as five million people live in the poor suburbs, and their livelihood is in part determined by this "parallel economy."[5]

In these suburbs the number of lower-income people who pay no taxes is more than 60 percent of the population, compared to 37 percent in French cities. The rate of joblessness is more than double the national average. Twenty percent of children in poor suburbs have health problems, and the gap between the cities and their poor suburbs has largely increased in the past decade. The school system, paradoxically, increases the segregation effect through the stigmatization of the local schools, which children of poor districts attend with a high rate of failure. Urban segregation, in turn, packs in jobless and less educated people. In the ghettoes a typical slang develops, and social control is imposed through ethnicity and group control.[6]

In fact, poor suburbs (*banlieues, cités, zones sensibles,* and more recently *ghettoes*) are specific to France in many respects. In Germany, most of the second- and third-generation migrants of Turkish origin live in old working-class districts but are not as segregated from the town and the city as inhabitants of the *banlieues* in France. The Turkish origin of German migrants makes them more community-centered, with social bonds between the members of the community being preserved and cooperation among them being much stronger than among North African French in the *banlieues*. Contrary to French North Africans or English Pakistanis or Bangladeshis, German Turks have no colonial past that would heighten their sense of inferiority. French of Algerian descent are unembedded from their communities, and their families have typically been more disbanded than their Turkish counterparts. The same holds true in regard to Jihadist activities. Turkish communities in the West are more Fundamentalist in their creed than the others, particularly Algerians, but there aren't notable Jihadist activities among them, contrary to North African communities in France and, more generally, Europe (in Spain the Moroccan community and in England and Italy as well) and Pakistani communities in England. *Banlieues* that are periodically set ablaze in France (particularly in 2005, but also in 2007, with thousands of cars burned each year) do not see many Turkish youth involved, their main actors being North Africans, blacks, and some French middle-class youth who take part in the destruction as if they were festivities.

On the whole, *banlieues* are a French peculiarity related to the high concentration of poor people, the segregation process, and the subjective relation to the colonial past in the daily life of young "Arabs." Some of these ghettoes are theaters of radicalization and Jihadism. Some, like Lyon's and Paris's suburbs, have a long history of radicalization, first in the name of their secular claim to citizenship and then in the name of Islam. The Jacobin, centralized nature of the French state makes its identification as the chief enemy even easier than in the federal system in Germany or in the English political system, where considerable degrees of autonomy are granted to communities.

In the *banlieues*, young males are caught up between three possibilities: being no one, economically excluded and socially stigmatized; participating in the underground economy and adopting middle-class living standards, risking prison terms and a life behind bars as recidivists; and becoming Muslim. Generally speaking, adopting Islam as a way of life and a religion has a moderating effect on the young Muslims, who learn moral attitudes toward society through Allah's religion (e.g., prohibitions on stealing and drinking alcohol). In a minority of cases, Islamization has been synonymous with radicalization. Islam has been combined with the underground economy for the sake of

Jihad in some cases. The "normal" identity of the young people (more and more caught up between mafias and aggressive police) has been to adopt a vindictive attitude toward society: all men in uniform are rejected (fire fighters as well as bus drivers and police officers), the identity is mostly circumscribed within the district or even to tiny parts within the district—sometimes just a few blocks in a *quartier*. The norms are that of the "ghetto," and small gangs impose their rules—at least at night.

Islamic fundamentalism and, within a tiny minority, Islamic radicalism are developing as responses to a situation these young men perceive as hopeless. Their only plausible options are either deviance by participation in the underground economy or self-enclosure in a rigid identity within close-knit Islamic groups that have a life of their own, with moderating effects on the conduct of their members: reducing violence, helping them be at peace with their identity, curbing consumerism and the desire to be part of the consumer society, and so forth. Still, within the Fundamentalist framework, there are a wide variety of attitudes that develop in reaction to the utterly secular environment. For some of these born-again Muslims, Allah's religion is more attractive because people see it as dangerous. Islamic radicalism in this sense is, in part, the result of a social process in which victimization ("there is no future") is combined with the attraction of a radical religious view that rejects society as impure (Fundamentalism) or fights it as being against Islam (Jihadists). Victimization is contradicted by reality: sizeable minorities of "Arabs"[7] succeed in their social and economic life and become middle-class French, even though many of them have a lower-middle-class background.[8] But this does not prevent the majority of male "Arabs" from poor ghettoes to consider themselves without a future. Victimization closes even the narrow entry into society by discouraging any attempt at integration within the larger society.

The case of the French Jihadists, mostly of the lower classes or the lower end of the middle classes, can be extended to Spain and England. In the case of the Spanish cell that committed the train bombings of March 11, 2004, the majority belonged to the lower or lower-middle classes and had a low level of education. Most of them were from North Africa (mostly Morocco), the majority of them residing legally in Spain.[9]

JIHADIST NEO-UMMA OR THE POLITICS OF VICTIMIZATION

Fundamentalist and hyper-Fundamentalist circles in Europe have developed a view of the Umma that is very different from that held by traditional Islamic communities. The Fundamentalist Umma is a community based on the identity of culturally uprooted people whose religious socialization is not achieved within the family but through Fundamentalist associations that provide the religious education that is otherwise lacking. Religion serves to instill a moral code of conduct in the people who have not internalized the ethical code of society through the school system and the family.

For many young people, Islam is a substitute for the failing European secular code of ethics. In this respect, re-Islamization of second- and third-generation Muslim migrants makes most of them better citizens, law-abiding out of respect for their religion rather than fear of secular laws. For a second group, Islam is a means of legitimizing violent opposition to global society. Many young men of these poor districts generalize the image of their victimization to all of humanity. They commiserate with Palestinian youth suffering the effects of their unequal fight against the Israeli army by comparing it to their own suffering as "Arabs" in French ghettoes. The same holds for "Pakis" (second- or third-generation English of Pakistani origin), who denounce the misdeeds of English society and police against them by referring to the ill treatment of Kashmiris at the hands of the Indian army. Victimization of the self extends the frontiers of suffering to other Muslims, considered as oppressed members of the global Islamic Umma.

Victimization brings Muslims together within an imaginary community where suffering is the paramount feature: Bosnia, Iraq, Afghanistan, Palestine, Chechnya, etc. Disaffected youth extend their own mental agony to other parts of the world, their task being facilitated by TV and the Internet, which broadcast vividly Muslims' unequal fight. The relationship with this neo-Umma is not a "cold" one, as it used to be among people within the hierarchic, traditional Umma. Fundamentalists in the neo-Umma create, in their imaginary world, egalitarian communities where Muslims suffer from the mischief of Westerners through illegitimate domination. This neo-Umma is, on the other hand, characterized by the lack of any cultural specificity. It is solely a "religious" community, devoid of any peculiar culture and reproducing, in ideal terms, the Umma of the Prophet, in which Persians (Salman the Pure, the first Persian convert to Islam), Arabs, slaves (the Ethiopian Bilal), and men and women lived in harmony.

Having no specific culture, the neo-Umma is above all cultures, transcending them all, disconnecting the religious norms and duties from any cultural setting[10] and rejecting those features imposed on European Muslims by their host countries. The European cultures in which they grew up are illegitimate because they are the means of stigmatization rather than integration. Most of the "Arabs" (that is, French of North African origin) in France and "Pakis" (English of Pakistani origin) in Britain do not master the language of their parents and speak, instead, English or French with an identifiable accent. The new culture has become, for them, a stigma rather than a bridge to their fellow citizens, and they express their pain through music, thus avoiding physical violence by transcending and sublimating it in art—new French rap or hip-hop, in which verbal violence is frequent; Rai, a mixture of Algerian and French music; or Brithop, the British version of hip-hop, giving birth to new types of reggae, accompanied by break dancing. Sometimes, the very same music is put at the service of Jihad. The Outlandish, a Denmark-based Muslim rap crew that has been gaining worldwide fame, is composed of a Moroccan, a Honduran, and a Pakistani. They have produced militant songs, among which is "Guantanamo," in which they denounce the American war in Iraq. They practice a "symbolic Jihad." Furthermore, some lower-middle-class Muslims join excluded youth in their pain through psychological identification, although they are economically integrated. They lead groups of fragile youth to Jihad, using all cultural means at their disposal (writing, music, or sports) for the promotion of holy war.

Another characteristic of neo-Umma is its transnational outlook, distinct from the customary Umma. Neo-Umma is at best a minority phenomenon among Muslims in the West. Jihadist neo-Umma is triumphant and conquering in its representation of its relationship with other religions. Hyper-Fundamentalists share this feature as well. Hizbu Tahrir in England intends to create a caliphate worldwide, with England becoming a Muslim country in the future. Its policies to achieve this goal are peaceful, contrary to the Jihadists, but otherwise, the intents and purposes are the same. Hyper-Fundamentalists as well as Jihadists seek world conquest, the former choosing to play the democratic role, the latter rejecting peaceful ways and promoting violent Jihad as the only way to achieve that end.

Jihadist neo-Umma is puritanical to the extreme. Traditional Umma rejected consumption of alcohol and involvement in usury (*riba'*, lending with interest rates) or gambling but tolerated those practices in private under the heading "Allah covers up the faults" (*Sattar al uyub*). Jihadists intend to penetrate deeply into believers' souls and impose on them, from within, religious commandments and prohibitions. In this respect, they are more "modern," since they refer to the faithful's conscience and ordain strict obedience to the interdictions decreed by Allah. Like many extremist movements in the West, they do not have the tolerance of traditional groups. They reject compromise and moderation and call it *jahiliya* (godlessness). More restrictive, holistic, and puritanical than customary Muslims, Jihadists fight for an Islam that is not embedded in diaspora culture and therefore denies its Western origin. Their religion is a double denial put into a sacred idiom: they reject the culture of migrant families as well as that of the Western world, in search of a new identity that finds its calling in an agonistic universalism extended to the entire world. World Jihad is world identity.

Neo-Umma politicizes Islam to the extreme, encompassing juridical, legislative, and executive powers. Besides the Prophet's rule in Medina (622–632) and those of the Four Well-Guided Caliphs, the Muslim world has never been politically unified or strictly ruled according to Allah's laws. The idea of an exclusively Islamic rule, shared by Shi'ite radicals (the *Velayat Faqih* of Khomeini) and Sunni Jihadists (*Hakimiya* by Mawdudi and later Qutb), is a rather late phenomenon, linked to the modernization of Muslims and in reaction to secularization within Muslim countries where social change occurred without democratization.[11] *Hakamiya* as well as *Velayat Faqih* are also inspired by the example of the very same despotic governments with secular leaders in Muslim countries, which imposed a more autocratic rule on Islamic societies than the traditional ones, which were more in accordance with the community and generally more respectful toward its customs, even those predating Islam.

Modern states (be it Atatürk's Turkey, Reza Shah's Iran, military Pakistan and Algeria, or Nasser's Egypt) have deeply influenced Muslim radicals in their conception of the new Islamic government, in which governors have almost absolute power in the name of Islam (they are called emirs, imams, and caliphs by the Jihadists and *Faqih*, Islamic revolutionary leader, and *Vali Faqih* by radical Shi'ites). Theocratic rule proposed as an alternative to secular rule in the Muslim world is in continuity with the Jacobin autocracy of despotic governments. Fascist governments in Europe between the two World Wars also inspire them. Fascist European political parties inspired the secular Ba'thist parties in Syria and Iraq, and they in turn left their imprint on the Islamic radicals who fought them.

The neo-Umma does not mean a return to Islamic tradition, but in general it represents a regressive but modern rejection of secular modernity in the name of a mythical tradition, largely reinvented. It reproduces many biases of authoritarian secular governments in the Muslim world, accentuating some of them while intent on re-Islamizing through violence Muslim societies that have been, from their perspective, at the mercy of the West and led astray by "depraved" secularizers. In the Western world, Jihadists push toward a system that not only puts an end to the rule of "Crusaders" but also converts them to Islam, so as to impose Allah's religion all over the world. Jihadism intends as well to re-Islamize Muslim diasporas, de-Islamized by their sojourn in the West.

In many European countries, the rate of secular Muslims in the second and third generations is moving closer to that of other groups, with the exception of a minority of Fundamentalist groups (which exist also within other religions in Europe).[12] Even though for some sociologists Muslims are a specific case in Europe and do not secularize alongside mainstream European trends, Jihadists in general regard the evolution of Muslims in Europe and the United States as leading them astray of Islam, perverting them through a rampant secularization—thus bringing core Muslims closer to Westerners, dulling their sense of holy war, and preparing the majority of the faithful for peaceful coexistence with Western unbelievers. The neo-Umma prescribes a task: to bring diaspora Muslims back to the genuine faith and push them toward Jihad against the West. In this respect, the neo-Umma's identity is exclusive of any other.

In the traditional Muslim world, religious identity existed side by side with ethnic, tribal, and regional identities. Although Islam exclusively promotes religious identity, this never happened in its history. Tribal allegiance, the so-called *asabiya*, was depicted by the Islamic grandfather of social sciences Ibn Khaldun (1332–1406) as the decisive element in the formation of empires in Islam. In the late nineteenth and twentieth centuries, nationalism superseded religious identity, but its failure in Muslim countries resulted in the resurgence of Islamic radicalism—this time as an exclusive identity, making Islamic faith the sole ground for any legitimate claims of political belonging. The monopolizing of Islamic identity, one of the main features of Muslim Fundamentalism and Jihadism, is in fact a theocratic version of nationalism, extended to the entire Islamic Umma as well as a religious reaction against the violence exerted by harsh secularization from above against Muslim cultures. For example, the case of Iran's forced unveiling of women by Reza Shah in the 1920s became one of the signs of the Pahlavi dynasty's anti-Islamic nature among its opponents.

According to the Jihadists, to realize the neo-Umma Muslims have to indulge in violence against Westerners, even if they are born and raised there. In Jihadist attacks in Madrid in 2004 and London in 2005 (and that would have been the case in Germany in 2006 if the bombs had exploded) the number of those killed through indiscriminate explosions was so high as to raise the question How could they kill their own fellow citizens? The answer is that Jihadists reject their European citizenship and become involved in a neo-Umma that is exclusive of such citizenship. Other citizens become their enemies, and spilling their blood, if it serves their cause, is not only tolerated but also commended through this radical interpretation of Islam. Jihadists do not sympathize with people outside the neo-Umma, which they are supposed to create by being self-proclaimed vanguards of the world Jihad.

Another feature of the neo-Umma is its extension through modern forms of communication to the entire world. Before modernization, news would not reach Muslims for months and sometimes even years, each region being *de facto* separated from the others, even within Muslim empires. At the time of colonization, news was spread to the modern world by journalists and the telegraph, but the Muslim world was still marginalized because most Muslims couldn't read. Beginning in the 1960s, the number of Muslims being schooled and finding their way into the universities began to swell. With the proliferation of schools and modern universities in the Islamic world in the following decades, Muslims have never been as well educated and aware of the world as they are today.

The neo-Umma is the consciousness of the Muslim community extended to the furthest frontiers of Islam through radicalized groups. The notion of the worldwide Muslim community is no longer an abstract one, confined to the sacred texts or the Koran. It has become a body of believers based on the awareness of new Muslim Fundamentalists and Jihadists. Someone like the soldier and the young intellectual Uyayri, killed by Saudi forces in street fights in 2003, sees this reality clearly, referring to its different parts, far from each other, through different regions and continents:

> In this time of weakness in which we currently find the Umma, from the *Kufr* [heretic] dictators in charge over their affairs to the situation in Palestine where Jews hold sway over Muslims and where we see the daily slaughter of our brothers, to the situation in Afghanistan where Christians have taken authority, killing thousands of innocent Muslims—thus revealing their true animosity and hatred toward the religion of Islam and its people—to the Atheistic Russians and their authority over Muslim Chechnya, to the worshippers of the cow [that is, Hindus] and their crimes committed against Muslims in India and Kashmir, to the captivity of Muslim children at the hands of Disbelievers—and there is no change or power except through Allah, it has now become incumbent upon Muslims to return to the Shari'ah [Islamic rulings and guidance] of their Lord and to know what duties He has prescribed upon them. It is known

that knowledge pertaining to matters of Shari'ah is an obligation upon all Muslims. Likewise, to act upon this knowledge too is an obligation. Jihad is one of the rulings that has escaped the mind of Muslims, so much so that some of them have even forgotten that there is something known as Jihad in Islam, whilst others who talk about Jihad are unaware about its jurisprudence.[13]

For the first time in their history, Muslims have become concretely aware of their belonging to the same Umma extending to all continents, mainly through modern communications in the hands of a minority of radicalized believers. The latter exploit Muslims' malaise by emphasizing their membership in the worldwide neo-Umma, defined as a "suffering Umma," at perpetual war with unbelievers. It is through Jihadists that Muslims have massively become conscious of a universal Islamic community that can act globally, mainly through violence. Previously, their sense of belonging was abstract and weakened through tribal and regional allegiances. If we compare the declaration of Jihad by the Ottoman Sultan in the First World War against the Allies (United Kingdom, France, and the United States) and its very limited results in mobilizing Muslims, even though the German government made a great effort to spread it all over the Muslim world, with the much more successful Jihadist activism nowadays, we clearly see the differences between the traditional Umma and the neo-Umma. Today most Muslims have access to the media, and they are also better educated; tribal and ethnic divisions are not as powerful as in the past, and the sense of belonging to the same Muslim community, mistreated and attacked by the West, is much more powerful than ever. Now belonging to the neo-Umma is subjectively within reach and objectively achievable, mainly in a destructive manner. Jihadism is the expression of the new imagined global Islamic community, politicized worldwide. This type of movement evolves only in the Islamic world; there is no similar movement in Christianity or any other universal body that would bring such a vision so close to its worldwide symbolic expression, mainly through vivid images of "apocalypse now."[14]

THE ROLE OF HUMILIATION

The major symbolic ingredient of Jihadism is the prevalence of a subculture of indignity and internalized humiliation among a large majority of Muslims. The Jihadist intellectual Uyayri summarizes it eloquently: "Muslims are at war today. What distinguishes our time from other times is the humiliation and the contempt suffered by the Umma, which was unheard of in the past. At the same time, Muslims are in a state of lethargy and anemia (*wahn*), instead of mobilizing and fighting against this humiliation. There is a Saying of the Prophet attributing anemia to the love of this world and the aversion of death. In another version of the same Saying, it is the aversion against fighting (*qitâl*) that is underscored. Nowadays this is the deadly illness of which the Muslim world suffers."[15]

Besides its military and political dimensions, humiliation has a deep cultural aspect, underlined by Uyayri, related to Muslims' honor: "[Muslim] women of 'yesterday' brought up men who became masters of the realms of Disbelievers, but [Muslim] women of 'today' breed men who are slaves to worshippers of cow, stonetree, and Cross [Christians] and are humiliated by them."[16] Women's behavior vilifies Muslim men, who kowtow to worshippers of the cows (in India and other heretical countries with which Muslim governments have established diplomatic and economic ties), stone (Buddhists in Thailand and elsewhere?) and the Cross (Christians). The remedy proposed by Uyayri is the readiness to die in an all-out war initiated by the West. The occurrence of the word "humiliation" in the Jihadist discourse is very frequent.[17] Still, humiliation is not a monolithic category, and there is a major anthropological and political difference between humiliation in the Muslim world and humiliation in Europe.

One can distinguish three major kinds of humiliation.[18] The first type, physical and independent of culture, is related to direct violence. The physical mistreatment of Chechnyans by the Russians, Kahsmiris by the Indians, or Palestinians by the Israelis are cases in point, noted by many Muslims in the Muslim world and even in Europe. Body searches or collective punishments against the population engender a sense of direct and intolerable humiliation. The same holds true in Iraq by American and, less often, British soldiers (e.g., at the Abu Ghraib prison during the first years of the Iraqi war). The fact that those who impose this type of humiliation are "occupying foreigners" exponentially increases its effect. Obviously, the feeling accompanying this form of humbling is not specifically Islamic. But the sentiment of abasement is translated into a religious framework: infidels demean Muslims and are disrespectful of Allah's religion.

When Muslims were not modernized, this attitude was interpreted as mutual mistreatment imposed by enemies against each other. Now that modernization has changed Muslims' mental framework, violence by a foreign enemy, militarily superior and religiously different, entails another consequence: the enemy not only intends to vanquish Muslims but wants to destroy Islam itself, with the aim of uprooting Allah's religion—not simply to fight against specific groups of Muslims. This attitude, paradoxically, is less characteristic of the people who are exposed to direct humiliation in their confrontation against occupying armies (Palestinians, Chechnyans, Iraqis, Kashmiris[19]) and more often seen among other Muslims who, through new media and communication networks, interpret this humiliation as intended to uproot Muslims from the face of the earth. Humiliation becomes vicarious; it is felt and internalized by proxy—by Muslims all over the world.

Radicalization occurs through the encounter of this second kind of humiliation, humiliation by proxy, among those European Muslims who live in situations of stigmatization. Among them, some groups develop a subculture of self-estrangement and indignity. Racism, remnants of colonial prejudice, and Islamophobia actively contribute to this feeling by providing it with objective support. These Muslims believe that they are rejected as citizens and even believe that they are considered inferior human beings. A deep sense of self-victimization dominates them, and their feeling of disaffectedness is intensified by spatial segregation (ghettoes in poor suburbs or poor districts) and their historical background (their parents immigrated as menial workers, and they belonged to former European colonies, with the notable exception of the Turks). Europe's racism certainly exists but is not as absolute as this vision of self-victimization implies, if only because part of the very same population succeeds, with a lot of pain, in joining the middle classes. The subculture of internalized indignity results in an abysmal sense of helplessness and lack of self-esteem, with victimization leading to withdrawal into the imaginary world of estrangement.

Islam, in its extremist version, inverts the vector of victimization. From the predicament of a victim, the new Jihadist actor intends to transform the other to a victim. He breaks down the barriers of confinement into indignity, declaring the other inhuman. Death looms large in this metamorphosis. The European "infidel" is humiliated by the Jihadist, who imposes on him the ultimate ordeal: confrontation with death. The European becomes inferior because he fears death, unlike the Muslim, who is fearless and accepts death as a martyr. The former is a coward, whereas the latter is valiant. Death transforms the Muslim's situation from "slave" to "master." The Westerner is superior militarily and economically; he is inferior when confronting the test of death. Absolute victimization is subdued by reducing the other to the situation of absolute victim. Within this framework, martyrdom, in its symbolic meaning, is the process of moving the victimized to the envied position of victimizer. This transformation confers a new dignity and a sense of pride that are the opposite of the former indignity and low self-regard.

Humiliated and contemptuous of himself before his religious metamorphosis, the new Jihadist becomes the subject who imposes symbolic humiliation on others in the name of his faith within a context marked by a deep antagonism toward society. Humiliation is the more intensified as disaffected Muslims believe that their qualms are the same as those of the Palestinians, Kashmiris, or Chechnyans. We witness an imaginary construction of a global, de-contextualized humiliation: the humiliation of the former (Palestinians, Kashmiris, Chechnyans, etc.) has nothing to do with that of the ghetto youth in France or England. Still, the imagination of the neo-Umma builds up this type of abasement and postulates an equivalence between these different experiences. The result, once Jihadism is internalized, is an all-out war against "disbelievers."

A third type of humiliation is notably different from the two others (the direct and the vicarious) and supposes some roots in Islamic culture. In the history of Islam, the relationship with the "People of the Book" (Christians and Jews) and those who have ties to monotheism (Zoroastrians) has been conflict-ridden. A late Koranic text enjoins Muslims to coerce both these groups so that they agree to pay an individual tax (*jizyah*) "with humiliation" (9:29). The status of the *dhimmi* (Christians and Jews under Muslim protection and rule) was inferior in Muslim empires, and their relationship was based on the symbolic reiteration of humiliation so as to remind them of the superiority of Islam.[20] Modern Jihadists have borrowed this tenet from historical Islam and aim at humiliating "infidels" in the name of the superiority of Allah's religion to all others. Once becoming Jihadists, the former victimized Muslims embody this ideal of historical Islam within the Christian world. Its application out of the Islamic context does not seem to them a major obstacle because humiliating the Westerner is, at the same time, changing the position of the dominated into that of the dominant.

These different types of humiliation are embedded in a subculture of victimization that justifies all excesses in response to the intolerable injustice against "downtrodden" Muslims. Moral issues become insignificant for Jihadists, who can cause massive deaths in the name of a lofty Islamic ideal, disconnected from its historical background. Jihadism, in this sense, is the result of the massive dissociation of the culture's embedded moral code from religion, integrally supported by global media coverage of Muslim humiliation: the images of September 11 are part and parcel of the symbolic war against the "arrogant West" by the self-proclaimed knights of Allah, who demean the infidel Occident as much through their deeds as through images.

In statements by Muslim prisoners in Europe, it is clear that the humiliation they feel in daily life extends from Europe to the United States. These prisoners interpreted the September 11 attacks in few distinct ways.[21]

Benamar, age twenty-six, believes that September 11 has been falsely attributed to Muslims by the media, controlled by Jews. Still, humiliation plays a significant role in his mind. This event humiliated the United States, which humiliates Muslims, although Benamar has compassion for the innocent people who died in the Twin Towers: "It is the media, especially here. On TV, they say it's the Islamists [who have committed the September 11 attacks] without the slightest proof. Bin Laden is an idol, a star for the young people at the moment because of the media. But the Americans deserve it. They think they rule the world. They have been humiliated. Nobody is at anybody's beck and call. But it's not good for the innocent people who died. . . . It would have been better if the attacks had targeted the government [buildings]. And all that comes from Israel and Palestine. The Jews control the media and the judiciary. Well, they do what they like."[22]

Omar, age twenty-five, explains the September 11 killings as the reaction against Americans killing innocent people, particularly the Palestinians:

> You shouldn't kill innocent people. The Americans do that to the Palestinian Liberation Organization and in Afghanistan. They sell their tanks to the Israelis to kill the Palestinians. Bin Laden doesn't do all that for money. He's already rich. The Americans make people hate them with their policies, and what Bin Laden did was not good but he is paying too. It is better to attack the government. The US does serious things in secret, everywhere. All these people have to be woken up so that they will come to know the whole truth and maybe the goodies are really the baddies, or worse still. They left the Muslims in Bosnia to die just for money! Then, when people of North African descent go to Afghanistan, I say it is normal. Young people [Muslims in France] don't have plans any more. They don't have anything any more. . . . There are people who come to recruit them. They are good talkers and promise things and off they go. They sacrifice themselves. It is religion. We are attacked. We have

to strike back. They are slowly killing us. A small part of it is religion, but it is mostly the anger inside them that makes these young
people leave and sacrifice their lives in Afghanistan. The TV stirs
up the hatred. They show the injustice every day, politicians who
are never imprisoned, dreadful pictures and it's not good.[23]

The two dimensions, the internal life of Muslims in Europe and
the external life of Muslims adversely affected by American policies,
are thus jointly analyzed. In France, many young "Arabs" sincerely
are convinced that they have no future, and hitherto they have no
plans. They see images of Muslims on TV, and they are exposed to
Islamist recruiters. They feel that the Americans are "slowly" killing
Muslims everywhere. They go to Afghanistan, where they can fight
them. Although Omar believes that Bin Laden should have attacked
government buildings in the United States instead of civilians, he
understands Al Qaeda's line of conduct, if not entirely approves of it.
Omar does not deny that Bin Laden masterminded the September
11 attacks. He finds them at least partially legitimate. Humiliation
is not directly mentioned but implied with references to the feeling
of being "slowly" killed by the Westerners (the United States is the
symbol of the West) and the fact that "young people" (a euphemism
for French Muslims in the poor suburbs) have no future.

Nabil, age thirty-one, believes that there is a deep relation
between the humiliation felt by the Muslims and the September 11
attacks. He particularly has in mind the plight of Muslims around
the world. The humiliation by proxy that he feels in their stead is for
him the key to the attacks: "It is injustice which is the cause of these
attacks. I can understand the kamikaze Palestinians. I wouldn't do
that but I understand them, and the guilty ones are those who pushed
them to do that. As far as the attacks in America are concerned, I
am sorry for the innocent who died but it is a good thing that the
Americans were humiliated . . . the injustice which exists in Palestine,
in Iraq, in Pakistan, in Afghanistan won't continue for long, God will
see to it."

The common thread in these interviews is primarily the Palestinian humiliation, as if Bin Laden had acted on their behalf. Nabil
expresses the general opinion on this matter, adding to it his hatred of
Jews: "For me, the most important thing is Palestine. . . . There have
been too many massacres. Frankly, I hate the Jews—it is just too much
all that. But I live near Belleville in Paris. It is a Jewish area and I have
Jewish friends, but when I get out [of prison], I'll ditch them."[24]

Humiliation, spite, rancor, and resentment are the main components of this attitude toward the United States and, more generally,

the West. The combination of abasement as a second-class citizen with no future (a mistreated, victimized Muslim in Europe) with a projection onto the West through America (the United States repressing Muslims in the Middle East and elsewhere) gives birth to an imaginary Occident at war with Islam. This symbolic construction is at the root of the tacit support that many Muslims, be they secularized or devout, give to Jihadism. Its substrate is American policy in the Middle East.

Humiliation can reach paranoid dimensions when coupled with the rebirth of the individual through his adhesion to Allah's religion. A broken identity that finds healing through Islam antagonizes the Westerner, who insults the Muslim's sacred faith. A poem written by Mohammed Bouyeri, the assassin of the Dutch film director Theo van Gogh, who was critical of Islam and its supposed mistreatment of women, gives some clues to this kind of radicalism. Bouyeri composed his poem, "*In bloed gedoopt*" (Drenched in Blood), in Dutch—his command of Arabic being sketchy—and had it in his pocket when he was arrested by police just after his murderous act in November 2004:

> So this is my final word . . .
> Riddled with bullets . . .
> Baptized in blood . . .
> As I had hoped.
> I am leaving a message . . .
> For you . . . the fighter . . .
> The tree of Tawhid is waiting . . .
> Yearning for your blood . . .
> Enter the bargain . . .
> And Allah opens the way . . .
> He gives you the Garden . . .
> Instead of the earthly rubble.
> To the enemy I have something to say . . .
> You will surely die . . .
> Wherever in the world you go . . .
> Death is waiting for you . . .
> Chased by the knights of DEATH . . .
> Who paint the streets with red.
> For the Hypocrites I have one final word . . .
> Wish DEATH or hold your tongue and . . . sit.
> Dear brothers and sisters, my end is nigh . . .
> But this certainly does not end the story.[25]

Neither "Jihad" nor "martyrdom" appears in the poem, but Bouyeri implies both. The notion of a "bargain" with Allah to die in His path and, in exchange, enter the innumerable gardens of paradise is part of the traditional notion of martyrdom, developed by scholars according to the Koran. He imagines himself riddled with bullets, already dead, similar to the hopes of the Iranian Shi'ite martyrs of Bassij, Sunni Palestinian martyrs, and martyrs of Al Qaeda. The traditional pure intention (*niyya*) that would justify entering paradise upon one's holy death is underlined here, as in traditional Islam. The image of the tree of Tawhid (Islam) waiting to be sprinkled by the blood of the martyr also appears in the classical martyrdom literature of the Iranian Bassij, the Palestinian suicide bombers, and many other Jihadist candidates for holy death. He refers to the enemy whom he threatens with death, his execution being the task of the "knights of death," the Muslim combatants of holy war (*mujahedeen*). The potential martyr wishes to die and to impose death on the adversaries of Islam, this death-centered action characterizing their relationship. He also wishes death on the fake Muslims, the "Hypocrites."

This poem, written by a Muslim whose return to religion barely dates back to a decade previous, is similar to Jihadist literature. The two, Muslim world martyrdom literature and European Jihadist pamphlets and poetry, use the same themes, ideas, metaphors, and motives. They aim at going beyond any specific national or cultural frontier. They refuse any embedding in a specific culture or society, transcending all cultures toward the attainment of a cultureless religion that crosses all boundaries. Killing those who insult Allah's religion or its Prophet (*sabb*) becomes a religious duty that has to be accomplished by the Muslim as a personal assignment (*fardh eyn*), in contempt of human-made law.

By insulting Islam, Theo van Gogh slurs not only Allah, but also all those who believe that he intends to humiliate them twice. Muslims are already in the humiliated position of a dominated, formerly colonized people, with a strangled identity, torn between two impossibilities: feeling European (French, English, Dutch) or belonging to the country of their parents or grandparents (Morocco, Algeria, Tunisia, Pakistan). These people belong to nowhere, and their identity is not only divided but broken. Islam heals the wound of this painful split identity by unifying it through focusing on a single issue: abiding by Allah's laws.[26] Criticizing Islam is intolerably humiliating, since it recalls the predicament of denying one's identity: insulting Allah's faith sends the born-again Muslim back to his former situation of nonidentity. Humiliation reaches paranoid levels that can hardly be attained other than in sectarian, close-knit groups.

JIHADIST BORN-AGAIN MUSLIMS AND CONVERTS

Jihadism in its Al Qaeda version is the first truly transnational movement within international terrorism. Among its members various nationalities are present, and many have multiple citizenships, as Europeans, North Africans, Middle Easterners, Africans, Indonesians, Americans, Canadians, etc.[27]

One of the effects of the September 11 bombings is the seduction exerted by Allah's religion on many people, particularly among ethnic minorities in the West and in Latin America among indigenous people. The return to "Moorish Spain" (Islamic Spain before the Reconquista, achieved in 1492) is part of the myth of the Muslims and shared by some indigenous people in Latin America. They believe that Christians in Spain defeated Muslims in the same way as the Spanish vanquished natives in South America. The same Catholic, Spanish regime conquered Latin America and vanquished Muslims (Moors) in Spain. Both Muslims and indigenous people were victims; both shared the lot of the unjustly defeated. This induces what is called "the other September 11 effect" among the converted as well as members of some ethnic minorities in the United States and Europe. Although it is difficult to measure the extent of the phenomenon, there has probably been a temporary increase in the number of conversions to Islam in both the United States and Europe.[28] References to José Padilla, the so-called "dirty bomber," and Richard Reid, "the shoe bomber," both converts to Islam and both of ethnic minorities in the West, become iconic.

The "downtrodden" are especially attracted to this brand of Islam, symbolically contesting the hegemony of the "white man." Blacks, Latinos, Native Americans, and even South Asian minorities see in Islam the only effective revenge against an arrogant West, after the fall of the Soviet Union. Latin American converts consider themselves cultural descendants of the Moors. This kind of imaginary relationship is one of the results of cultural globalization. In the same fashion as French-born Arabs build up imaginary filiations with African Americans in their music and in their attitudes toward "white" French (they sometimes call themselves "gray" [*gris*], in comparison to "white" French and Blacks in France), Latino converts display a defiant attitude toward the West by expressing their pride in September 11, performed on their behalf by Bin Laden.

Among European Jihadists two categories are paramount: born-again Muslims and converts. Sometimes their cases are not dissimilar. Particularly in France, many young second- and third-generation people of North African descent have been brought up in total ignorance of Islam. Their return to it is somehow between the "born again" and the "convert."

Among the converts to radical Islam, many turn to Allah's religion to fight against the imperialist West. They are usually torn between multiple identities. The case of Christian Ganczarski (Muslim name: Abu Ibrahim) is a good example.[29] French juridical authorities indicted him for his involvement in the attack on a synagogue in Djerba, Tunisia, in 2002, in which twenty-one tourists were killed. He was born in 1966 in Poland, moved to Germany with his parents, acquired German citizenship, and married, and he and his wife converted to Islam. He spent time in Afghanistan and Bosnia, became a computer expert, was close to Bin Laden, and, according to some Jihadists arrested, gave insulin injections to Bin Laden. He became an important person within Al Qaeda. In spite of the fact that Al Qaeda's leadership was Arabic, people like Ganczarski reached high-level positions.

His profile is not exceptional: roaming between Europe and the Muslim world, multicultural, he is one type of European Jihadist convert who engages in a war against the West in the name of an anti-imperialist Islam. The other type is the French or English Jihadist, with little cultural knowledge of Allah's religion, who gets involved in holy war to take revenge against the West, where he suffers stigma from his non-European, colonial background.

One can try to have insights into the mind-set of converts and born-agains within the Jihadist movement, who are from all walks of life, by examining their biographies.

The fate of Willie Brigitte, a Jihadist convert, is a good case study. He was born in 1968 in Pointe-à-Pitre, in the Caribbean island of Guadaloupe, a French overseas territory, age thirty-eight in 2007. He converted to Islam and took the name of Abdel Rahman (like almost all converts, who choose a Muslim name to mark their new symbolic birth to Islam). He came into contact with radical Muslims in France's poor suburbs. In 1998 he traveled to Yemen and then made a journey to Pakistan, where he spent many months in a training camp in the Punjab Valley. He came back to France, where up until 2001 he supervised the training of volunteers who wanted to go to Afghanistan. He went to Afghanistan after the September 11 attacks and fought against American forces there. He then went to Australia, probably to study how to blow up a nuclear reactor in Lucas Heights. A Senegalese friend in Australia introduced him to his future wife, an Australian, who converted to Islam. It was his third marriage. He was deported from Australia to France on charges of staying illegally in Australia. He was prosecuted in France for having provided counterfeit identity cards to the assassins of the Commandant Masud in Afghanistan, two days before the September 11 attacks.

Brigitte's case, like that of many Jihadist converts, reveals the diversity of the contacts with different countries and cultures to which converts are exposed—the existential experiences, the marriages and friendships with people of other cultures (Brigitte married an Australian woman; another Jihadist had a Bosnian and a Japanese spouse, both converted to Islam under his influence[30]), the variety of countries and even continents they went to (Australia, Afghanistan, Pakistan, and France, among others, in the case of Brigitte). These converts look for adventure, for a stringent faith to which they can devote their lives as dedicated, revolutionary adepts combining personal faith and social, anti-imperialist commitment. Their anti-imperialist revolutionary stance borrows many conservative features, in particular in relation to women based on man's superiority in the name of patriarchal Islam. In their case Islam combines the rigidity of the faith with a male-centered sexual ethic (they can have up to four wives) and anti-imperialism.

Convert Jihadists play a significant role in Jihadist groups, which welcome them partly because as Westerners they attract less attention than native Muslims, partly because the media focus on them and give their organization a symbolic weight, and partly because they are the proof of the legitimacy of Jihad, since as former Christians or secular people they witness to the righteousness of Jihad. The media devote a lot of attention to them out of fascination mixed with horror.

One example is the Australian "Jihadi Jack," a former taxi driver. His real name is Joseph Jack Terrence Thomas. He was thirty-three years old in 2007; he had converted to Islam at the age of twenty-three. He chose the name "Jihad," which is not uncommon among Sunni Arabs and points to the fact that Jihad bears a positive meaning in Islam, contrary to its connotation in the West. He married a Muslim woman of Afghan origin. As a radicalized convert, he went to Afghanistan in March 2001 to fight on the side of the Taliban. He met there with Al Qaeda leaders, including Bin Laden. He was arrested at the Karachi airport and extradited to Australia in November 2004, before being indicted for terrorist activities. He was condemned, but for lack of evidence the Court rescinded the judgment. The Australian justice system still submits him to many restrictions.

The frontiers between organized crime and Jihadism are not watertight. Lionel Dumont is a case in point. He was born in 1971, one of the youngest among eight children of a modest Catholic family in Tourcoing, a French town close to the Belgian border. He finished secondary school and made his military service in Djibouti, where he was voluntary personnel in Somalia. He was indignant about Western politics in that region, and once back in Roubaix, he haunted the Fundamentalist mosque Da'wa. He converted to Islam in 1993 and took the name of Bilal or Abu Hamza.

In 1996 he was the leader of a group of ten thugs from Roubaix, "the gang of Roubaix," who had committed half a dozen armed robberies against supermarkets, banks, and vans transporting funds in the region. The group killed a driver and wounded three policemen and an escort for the funds transportation. Armed with grenades, machine guns, and a rocket launcher, they shot at those who blocked their way. In March 1996 the police attacked the house in which many members of the group lived. They did not surrender; four died, seriously burned, and two were grievously wounded. Belgian gendarmes killed another member of the gang during a gunfight. All the members of the group had fought against the Serbs in Bosnia, within the ranks of the "Soldiers of Islam." (In 1995, the Dayton Accords had divided Bosnia-Herzegovina into two entities; Jihadists had to leave the country.)

In 1997 Dumont was arrested for an armed attack and condemned to twenty years' imprisonment in Bosnia, but he escaped prison in May 1999, going to Malaysia, then Indonesia. There he was assisted by the Jama'a Islamiya, an organization involved in the Bali Jihadist attacks in 2002, when more than two hundred people died. He then went to Japan. He lived there from July 2002 to September 2003 with his second wife, a German of Portuguese origin who had converted to Islam. He roamed between Singapore, Malaysia, and Thailand, getting in touch with other Jihadists. He was arrested in Munich, Germany, in September 2003. For his involvement in the Roubaix murders, he already was condemned to thirty years' imprisonment by a French tribunal in 1996.

Dumont's case, as in many others, displays the incredible mixture of cultures (as a Frenchman he becomes a Muslim, marries a Bosnian, then a German, and moves between Japan, Singapore, Malaysia, Indonesia, and Bosnia, ending up in Germany). This is a generation that is caught up between many cultures and countries, with Islam becoming a means to transcend all these cultures by subordinating them to a sacred, transcultural identity that goes beyond a disorienting world. These Muslims are multicultural, multilingual, living in a globalized society but identifying with Islam in part because they do not accept the "grey zone" created by cultural relativism (the transition from multiple identities to no identity at all is frequent), but also because they see no alternative to Western hegemony in the post-Soviet era other than radical Islam.

The same pattern roughly holds for another member of the Roubaix gang, Christophe Caze.[31] In his fifth year of medical studies he went to Bosnia for humanitarian reasons. He converted to radical Islam. In Zenica rumors had it that he had killed and tortured Serbs. Once back in France, he pushed his friends to join Jihadist groups. After the end of the war in Bosnia, along with Dumont and other friends, mainly of North African origin, he founded the gang of Roubaix. He was in touch with Abu Hamza, the radical imam of Finsbury Park who probably sent him money from London. He was connected as well to Fatah Kamel, a French Canadian of Algerian descent whose network was connected to Bin Laden's camps in Afghanistan.

The multinational, multicultural, multilingual ties and networks are there, to make out of these converts citizens of a new world in which their faith in a revolutionary Islam supersedes all cultures and national politics. In its name they declare open war on the West. The anti-imperialist dimension of Islam is paramount. Its capacity to give sense, beyond any doubt, to this fight in the name of Allah makes it the most comprehensive ideology, satisfying extreme left and extreme right aspirations in an age of skepticism and suspicion. Islam is, all at once, a vision of holiness and a doctrine of sacred war. It casts doubt out of the minds of the very same people who were brought up and educated within the Western world of democracy, criticism, and "reflexivity," where doubt and uncertainty are major hallmarks of the culture. Their belief in the religion of Allah makes doubt impossible, skepticism sinful, and the rejection of the West irrefutable.[32] In this respect, Allah's religion assumes a new role, much beyond its traditional garb of unsophisticated and un-modern appearance. Its role is an alternative to the lingering doubt and skepticism in late modernity in the name of a transcultural ideal of universality. Violence is seen as an antidote to the Western diffuse culture of nonviolence and legality, based on "hypocrisy" and "duality": softness and democracy on the one side, brutality and the rule by an elite of idol worshippers, on the other.

The case of Hervé-Djamel Loiseau is noteworthy. He is one of the first converts who attained martyrdom through Jihad in the Tora Bora Mountains of Afghanistan, where he died in December 2001, trying to escape American bombardments. Hervé Loiseau became Djamel since his return to Islam, as a born-again Muslim. He was born in Paris in March 1973, in the popular district of Belleville, of a father from Kabylie, Algeria, and a French Catholic mother. His parents divorced when he was five, and his father disappeared from sight. Loiseau grew up in ignorance of Islam until his twenties. He first joined Tabligh, the multinational Fundamentalist and pietist movement that is deeply rooted in France, and he was exposed to Salafist influence through North African mentors. He went to Saudi Arabia, where he seems to have met Salman al Awsah, the spiritual father of many Saudi Jihadists. On his return from Mecca in 1998, the French Intelligence (Renseignements Généraux) arrested him. He was freed, pending trial. At the beginning of 2000 he went to London, later flew to Lahore, and from there went to Afghanistan. A year later, his dead body was found in Tora Bora.

His case is akin to that of Zacarias Moussaoui in more than one respect. He is between what might be called the born-again Muslim and the convert. In both cases, parents did not provide their children with any Islamic culture. Instead these men found Islam through radicals, their "conversion" being an imaginary return to Islam, a rupture with cultural rootlessness. They became the prey of Jihadist preachers, who easily enrolled them in the holy war against the West, toward which they bore a grudge for having found themselves between two worlds, in neither of which they felt at home. In France Moussaoui felt he was a "dirty Arab" and in Morocco a "dirty Frenchman," the same holding true for many North Africans in France, even among those resulting from mixed marriages. This is also the case for the English of Pakistani origin in the United Kingdom who wield a denied dual identity, neither English nor Pakistani.

Islam operates also against the disorganization of daily life and the many unhealthy enticements to which people are exposed in modern life, like drug or alcohol addiction. The Courtailler brothers are symptomatic among Jihadist converts. David, alias Daoud (his Islamic name), and his younger brother Jérôme (alias Souleiman) were the sons of a pork butcher of a small town close to Annecy, France. The two brothers lived in an Arab environment and were exposed to the influence of "French Afghans" (mainly French of North African descent who went to fight in Afghanistan against the former Soviet Union and then returned home with their mind set on Jihad). They appear to have known Kamel Daoudi, who was indicted for his involvement in the attempt to blow up the American embassy in France in 2001.

Jérôme was arrested in Rotterdam, with false papers and a machine to fabricate credit cards. The elder, David, had taken accounting classes. This young secular Catholic was a drug addict. He left France for Great Britain, but during his time in Brighton he met Pakistanis who acquainted him with radical Islam. He officially converted to this religion, went assiduously to the mosque, and began earnestly learning Arabic. In the meantime he made trips to Pakistan and Afghanistan, his expenses being covered by Jihadists in Pakistan. There, he said, he overcame his feeling of being lost and clueless. He followed military training at Bin Laden's camps in Afghanistan. Between 1997 and 1998 he spent around nine months in the brigades of Bin Laden. He made the trip to Spain many times. He went to Peshawar, Djalalabad, and Kabul before joining the training camps in Khost, where he learned how to use weapons.

In his testimony to the French tribunal in March 2004 he described his feeling toward Christianity:

> The Judge: Your parents are Catholics?
> David: Yes, but I did not practice. I find churches cold and lugubrious.
> Judge: Why [did you choose] Islam?
> David: I had lots of problems with alcohol and drugs. I needed a religion.[33]

After returning to Brighton, he went to Morocco, where he took Koranic lessons at a school close to Sheikh Yassine, the leader of the Fundamentalist movement *Al Adl wal Ihsane* (Justice and Charity). Then he went to Spain, where a Syrian veteran of the Bosnian war hosted him. There he met Jamel Zougam, who was later indicted for his participation in the Madrid bombings of 2004. (On October 31, 2007, Zougam was convicted of 191 charges of murder and 1,856 charges of attempted murder and received a sentence of 42,922 years in prison.) David was arrested in September 2003 in Holland. In May 2004 he was condemned in France to four years' imprisonment for his involvement with the "Afghan network."

His case is similar to that of many other European converts, devoid of cultural benchmarks, exposed to drugs and addictions. For them, Islam has a twofold meaning: it takes them away from a life of addiction and loss of purpose, on the one hand, and gives them, on the other, a moral role in world history as new actors in holy war. Their fight for good against evil makes them new knights of a noble cause, mainly against a wicked West, where they have been at a loss to find a sense to their lives and a justification for the social and economic injustices worldwide.

Richard Reid, alias Abdel Rahim, combines many features of a stigmatized and derelict individual. He was born in 1973 in Bromley, south of London, to an English mother and a Jamaican father. He had a difficult childhood and adolescence, spending many years in jail for various offenses. He converted to Islam in the Feldham Young Offenders' Prison. He was approached by members of Al Qaeda at the Brixton mosque, one of the major places in south London where ideological Jihadism flourished and a place he haunted assiduously. Before his attempt at exploding the plane on December 22, 2001, he went to Amsterdam and Paris. His traces have been found in Egypt, Israel, Turkey, Pakistan, and probably Afghanistan.

In his case, we are close to a model of pluralistic culture, with Islam serving as an anti-Western ideology, this dimension superseding the strictly religious, ritualistic one, as in the case of many Western converts. Within Western civilization many turn against "occidental arrogance," declaring war on it in the name of an ideology that was not, up to now, native to the West. Jihadism achieves "indigenization" in the West by blending leftist, rightist, and Islamic themes into a new radicalism. This directly contradicts the "clash of civilizations" theory[34] propounded by Samuel Huntington, since these young converts or born-again Muslims belong to Western civilization but develop a hostile attitude toward it for social and existential reasons. Islam is an imaginary "anti-Western" ideology they hold to for lack of any other alternative; it is attractive to them for another reason as well: it is for the restoration of the "natural" order, the hierarchy between man and woman, child and father, good and evil (homosexuality being the evil), etc. The reactionary attitude toward women and many other moral issues finds an outlet in this neo-Islamic tenet that becomes a substitute for the old extreme-right ideologies. Anti-Westernism can be triggered as a result of humanitarian work done in a Muslim country (the case of the members of the gang of Roubaix). It can be due to relations with Muslim radicals (the Brixton mosque and the Finsbury Park in England) or be related to a specific type of urbanism (the *banlieues* in France, where there is a simmering rejection of French politics and culture).

The case of Jason Walters reveals the significance of the Internet to the new Jihadist groups. The Web facilitates connections between members but weakens them as well, since the traces can easily be followed by intelligence organizations. Walters was born in 1985 of a black American father, Carl, who was a US soldier, and a Dutch mother. The marriage ended in 1997, when Carl lapsed into alcoholism, moved out of his home district, and lost his job. He began spending time with Muslims he met by chance and convinced his two sons, Jason and Jermaine, to convert to Islam as well in 1998. Both began studying the Koran and were outraged by the fate of the Palestinians and Chechnyans. After September 11, Jason, who used to be proud of his American origins, began hating the United States. The two brothers radicalized, pushing their mother and sister to convert and to adopt the veil and submit to Islamic norms. The father remained far from radicalization and did not approve of his sons' Islamism. Jason changed his name and became Jamal; Jermaine was called Nordin.

Beginning in 2003, Jason came in contact with Jihadists through the Internet, specifically with a young Dutchman of Moroccan origin, Samir Azzouz, who was arrested in Ukraine trying to enter Chechnya and extradited to Holland. At the same time, another group of born-again Muslims and converts used to gather in a cyber café close to Rotterdam and in Amsterdam at the house of Mohammed Bouyeri. They were members of the so-called Hofstad group. The online chats and e-mails among Jason, Samir, and others were an immense help to the police in detecting the other members of the group and eventually arresting them. Jason made at least two journeys to Pakistan. In the first one, he learned how to use grenades and a Kalashnikov and other machine guns. Pakistani authorities, alerted by Dutch intelligence, closely followed his second stay in Pakistan in December 2003. Zacaria Taybi, a Moroccan born in Amsterdam in 1984 and also a member of the Hofstad group, accompanied him. From September to December 2003, Jason attempted to recruit new members through the Internet, sending them to Pakistan. On November 9, 2004, the police attempted to penetrate the group's house, but Jason threw a grenade that wounded four policemen. After a twelve-hour siege, the group surrendered.[35]

Jason's bicultural origins (black American father, Dutch mother), the influence of Islam (conversion of the father followed by the sons), the role of the Internet in recruitment and radicalization as well as the role of the Moroccan radicalized groups in Holland and in many parts of Europe are quite relevant in this case.

Most Jihadists are in their twenties and thirties, but a few are older. Jack Roche was born in 1953 in Great Britain, migrated to Australia in 1978, and converted to Islam in 1992. He married an Indonesian woman. Al Qaeda members approached him in a mosque in Sydney. He was provided with $8,000 by Khalid Shaikh Mohammad (one of the main organizers of the September 11 attacks) and Riduan Issamuddin, the leader of the Jamaah Islamiya in Southeast Asia and one of the people responsible for the 2002 Bali attacks in which 202 people died, including 88 Australians. Roche made trips to Malaysia, Pakistan, and Afghanistan under the aegis of Riduan Isamuddin. Arrested in 2002 by the Australian authorities, he was accused of being a member of the cell that plotted to blow up the Israeli embassy in Canberra. He was condemned to nine years' imprisonment.

Pierre Antoine Robert was born in 1972 in a town close to Saint-Étienne, France. His father was a glass blower. There were three sons in the family. A Turkish community lived a few kilometers further, and he connected with people in it. Under the influence of a proselytizing Turk, he converted to Islam at the age of eighteen and became Yacoub. He was eager to learn more about Allah's religion and got in touch with many Moroccans and Algerians at the local mosque. He traveled to the Turkish region of Konya, where he learned Arabic in a Koranic school. He went to Iran and Afghanistan, mainly the Khalden camp, on the frontiers of Pakistani tribal zones, and there, in 1994, he engaged in military training for many months and learned how to deal with explosives and different types of weapons. He made many trips to Germany, Belgium, Spain, and France, indulging in contraband and smuggling activities.

In 1996, he was in Tangier, where he met a Moroccan woman, Fatima, whom he married and who gave birth to two sons, Ibrahim and Selma. Later on, Robert settled in Ricamarie, close to Saint-Étienne. The couple seemed odd to the inhabitants: he, a blond convert, she, veiled in black from head to toe. He was a car reseller. Also in 1996, he left France for Morocco to fully live his faith in Tangier, in a flat belonging to a mosque. He regularly visited the Mosque Mohamed V and explained that he was a car seller in Europe. He regularly visited a cyber café on Mahatma Gandhi Street, where he pretended to be German. He received his messages there. He swindled stowaway Moroccans, who intended to go to France illegally, and built ties with racketeers to obtain arms.

The arrest of a young computer specialist, Rachid Larabi, born in 1971, who had learned how to use mobile phones as detonators and how to mix up chemical products for the manufacture of bombs, resulted in the identification of his boss, Abu Abderrahman, alias Pierre Robert. By August 2001 Robert had received military training in Afghanistan and was nominated "emir" by a clandestine network made of Jihadist groups in Tangier, Fez, and Casablanca in Morocco. He taught members how to use explosives and trained them in the forest of Gueznaya. He was arrested in June 2003 in the forest close to Tangier, in possession of seven French passports, and was condemned to life imprisonment by a Rabat court in September 2003.

In Robert's case, too, there are many journeys to different parts of Europe, the Middle East, North Africa, and elsewhere. His desire to be a full-fledged Muslim brought him to marry a Muslim woman who shared his radical religious views. He used underground economic activities of smuggling, trafficking, and swindling to finance his Jihadist involvement. As a French convert, he acceded to high levels ("emir") within an Arab, North African, and Jihadist organization. These groups are, in fact, a ladder for the rise of radicalized converts whom Arab Muslims generally consider with suspicion. Converts' claims to leadership are usually rejected because they are considered a disguised perpetuation of former colonial supremacy over Muslims. These suspicions notwithstanding, Jihadist groups give converts the opportunity to achieve prominent positions within their networks. These groups are "modern" in the sense that they are "meritocratic"; they grant to French, English, or Australian Jihadists high status, independent of their origins and only according to their "capacities" (a case in point is the Polish-German-Muslim Ganczarski, who became very close to Bin Laden).

The role of charismatic imams in radicalizing young people is obvious in the case of Yong Ki Kwon. He is a South Korean, naturalized American, and thirty years old in 2007. He was born of Christian parents and converted to Islam in 1997. He received a diploma from Virginia Tech. He left the United States for Pakistan nine days after September 11 attacks. He received military training in the camps of Lashkar Tayiba, a militant Kashmiri group based near Lahore that operates against India and is declared a terrorist organization by the United States. He did all he could to reach Afghanistan, to fight on the side of the Taliban against the United States. He could not enter the country, however, because the frontier was closed and American forces had already taken over. He had to return to the United States to gather information for Jihad there. Kwon was the member of an informal group, the Jihadist network of Virginia.

On December 16, 2001, Kwon and many of his friends swore to respond positively to the appeal of their spiritual guide, Ali Al-Timmi, for Jihad. Al-Timmi, who had recently obtained a doctorate from George Mason University in cancer research, is a US citizen born in Washington, DC. He studied Islamic theology under a prominent Saudi cleric, Safar al-Hawali, a radical scholar close to Bin Laden. Many of al-Timmi's speeches and writings are posted on various Islamic Web sites. He denounced the United States as "Islam's greatest enemy" and induced some of his followers to take up arms against US forces.[36]

José Padilla is an American citizen, born in Brooklyn, New York, in 1970, to a Catholic family from Puerto Rico. The young José became a juvenile offender as a member of the Latin Kings gang and was arrested and put in jail many times. He was eventually incarcerated for his involvement in a murder. In prison he converted to Islam. Later on, at the Al-Iman mosque in Fort Lauderdale, he met the Palestinian Adham Amin Hassoun, who presented himself as the member of a charity association, Benevolence International Foundation. The association was later accused by the American government of being involved in terrorist activities. Padilla became a close friend of Hassoun, who was arrested in 2002. After his conversion to Islam, Padilla married an eighteen-year-old Egyptian Muslim and chose an Arab name like the other converts, Abdullah al Muhajir. He decided to convert to Islam after a dream in which he saw a holy turbaned man in a desert sand storm.

Beginning in 1998, he traveled to many countries, including Egypt, Saudi Arabia, Afghanistan, Pakistan, and probably Iraq. Padilla was arrested in Chicago on May 8, 2002. On August 16, 2007, he was found guilty of all charges against him by a federal jury, which found that he had conspired to kill people in an overseas Jihad and to fund and support overseas terrorism.[37] In his case, as in many others, the passage through juvenile delinquency, the meeting of a charismatic person (an imam or a strong personality), and, above all, finding a group of people ready to engage in a common action seem of paramount importance.

Another American Jihadist is Adam Pearlman Gadahn, alias the emir Yahya Gadahn, born in 1978. He figured in a video of Al Qaeda, just before the fifth anniversary of the September 11 attacks. In that video Ayman al Zawahiri in person introduced him as Azzam al Amiriki (Azzam the American). Speaking in English, Azzam claimed that the ignorance of Islam was at the root of the Western approval of Israel's massacres of Palestinians and Lebanese. During a period of forty-four minutes, he preached about Islam, and among other things he said, "If the Zionist crusader missionaries of hate and counter-Islam consultants like Daniel Pipes, Robert Spencer, Michael Scheuer, Steven Emerson, and yes, even the crusader-in-chief George W. Bush were to abandon their unbelief and repent and enter into the light of Islam and turn their swords against the enemies of God, it would be accepted of them and they would be our brothers in Islam."[38]

He also called upon Westerners to convert to Islam, denouncing the wrongdoings of Christianity and Judaism and proclaiming the legitimacy of Allah's religion. Azzam al Amiriki is the English translator of the messages of Al Qaeda leaders. He praised the "echo of explosions and the slitting of the throats of the infidels" and attacked US foreign policy and military activity, particularly in Iraq and Afghanistan. He predicted future attacks: "Yesterday, London and Madrid. Tomorrow, Los Angeles and Melbourne, God willing. At this time, don't count on us demonstrating restraint or compassion."[39] He also created an eleven-minute video about the glory of Al Qaeda, broadcast by ABC.

On May 29, 2007, Gadahn again spoke through another video, *Al-Qaeda Video Warning to US by American Adam Gadahn*, broadcast over the Internet. In this video Gadahn listed six actions that the United States should take to prevent future Jihadist attacks:

> Pull every last one of your soldiers, spies, security advisors, train-ers, attachés, . . . out of every Muslim land from Afghanistan to Zanzibar. . . .
>
> End all support and aid, military, political, economic, or oth-erwise, to the fifty-six-plus apostate regimes of the Muslim world, and abandon them to their well-deserved fate. . . .
>
> End all support, moral, military, economic, political, or other-wise, to the bastard state of Israel, and ban your citizens, Zionist Jews, Zionist Christians, and the rest from traveling to occupied Palestine or settling there. Even one penny of aid will be considered sufficient justification to continue the fight. . . . Impose a blanket ban on all broadcasts to our region. . . .
>
> Free all Muslim captives from your prisons, detention facilities, and concentration camps, regardless of whether they have been recipients of what you call a fair trial or not.

He warned, "Your failure to heed our demands and the demands of reason means that you and your people will—Allah willing—experience things which will make you forget all about the horrors of September 11, Afghanistan and Iraq and Virginia Tech."[40]

Gadahn's grandfather was a well-known Jewish surgeon, but his parents converted to Christianity. He describes himself as having experienced a "yawning emptiness," seeking ways "to fill that void." He explored Christianity but later found evangelical Christianity's "apocalyptic ramblings" to be "paranoid" and hollow. In 1995, at age seventeen, Gadahn began studying Islam at the Islamic Society of Orange County. He converted the same year. In 1998 Gadahn moved to Pakistan, where he married an Afghan refugee.

In his case, the family tradition of seeking one's own religion, his existential feeling of emptiness, Islam as clearly identifying the enemy (America, Jews, depraved Muslim governments, among oth-ers), and Allah's religion being at the same time anti-imperialist (left-ist charm) and for the restoration of "sane" family and social values (rightist lure) seem decisive. On the other hand, Al Qaeda has given him a prominence that manifests the capacity of this organization to exploit people's talents and merits, independent of their ethnic background.

Another American, Earnest James Thompson, born in Denver in 1966, converted to Islam and changed his name to Ujaama. For years, James Ujaama was known as a prominent community activist in Seattle. He wrote at least three books on how to succeed in business, including one titled, *The Young People's Guide to Starting a Business Without Selling Drugs.*[41] Washington state lawmakers declared June 10, 1994, James Ujaama Day for his community service and gave him a key to the city of Las Vegas with a Certificate of Special Congressional Recognition. But according to US authorities, there is another side to Ujaama.

During a trip to England in 1999, Ujaama met Abu Hamza al Masri, the radical Muslim cleric who is serving a seven-year sentence in England for inciting to murder and racial hatred. Also in 1999 Ujaama traveled to Afghanistan, where he offered his support to Al Qaeda, according to family friends. Ujaama was arrested in Denver on July 22, 2002. He was accused, among other charges, of attempting to create a camp for training terrorists near Bly, Oregon, between October and December 1999. Ujaama pleaded guilty only after videos were uncovered showing him sitting next to Abu Hamza and talking about Jihad. He was sentenced to a two-year imprisonment after cooperating with the authorities.

As an African American, he became involved in Jihadist Islam after years of living a moderate version of it. The shift from one version to the other happened through the influence of a charismatic imam, Abu Hamza al Misri. This case, that of a successful person putting an end to his social ambitions in the name of radical Islam, is reminiscent of the Frenchman of Algerian origin who studied in a prestigious Parisian university and turned toward radical Islam, ending his promising career.[42]

Another example is Wadih El Hage, born in 1960 into a Catholic family in Sidon, Lebanon. He grew up in Kuwait, where his father worked for an oil company. He converted to Islam as a teenager, after reading the Koran.[43] His family disapproved of his conversion and rejected him, but a Muslim sheikh in Kuwait who paid for his education in the United States took him in, and he became a deeply religious young man. In 1978 El Hage moved to Lafayette, Louisiana, to attend college. He studied urban planning and obtained a job at a donut shop where many young Arab men worked. At the beginning of the Afghan war against the Soviet Union, El Hage left Louisiana and traveled to Pakistan to enroll in *mujahedeen* war-training programs. Thousands of young Arab men from around the world flocked to Pakistan to help Afghans expel the Soviets. El Hage was a follower of Sheikh Abdullah Azzam, one of the most important Ulama of the Arab *mujahedeen* forces. By January 1985 El Hage returned to the United States and university. Later that year, he traveled to Arizona to marry an eighteen-year-old American Muslim; the two were presented to each other through an arranged marriage. In May 1986 El Hage graduated and moved permanently to Arizona to start family life. He and his wife returned to Pakistan several times over the next few years. When they returned to Arizona, El Hage worked at several minimum wage jobs, including as a city custodian. In 1989 he was granted US citizenship.

In early 1991, according to his grand jury testimony, he was called to New York to help direct the Alkifah Refugee Center, a Brooklyn-based group that raised money to support veterans of the Afghan war. According to documents from the World Trade Center case, Alkifah had a Tucson office and contacts with the main mosque in Arlington, Texas, and family members confirmed that El Hage had been in contact with the group. In early 1992 El Hage moved his family to Sudan, and he began working as a secretary for Osama Bin Laden. Family members say El Hage worked only in Bin Laden's legitimate businesses in the Sudan. El Hage frequently took international trips to Europe and elsewhere on business for Bin Laden. In 1994 he left Sudan for Kenya and became director of a Muslim charity organization called Help Africa People. Kenyan government documents state that the organization was dedicated to malaria control projects. He also worked in the gem business for extra income. During his time in Kenya, he stayed in contact with members of Bin Laden's inner circle. Later he moved back to the suburban community of Arlington, Texas, and secured a job in a local tire store. The family moved into a small apartment near the University of Texas, and the children enrolled in a local Muslim school.

El Hage serves life imprisonment in the United States for his part in the 1998 US embassy bombings. The fact that he was an American citizen and could travel everywhere with his passport was one of the reasons Al Qaeda often used his services. In his case as in that of other foreigners, Al Qaeda has given them prominent roles, going beyond the "ethnic" divisions of action of many local Jihadist movements. He traveled extensively in many parts of the world, leading a dual life: that of a worker and leader of charity associations within the United States and that of a Jihadist who helped the cause of the holy war. The ability of converts like him to play a role "in between" and to combine so many different and contradictory dimensions of their actions testifies to their utter modernity and the capacity of Jihadist organizations to adapt to modern conditions, in the name of a long tradition of war-mongering.

The case of Randall Royer is exemplary of gangs, small groups, or "cliques."[44] He converted to Islam in 1992 in Saint Louis, after the Los Angeles riots caused by racial tensions. The nineteen-year-old

Royer by chance entered a mosque on a university campus, where he found a white, a black, an Arab, and a Pakistani. They began to talk, and he found that they were similar people, without any barrier between them, linked through Islam. Something was triggered in him, provoked by Allah's religion. He had already given up his Christian faith, believing that the Trinity was in fact a unity, the unique God. His contact with his Muslim friends pushed him toward Islam. He came to believe that Allah could set the direction of a person's life. He announced it in an interview published online in June 2003.[45] His father, a Christian Baptist, and his mother, a former Catholic nun, believed that their son was undergoing a transitional mystical experience. But Royer became a steadfast Muslim.

In 1994 he joined the Bosnian forces that fought against the Serbs in Bosnia-Herzegovina. He chose the Islamic name of Ismail. There he rallied a group of Arab combatants, with some Kashmiris among them. Afterward he went to Pakistan. He made many trips to Bosnia, where he met his future wife with whom he returned to the United States. He joined Cair, the largest Muslim association in the United States. He made a third trip to Bosnia just after the September 11 attacks, this time apparently following the advice of Ali Al-Timmi, who advised him to wage Jihad outside the United States, for fear of repression against Muslims after September 11.

A December 16, 2004, decision by a US district court dealing with the "Virginia paintball" case convicted Randall Royer and Ibrahim al-Hamdi for their participation in what prosecutors called a "Virginia jihad network." Royer and al-Hamdi received long prison terms; seven others pleaded guilty or were convicted in that case, and two were acquitted.[46]

The conversion of Royer to Islam is similar to that of Yahya Gadahn; both went in search of a faith within a Christian world where the belief system seems somehow worn-out, looking for intense sensations and direct action. Islam provides a strong and vigorous creed, asking the believer to scrupulously abide by its rules, breaking the "grey zone" and replacing it with a dichotomy between God and evil, which is no longer shared by institutional Christianity. The passage between Fundamentalist Islam and its Jihadist version is also clear here, as in other cases. The trigger is threefold, according to different groups of Jihadists: the Bosnia repression of Muslims, the Afghanistan war and its aftermath, and, nowadays, the war in Iraq. These three world events have in many cases triggered the transition from Fundamentalist Islam to its Jihadist version by many converts. Among the born-again Muslims, events in Algeria (the military coup of 1991), in conjunction with Western involvement in Afghanistan and Iraq (the English participation in the war in Iraq), have played a major role. This proves that joining Jihadism is not only related to "identity problems" but also linked to the political and social problems of the Muslim world where the intervention of foreign, non-Muslim governments (the United States in most cases, France in the Algerian military coup of 1991–92) plays a decisive role.

Shane Kent is an Australian, born in 1976 in the suburbs of Melbourne. He converted to Islam while he patronized the mosque of Brunswick, where the Fundamentalist sheikh Mohammad Omran preached. Another preacher, Abdul Nacer Benbrika, called Abu Bakr, forty-six years old and the spiritual master of the so-called "terrorist cell of Melbourne," influenced him. Kent married a woman of Turkish origin. Abu Bakr sent him in 2001 for military training at Al-Faro, the famous Jihadist camp in Afghanistan managed by Al Qaeda. In the trial of the "terrorist cell of Melbourne" in December 2005, Kent was also accused for his illegal activities in raising funds by falsifying credit cards and hold-ups. In his case, the influence of a hyper-Fundamentalist mosque as well as a charismatic preacher seems essential.

A closer look at the biography of some of the Jihadists in Europe, either born-again Muslims or converts, attests to their identity problems and the "grey" picture of many second- and third-generation Muslims there. The comparison with the United States yields many insights. Whereas most Muslims in the world reckon American policies toward them as unbalanced, unjust, and even repressive, American Muslims, up to now, have shown far fewer cases of radicalization than the Europeans, even in terms of their proportion vis-à-vis non-Muslims in their respective societies.[47] This has certainly to do with the social class of the former compared to the latter: "white" American Muslims are middle class and mostly share the American dream; they enjoy a high educational level, whereas European Muslims are mostly from the lower classes with less education. They are in the doldrums concerning their own identity and their integration within the European landscape.[48] Although a sizeable minority of European Muslims has reached the status of the middle classes, still many of them are economically excluded and socially marginalized. The plight of the latter pushes some of the former toward radicalization much in the same way as many middle-class people turned to the extreme left movements in Europe in the 1970s in the name of the exploitation of working-class people. The case of Mohammad Sidique Khan, the leader of the London bombings of July 7, 2005, proves the difficulty of integrating second- and third-generation Muslim youth in Europe. Sidique was the ringleader of the bombings. He was born in Leeds, the youngest child of four. His father was a foundry worker in his fifties. Sidique was thirty at the time of his father's death. He had been married and had a small child. He worked as a youth worker and school mentor. The other two bombers, Shehrzad Tanweer and Hasib Hussain, had known Khan through his youth work. Tanweer, twenty-two, was working in his father's fish and chip shop after having completed a two-year further education course in sports science at Leeds Metropolitan University. Hussain, just eighteen, was awaiting results of a series of courses at a local college.[49]

The role of the district is important in Britain, much in the same way as the so-called *banlieues* in France. The shabby situation of the Muslim community, partly of Pakistani origin, in the suburbs of Leeds was alarming, with the number of drug-addicted youth rising steadily. In the mid-1990s, a group of second-generation young Pakistanis, called the "Mullah Boys," with about twenty members, tried to intervene locally to stop the addiction. Sidique Khan was a leading figure in the effort: "On several occasions, the group kidnapped young Pakistani drug addicts and, with the consent of their families, held them in a flat near the Wahhabi mosque on Stratford Street—and forcibly cleansed them of their drug habits."[50]

After September 11, 2001, the group became more and more religious. It expressed new tendencies and more individualization, compared to what was expected from Pakistanis. Its members began to choose their own wives instead of submitting to the choice of their families. They privileged Islam over the tribal and family ties within their district by refusing to marry their cousins.

Sidique was involved in a Wahhabi type of Islam; paradoxically, it was in a way more modern. Whereas Pakistani imams who mainly spoke Urdu held the traditional Muslim mosque on the corner, the Wahhabis spoke English. The poor quality of Sidique Khan's Urdu was a stumbling block to his understanding the Pakistani imam's preaching. The same phenomenon is true in France. Most of the traditional mosques are held by imams of Moroccan or Algerian origin who do not speak fluent French and whose preaching is in Arabic, which is not mastered by the second- or third-generation Muslim youth. By contrast, in the 1990s, the preaching of radical imams was mainly in French, in tiny groups or even in some radical or Fundamentalist mosques.

Another fact about Sidique Khan is his gradual adherence to radical Islam. In many other cases (Moussaoui in France and in England and many other Muslims or converts[51]) the same fact holds true. The identification with the Jihadist version of Islam does not usually happen suddenly, but through a long period of "incubation." In Sidique's case, the conversion of some of the other members of the

"Mullah boys" to Jihadist Islam reinforced his bent. He fell in love with an Indian Muslim girl of Deobandi tradition (the equivalent of the Wahhabi brand of Islam in Saudi Arabia), and this added to the friction with his family, whose Islam was of Barelvi tradition (the Deobandi are close to the Hanafi school of Sunnism and deem the Barelvis infidels). The couple met at the university, outside the realm of family influence; his wife was studying sociology. Their marriage in 2001 cut Sidique off from his family, pushing him toward Islamic radicals, who acted as a substitute for his family. (His mother had died a few years before, and his father and his second wife moved to Nottingham.)

Investigations reveal that Sidique was associating with radical Muslims related to Al Qaeda. He and Shehrzad Tanweer were sent to Pakistan to learn bomb making. In March 2001 Sidique took on a £17,000 a year job as a mentor at the local primary school. Tanweer was also involved, from 2001 onward, in local youth projects, and Sidique visited his family regularly. The other member of the group, Jermaine Lindsay, born in Jamaica in a Catholic family but brought up in Huddersfield, was in regular contact with Khan since late 2004. A radical preacher, Abdullah Al-Faisal, who twice preached in Beeston before being jailed for inciting racial hatred, probably introduced them to each other. Khan and Tanweer went for a long trip to Pakistan in November 2004 and went on a reconnaissance journey to London, where they met Lindsay. Sidique's wife gave birth in the same year to a girl.

In his video-suicide note produced by Al Qaeda, Sidique criticizes British foreign policy and then addresses his critiques to Muslim scholars in Britain: "Our so-called scholars today are content with their Toyotas and semi-detached houses. They seem to think that their responsibilities lie in pleasing the *kufr* (Unbelief) instead of Allah. So they tell us ludicrous things, like you must obey the law of the land. Praise be Allah! How did we ever conquer lands in the past if we were to obey this law? . . . By Allah these scholars will be brought to account, and if they fear the British government more than they fear Allah then they must desist in giving talks, lectures and passing fatwas, and they need to sit at home and leave the job to the real men, the true inheritors of the prophets."[52]

Sidique was imbued with rudimentary Jihadist ideology about the fact that martyrs don't die and go to paradise, opening the way to their families and people close to them: "According to the official account of 7/7, at around 8.30 AM at King's Cross station on the day of the bombings, "four men fitting their descriptions are seen hugging. They appear happy, even euphoric." In the closing scenes of the BBC drama that never was, Jermaine Lindsay turns to Khan and says, "I want my children to be proud of me." Khan replies, "They will be." And as the four bombers move through King's Cross, Khan suddenly stops, turns to the rest of the group, and says: "There are no goodbyes, only a lapse of time. We will see our families soon."[53]

Some interpretations put into question the Mullah boys' importance as well as Sidique's long period of radicalization. From this point of view, his radicalization happened much later, in 2003, rather than over a decade. The interpretation by Shiv Malik, as summarized above, mainly stresses Sidique's identity crisis: being caught between two cultures, the parents with their traditional Islam and secular society. He identified with radical Islam to escape the impasse of this dual identity. The British war in Iraq played an important role insofar as it proved the antagonism of Britain to Islam.[54]

Zacarias Moussaoui's case is also a pertinent example in many respects. He is the youngest son of a Moroccan who was violent, alcoholic, and paranoid. He was one of four children of the family: two girls and two boys. The father was a two-faced man according to some accounts, pleasant with outsiders, extremely violent within the family, often beating his wife and children, sometimes with an extreme cruelty. In his youth, before becoming a radical Muslim, Moussaoui had many secular French friends, among them secular Jews. His girlfriend, with whom he lived many years before leaving for London, was the daughter of a "pied noir" (a Frenchman forced to leave Algeria after the war of independence [1954–1962]). He did not practice Islamic rituals before leaving France. His mother, Wafi, worked hard to make ends meet; her husband became a drunkard and was absent for long periods. She had married him in Morocco at the age of fourteen, in a marriage settled by the parents without her consent. She divorced in 1972. Wafi had to work for the family subsistence and as a single parent; she took care of her four children. They had hard times, but she still was able to buy a house on credit. She did not give any religious education to her children; they did not know anything about Islam and were totally secular, according to the French model. She thought that integration into the French society meant breaking ties with Islam.

The children developed many psychological problems late in life. The two daughters suffered from a form of schizophrenia, one of them having to be under intense medical care. The father, too, was paranoiac, certified by French doctors. The brother Abd Samad married a cousin in Morocco who was a religious Fundamentalist and member of the Ahbash group, according to her mother, converting him to that brand of Islam.

Zacarias Moussaoui went to London in 1993 to improve his English and get a diploma in business. There he came into contact with radical Muslims. In the 1990s London (or in the language of the Islamic Fundamentalists, Londonistan) was a hotbed of Jihadism in Europe. Because of England's liberal policies, many Islamic radicals who could not stay anymore in France or in other European countries went there, benefiting from a safe haven. Many North African Islamists went there as well, to escape repression in Algeria, Tunisia, or Morocco. Moussaoui fell under the influence of radical Muslims, who helped him financially and provided him with a new community in a society where he was alone and had no ties. When he went back for holidays in France, he tried to convert his mother and sisters to a strict Islam, without success. His Islamization meant his rupture with the French language, his old friends, and even his family (including his mother, she has said).

In his preconversion life he drank alcohol, smoked pot, had sex outside marriage, and befriended secular, even secular Jewish, people. Now he abstained from alcoholic beverages, broke off ties with all his former friends, put an end to his relations with his girlfriend and his family, reneged his French identity, denounced Jews, and changed his appearance: he grew a long beard, shaved his head, and put on traditional Afghan dress. He went to Morocco to visit his grandmother, and there the police arrested him for his "extremist" look; he was released after the intervention of a family member. His only relation with one of his sisters was accompanied by his intense insistence on converting her to his brand of Islam, asking her to stay home, put on the veil, not watch the TV, read the Islamic books he brought to her, and open up a *halal* business.

The extremist version of religion professed in London by Islamists around radical imams fascinated Moussaoui, who found a religion that was not congenial to the West, treating Westerners as equals instead of putting them on a pedestal as former colonialists or as the masters of the world. His lack of knowledge of Islam made him easy prey for Jihadists, who portrayed "true Islam" as alien to any compromise with the West, in particular in respect to the political handling of the Muslims' affairs in which the latter were unjustly treated.

In England, once the radicalization process had progressed to a certain degree, Moussaoui changed his outlook: he shaved the beard, the "traditional" clothing gave way to casual clothes, and the fervency and aggressiveness of the former period were carefully hidden. The new attitude can usually mean either that the individual has given up his former rigid religious belief or that he needs to cover up his Jihadist identity for the sake of escaping police investigation.

Moussaoui's connection to Al Qaeda seems established because of his stay in Britain. Before the tribunal in Alexandria he justified turning down his lawyer for the following reason, in his somewhat imperfect English: "From the first day when I was in New York, I understood that America wanted blood, okay. So I didn't have to make all this lawyer argument. And I am not a lawyer anyway. And I was attacking. I take the position that the judge was my enemy, you were my enemy, everybody was my enemy because that is the way to assume. I want to kill you, I just admit that you want to kill me. I want to kill American people, I believe that every American want(s) to kill me, somehow."[55] His major assumption is that he wants to kill Americans without distinction, and they want to kill him in the same way. In his agonistic religious feeling, with his sense of being besieged, there is no room for neutral, let alone sympathetic attitudes toward others, globally identified as enemies. The only way of relating to them is killing or getting killed in the name of a radical version of Islam. His "religiosity" is death-centered in the way he relates to himself (getting killed by the enemy) or to the others (killing them as enemies of Allah).

Moussaoui's attitude toward the West is inverted colonialism. He bears in mind colonization and the inferiority of the colonized (the Moroccans in his case). By adopting the agonistic version of Islam, he vindicates Muslims' superiority over the pagans in the name of Allah:

> I mean there is two . . . aspects, okay? Here is one aspect that I would say purely theological, based on my religion. And after, there is my life experience.
>
> So theological aspect refer to the Koran who on chapter 9, Verse 29 place the obligation of the Muslim to be the Superpower. . . . So, from an Islamic point of view, we have to be the Superpower. We have to be above you. And you have to be subdued. And you have to pick words which we call the *jizyah*. Some people, I mean, translate it as a tax but it is not a tax, it is a tribute. . . . After that, it is because America, you are the Superpower and you want to eradicate us, Islam, you or a crusader, like George Bush said. . . . We have been at war with the Jews and the Christians for 1427 years [since the inception of Islam]. To the point that I will say the word "Crusade" in English is being used as something ongoing, without an end. You say Mother Teresa was in a crusade against poverty in India. Do you understand? Crusade is something ongoing. . . . The relation between Muslims and Jews and Christians has always been at war, okay? You have created the State of Israel, the Jewish

state of Palestine. This country, to give you a very specific example why I am up to destroying this country . . . There is no difference between the Jewish state of Palestine and Hawaii. . . . Without America, there is no Jewish State. . . . And if we want to destroy this Jewish state and re-establish Islam, we will have to destroy you first.[56]

Moussaoui refers to the verses that define the relationship between Muslims on the one hand, Jews and Christians on the other, in a compound way: either the latter's submission and tribute, conversion to Islam, or holy war. But he adds to this traditional attitude another, existential notion: the West has been intent on destroying Islam since its beginning. The idea of the Occident as the archenemy that would not only subdue Muslims but wreck havoc on Islam is a new one, related to the modern world, not a part of the traditional Islamic perception. The colonial experience and the trauma of the build up of the Israeli state are among the ingredients of this existential experience, but, at the root of it, there is a feeling of failure that induces the absolute Jihad and absolute rejection of the other as the enemy. Traditional Muslims did not consider non-Muslims in this radical way. For them "people of the Book" were "impure" but not absolute enemies.[57] Radicalization means that the others—not only the non-Muslims but also all those Muslims who do not share the Jihadist view—are absolute, dehumanized enemies, to be annihilated.

Moussaoui's feeling of being encircled by an all-powerful enemy goes back to the old leftist idea of imperialism, integrated into his framework of Islam: "[The world] is organized to your great benefit, to your only benefit. Because in 1948 you changed from the Gold Standard to the dollar standard. . . . You have the Wall Street, the Stock Exchange, and you organize, train, sponsor in every sense, every puppet government around the world, especially in Muslim countries and in African countries. And they are all your slave(s) because you have a superior military technology. You have a superior intelligence, you have the know-how and you do this very skillfully. And everything is done by the CIA and you pretend not to know about this."[58]

America has shaped the world to dominate it, and Islam is the only ideology able to fight against the submission of the world. Islam replaces the old leftist ideology that lost its momentum with the fall of the Berlin wall in 1989. Particularly among the converts or the European born-again Muslims, this aspect of Islamic radicalism is highly attractive. The recriminations are the same: all the responsibility is borne by America, be it in the street fights in Palestine or the war in Bosnia: "Every child in Palestine is being killed because of you. What happened in Bosnia is because of you. You run the show. You are the United Nations. Where are they? In New York. The Security Council, who is sitting there? It is America. You just manufactured reality and you talk about justice, Human Rights, and you set the mind of the fool. But you didn't set my mind."[59] The notion of "false consciousness" is taken up here, this time in reference to Islam. The alienated masses have their mind set by the ideological issues invented by the United States, like human rights. But genuine Muslims, like genuine revolutionaries, are not fooled by this masquerade. They know where the ultimate reality stands.

Islam allows its followers to claim power in the name of a righteous holistic conception and to contest American hegemony: "You have power and you are going to—you run the show. And I want power and I will run the show."[60] Before embracing Islam, the individual had only specific and personal claims. Once armed with the faith in Allah, he can claim global power; he no longer feels inferior to the domineering elites who are under the aegis of the United States. Islam makes possible the claim of a new world order, through the belief in Allah.

During the trial, members of the families of the victims of September 11 testified and expressed their grief and anguish. Moussaoui was not moved by their distress as human beings. He was so much imbued with his ideology that he totally dehumanized those who suffered pain at the loss of their loved one. He was totally insensitive to their sufferings, his ideology making compassion impossible, the sufferings of the "enemy" being no cause for sympathy: "As a person I find it disgusting that some people will come here to share their grief [on September 11] in order to obtain the death of somebody else [referring to his own death sentence]."[61]

He goes further, expressing joy at the spectacle of the enemy's woes: "We want to inflict pain on your country. We wanted—I am glad they have received pain, I am glad their family are suffering pain, and I wish there would be more pain because I already can forecast, after tomorrow, next week, the week after, the children of Palestine will be in pain. The children of Chechnya will be in pain. So this would strike me that lots more of your people are in pain so they will share in the pain. Because you enjoy life, you have so many this and that, okay, but I want you to share in the pain."[62]

Here we witness what Nietzsche called pure resentment. Since elsewhere people are suffering, and since the suffering is caused by America, so the Americans should suffer in order to restore the balance. The Chechnya children who are repressed by the Russians are mentioned here as another face of American imperialism. More so, the fact that Americans are rich and the others poor is seen as another sign of their guilt. The entire mechanism is based on a resentment-laden attitude and not on a balanced view of the adversary. All the ills of the world are attributed to America, and the problem is not how to lessen others' pain by legitimately fighting the American (or Western) hegemony but how to make the enemy suffer in a way that becomes an enjoyment in itself for those who have previously suffered.

Many Muslims, even among the most radical, reject this attitude. In the past, at the inception of the Islamic conquest, the rulers prohibited the armies from harming those who did not directly take part in the war. The caliph Abu Bakr (the first ruler after the Prophet) gave orders to the army he sent to conquer the neighboring countries: "If you are victorious, do not kill neither women nor children, do not destroy anything, do not cut fruit trees, and do not cut the throat of the cattle, except for what you eat. In Syria there are Christian anchorites living in hermitages where they profess Christianity, far from the world. They do not attack nor trouble anyone. Do not trouble them and don't kill any of them."[63]

With Moussaoui, we are worlds apart from the temperance of the original Muslims, supposedly the models of the Jihadists. Even someone like the medieval theologian Ibn Taymiyah, who professed a radical vision of Islam that called into question the interdiction of killing Muslims under specific circumstances (when the army of the heretics had Muslims in their ranks, like the Mongols in the thirteenth and fourteenth centuries), did not view the suffering of others as the off-setting of one's sufferings. Islam, in their view, was justice, and one should not inflict sufferings on the enemy under the pretext of having suffered at his hands. In this perspective "justice" means applying the rules of Allah instead of seeking Schadenfreude.

Moussaoui's case is one of a radical born-again Muslim who becomes a Jihadist through a complex web of relations in which the following factors play a major role:

- The family crisis. His father had schizophrenia, according to French medical documents, as did his two sisters, to different degrees (one under constant medication). The single parent family, the oppressive presence of the violent father, and then his disappearance made the psychic structure of the family all the more fragile. Moussaoui's brother later embraced a Fundamentalist brand of Islam, the Ahbash. More generally, the anthropological crisis within North African families in Europe is a factor in the social problems of young males. The transition from the rigidly patriarchal family to a loose, single-family structure particularly traumatizes the males in an egalitarian environment of gender relations for which they are not prepared. The identification with Jihadist Islam grants the males their superiority in gender relations they had lost in Western society.

- Total ignorance of Islam and identification with French society and its brand of secularism (laïcité) in a situation of cultural up-rootedness. (Many other European Jihadists share this feature to some degree, even in England.)
- The feeling of malaise from being "in-between," within a frame-work that did not give him the opportunity to find his real self. Moussaoui was caught between a fragile sense of Frenchness and a reference to his Moroccan origin that was constantly emphasized (his accent, his skin color, his Arabic name, the colonial past vividly present in society) by the very same French environment that was supposed to integrate him. Islam provided him with an identity that solved this insurmountable duality; his new religious identity was at war with both fragments of his former split self, the Moroccan and the French.
- The Jihadist environment in London that allowed him to find people who could connect him to radical groups. This played a major role in his radicalization; "Londonistan" had the Jihadist intellectuals, the Jihadist setting in a few mosques or their environment, and Jihadist networks, unimpaired by British intelligence until after September 11.
- Total identification with the extremist brand of Islam, ignoring its civilization, culture, and history. Ignorance of Islam in the Muslim diasporas where people bear a grudge against society makes identification with Jihadism easier.
- The generalization of his hatred of France (the colonial power, the country where he was raised without entirely belonging to it) to the West through radical Islam as a catalyst and a legitimizing instance.
- The dual role of the global ideology of Jihadism that articulates the leftist critique of imperialism (American "arrogance") with the rightist critique of Western bestiality and depravity (Moussaoui calls Americans the "Slaves of Sodom" in one of his letters). This duality seduces a wide range of people, from those seeking social justice to those fighting for a "sane society" within the ambit of radical Islam.

The case of Mohammed Bouyeri is also worth mentioning. He was born in 1978 in Amsterdam of Moroccan parents. After finishing his secondary education, he went to a college but never obtained a degree, even after five years of study. In his youth, he was a member of a Moroccan street gang. After his unsuccessful studies, he began working as a volunteer in a neighborhood organization in a suburb of Amsterdam. On the existential side, his radicalization occurred after the death of his mother and the remarriage of his father, reinforced by the September 11 attacks and the war in Iraq.[64] He began to refuse to serve alcohol to clients or to attend mixed-gender meetings. Finally, he put an end to his activities there. He wore a *Jellaba* (traditional Islamic garb) and grew a beard. He regularly attended the Al Tawheed mosque, where he met with Samir Azzouz, a radical Muslim, and other Islamists. With them he founded the Hofstad group, a loose network of multicultural people who met now and then in his flat, among whom were two brothers, Jason Walters, (alias Abu Mujahied Amriki or Jamal; see his case above), later sentenced to fifteen years imprisonment, and his brother Jermaine, who was acquitted by the tribunal.

According to Bouyeri, he fulfilled his Islamic duty by perpetrating the murder of Theo van Gogh in November 2004. His deep belief was that only through Jihad could Muslims cope with the West's antagonism toward Islam. Bouyeri's case does not reveal any direct connection to international Jihadist organizations. He and his friends were from Amsterdam; all of them were of Moroccan origin, besides two or three converts to Islam. Here, as in some other cases, one can speak of "homegrown Jihadism," in contrast to those groups linked to outside terrorist organizations.

Apart from born-again Muslims who are born and raised in Europe, one can also find those who spent long years in Europe, underwent intense cultural influence, but then violently rejected it and turned to Jihadism for existential reasons (racism or fear of losing one's soul) or political reasons (the war in Afghanistan, Iraq, among others). The case of Sarhane Ben Abdelmajid Fakhet, the presumed leader of the Madrid bombings on March 11, 2004, is a case in point. He grew up in a middle-class family in Tunisia and received a Spanish government scholarship to study economics in Madrid in 1994. He was a serious student of the Autonomous University of Madrid, one of the best Spanish universities for economics. He worked as well in the real estate sector and was proficient in that job. After a few years, he gave up his studies and became a devout Muslim. Progressively, he became a pillar of the mosques, turning more and more radical. The war in Iraq and the participation of the Spanish government in it made Jihadist activity inevitable for him. He died at the age of thirty-five, in a flat at Legane, a suburb of Madrid, blowing it up when the police raided it. In a video left in the rubble, he compared the invasion of

Afghanistan and Iraq to that of Muslim Spain by the Christians and the expulsion of Muslims from Spain in the sixteenth century. He claimed "blood for blood" and "destruction for destruction" as the justification for the Madrid bombings.

Islam becomes a sacred identity when the former identity (the parents' or the one to which one clung before living a long time in the West) becomes fuzzy or impossible to embody and the Western identity is denied (as in the case of many European Jihadists who feel rejected as full citizens) or simply out of reach. Any disrespect toward Islam becomes a matter of life or death for these new zealots, for whom Islam is not only a religion but a new identity, antagonistic to the societies in which they live. The conjunction of many factors is significant, the wars in Afghanistan and Iraq to which many European countries participated being a political catalyst for their hatred of the West.

TYPES OF JIHADIST GROUPS

There are many types of Jihadist groups in the West. The first is the cultic one, built mostly around a charismatic figure. At the beginning, it is more or less open to the outside world, but the psychosocial dynamics push it toward being closed. Certain events—triggers— encourage the members of the group to act violently. The target can be specific (for instance, Theo Van Gogh as an anti-Islamic public figure for the Hofstad group) or more general (the attack on an entire society, a government, or a large group as the case of Al Qaeda attacking the Twin Towers in New York, a hotel in Egypt, or in Jordan killing tourists, workers, and the man on the street). This type of cultic group usually has a leader and more or less follows his orders. After September 11, this type has been in decline in the West, though not in the Muslim world.

A second type of Jihadist group is made of friends and "buddies." There is no rigid hierarchy within the group, and they act together in an informal way, without much hierarchy. Many new groups building up in Europe and elsewhere seem to have some kind of affinity with this type, which is egalitarian, friendly, loose, and nonhierarchical. This sort of group, mainly identified by Marc Sageman,[65] is supposed not to have a formal leadership. It is difficult to identify specific groups that entirely satisfy this category. Still, one can say that this type of loose group based on the affinity of the members (friendship, local ties, and family relations) is one of the major components of post–September 11 Jihadism, at least in the Western world.

A third type of group is mainly based on family ties along generational linkages, sometimes bringing together fathers, sons, uncles, cousins, and even daughters, sisters, or wives. The family group can constitute a subgroup within a larger one. The Benchellali cell, made of the father, three sons, and the mother has been part of a much larger Jihadist cell, the so-called Chechnyan group, made of some twenty-five people, convicted by a French tribunal in 2006. One of the brothers, Menad Benchellali, participated as an expert in the fabrication of the poison ricin. In the United States the group is referred to as the "French poison cell." These families are usually made of people belonging to different cultures, and the younger generation is caught up between two or more cultures and worlds. The Benchellali family consists of people of Algerian nationality (the father and one brother, Merouane Benahmed), and one, Menad, of French citizenship. Usually, they are ill at ease existing between two extremely different worlds.

The Canadian case of the Khadr family extends over three generations. The grandfather, Ahmed Saïd Khadr, left Egypt in the 1970s and migrated to Canada, where the entire family settled. They had four sons and two daughters. The father traveled extensively to Pakistan and Afghanistan, as a member of Al Qaeda, in the 1990s. The family moved from Canada to Pakistan in 1990. In 1994 Pakistani authorities arrested Ahmed Khadr. His brother Omar Khadr returned with his other brothers and sisters to Canada, to stay with their grandparents. Omar returned to Pakistan and then to Afghanistan. In 2002 he was arrested by the United States after fighting the Americans. He was imprisoned in Guantanamo. In 2005 he was charged with criminal activity within Al Qaeda—for killing a US soldier. Another brother, Abdulraham, was arrested in Kabul and handed over to the Americans. The father was killed in the battle against the United States after his release through bribery in Pakistan and his return to Afghanistan.

Although much of the story is still a matter of conjecture, one fact remains: the father had an Egyptian identity; the family became involved in Pakistan through Al Qaeda links; the father traveled extensively between Canada, Pakistan, and Afghanistan; and the younger generation partially did the same, belonging to the "in-between." The cultural factor by itself certainly does not explain their involvement in Jihadist activities, but the fact that the father was involved played a major role, as in the case of the Benchellali family. The conflation of cultural factors and the figurehead of the father facilitates the membership of the sons (and even the mother in the Benchellali case). Usually, in Jihadist cases, the family ignores the involvement of their son. Within the model of the family cell, the enlarged Jihadist identity attracts the younger generation in a characteristic inversion (usually the son joins the Jihad, unlike the father, who is traditionally minded and quietist). The involvement of the younger generation sometimes occurs in a way that is not always fully conscious. Some members claim that they were enrolled in Jihad without truly appreciating their new role and once caught up in the new system, they had almost no choice.[66]

A fourth type of Jihadist group is made of people identifying with a set of charismatic people who "share" their charisma: one is charismatic in the field of organization, the other in money making and relating to the outside world, another in the field of technical skills (explosives, for example). There is an implicit hierarchy within the group, but there is no formal leader. The Jihadist group that bombed the train in Madrid in 2004 seems to belong to this category.

After September 11 there was no more room for large groups in the West. The small groups that form around a single person are not strictly hierarchical, but there is still one who plays the role of the ringleader. In the French case, the group that sent its members in Iraq to fight the US army had a leader, Farid Benyettou. One of the members, Boubaker el Hakim, a Frenchman of Tunisian origin, was sent to France from Syria to be indicted as a member of a terrorist organization. His brother Redouane, nineteen years old, was killed in Iraq. He was from the nineteenth district of Paris, and he knew Farid Benyettou, the spiritual leader of the group and the recruiter who was indicted in January 2005 and jailed for organizing the departure of the group members to Iraq.[67]

In the Western world, where large-scale Jihadist operations are becoming highly improbable, the new cells, small in size, are usually animated by a new type of leader who does not hold a rigidly hierarchical position within the group but still enjoys a spiritual privilege of primus inter pares rather than an absolute position of an undisputed leader. The new figureheads more and more look like the "leopard chief" of primitive societies, where their privileges are not so much in making decisions in an absolute manner but in having a diffuse influence within the group that makes them slightly above the average and makes possible some crucial orientations within the group.

TYPES OF JIHADIST INDIVIDUALS

One can distinguish five types of Jihadist personalities: the missionary, the macho, the upholder of justice, the adventurer, and the existential man.

The missionary seeks to expand Islam to the world, according to the religious writ. Among the Jihadists some would like to behave according to the letter of the holy text. They firmly believe that Islam has the calling of becoming universal and no compromise should be made on this mission. The relation between Muslims and others is only three-fold: either their conversion to Islam or their paying taxes (*jizyah*) or Jihad. These people believe that humiliation of others through bombing, maiming, and killing is a necessity to implement Allah's sentence at the present time, because of Muslims' military inferiority toward the West. This type of warrior intends to spread Islam through holy war, unlike the Muslim Fundamentalists, who aim at the same goal through peaceful means.

The second type is the macho. For him Islam restores the family and social bonds on a sane basis, according to men's needs. According to the Koran, a man has the right to marry up to four wives,[68] on condition of being "just" toward them; he can impose, in the name of Allah, "modesty" on women and exert his authority toward children within a patriarchal family. In the Jihadists' minds, this dimension is connected to another, the rejection of Western sexual and, more generally, gender values. Homosexuality has to be banned as well as "pornography"—that is, the "nudity" of women, their appearance in the public sphere, their work outside the home, and even sometimes their education on parity with men. A patriarchal version of Islam is still legitimate for many orthodox Muslims all over the world, and Jihadists exploit this convergence of their view with that of the Fundamentalists and even merely orthodox Muslims to attract them. Contrary to Islam, the same patriarchal version of family and gender vision in Christianity or Judaism cannot be anything but a sectarian or, at best, marginal conception. A stringent form of machismo in the name of traditional Islam is thus shared by orthodox Muslims, Fundamentalists, and Jihadists alike. But violence is justified only by Jihadists to oppose Western culture that contaminates Muslims in the Western diasporas and in the Muslim world through illegitimate governments, which are subservient to the West.

The second type makes cultural values one of the main reasons for violently rejecting the West and the spread of its values to the world. Among Western Jihadists, the fascination with this aspect of Islam goes hand in hand with the "castration" feeling of many men who have experienced the "dispossession" of their virility and manhood by emancipated women. Islam, in its Fundamentalist and Jihadist versions, is the major proponent of this type of machismo because many Jihadists consider it as the only genuine opponent of Western depravity. This dimension of patriarchal Islam is akin to the

archconservative movements in the West, but Jihadism makes violence legitimate in other perspectives as well, allowing the adherents
to combine different logics of action within this framework (which
Christian conservative groups cannot easily afford to realize). Anti-
imperialist logic is one of them.

The third type is the justice seeker. Injustice in the world is due
to the Western and, more particularly, American hegemony. The fight
against it cannot be based on leftist ideologies anymore. Muslims
are the "oppressed" (*mustadh'afin*), and the legitimacy of the fight
against the "oppressors" (*mustakbirin*) is recognized by the Koran.
Many dimensions of the extreme left ideologies are coupled with the
lure of taking a "holy" revenge against the West. The humiliations
endured by Muslims in many parts of the world, related in a real or
imaginary way to Occidental hegemony, makes Jihadist Islam the only
major bearer of the anti-imperialist standard in the West, particularly
among the converts.[69]

The fourth type is the adventurer. Jihadism has a play dimension that can be satisfied in many ways. The adventure involved in
taking trips and journeys all over the world (up to a few years ago it
was much easier; since September 11, it has become riskier and, in a
way, more exciting) is one of the stimulating dimensions of Jihadism;
the adventure of meeting "extraordinary" people who make history is
another one. Socialization within these groups through the Internet
or direct links breathes life into an otherwise grey existence, usually
without any major excitement; another aspect is the multicultural one:
many people, with different backgrounds and cultures mix up within
Jihadist groups. They thus realize a universalistic calling in the name
of Allah's faith. The adventurer can be as well motivated by what is
in "vogue" and "fashion," in the same way as martyrs in the Iranian
revolution who were proud to follow a "martyrdom fashion." They thus
modernized martyrdom through the identification with the "vogue"
and Islamized modernity by converting the "fad" to a "sacred" act.[70]
Within the figurehead of the holy adventurer, Jihadism integrates many
dimensions of modern exhibitionism, fashion, and emotionalism.

Adventurers need to become "someone" through excitement.
From the status of "nobody" they accede to the rank of a world figure
through the media. They revere Bin Laden not only because of his
role as an Islamic Robin Hood who takes revenge against the powerful for the sake of the "oppressed," but also because of his stardom.
Contrary to Western stars, he is a "sacred star"; he combines the
logic of stardom with that of nobility. Unlike "cheap" Western stars,
who just imitate action in their fake heroism, he does what he says.
Bin Laden and other figures of Jihadism become icons for the young

Jihadists in Europe who need to be "somebody," satisfy their hopes for excitement, and realize their desire of surpassing the Western "masters" who colonized their fathers and marginalized their "sons" in poor districts. The sense of adventure, combined with the logic of realizing one's self by humiliating the "damned Westerners" is part of the fascination exerted by Jihadism on the mind of many young uprooted European Muslims. Through violence in the name of the holy war, they would like to shake the yoke of internalized humiliation by combining it with hyper-excitement.

In many European countries, in spite of the passing of more than half a century, the colonial memory is still at the back of their minds. Particularly in France, the Algerian drama of the war of independence, the deaths of hunderds of thousands, and the forced departure of more than one million French born and raised in Algeria is far from over in the minds and hearts of many people. In England, a country with a multicultural policy, ethnic minorities do not mix easily, and the rate of intermarriage is not high. The colonial past is present in the form of mutual avoidance and "leaving apart." The policies of Britain toward Iraq and Afghanistan and its siding with the American government for the occupation of the two countries from 2003 onward has been interpreted by many Muslim citizens as an anti-Islamic policy, reminiscent of colonial arrogance. Generally speaking, the anti-colonial dimension of Jihadism in Europe is not negligible and, conflated with the feeling of being second-class citizens, predisposes part of the new generations toward radicalization in the name of Allah.

The last type of Jihadist is the existential man. The deep crisis between multiple identities rejected by the host societies is a major problem for this group. The "neither/nor" is paramount: neither Algerian nor French (in France, the second and third generation of youth rejected for being "Arab" and in Algeria for being "French," the same situation holding true for the English Pakistanis). This dual identity is in fact a double denial of identity since each dimension (Frenchness for France and Algerianness for Algeria) is discarded by both societies (France and Algeria, England and Pakistan).

The split self can be pushed toward Jihadism through two major factors. The first is the deep humiliation from not being seen as equal to the others in Western culture, where equality is a major ingredient of collective identity. Not being "the same" means, in the ethnic English ghettoes or in the poor French *banlieues*, being "inferior" to the others. There is no status in the dominant European culture for this type of inferiority, contrary to the traditional cultures that impose a hierarchy (like the Indian caste system). In an egalitarian culture, the feeling of insurmountable inferiority is the more excruciating, since it has no legitimacy and no locus within the culture. Radical Islam resolves the dilemma by rejecting both of the ingredients of the former split identity: the French and Algerian components are declared illegitimate and godless in the same manner as the Pakistani and English ones. Jihadism, in its modern version in the West, is deeply egalitarian: blacks, whites, ethnic people from all over the world become members of a new "international Jihadism" that realizes, through the fight against the West, the very egalitarian values promoted by the West. It washes away humiliation and replaces it with a deep sense of pride; it erases a painful dual identity with a solid, even monolithic one based on religion, in which doubt is rejected as an evil characteristic, peculiar to the "depraved Westerner."

The existential Jihadist realizes his dream through the identification with holy war: hitherto, he belongs to a "warm" community, the neo-Umma, in sharp contrast with before, when he belonged to nowhere in societies that are, at best, "cold." The neo-Umma is more than warm; it is "effervescent," and it brings meaning to the life of the believer and assigns an ideal to it, namely the merciless combat against the arrogant Occident where imperialism goes hand in hand with godlessness and moral depravity.

WOMEN AND MARTYRDOM

During the long war between Iran and Iraq (1980–1988), women's role as martyrs in the young Islamic Republic was only an indirect one: they could not take part in the war as soldiers and meet martyrdom in the same fashion as men. They could die as martyrs by nursing wounded soldiers and succumbing under the Iraqi bombings. They even could be recognized as martyrs if they died, like many men, as a result of the air strikes by Iraqi fighter jets.[71] Women were denied direct participation as "martyr soldiers" in Bassij, the organization that mainly enrolled young volunteers in Iran, although there was a demand in that direction by many young revolutionary girls.

In many other countries, women have gained some foothold within Jihadist organizations. In Chechnya their role has been important. In Palestine an increasing number of women have been involved in suicide attacks in recent years, whereas in the Jihadist movement in Jordan, Egypt, and Iraq there has been marginal involvement of women up to now. But their role has always been close to that of the foot soldier and not within the leadership of these movements.

There is a paradox in the Jihadist movement vis-à-vis women. On the one hand, Jihadists denounce the presence of women in the public sphere and fight for their return to the family. They reject the Western idea of the equality of men and women and propose a rigid view of the Shari'ah that refuses to recognize a formal role for women in the political or even the economic and cultural sphere, other than that of the mother, sister, or wife. But on the other hand, the hard facts of the modern world push Jihadists to accept with some reluctance the participation of women, at least within the family and the city, to spread Jihadist ideology.

Among the Jihadist ideologues, Yusuf al Uyayri was one of those young "soldier intellectuals" who attached a major importance to women. In his writings on women and their role in the Jihad he calls out to Muslim women and asks for their assistance in a situation where there is a "new crusaders' war" against the world of Islam. Uyayri summons women to help because many Muslims and, in particular, women believe that Jihad should be avoided because it is the path to death for their family. According to Uyayri, the predicament of the Muslims is their willingness to acquiesce to inferiority and humiliation and their lack of determination for Jihad because of their lethargy and love of life in this world. The only way to resolve the problem is violent Jihad.

Today, Uyayri contends that women as mothers, wives, daughters, or sisters are an obstacle to Jihad, since they forbid their men to engage in the fight against the unbelievers. On the contrary, he argues, as true believers women should educate their children for the sake of Jihad; they should protect the sexual honor (*irdh*) of their men, once they choose the path of Jihad; and they should become more active in preparing men for holy war: "Women should become conscious that the fight between Islam and the people of disbelief is inescapable. This is the continuation of the Crusades, headed by the United States against the Muslims, all over the world. Women should imitate the role of the women in the Golden Age of Islam. In this war some Muslim women are enticed to the ranks of the enemy through dancing, prostitution, singing, and the like. Another way of behaving is the case of Umm Amarah, who participated also in the jihad. Many other women took part in the wars of the Prophet by distributing water and serving as nurses to the wounded."[72]

Uyayri asks women to end their role as "prostitutes" within the new sick culture, spread by the West, where dancing or singing is given precedence over the genuinely Islamic role of taking part in the Jihad, like many women during the time of the Prophet, when they helped men in holy war: "To become genuine Muslims, women should behave in the same way as those who entered the fight during the first centuries of Islam. They fought side by side with men, not because of the paucity of the latter but because of their love for sacrifice in the path of Allah. Aïcha, the young wife of the Prophet, was an example. She told the Prophet that she chose the Jihad because there was nothing higher than Jihad in the Koran."[73]

Uyayri does not push women to become directly involved in Jihad as fighting soldiers. Instead, he asks them to accept the sacrifice of their sons, husbands, or fathers and actively prepare them for this holy task, emulating the women of the Golden Age of Islam. Women should instill men with the love of Jihad and martyrdom and make them renounce their personal, worldly desires for the sake of the Muslim community: "Women like men should accept the ultimate sacrifice for the Umma and renounce their own personal welfare for the sake of jihad. The Umma is paramount, and the individual is only a mere member of it. The case of Umm al Sahba is instructive: seven of her sons embraced martyrdom in the Prophet's wars, and she still was devoted to the Prophet. In summary, genuine Muslim women encourage men to take part in Jihad and to accept the sacrifice of their life for this sacred mission."[74]

For Uyayri, women can be an impediment in the way of Jihad but can as well be among those who encourage men to engage in it. Women can make men conscious of the fact that the love of Jihad should trump the love of this petty world and its enticements, according to the model of the forefathers, who devoted their life to the Umma and joyfully accepted martyrdom in this path.

Uyayri makes a critique of modern individualism that gives priority to personal aspirations against the higher interests of the community. Jihadism is in this respect anti-individualism. Love of Jihad supposes recognizing the priority of the community over the self. Selflessness, willingness to make the ultimate sacrifice, and Jihad go hand in hand, in his view.

Shariati, the ideologue of revolutionary Shi'ism, devotes a whole book to the role of women in modern Islam.[75] For him two models are irrelevant: the traditional Islamic woman and the modern Western one. He proposes a third model, that of Fatima, the daughter of the Prophet and the wife of Ali, the first Shi'ite imam and the fourth Well-Guided Caliph. For him, Fatima (Fatemeh in Persian) was the heroic woman who assisted both the Prophet and her husband, Ali, in their ordeal for the sake of Islam. Traditional Muslim women were devoid of any public role, contrary to Fatima. Modern Western women are devoid of any aspiration for revolutionary feeling, being alienated like Western men by the desires of this world. There is no ideal of realizing a new world of justice in either of these models. Fatima was a woman who presented a model of womanhood distinct from the two others. Shariati is not clear about the real role of this third model besides the fact that he rejects the two others, but his conception of women's role is no different in its key features from that of Uyayri. Writing more than three decades later, Uyayri celebrated the sense of abnegation and self-sacrifice among men who are influenced by women, renouncing the pleasures of this world and promoting the heroic ideology of revolutionary Islam based on self-sacrifice for the sake of the Umma.

The effective role of women in suicide operations has been increasing in the last decade, particularly since 2000. In Chechnya, Iraq, Jordan, Egypt, Uzbekistan, and Palestine women have played a role in suicide bombings. What makes them attractive for the plots is that they are seen as unable to commit violent acts, and they can hide their weapons, sometimes appearing pregnant, under their veils. The *mujahidat* (feminine form of *Mujahidun*, those who make the Jihad) are involved in many cases as sisters, mothers, or wives. The Jordanian Sajida Mubarak Arrous al-Rishawi and her husband detonated explosives in November 2005 in three hotels in Amman. Her husband died, but she survived because of the failure of the ignition system. In April 2003 two women in Iraq blew up their car at a checkpoint and killed three soldiers. In September 2005 an Iraqi woman took part in the assassination of job applicants, under the leadership of Al Qaeda.[76] Other incidents involve women as soldiers, like the April 2005 shootings by two veiled Egyptian women of a tourist bus in Cairo. In the latter case, the two women, both in their twenties, were related to a male activist, Ehab Yousri Yassin. One was his sister (Negat Yassin) and the other, his fiancée (Iman ibrahim Khamis). They acted out of revenge for Yassin's death by the Egyptian authorities. The two women then shot themselves.

A young Uzbek woman played a major role in a suicide attack in March 2003: the nineteen-year-old Dilnoza Holmuradova detonated explosives at Tashkent's Chorsu Market, killing at least forty-seven people, including ten police officers. She came from a middle-class background, was well educated, spoke five languages, and, unlike the vast majority of Uzbek women, had a driver's license. In her case, intense modernization in a society without any social orientation after the collapse of the Soviet Union and the attraction of Islam in its radical version through the Islamic Jihad group seem to have played an important role. In this case, she seems not to have acted as a sister or a mother or even as a wife but as a woman, too modern to be understood by society and dead set against the state.

In the Palestinian suicide attacks, Wafa Idriss was the first to act in January 2002. She killed one Israeli and injured more than a hundred fifty others in a Jerusalem shopping district. Four other Palestinian women committed suicide attacks in the four months following Wafa Idriss. Some women seem to have been involved as "mere women," contrary to the general rule in women's martyrdom operations, where they are involved as relatives of men. This is the case of Hanadi Jaradat, who detonated a bomb in an Arab-owned restaurant in Haifa, killing nineteen people. In a prerecorded video aired by Al Jazeera on August 24, 2005, she said, "By the power of Allah, I have decided to become the sixth female martyrdom seeker who will turn her body into shrapnel, which will reach the heart of every Zionist colonialist in my country."[77]

The nationalist motive is given in an Islamic idiom. On the whole, Islamic nationalist movements, like those in Palestine, Chechnya, or Kashmir, are different from the transnational Jihadism of Al Qaeda. In the first case, the national issues are vindicated through Islam. These movements mark no affinity with Al Qaeda or transnational Jihadism in general: they have national goals, which usually precludes affinity with transnational Jihadism.[78] Only a marginal number of their followers take the path of global Jihad.[79]

In Muslim societies, women can play a significant role in mobilizing men: if they accept defending the honor of the Umma by sacrificing their lives, then men should do more, otherwise they are less than women. Not acting to surpass women in courage and heroism would put man's superiority into question. Women's involvement in suicide operations also has some long-term implications for orthodox Islam. If women directly take part in Jihad, they will be exposed to men who are "strangers" and whom, according to traditional Islam, they should not meet. The Jihadist motto would put into question some of the tenets of orthodoxy in relation to the segregation of men and women and the implicit inferiority of the latter to the former: if women can die like men, there is little grounds for claiming that they should not be equal to them in other respects.

The martyrdom of women can not only incite men to take part in Jihad but also entice other women to become more involved in suicide operations. Women's martyrdom thus has a dual role: it calls into question men's sense of honor and pride (*gheyra, irdh*), and it provides a heroic example that other women can imitate. In the media women suicide bombers present a more spectacular case, their coverage being greater than that of men. Their enrollment in Jihadist operations can be as well a quest for empowerment within Muslim societies that are deeply patriarchal, even though their primary aim might not be to assert their equality with men.[80]

Among converts there are some women who engaged in holy war against the Americans or their allies. The case of Murielle Degauque is rather exceptional, since there aren't many women converts directly involved in global Jihad so far. She was a young convert from Charleroi, Belgium. On November 9, 2005, she triggered her explosive belt in Baquba, Iraq, killing five policemen and wounding civilians. Few days later, Americans killed her husband, a Belgian citizen of Moroccan origin. Another convert, Pascal Cruypenninck, wanted to commit a suicide bombing with his fiancée, a young African woman, but he was arrested.

The media play a role in the mobilization of women in the path of Jihad. New technologies, particularly the Internet, enable women to act more freely than within traditional social networks, which are dominated by men. Jihadist media like *Sawt al Jihad* or *Minbar al Tawhid* urge women to take part in Jihad. *Sawt al Jihad*, produced by Al Qaeda in Saudi Arabia, devotes part of its editorials to women. The work of Al Khansaa (the name of a pre-Islamic female poet who lost four sons in Jihad) exhorts women to take part in holy war against the enemies of Islam. What kind of role is assigned to women? "There are many ways a Muslim woman can participate in Jihad. . . . The sisters' role on the battlefield is: 1. Participation in the actual fighting; 2. Supporting the fighters in the battlefield; 3. Providing guard duty and protection.[81]

THE EVOLUTION OF THE GLOBAL AL QAEDA IN THE WEST

Among social scientists, the overwhelming majority agrees that since September 11, 2001, Al Qaeda has evolved into an organization with new leadership styles and patterns of recruitment and training. It mounts its operations within a transnational network of cells acting on the local level with a high degree of autonomy and sometimes even in total independence from the formal leadership of Bin Laden or al Zawahiri. This new structure is much more adaptable and flexible than the centralized model of the old leftist radical groups of the 1970s or even the hierarchical structure of Al Qaeda prior to September 11. What binds the members together is a common vision of religion, one's duties, and a worldwide calling.[82] The changes within the organizational structure of Al Qaeda have been analyzed by some of their protagonists. On the basis of the writings of Al Qaeda's main strategists and intellectuals, they propose a decentralized, individual-ized Jihad for the future.[83]

More and more, Jihadist terrorism in Europe is a jumble of basically autonomous radicalized cells that have contacts with the outside world and no central organizational scheme. According to Coolsaet, self-radicalization and self-recruitment of individuals at the fringe of migrant Muslim communities in Europe is more important for Jihadist recruitment than any organized network of international recruiters,[84] Iraq being a possible exception. Nesser and Hegghammer believe that there is no top-down recruitment apparatus but a "horizontal recruitment," which makes Al Qaeda more organized than other Jihadist groups. There are people who fulfill the role of recruiters for Al Qaeda, creating a "culture for recruitment" and making it possible for militant Jihadists to create links with potential recruits through their ties with converts, friends, and family members.[85] Al Qaeda's aim is, according to Bartley, to use unconventional tactics of "indirect—namely asymmetric warfare" in order to provoke previously unimaginable destruction and spread fear.[86]

Major changes have occurred also in the nature of Jihadist groups, mainly Al Qaeda. Large-scale operations like the September 11 attacks are henceforward highly improbable, for technological and intelligence reasons: American and, more generally, Western governments are able to monitor phone calls and Internet exchanges in order to prevent plots. Many cases of Jihadist plots that have been detected are related to the question of hyper-sized Jihadist cells. From September 11, 2001, to November 2007, the American government has thwarted some nineteen terrorist attacks against the United States.[87]

In England, in August 2006, the attempt to blow up many air-planes en route to the United States by mixing up liquids within the aircraft failed in the same way as other Jihadist plots in some other European countries. Fifteen persons suspected of being involved in the UK-based plot were arrested. The cooperation between the British, the United States, and Pakistan were essential to putting an end to the plot.[88]

On July 31, 2006, two Lebanese students, Youssef el Hajdib, twenty-one, and Jihad Hamad, twenty, planted two suitcase bombs aboard German regional trains in Dortmund and Koblenz. The devices, fitted with alarm clocks for timers, failed to detonate. If they had, they would have created a fireball up to fifteen meters wide and hurled deadly shrapnel up to a hundred meters, according to explosive experts. It could have been the worst terrorist attack on German soil in the country's history. Unlike the August 2006 plots, this one was not detected by the police before it took place. It didn't succeed because of the technical failure of the ignition system. The main reason for the authorities' inability to cope with the plot was the sheer number of terrorists (probably fewer than five).

On January 26, 2005, French police arrested eleven people, three of whom eventually were charged with terrorism conspiracy, in Paris's nineteenth district for recruiting young French residents to launch terrorist attacks in Iraq. It was the first arrest since the opening in September 2004 of an investigation by the Paris prosecutor's office into Jihadists in Iraq. French officials stated in November 2004 that twenty-two young people had left for Iraq, and at least seven were killed there, including two suicide bombers.[89] The group was seemingly identified from the demonstration of some of its members against the banning of the veil in French government-sponsored schools in 2004. Otherwise, it would have been much more difficult to detect them, because of the low number of the group's core members and their lack of any terrorist records.

In summary, the kind of Jihadist terrorism that is still possible in the West is the one with only a few people involved (fewer than five or six people) or the lone wolf (e.g., the Unabomber). The new awareness of the Western governments after September 11, the lessons drawn from the Madrid and London attacks of 2004 and 2005, and the coordination between the intelligence services of the West and their friendly Islamic countries' counterparts, under the aegis of the United States, make large-scale attacks involving high number of Jihadists unlikely to succeed. This does not mean that their plots could not be deadly, but they probably could not reach the high numbers of the September 11 attacks, unless new techniques were put into effect.

Whereas large Jihadist groups can be identified through shared intelligence between the United States and other allies and the use of new technological devices, the small Jihadist cells are much more difficult to locate. The major concern, within the intelligence services of the West, is not large-scale groups but small, ad hoc ones. What can help identify them is the fact that radicalization of Muslims as a general rule is a rather lengthy process and not an event occurring in the short term. Another possibility is the so-called "lone wolf" operative: what to do if a single person, among the sympathizers or members of the dormant cells of Al Qaeda, engages in a terrorist activity. Since he won't be in touch with anyone, he cannot be detected. The Jihadist sites mention this possibility, scoffing at Western intelligence services: "What frightens [the FBI] and deprives them of sleep at night and peace during the day are . . . the lone wolves of Al Qaeda."[90]

On the other hand, Jihadists are facing a major dilemma. In the West, at the back of many Jihadists' minds is their desire for large-scale, spectacular terrorist action like September 11 with apocalyptic results, as much in terms of mass killing as media coverage. This opportunity is denied to them. In Europe, all those attempts with numerous people and large-scale Jihadist involvement were neutralized by the surveillance and infiltration of the intelligence and police services into the Jihadist circles and a closer cooperation between different Western nations.[91] In the Muslim world, plots of high magnitude are still possible, although there has never been as spectacular a terrorist act as September 11. In Iraq, in Pakistan, and in some other Muslim countries, still many dozens, and sometimes a few hundred, have been killed in the terrorist attacks. By means of media coverage all over the world, the terrorist act of September 11 has become iconic, not only in the West, but also in the Muslim world and the dream of the Jihadists is to reproduce it, in particular in the West, to put on display the powerlessness of the American and other Western governments in countering worldwide Jihad.

Abu Mus'ab al Suri, the Jihadist intellectual most versed in the social sciences, proposes a new type of Jihadism, based on decentralized, small, nonhierarchical groups, operating in a totally autonomous manner. His proposal, after the September 11 attacks and the reorganization of the Western intelligence and military services[92] is amazingly modern. His advice to Jihadists is terrifying, but in another sense would rob them of the world coverage in the manner of September 11. The only way Al Qaeda–type Jihadist movements can operate in the West is through small and decentralized groups that cannot achieve the same scale of damages and killings as in September 11. The dilemma is there: either kill a limited number of people each time, become a kind of "news in brief" in the media, or risk arrest and deterrence by launching a large-scale terrorist attack. Up to now, Jihadists have overwhelmingly chosen the second alternative, with few exceptions. Their neutralization by the police forces has been almost general in the United States, United Kingdom, France, and a few other European countries since the last attack in Great Britain in July 2005. Still, al Suri's proposal is the most realistic one for the survival of Al Qaeda–type organizations in the West.

TABLE 6.1: CORRESPONDENCE BETWEEN JIHADISTS IN THE MUSLIM WORLD AND JIHADISTS IN THE WEST

Jihadists in the Muslim World: Their Attitudes and Perceptions	Jihadists in the West: Their Attitudes and Perceptions	Differences and Similarities
The history of the West as corrupt, godless, and domineering.	Europe as a racist and hypersecular society that stigmatizes Muslims. The image is extended to the United States through media coverage of the Palestinian, Iraqi, and Afghan situations.	The West's picture is negative for different reasons in the two cases.
Muslim lands are under the yoke of disbelievers from within (rulers who do not apply Islamic law) and without (America as an imperialist, domineering, and arrogant power imposing on Muslims their crusaders' law)	Western countries repress Western Muslims of second and third generations by denying them equal rights and by making them second-class citizens. The West denies Muslims their religious rights by imposing secular laws on them.	The nature of the repression is different in each case, but the fact of repression is considered to be common by the Jihadists who distinguish between the close enemy (*adu al qarib*) and the far enemy (*adu al ba'id*), some prone to attack the former, the others proposing to attack the latter.
Direct humiliation by Western powers or Western armies (Israel is seen as a Western presence in the Middle East; the same holds true for the colonial presence of Russia in Chechnya): the West represses Muslims through illegitimate governments in the realm of Islam.	Humiliation by proxy on Muslims in the West: they are mistreated in France in the same fashion as Palestinians by the Israeli army, and in England Muslims are abused as Kashmiris are by the Indian army.	Many Muslims identify these two very different types of humiliation as being identical, particularly in Europe.

Jihadists in the Muslim World	Jihadists in the West	Differences and Similarities
The West is sexually corrupt and morally depraved. It is destroying itself and the Muslim world through the imposition of its model of sexuality, godless morality, gender equality, and consumerism.	The West perverts Muslims by pushing them toward immorality and corrupt cultural mores. In particular, Europe has broken the structure of the Islamic family among the Muslim diaspora and is pushing young Muslims toward sexual debauchery. Muslims are denied middle-class status but are pushed toward the denial of their religious tenets through the seduction of consumerism.	There is a consensus among the Jihadists on both sides on the dual depravity of the West through "sexual debauchery" and "moral corruption," but in each case the type of perversion is different: in the Muslim world it is the imitation of the West, while in the West it is the corruption of the Muslim diasporas from within that makes the occidental influence dangerous.
The West is godless and ignorant of Allah (*jahiliya*): it is an anathema to the Muslims who believe in the Koran and the rule of Allah. Jihad is the only way to cope with this predicament.	Living in the West within a diaspora makes it impossible to practice the laws of Islam that are the only valid ones. Jihad is the only means of imposing the Islamic law.	The two visions have in common the perception of the godless nature of the West (*jahiliya*) and the necessity of Jihad to restore God's law.
Democracy is not only a political system but also a religion of unbelief and idolatry (*taqut*). It is important for the West to destroy Islam from within, using their lackeys. Muslims have to wage Jihad against it, to establish Allah's rule on Earth.	Democracy is a political system that prevents Muslims from following their religion. Muslim diasporas will, in the long run, be deprived of their Muslim identity. Muslims have to migrate back to their Islamic land or wage Jihad against the West.	In the first case, the fight against Democracy is the same as the fight against idol worshippers in Muslim land (the close enemy); in the second case, Muslims have to fight for their rights within the West (the close enemy) and from without (the far enemy).

Continued

Jihadists in the Muslim World	Jihadists in the West	Differences and Similarities
Democracy as a system of human-made law, legislative assemblies, and governments elected by the people is in its principle against the laws of Islam. Muslims should fight it as an illegitimate way of holding power by illegitimate rulers.	Democracy is a system that excludes, de facto, Muslims from the circles of power (the proportion of Muslims in the political system in Europe is by far inferior to their proportion in society). The Jihadists reject it less on a theoretical basis and more on its practical effects. Fundamentalists, on the contrary, ask for more democracy to have a better footing in political institutions.	In both cases democracy is to be rejected, mainly through violent Jihad. The attitude of playing the democratic game in order to have access to parliaments by the Muslim Fundamentalists is denounced as anti-Islamic.
The role of long-term history and the relation with Islam are important in terms of historical continuity in Jihadists' representation of the self and the enemy (the West). Colonial rule and the creation of Israel are seen as proceeding from the same domineering attitude of the West toward Muslims.	The role of short-term history, the uprootedness of European Muslims through emigration, and the constitution of diasporas in Europe are more important in building up Jihadism there than the long-term history of Islam. The success of Jihad among the second- and third-generation Muslims in Europe is related to their feeling of being neither Arab (or Pakistani) nor French (or English), rejected by both countries of reference and having thus lost their identity. Radical Islam becomes a new identity at loggerheads against the West and their country of origin (Algeria and France, Pakistan and England).	Jihadists in the two parts of the world, for different reasons and from different perspectives identify the West as the enemy: in the Muslim world, in accordance with the historical continuity and long-term perspective; in the European diasporas, in relation to the discontinuity resulting from emigration to the West and the social problems related to their presence in Europe.

Jihadists in the Muslim World	Jihadists in the West	Differences and Similarities
Jihadism is an ideological movement with major intellectuals, martyrs, figures, and deep roots in the history of the Muslim world. Jihadism has rejuvenated and modernized the radical trends within Islam, which were formerly marginal and local, and created a new worldwide movement.	Jihadism is a social movement with no major intellectual figures, no notable martyrs, and no roots in history, due to the low intellectual level of the Jihadist Muslims in Europe. Only Arab intellectuals in London have been leading figures in Jihadist constellations.	The two Jihadist movements are profoundly different in their meaning, scope, and depth in their respective societies.
The Jihadist movement is based on Arabic as the major language, with a large library of works, contemporary and ancient, vindicating Jihad. Persian and Urdu are the two other major languages of Jihad.	The Jihadist movement has no major intellectual production and is based on the simplified version of the mainly Arab intellectual productions by local imams and migrant popularizers and a few Arab leading figures in "Londonistan."	Ideologically, Western Jihadism is dependent on Jihadist intellectuals and imams of the Muslim world, some of them having migrated to Europe.
The Jihadist movement's members are from Muslim countries, with the exception of some converts.	The Jihadist movement's members are mainly Western Muslims, with high numbers of converts and some followers from Muslim countries. They constitute "homegrown terrorism" in the West, although some have links with Jihadist movements in the Muslim world.	The social compositions of the Jihadist movements are different in the West and the Muslim world, with some Arabs, Pakistanis, and others from the Muslim world participating in the Jihadist movements in the West. Still, their members are mainly Muslims in Europe or converts.

Continued

Jihadists in the Muslim World	Jihadists in the West	Differences and Similarities
The Jihadist movement in the Muslim world is in reaction to autocratic regimes that combine political repression and allegiance to the West and the trauma caused by the constitution of the state of Israel and its aftermath.	The Jihadist movement in the West is in part in reaction to the democratic rule under which many Islamic taboos are not only permitted but also sometimes encouraged (women's "nakedness," free love, abuse of the Prophet in the media, etc.) from the Jihadists' point of view and the constitution of marginalized diasporas in Europe.	In both cases the political structure plays an undeniable role in Jihadism, for different reasons. Cultural factors play an important role.
The Jihadist movement is in reaction to secularization processes that are not embedded in Muslim societies but are becoming part of the identity of important minorities within the Muslim world (Turkey, Egypt, Pakistan, Iran, etc.). Jihadism operates as a de-secularizing movement. It has the tacit support, in this respect, of many Fundamentalist groups within Muslim countries.	The Jihadist movement is in reaction to the major secular tendencies within European societies in which sometimes the practice of Islamic rituals is considered as illegitimate (the veil in France, respect for the Prophet in Denmark, etc.). Jihadism calls Muslims to save their identity through violent means, rejecting society at large and appealing to the majority of Muslims, who are reluctant to directly break with secular tendencies of the European population.	In both cases Jihadism is a movement against secularization. In the Muslim countries, they fight against secularism as induced by modernization and imitation of the West. In the West, Jihadism fights against secular environments that have a tremendous impact on Muslim diasporas. In both cases Jihadism lauds violence as the only means to combat secularization. This distinguishes it from Islamic Fundamentalism that operates through peaceful means.

Jihadists in the Muslim World	Jihadists in the West	Differences and Similarities
Muslim youth would join the ranks of Jihadist heroes to perform their duty toward Allah.	The "blond convert" nicknamed "Rakan bin Williams" helps promote Jihad in the West. He looks like Westerners and cannot be identified as an "ethnic" Muslim. This is the ideal of Jihadists in the Muslim world and has been partially realized in Europe.	Mainly people from their own region will promote Jihad: in the West the Muslims from the Western diasporas and the converts, in the Muslim countries by Muslims from all the lands of Islam. Those from the Muslim world in the West who engage in Jihadism have been there for at least a few years. The few mixed cases do not change the general rule.
In Muslim countries, from the Jihadist viewpoint Jihad is an individual duty (*fardh al ayn*), a religious obligation incumbent on every able-bodied male Muslim.	Muslim communities in the West (Muslim diasporas) should either return to Muslim countries or enroll in Jihad as an individual duty, according to Jihadists. In Europe Muslims are running the risk of losing their Islamic identity. This view is also shared by Islamic fundamentalists.	In both cases, able-bodied Muslims should engage in Jihad, which is an imperious religious obligation (*fardh al ayn*). There is no peace within the Muslim world or outside of it for Muslims. Muslims live in a state of war imposed by the Western world order and the only way to cope with it is merciless war, Jihad, which is at the same time a just and holy war.
Jihadists in the Muslim world are based on groups led by charismatic chiefs or new, modernized cells with experienced leaders related to the world of modern technology (engineers, technicians) or religious leaders (belonging to Jihadist schools). Hierarchy is still important.	Jihadist groups in the West are mostly related to each other through the Internet or close friendship, ethnic, family, or professional ties (teachers, doctors, etc.) in ways excluding rigid hierarchy, especially after September 11.	In both cases Jihadism innovates in terms of organizational structure and technology, in comparison to the violent opposition groups of the past. The Internet plays a major role in both cases.

Continued

Jihadists in the Muslim World	Jihadists in the West	Differences and Similarities
The Marxist notion of the fight between the working class and the ruling class is transposed into the fight between *Mustadh'afin* (the oppressed) and *Mustakbarin* (the oppressors) (Shi'ism, and marginally Sunnism) or against idolatrous political regimes, *Taqut* (Shi'ism and Sunnism).	The Marxist notion of the fight against imperialism is transposed into the fight against *Taqut* (idolatrous governments).	Jihadism takes up many notions of extreme-left Marxism by renaming it through Islamic idioms. Imperialism becomes "world arrogance" (*istikbar*) or idolatry (*taqut*); the working class becomes the oppressed (*mustadh'afin*); the repressive ruling classes become the oppressors (*mustakbirin*)
Islamic Unity means Muslims' obligation to fight against their depraved governments that are subservient to the West (mainly to America for the Middle East, to France in North Africa), in order to achieve the Unity of the Umma.	Muslims should fight the West as the enemy who aims at destroying Muslim's Unity embodied in the Umma.	The Jihadist neo-Umma restructures the traditional Muslim community into a neo-Umma with new features: it is organically unified, it is tied by a new Jihadist elite, it is anti-imperialist and anti-secular in a violent manner, it is based on an effervescent unity of the heart, and it is staunchly anti-Western, anti-Shi'ite, and anti-democratic.

JIHADISTS' NEGATIVE ATTITUDE TOWARD RECENT MUSLIM MIGRATIONS TO THE WEST

In the world of Islam, migration (*hijra*) has a solidly religious meaning within the Prophetic tradition. For the Jihadists, the justification for the migration of Muslims to the West should be the same as the Prophet's exodus from Mecca to Medina. Mohammad felt threatened in Mecca, and he wasn't strong enough to fight against his powerful opponents in that city, to protect the fragile Muslim community. He chose to migrate to Medina (known at the time as Yathrib), where he gathered strength. Once powerful enough, he returned to Mecca and conquered it. Thus emigration precedes Jihad, to which it is a prelude. Abdullah Azzam, the Palestinian Jihadist intellectual, says, "Jihad is the apogee of Islam, and we accede to it through emigration (*hijra*), then the preparation (*i'dâd*), then the guarding of the frontiers (*ribât*), then the combat (*qital*). The emigration is indispensable for jihad."[93]

Emigration to a non-Muslim land is forbidden for any reason other than preparing for Jihad. Tartusi summarizes this idea, underscoring the unbreakable link between migration and Jihad from the Islamic perspective:

> The causes and aims of migration are . . . :
> 1. The safety of worship and religion . . .
> 2. The security of the person: if the oppressors threaten someone with certain death and he has no power to neutralize them by himself, then he should migrate and seek elsewhere security for himself and his family. . . .
> 3. Strengthening the Muslims and weakening the Infidels: one of the causes and aims of migration is the revival of the duty of Jihad, the strengthening of the Muslims and the increase of their numbers against the Infidels. Migration and Jihad are two inseparable things and each of them is the cause of the other and necessary to it, and the continuance of each of them is necessary to the continuance of the other. . . . Even if the sun rises from the West, Jihad lasts up to the Day of Judgment.[94]

In the second half of the twentieth century, Muslims massively migrated to Europe, mainly for economic reasons, to work there and earn their living, thus escaping poverty and joblessness. This mass migration, the first of this nature in Islam to non-Muslim societies, does not follow the Prophetic model. In the same way, the migration of middle-class Muslims to the United States and Canada is totally different from the Prophetic pattern of migration. In Europe as in America, Muslims are living as a minority within secular though culturally Christian societies, and their explicit aims, at least for the overwhelming majority of them, is not to wage Jihad but to live peacefully with other citizens, finding compromises with the host societies in order to live according to their faith.

The new pattern of migration does not escape Jihadists' attention. They are deeply disturbed by the attitude of the majority in the Muslim diaspora, and therefore many of them strongly recommend return to Muslim countries. Living in the "House of War" (countries that are neither dominated by Muslims nor converted to Islam) might be a curse in the war between Islam and the West: the Western heretics might use them as "shields": "The lack of migration from the House of War [back to the Muslim countries] ends up most of the time in Muslims becoming shields behind which the Infidels protect themselves when there is war between them and the Muslims. . . . This happened lately to the Muslims residing in the US and having acquired its nationality. They were forced to cooperate with the infidel American Army in its offensive against the Muslims in Afghanistan [invasion of Afghanistan and overthrow of the Taliban by a coalition led by the American army in 2001–2002]."

Tartusi mentions the Islamic jurisprudence on migration:

> The religious commandments for migration are divided into four kinds: necessary, religiously preferred, religiously forbidden, and neither necessary nor forbidden (indifferent) religiously.
>
> The necessary migration [back to a Muslim country]: when the Muslim is fearful for his safety and his religion from *fitna* and death and cannot publicly show his religion and cannot accomplish the religious obligations [he has to emigrate]. . . .
>
> • The religiously preferred migration [back to a Muslim country]: when the Muslim can display his religion in the country of his residence and accomplishes the necessary religious acts that are imposed by Allah, and it is warranted that he is not forced to help the Infidels in their fight against the Muslims, then the emigration [back to the Muslim country] is religiously preferred but not compulsory.
>
> • The religiously neither compulsory nor preferred migration: this is when the Muslim is powerless, and his weakness prevents him from emigrating.
>
> • The [religiously] forbidden emigration: this is the case when [the emigration] results [in the weakening of the Muslim interests] that cannot be otherwise promoted by the emigration or [by] the House of emigration. When being in the House of Infidelity one is protected from the dissension (*fitna*) and can display his religion, accomplish the religious obligations and in addition to that, he can call people to join Islam (*da'wa*) [then emigration back to the Muslim country is forbidden].[95]

For the Jihadists, the presence of the Muslim diaspora in the West is not, in general, an asset for Islam. On the contrary, Muslims in the West are running the risk of losing their souls and getting secularized. Even if they hold onto their Islamic identity, they might be used by the Western powers against the Muslim world, be it in terms of enrollment (in the army or elsewhere) or in terms of becoming submissive Muslims, incapable of Jihad.

Unlike the Jihadists, many Fundamentalist Muslim groups like Hizbu Tahrir argue that by remaining in the West and not returning to Islamic countries, Muslims can promote the Islamization of the West, and therefore their stay is legitimate—even necessary from the religious point of view. Jihadists usually reject this argument, pointing out that the majority of the Muslims who migrate to the West are not prone to Jihad. These two attitudes toward Islam in the West underscore the differences between the Jihadists, who believe in the inevitable and inescapable war with the West so as to establish Islam, and the Fundamentalists, who believe that they can contribute to the universal caliphate by promoting Islam in the West in a peaceful (or at least nonviolent) manner. In both cases the ultimate aim remains the expansion of Islam, but the understanding of the means to achieve that end is different in each case.

A major event that took place in the second half of the twentieth century was the formation of sizeable Islamic diasporas in the West. In many European countries, Islam has become the second largest religious group, and in Western Europe the number of Muslims is around fifteen million (between twelve and eighteen million). The first generation of migrants in Europe was religious in the traditional way: "orthopraxy" rather than "orthodoxy," submitting to religious rituals and restrictions (daily prayers, prohibition of eating pork or drinking alcohol, etc.) rather than asking any existential or political questions about Islam and, in particular, Jihad. The second- and third-generation Muslims began to ask themselves identity questions related to Islam, in part because their national identity in Europe was in crisis and their economic status was slow to improve. At the same time, most European Muslims are influenced by secular trends within Europe. In Western Europe, the major trend is the progressive secularization of the majority of Muslims: they do not practice the five daily prayers regularly, and in fact many do not perform them at all; the use of alcohol is spreading among Islamic youth; and premarital relationships are making inroads into many Muslim families. Some resist this process, but many give up, and the result is, in the eyes of many Fundamentalists and Jihadists, moral decay.

European prisons have a disproportionately high number of young, male, uneducated, and religiously ignorant Muslims.[96] The lure of Western mores seduces many young Muslims, who give up the traditional way of life of their parents and grandparents and indulge in the new ways of the Western world, sometimes with a deep remorse in the back of their conscience. The result is sometimes a brutal return to Islam, not to its traditional, nonpolitical versions but to rigid, intolerant versions. These born-again Muslims push their parents to return to their version of Islam, their sisters to wear the scarf, and their fathers to renounce alcohol, and the family to reject the sick seductions of Western life. This is the case of Zacarias Moussaoui and other Islamists interviewed in French prisons.[97] Some of these born-again Muslims join extremist groups and point an accusing finger at the West. Again, Moussaoui fits very well in this model,[98] not to mention Khaled Kelkal[99] and Mohammed Bouyeri.[100]

Particularly in Europe, the anthropological structure of Muslim families has been shattered, mostly among the poor and the downtrodden, who have no cultural and economic protection against the dislocation of their social bonds. In many cases, family structure has been subverted: the father left home, and the family is led by the mother, who has to work and take care of the children at the same time. This situation pushes the children (mainly the boys) toward delinquency. The result has been a much higher rate of deviance and crime among the male members of the family and a fragile anthropological structure with many uncontrolled tensions toward sexuality and men-women relationships (gender equality in the larger society versus deep inequality within the family) and a deep grudge against society. The return to Islam in its Fundamentalist or Jihadist versions is a way of overcoming the unbearable contradictions without means of integrating internal conflicts within European countries, where colonial prejudice toward Muslim migrants, their children, and their grandchildren still prevails.

What many religious Muslims in Europe see is, on the one hand, the "obscene secularization" of their brethren and children who become addicts, consume alcohol, date non-Muslims, indulge in nonmarital sexual relations, and do not practice their ancestral religion; on the other hand, they helplessly witness the loss of self-respect and dignity among many of those "depraved" Muslims who become petty thieves and offenders, thus trampling on Islamic moral values. Some turn the grudge toward the Western world that corrupts Muslims. Embracing Islam can mean either breaking off ties with a sinful society and finding solace within a close-knit Fundamentalist group or turning to a Jihadist group in order to take revenge against a godless society that has been inhospitable to Muslims and the enemy of Islam in many parts of the world (Bosnia, Afghanistan, and Iraq among others).

Jihadist intellectuals and networks are happy with this tiny minority of radicalized Muslims, but they are very critical toward the Muslim majority who give up the Islamic way of life and adopt

Western-style modernity and a conciliatory attitude toward the devilish West. That is why in most cases when Muslims perish with non-Muslims in terrorist attacks, Jihadists justify their death officially as inevitable and regrettable. But in their mind, these lukewarm Muslims are paying for their nonmilitant attitude toward the West. They refuse to go back to Muslim countries, to get involved in Jihad, and they are slack in their religious duties. Their death with the sinful Westerners is no matter for remorse among the Jihadists.

The new Muslim middle classes in Europe, unlike their American counterparts, are not exuberant about their achievements and have a much more discreet attitude, in line with European culture. Moreover, as a new middle class, they would like to become anonymous rather than being singled out as successful Muslims. Many choose to "disappear" within the larger society, particularly in France, with its culture of total assimilation. Few of them resent the fate of the Muslim community in Europe or have deep guilt toward them and Islam as such. They are much more resourceful and proficient than the downtrodden Muslims. Some of the resourceful new middle-class Muslims cross over the forbidden line and join the Jihadist groups. Their attitude toward their Muslim brothers is akin to that of the radical leftists who were self-proclaimed leaders of the working-class people. These Jihadist middle-class Muslims choose to fight against the West in a combined sense of religious duty and personal revenge against a society where being the son of immigrants is still degrading, as descendants of the former colonies.

The case of Mohammad Siddiq Khan is that of a lower-middle-class teacher, born in England of Pakistani parents, who became a Jihadist and led a group of terrorists to bomb the London underground and buses.[101] Zacarias Moussaoui's case is of the same type. Muslim middle classes in Europe suffer a malaise related to the difficulties of their upward mobility in rather rigid societies in which being a Muslim from former colonies is stigmatizing. The lot of the Muslim lower classes in Europe and the participation of the European countries in the war against Muslims (Britain in Iraq and Afghanistan, France and Germany in Afghanistan, etc.) push a tiny minority of them to Jihad.

Jihadists attempt to organize the very limited number of those Muslims in Europe who opt for the radical version of Islam, but they clearly see that most Muslims are not on their side, their life in Europe gradually secularizing the majority and pushing some minorities toward pietistic, Fundamentalist, or individualist Islam rather than the Jihadist one. That is why they are mostly in favor of the return of Muslims to Muslim lands. By contrast, Fundamentalists (like Hizbu

Tahrir or the offshoots of Muslim Brotherhood or Tabligh) believe that Islam can thrive and eventually become the dominant religion in the West.

On the whole, Jihadists are keenly aware that the exodus of mainstream Muslims to the West does not aim at Jihad, unlike the Hijra of the Prophet, who, according to them, migrated from Mecca in order to return to it forcefully. In the Western world, many Jihadist intellectuals find themselves in the paradoxical situation of preaching the migration of Muslims back to Muslim lands, whereas they, as radicals, remain in the West for fear of being jailed and tortured if they return to their home country in the Muslim world.

Notes

1. See Jocelyne Césari, *When Islam and Democracy Meet: Muslims in Europe and in the United States* (New York: Palgrave Macmillan, 2006).

2. Pew Research Center, *Muslim Americans: Middle Class and Mostly Mainstream*, May 22, 2007, http://pewresearch.org/pubs/483/muslim-americans.

3. This is of course based on extrapolations rather than exact calculations. See www.youtube.com/watch?v=Z6y3lVfDIGo&feature=related.

4. See the journalistic account of Jérôme Pierrat, *La mafia des cités: Economie souterraine et crime organisé dans les banlieues* (Paris: Denoël, 2006).

5. See Alain Tarrius, *La Mondialisation par le bas: Les nouveaux nomades de l'économie souterraine* (Paris: Balland, 2002).

6. See Didier Lapeyronnie, "La formation du 'ghetto' dans les banlieues françaises," Lectures at the Université Victore Segalen (Bordeaux III) 2007, http://www.ihedate.com/generated/objects/ACTES%20SEMINAIRES//SEM1_ACTES_LAPEYRONNIE.htm.

7. Other designations used by the migrant youth in a self-derisory way are obtained by inverting the word for "Arab," *Arabe*, which becomes *beur*, and inverting the inversion, that is, *robeux,* which means French of North African descent living in the poor suburbs.

8. Rémy Leveau and Catherine Wihtol de Wenden, *La beurgeoisie: Les trois âges de la vie associative issue de l'immigration* (Paris: CNRS Editions, 2001).

9. See Fernando Reinares, "Hacia una caracterización social del terrorismo yihadista en España: Implicaciones en seguridad interior y acción exterior," http://www.realinstitutoelcano.org.

10. See Olivier Roy, *Globalized Islam: The Search for a New Ummah*, CERI Series in Comparative politics and International Studies (New York: Columbia University Press, 2004).

11. The idea of the *Velayat Faqih* can be traced back to the eighteenth century, in which it was limited to juridical matters in which the Islamic

jurist had to rule (the limited guardianship). The political guardianship (*Velayat Motlaqeh*) was for first explicitly developed by the late Ayatollah Khomeini, although indirectly it can be found in some of the Sayings of the Shi'ite imams.

12. According to an opinion poll taken in 2006 for CSA-La Vie, in France 49 percent of the Muslims never go to mosques, but the rate of those practicing Ramadan is higher than before: 88 percent respect Ramadan's fasting versus 60 percent in 1989. The practice of Ramadan is more and more part of Muslims' festivities, and many Muslims fast without accomplishing other religious duties that are compulsory within traditional Islam (the five daily prayers, the ablutions before prayer, etc.).

13. Shaykh Yusuf al Uyayri, "The Ruling on Jihad and Its Divisions," Series of Researches and Studies in Shari'ah no. 2, English Translation by Abu Osama for at-Tawheed Publications (al-Muwahhideen), http://www.prism.org.

14. Transition from global violence to peaceful coexistence would make the neo-Umma a vector of worldwide Islamic humanism, once Jihadism is overcome as the exclusive way of self-assertion.

15. Youssef Bin Saleh al Uyayri, *Dowr al nisa' fi jihad al a'dâ* (The Role of the Woman in the Jihad against the Enemies), *Minbar al Tawhid wal Jihad.*

16. Al Uyayri, *Dowr al nisa'.*

17. The number of occurrences for the word "humiliation" (*dhill*) and its derivatives is respectively: 555, 621, 166, and 4,149 times in the four major books chosen for a quantitative analysis (see chapter 3).

18. I proposed this typology in 2002 in my book *Les Nouveaux Martyrs d'Allah* (Paris: Flammarion, 2002), appearing in translation as *Suicide Bombers: The New Martyrs of Allah* (London: Pluto Press, 2005). Jessica Stern also talks about humiliation, without distinguishing different types, in *Terror in the Name of God: Why Religious Militants Kill* (New York: HarperCollins, 2003).

19. Few Palestinians, Kashmiris, or even Chechnyans embrace global Jihad within the framework of their national movements. In general, being a Palestinian within Hamas or Islamic Jihad means rejecting Al Qaeda or other global Jihadist groups. National aims overshadow global Jihad in this case. When there is no hope for realizing national claims, national Jihad may change into global Jihad.

20. Still, Christians and Jews were allowed to live under Muslim rule, whereas Christians expelled Muslims (and Jews) from Spain, once they reconquered it (in 1492 the last Muslim ruler in Andalusia was vanquished, and a few years later Muslims and Jews were forced to convert or flee the country).

21. The study was done between 2001 and 2003 in three French prisons where the number of Muslims was high. The results have been published in Farhad Khosrokhavar, *Islam dans les prisons* (Paris: Balland, 2004), and idem, *Quand Al Qaeda parle: Témoignage derrière les barreaux* (Paris: Grasset, 2006).

22. See Farhad Khosrokhavar, "Muslim Anti-Semitism: The View from Prison," in *The Lure of Anti-Semitism: Hatred of Jews in Present-Day France,* ed. Michel Wieviorka (Boston: Brill, 2007).

23. Khosrokhavar, "Muslim Anti-Semitism."

24. Khosrokhavar, "Muslim Anti-Semitism."

25. See http://en.wikipedia.org/wiki/Mohamed_Bouyeri.

26. The transition from the divided to the unified self can be achieved by Islam, either in a peaceful way, through Fundamentalism, or in a violent manner, through Jihadism.

27. So far, non-Palestinian Israelis, Chinese, and Latin Americans are absent. Palestinian suicide bombers belong to the Islamic nationalist Jihadists (Hamas, Islamic Jihad), but not to the transnational Jihadist organizations.

28. See Hisham Aidi, "Let Us Be Moors: Islam, Race and 'Connected Histories,'" *Middle East Report* 229 (Winter 2003).

29. The following cases are based on the media and other open sources available. If some of the data is subject to limitations, the aim is not so much to trace their biographies as to show how their life is "modern," "global" and based on what is to come rather than what belongs to the past.

30. See Khosrokhavar, *Quand Al Qaeda parle,* interview with Moham-mad (a pseudonym).

31. See http://www.raid.admi.free.

32. In the Jihadist literature, this dimension of doubtlessness is often stressed. Against the nagging doubt of late modernity, Jihadists brandish the second verse of the sura "The Cow" (Al Baqara): "This is the Book; in it is guidance sure, without doubt, to those who fear Allah."

33. See the transcript of the tribunal in *Le Figaro,* March 31, 2004.

34. Samuel P. Huntington, *The Clash of Civilizations and the Remaking of World Order* (New York: Simon & Schuster, 1996).

35. See Emerson Vermaat, "Jason Walters, from Muslim Convert to Jihadist," http://www.militantislammonitor.org, December 20, 2005.

36. See http://www.militantislammonitor.org/article/id/532.

37. See http://en.wikipedia.org/wiki/Jos%C3%A9_Padilla_%28pris-oner%29.

38. See http://en.wikipedia.org/wiki/Adam_Yahiye_Gadahn.

39. See http://en.wikipedia.org/wiki/Adam_Yahiye_Gadahn.

40. See http://en.wikipedia.org/wiki/Adam_Yahiye_Gadahn.

41. See http://archives.cnn.com/2002/LAW/08/29/ujaama.back-ground/index.html.

42. See Khosrokhavar, *Quand Al Qaeda parle,* interview with Hassan (a pseudonym).

43. See for Wadih El Hage: http://www.pbs.org/wgbh/pages/frontline/shows/binladen/upclose/elhage.html.

44. See Marc Sageman, *Understanding Terror Networks* (Philadelphia: University of Pennsylvania Press, 2004).

45. See "Islam Set Direction in Man's Life," http://colorado.indymedia.org.

46. See http://counterterror.typepad.com/the_counterterrorism_blog/2005/02/defendant_ahmed.html.

47. As of June 2008 more than twenty-four hundred people had been arrested in Europe and condemned or were awaiting trials for their participation in Jihadist activities. The number is around sixty in the US. Even taking into account the higher number of Muslims in Europe (four times more, estimating around 15 million Muslims in Europe and 4 million in the United States, including African-American Muslims), still the proportion of Jihadists in Europe is at least ten times more than in the United States. These figures are somewhat tentative, but about a thousand people are being charged in Britain for participating in terrorist activities or related topics and at least the same number in France.

48. See Paul M. Barrett, "American Muslims and the Question of Assimilation," in *Muslim Integration: Challenging Conventional Wisdom in Europe and the United States,* Center for Strategic and International Studies Transatlantic Dialogue on Terrorism, September 2007.

49. See Shiv Malik, "My Brother the Bomber," *Issue* 135, June 2007.

50. Malik, "My Brother."

51. See the interviews and analyses in Khosrokhavar, *Quand Al Qaeda parle,* and idem, *L'Islam en Prison.*

52. Malik, "My Brother."

53. Malik, "My Brother."

54. See Yahya Birt, "Beyond Sidique," *Issue* 135 (June 2007).

55. From the transcripts of Moussaoui's trial.

56. Moussaoui trial transcript, 3657–660.

57. In India, during the Moghol rule by Muslims from the sixteenth to the nineteenth century, Hindus were not generally forced to convert, and in some periods even the Islamic tax (*Jiziyah*) was not levied on them. This shows that even religious people other than the "people of the Book" (Christians, Jews, and occasionally Zoroastrians) were tolerated within Muslim empires.

58. Moussaoui trial transcript, 3662.

59. Moussaoui trial transcript, 3663.

60. Moussaoui trial transcript, 3663.

61. Moussaoui trial transcript, 3664.

62. Moussaoui trial transcript, 3665.

63. See Tabari, *La Chronique: Les quatre premiers caliphes* (Paris: Sindbad, 1989).

64. See http://en.wikipedia.org/wiki/Mohammed_Bouyeri.

65. See Sageman, *Understanding Terror Networks.*

66. See Mourad Benchellali, *Voyage vers l'Enfer* (Paris: Robert Laffont, 2006).

67. See Agence France Presse, "Terrorisme: Un franco-tunisien expulsé de Syrie écroué à Paris," Paris, June 4, 2005.

68. "And if you be apprehensive that you will not be able to do justice to the orphans, you may marry two or three or four women whom you

choose. But if you apprehend that you might not be able to do justice to them, then marry only one wife, or marry those who have fallen in your possession" (Sura An'nisa [Women], verse 3).

69. This category, the justice seeker, and the next, the adventurer, correspond to Marc Sageman's heroes, fighting for justice and fairness, being moved by moral outrage. The two ingredients (heroism and moral outrage) are somehow autonomous, although related to each other. See Marc Sageman, *Leaderless Jihad: Terror Networks in the Twenty-First Century* (Philadelphia: University of Pennsylvania Press, 2008).

70. See Farhad Khosrokhavar, *L'islamisme et la mort: Le martyre révolutionnaire en Iran* (Paris: L'Harmattan, 1995).

71. This kind of accidental martyrdom has many antecedents in the history of martyrdom in Islam, after the first centuries of Allah's religion. See David Cook, *Martyrdom in Islam* (Cambridge: Cambridge University Press, 2007).

72. Al Uyayri, *Dowr al nisa'*.

73. Al Uyayri, *Dowr al nisa'*.

74. Al Uyayri, *Dowr al nisa'*.

75. Ali Shariati, *"Fatemeh Fatemeh Ast* [Fatima Is Fatima] (Tehran: Shabdiz, 1978).

76. Farhana Ali, "Ready to Detonate: The Diverse Profiles of Female Bombers," *The MIPT Terrorism Annual*, Jaffee Center for Strategic Studies, Tel Aviv University, 2006.

77. Ali, "Ready."

78. For a discussion see Khosrokhavar, *Suicide Bombers*.

79. The transition from national to transnational Jihadism can be observed in Pakistan, among some Kashmiri movements (Lashkar Tayiba) or Palestinian groups outside Palestine, and in Lebanon. See Bernard Rougier, *Everyday Jihad: The Rise of Militant Islam among Palestinians in Lebanon* (Cambridge: Harvard University Press, 2007).

80. See Yoam Schweitzer, editor, "Female Suicide Bombers: Dying for Equality?" Memorandum no. 84 (Tel Aviv: Jafee Center for Strategic Studies, Tel Aviv University, August 2006).

81. Strategic Arabic Translations, *Al Khansaa*, August 2004. See *Al Khansaa* web magazine, Al Qaeda's online women's magazine, which is published on different Al Qaeda websites

82. See R. Borum and M. Gelles, "Al Qaeda's Operational Evolution: Behavioural and Organizational Perspectives," *Behavioural Sciences and the Law* 23, no. 4 (2005).

83. Michael Scheuer, "Al-Qaeda Doctrine: Training the Individual Warrior," *Terrorism Focus* 2, no. 11 (June 10, 2005); Brynjar Lia, *Architect of Global Jihad: The Life of Al Qaeda Strategist Abu Mus'ab Al-Suri* (New York: Columbia University Press, 2008).

84. R. Coolsaet, *Radicalisation and Europe's Counter-Terrorism Strategy*, Royal Institute for International Relations and Ghent University, Transatlantic Dialogue on Terrorism, CSIS/Clingendael, The Hague, December 8–9, 2005.

85. See P. Nesser, "Jihad in Europe: Recruitment for Terrorist Cells in Europe," in *Path to Global Jihad: Radicalisation and Recruitment to Terror Networks*, http://www.ffi.no/TERRA; T. Hegghammer, "Global Jihadism After the Iraq War," *Middle East Journal* 60, no. 1 (2006).

86. C. M. Bartley, "The Art of Terrorism: What Sun Tzun Can Teach Us about International Terrorism," *Comparative Strategy* 24 (2005).

87. *U.S. Thwarts 19 Terrorist Attacks Against America Since 9/11*, The Heritage Foundation, November 13, 2007.

88. The August 10, 2006, transatlantic aircraft plot was a Jihadist act to detonate liquid explosives carried on board several airliners traveling from the United Kingdom to the United States. Unprecedented security measures were immediately put in place. This sudden imposition caused chaos and delayed flights for days. Of the twenty-four suspects who were arrested in and around London on the night of August 9, 2006, eleven were charged with terrorism offenses on August 21, two on August 25 (subsequently discharged on November 1), and a further three on August 30. See US Department of State, *Country Reports on Terrorism Released by the Office of the Coordinator for Counterterrorism*, April 30, 2007.

89. See MIPT Terrorism Knowledge Base, *France: 2005 Overview.*

90. See the Islamist website http://www.ek-ls.org, published on November 19, 2007. See http://www.memri.org, Special Dispatch Series no. 1772.

91. There is a disproportion between the number of terrorist attacks in Europe and the European and international focus on Islamist terrorism. Out of 498 attacks that were carried out in the European Union in 2006, only the failed suitcase bomb attacks in Germany and the foiled airplane mass bomb attacks in Britain were perpetrated by Islamist terrorists. The vast majority of terrorist attacks were carried out by separatist terror groups targeting France and Spain. Almost all attacks resulted in mostly material damage and did not intend to kill. On the contrary, Jihadist attacks aim at mass casualties. As a result, Islamist terrorism is a priority for European states' law enforcement services. Half of the 706 terrorism-related arrests made in 2006 were related to Islamist terrorism, with France, Spain, Italy, and the Netherlands having the highest number of arrests of Islamist terrorist suspects.

92. Abu Mus'ab al Suri, *Da'wa al muqawama al alamiya* (Call for a Worldwide Islamic Resistance), *Minbar al Tawhid wal Jihad.*

93. Abdullah Azzam, *Join the Caravan!* www.al-haqq.org.

94. Abu Basir Tartusi (Abdul Mon'im Mustafa Halimah), *Al hijrah: Masa'il wa ahkam* (The Emigration: The Problems . . . and the Power), *Minbar al Tawhid wal Jihad.*

95. Tartusi, *Al hijrah.*

96. For the French and British cases, where the proportion of Muslim prisoners is more than five times higher than the rate of Muslim in society, see James A. Beckford, Danièle Joly, and Farhad Khosrokhavar, *Muslims in Prison: Challenge and Change in Britain and France* (London: Palgrave Macmillan, 2005); Khosrokhavar, *L'islam dans les prisons.*

97. See Khosrokhavar, *Quand Al Qaeda parle*. For a general account of this book in English, see John Rosenthal, "The French Path to Jihad," *Policy Review* 139 (October/November 2006).

98. Zacarias Moussaoui, a Frenchman of Moroccan origin, lived a totally secular life with his mother, brother, and sisters. He went to London and there embraced Jihadist Islam and became a member of Al Qaeda. He was condemned in 2006 to life imprisonment.

99. Khaled Kelkal, born in 1971 and killed by French police on September 29, 1995, was a French terrorist of Algerian origin affiliated with the GIA. He was involved in the metro attack on July 25, 1995 in the Saint-Michel RER station in Paris.

100. Born in 1978 in Amsterdam, Mohamed Bouyeri is currently serving a life sentence for the murder of Dutch film director Theo van Gogh. He holds both Dutch and Moroccan citizenship.

101. Mohammad Sidique Khan (1974–July 7, 2005) was the oldest of the four suicide bombers responsible for the July 7, 2005, London bombings that killed fifty-two people and injured over seven hundred.

7

Jihadist Intelligentsia
around the World

Islam wields a radical intelligentsia that is probably lacking in the two other monotheist religions. Although Christians have Fundamentalist theologians, they have no continuous tradition that sustains them and provides a set of justifications for physical violence in such a substantial manner as in Islam. Secularization has also weaned Christianity of radicalization in the name of God. In Islam, radicals are not only contemporary, but also go back to the death of the Prophet, and since then, although disparaged, they have been a constant source of inspiration in the Muslim world, among extremist minorities.

The impact of modernization among Muslim intellectuals is at best ambivalent. The first Reformist movement in Islam, in the late nineteenth century (led by Al Afghani, Abduh, Rashid Rida, and others), tried to modernize Islam by reviving the notion of *ijtihad* (active reinterpretation of the Islamic laws in the historical world), taking part in journalistic activities, and rationalizing the Islamic laws. They failed because of the ambivalence of their references (the Salaf or first generations of devout Muslims, the Islamic Golden Age, the Prophet's rule, etc.). The relation between the major Reformist movements and the Fundamentalist trends within Islam are much more complex than in the two other major world religions, for internal and external reasons. The internal reasons are the institutional conservatism of the major centers of learning and education in the Muslim world, the rigidity of the Islamic tradition (the only major reference, the Koran, is interpreted according to rules that favor closure of the mind rather than openness), the autocratic governments that find it easier to reach compromises with conservative religious authorities rather than Reformist ones, and the cult of "unity" based on the first pillar of Islam (*tawhid*), among others. The external reasons are the negative dimensions of change (colonialism, the creation of Israel, the successive wars in the Middle East between Israel and the Arab world, then Al Qaeda and the chain reactions caused by it). Muslim Reformists are squeezed between their desire for modernization and the traumatizing effects of modernity. They swing between identification with the modern world and frustration with it.

The modernization period in Islam, mainly from the nineteenth century onward, has given birth to secular intellectuals with a nationalist, socialist, or communist bent, but the more important fact has been the appearance of secular Muslim intellectuals, often with a radical disposition in the name of Allah because of the traumas caused by modernization. Be it among the Shi'ites, as in the cases of Ali Shariati (1933–1977), Jalal Al Ahmad (1923–1969), the late Ahmad Fardid (1909–1994), etc., or in the Sunni world, as in the cases of Hassan al Banna (1906–1949), Seyed Qutb (1906–1966), the agricultural engineer Shukri Mustafa (1942, 1978), the leader of the Jihadist group *Takfir wal Hijra* whose member Khaled Islambouli killed the Egyptian President Anwar al Sadat in 1977, Bin Laden (b. 1957), and Ayman al Zawahiri (b. 1951), many of the radical intellectuals do not belong to the Ulama. They lead a "nonreligious" life, and their earnings are mainly related to modern jobs (Ayman al Zawahiri was a physician, Bin Laden a businessman, Shariati a PhD holder from the Sorbonne, and so forth). These people are the paradoxical results of modernization and secularization, but they react to these tendencies and reject them. They are not unaware of modern life, since they usually are part of it, having lived in the West (Shariati lived many years in France; Abu Mus'ab al Suri, Abu Qatada, Abu Hamza al Misri, and many others lived in Britain, Spain, and Italy). Many of these new intellectuals, some of whom go back as far as the 1930s (like Eqbal Lahuri, the Indian Persian-writing poet and Fundamentalist), have taken the side of Islamic Fundamentalism against secular or Reformist thinkers.

The new generations of Jihadist intellectuals are not homogeneous. They are from all walks of life and belong to different Muslim societies (Arab, Pakistani, Persian, etc.). There are many scientists and engineers among them, as well as traditional people. Their intellectual production is considered legitimate by many Muslims around the world because they are considered to belong to a lineage of an Islamic tradition that has been vibrant throughout the history of Islam, with large periods of marginality, but without totally disappearing. The fact that secularization has been late in Islam's history makes their claim the more legitimate. We find a major difference between the Christian world, whose revolutionary, utopian, religious intellectuals disappeared in the late seventeenth century as central figures of Western history, and the Muslim world, where the Jihad was revived in the nineteenth century in reaction to European colonization (Algeria, India, Caucasus) after its eclipse for more than half a millennium, after the Mongol period of the late thirteenth and fourteenth centuries.

The secularization that took place in the West did not occur as such in the Islamic world. The adaptation to different situations happened mostly by the multiplication of sects and reinterpretation of the rules within established schools of law (four in Sunnism) rather than through the direct marginalization of the religion in matters related to the social and political realms, as it happened in the Occident. Even at moments of acute crisis (as when, in the late thirteenth century, the Mongols attacked and conquered Muslim lands and imposed their own legal code, known in Islam as the "Yasa" or "Yasaq") the legitimacy of religion was not put into question. Mongols imposed their rules in a violent manner, without any legitimacy on the side of the Muslims. They later converted to Islam, and from then on they applied Islamic law (or a combination of it with some of their own traditions). Many Jihadists compare the prevailing situation nowadays with that of the Mongol conquest of Muslim countries. They conclude that the current situation is worse than that time because Mongol rulers converted to Islam and restored Islamic law and education, whereas the West is "destroying" Islam irreparably, not only through conquest or political domination, but through dissemination of a secular, consumerist, hedonistic, and perverse culture that cuts off Muslims from their Islamic roots by enticing or even bewitching them.[1]

The Muslim intelligentsia is divided into the Ulama and non-clericals. Many of the most radical ones are from the second group, in an apparent paradoxical fashion. Lacking a formal institution, Muslim clerics do not have the same status as within Catholicism or even some institutionalized churches in the Protestant world. Still, belonging to Al Azhar University in Cairo or the higher institutions of learning in Saudi Arabia or elsewhere gives a status akin to that of organized churches. The nonclerical radical intellectuals apostrophize the new social groups that have arisen out of the disbanding of traditional bonds, namely the professionals with higher educational backgrounds and the downtrodden. In terms of gender, many young women, caught between the traditional restrictions without the traditional protection, particularly in large urban zones, join them. These new groups, abandoned by an erratic and nonpluralist modernization, are much more hurt than healed by change. Islamic radicalism, in its promise of restoring the God-created order, appeals to them. The fight against the godless, selfish, and heretical elites and secularized minorities motivate these people in the same way as those who have gone through modern education and wild urbanization but see themselves as victims of these soulless changes.

Ideologically, Islamic intellectuals can be divided into four main groups, their ideas gravitating around a few major themes: secularization and the question of its legitimacy, individualization and its limits, democracy and its status, women's emancipation and its meaning, apostasy and its status, new Muslim diasporas and the laws governing them, Jihad and its necessity, deviations like nonmarital sexual relations, homosexuality, consumption of alcohol and drugs, and the limits of tolerating them, etc.

The first group, the Reformists, strive to open up Islam to modern trends, mainly secular, democratic, and individualist, and promote tolerance of differences of opinion and religion by reading the Koran and the Prophetic Tradition according to new rules. They attempt to secure Islam for the spiritual life of believers and leave the public sphere to human laws, whose legitimacy is granted by their version of Islam. They fight against the ambivalences of Reformism that ballasted the major trends of reform in Islam since the end of the nineteenth century. Still, many ambiguities are still prevalent, and they don't dare directly question many traditional tenets of Islam. The three other groups, referring to themselves as "Salafi," that is, respectful of the Salaf, the founding fathers of the Islamic tradition, are the Fundamentalists, the hyper-Fundamentalists, and the Jihadists. They agree in their definition of Islam but differ in their strategies and the degree of intolerance toward the "deviant" Muslims and the non-Muslims, as well as toward political pluralism.

All four groups refer to the Islamic past to claim their legitimacy. The war among them, in particular among the Jihadists and the hyper-Fundamentalists on the one side, the Reformists and the Fundamentalists on the other, is raging, and they energetically reject each other in the name of their understanding of religion (Reformists and Fundamentalists versus the Jihadists and hyper-Fundamentalists) or in their strategies (Jihadists versus Fundamentalists). The fact that sizeable minorities in the Muslim world have secular daily lives complicates the picture. The latter have no legitimacy, but they disturb the global picture by introducing "disorder" (*fitna*) from within. Many orthodox Muslims see them as the Trojan horse of the West and devoid of any autonomy. This is, of course, a mythical view, since these "secular" Muslims, sometimes comprising a fourth or even a third of the population of large cities, are the internal products of social change in the Muslim world rather than the result of any diabolic manipulation by the West for the sake of destroying Islam. The secularization of sizable minorities in the Muslim world destroys the homogeneity of the Muslim worldview from within and makes it difficult for staunch Muslims to impose an exclusively Islamic political order without recourse to violence. Fundamentalists believe that they can restore an Islamic order by winning back secular Muslims through a long-term policy of persuasion; Jihadists are convinced that secular Muslims are nothing but the Western fifth column and that only intimidation and violence can force them to accept the rule of Islam, not persuasion. Within Muslim societies ruled by Islamic radicals (the Taliban in Afghanistan or Shi'ite theocracy in Iran), secular groups become culturally speaking an oppressed minority. They can thrive economically, but culturally they are denied public recognition and are forced to lead their way of life only privately, constantly fearing repression in the name of religion.

In respect to social and political issues, some Jihadists are radical when it comes to fighting in the political field, but they are more or less tolerant regarding the trespassing of Islamic rules on alcohol or illegal sexual intercourse (this is the case of Maqdisi, who is politically radical but less stringent vis-à-vis the personal transgressions of Islamic prohibitions). The malaise of the Muslim world is a reaction to the fact that reality has irretrievable changed in the last century with the advent of numerous new social groups with new subcultures and mores, but the majority is at pains to admit, even less to follow, these traumatizing cultural and social changes. In the past, the Islamic civilization had preserved its religious belief system in spite of the torments of world history. Today numerous Jihadists believe that Apocalypse should be the fate of Muslims, before they impose it on the rest of the world. The overwhelming majority of Muslims share a deep-seated malaise in their daily lives, particularly when the secular alternative to Islamic Radicalism and Fundamentalism seems unconvincing to Muslims who have recently experienced dictatorial secular regimes that governed in the name of nationalism, socialism, or both.

THE ISLAMIC REVOLUTIONARY VANGUARD

Leftist currents in the 1970s rejuvenated the ideology of the vanguard, which has the duty to set the revolution in motion and to encourage the exploited and alienated people to join them. In Islam, the vanguard theory predates to a very large extent that of Western revolutionaries of the nineteenth and twentieth centuries. Some Sayings of the Prophet point to the fact that small minorities of Muslims will carry on the fight against oppression and injustice in spite of the apathy of mainstream Muslims. Jihadist intellectuals are quick to use these Sayings of the Prophet to vindicate their position as an Islamic revolutionary minority that raises the standard of revolt against the idols and their worshippers in the name of Allah.

Tartusi refers to them in relation to the continuation of Jihad up to the end-time:

> The religious texts point explicitly and clearly and without any doubt to the fact that Jihad continues all the time until the Day of Judgment, be the Caliph or the Imam at the head of Muslims or not. . . .
>
> The Prophet said: "They don't leave this religion in a standstill; a group (*isabah*) of Muslims will fight for it up to the Last Judgment." (Mentioned by the trustworthy compiler of the Sayings of the Prophet, Muslim).
>
> The Prophet said: "A group (*ta'ifah*) of my Community keeps on fighting for the Truth appearing in the Day of Judgment." (Muslim)
>
> Salma bin Nufayl al Kindi said: I was sitting next to the Prophet and a man said: 'You, the Prophet of Allah, many people dismount the horses—that is, they leave them, lay down weapons and say: no more Jihad, the war has ended.' The Prophet turned his face toward him and said: 'They lie! Now, now, the fight is going on, and a small group within my community keeps on fighting for the Truth, and Allah frightens the other communities in their heart, and they live out of that until the Last Hour.' . . ."
>
> The Prophet said: "A group (*ta'ifah*) of my Umma will fight for the Truth, looming to those who are opposed to them until the last one of them is killed by the Dajjal [Islamic Anti-Christ]."
>
> The Prophet said: "A group (*ta'ifah*) will continue. . . ." This asserts the perpetuation of this group that fights in the way of Allah through all the times and places until the Day of Judgment and whose Jihad will not stop in an accidental way by the absence of the Caliph as in our time.[2]

Kharijites after the death of the Prophet, and then numerous sects and mystical groups within Islam during its history up to modern times, have exploited this notion of a minority elite of authentic Muslims, to promote Jihad, be it the "smaller Jihad" (*jihad asqar*), which is violent, or the "greater Jihad" (*jihad akbar*), which is spiritual.

According to the Jihadists, their own vanguard revolutionary group is this *ta'ifah*, this *isabah*, this minority Umma among the larger Umma that will never end Jihad. The Islamic world does not need a new theory of revolutionary vanguard; the theory already exists and has only to be modernized. The modernization consists in identifying the culprits (the idol worshippers in the West and the Muslim rulers deviating from Islam). The core of the Islamic theory of Jihad can be easily modernized and put at the service of a revolutionary cause. The new Jihadist intellectuals have begun, mostly in the second half of the twentieth century, to perform that duty.

THE ICONS, THE POPULARIZERS, AND THE LOCAL CHARISMATIC IMAMS

Nowadays there are three types of Jihadist intellectuals:

1. The icons are well versed in Islamic jurisprudence (*fiqh*) and reason in ways that bear witness to their deep knowledge of the Islamic Sunna (religious norms bequeathed by the tradition). They are prestigious among their disciples. They are, however, mostly "Arabs"; that is, their culture is overwhelmingly Arabic. There are a few non-Arabs among them, like Sheikh Abdallah el-Faisal, Jamaican by birth but living in Stratford, East London.[3] In the Shi'ite world people like Ayatollah Mesbah Yazdi[4] are closest to the Sunni Jihadists. The icons also include people like Maqdisi, Abu Qatada,[5] Abu Hamza al Misri, the so-called Captain Cook,[6] Sheikh Omar Abdel Rahman (the blind Egyptian imprisoned in the United States)[7], Abu Mus'ab al Suri,[8] and Tartusi,[9] among others. Their writings are quoted, translated, or simply spread by their disciples or themselves in Europe and the Western world in general. Their major center in the West has been London (the so-called Londonistan), where they spread their views and those of their colleagues up to 2001 without constraint.

2. The popularizers facilitate the understanding of the icons' complex religious thought. Their role is essential in Europe because the icons are usually difficult to understand by the new generations of European Muslims, who do not master Arabic and need the "translators" of complex ideas into simplified ones. Some of the icons like Abu Qatada or al Suri have also accomplished this task.

3. Local charismatic imams or intellectuals constitute the third group. The first two groups are usually identified by the intelligence services in Europe, and most of them are in jail or have been expelled from Europe. Local people who teach Jihad are more difficult to detect. They usually operate in small groups or cells and not only in Muslim

districts, but anywhere there are disenfranchised Muslim youth as in the so-called *banlieues* in France, poor districts in England, or old working-class districts in Germany. They also operate in European prisons, and their messages can be transmitted to the other inmates through private channels, which are difficult to locate. They can thrive as well in Western institutions and organizations like universities or charities.

Much of the socialization of Jihadists in Europe is based upon these three kinds of intellectuals who "facilitate" the understanding of Jihad to a Muslim youth, devoid of the credentials of Arab Muslims (direct access to the Koranic text, the Arabic interpretation of the text, etc.). Because Muslim youth in Europe are uprooted, Jihadist Islam can more easily indoctrinate them, exploiting their frustration and grudges against society. They find an outlet in Jihad, which they instinctively identify as the main tenet in Islam. Knowing little about Islam predisposes them to espouse Jihadism as a means to fight against those who have not been hospitable to them (according to their self-identification as victims).

The case of Mohammed Bouyeri, the murderer of Theo van Gogh, illustrates the overlaps of the three types of intellectuals. Bouyeri considered himself an intellectual, and in the so-called Hofstad group he was a central figure ("local intellectual" in our terminology). He translated some of the works of Abu Hamza al Misri, the militant imam of Finsbury Park Mosque in London, which were discussed in the meetings of the group, mainly in Bouyeri's home. In this case, Abu Khaled Redouan al Issa, a former Syrian army officer who introduced the thoughts of the forefathers of Jihadism (Seyed Qutb and Abul ala Mawdudi) to the group, played the role of the popularizer. Al Misri, who, in Bouyeri's case, was the major inspirer, played the role of the icon. Al Misri's work had become accessible to Bouyeri through English versions, some of which were translated by Bouyeri himself into Dutch.[10] In this particular case the triangular interactions of Jihadist intellectuals is clear.

Jihadist Islam becomes attractive to Muslim youth in Europe as much through radical intellectuals who profess it as through the "push factor" by the society that rejects them or does not recognize them as genuinely European. They are in a "neither/nor" predicament: Europeans do not recognize them as being part of their society, and in their parents' country of origin they are considered "dirty Frenchmen," "dirty Englishmen," etc.[11]

Some reformist intellectuals or Ulama in the West endeavor to adapt Islam to Western democracy by referring to Islam as a "minority religion," with Muslims having to adapt to the new situation by submitting to the prevailing secular laws, a situation previously unheard of (Muslims were either in a majority position or dominant as a minority, through conquest). This "*fiqh* of the minority"[12] accepts the laws of a non-Muslim government. The supremacy of non-Muslim governmental laws over Islamic laws is something Muslim jurists have been loath to admit in the name of a tradition, according to one of the forefathers of Jihadism, Ibn Taymiyah, that dictates that Islam has to gain the upper hand. This is tacitly approved of by many hyper-Fundamentalists and traditionalists: "Ibn Taymiyah says: any group of people continuously refusing to follow the law of Allah in a public way need Jihad so that their religion totally becomes Allah's religion."[13] Jihadists denounce the reformists' attitude by referring to the Islamic tradition that prohibits any compromise on this issue.

What is new among Jihadists is the arrival in high numbers of a new type of intellectual who is more than the "intellectuel engagé," a term coined by the French, or Gramsci's "organic intellectual," combining many peculiar features of Western intellectuals and traditional Islamic theologians and thinkers. The whole process began of course much earlier, in the second half of the twentieth century, with the advent of the new hyper-Fundamentalists like al Banna, Mawdudi, and Qutb in the Sunni world, Shariati and Khomeini in the Shi'ite. The novelty is the high number of the new-generation intellectuals and their capacity to use new communication technologies (mainly the Internet, but also videotapes and TV). They combine theological and military skills; they address Arabs in a new way, in a language much more accessible to them, at least in their journalistic writings; and they are more polemical and able to use modern words and social science terminology instead of the complicated idiom of the traditional Ulama and Fuqaha (the Islamic jurists). People like Jahiman al Oteibi,[14] Shukri Mustafa,[15] and later on Hamid al Ali,[16] Yusuf al Uyari,[17] and Abu Yahya al Libi,[18] are (or were) much younger than the old scholars, being in their thirties, forties, and fifties and having a much deeper understanding of Muslim youth in the Arab world.

Most of these intellectual-warriors are not known in the West, but their themes are popularized, and they are somehow worshipped as heroes, warriors of Islam by close circles of Islamic Ulama in Europe, who spread them either directly (to those living in London) or through local imams. In the European prisons, jailed Jihadists are highly regarded by many Muslim inmates. The admiration is the greater, as most of the Muslims in Europe are considered to be "nobody," economically and culturally, at best second-class citizens, whereas the imprisoned Jihadists are seen as world figures. Behaving heroically, inspiring fear in Europeans, and becoming famous through the media are considered feats they cannot themselves achieve. The new Jihadist warriors, following intellectual warriors, become models for some European Muslims who look for reasons to fight against societies they hate for making them unwelcome. Jihad becomes a path to escape victimization. It is a vindication, and Jihadist intellectuals are heroic paragons, the more so as many have been killed (like Jahiman or Uyayri) in street fights in the Muslim world.

THE POSTMODERN JIHADIST POPULARIZER: THE CASE OF LEWIS ATIYAT-OLLAH

Lewis Atiyat-Ollah is a Jihadist intellectual who has chosen his pen name for obscure reasons he does not explain in his book.[19] Perhaps he intended to prove that the Jihadist movement is not confined to a single nation but encompasses the entire world, inclusive of the West. Perhaps he aimed to prove that he is the Jihadist counterpart to Bernard Lewis, the historian of the Islamic world whose stance on Islam has been controversial in the last decade. His case is noteworthy because his thought combines many features of the Jihadist icons who are known for their Islamic theology and sometimes social science knowledge but has postmodern aspects, lacking in most of the other Jihadists. He thus popularizes in a creative way their ideology by modernizing them. He integrates many dimensions of Western modernity, like tolerance of opposing views, the capacity to argue in a style that is far from the Jihadist diktat style, and an ability to argue from a globalized perspective that is lacking among the traditionalist icons like Maqdisi and even the other major Jihadist thinkers I have mentioned in previous chapters.

Atiyat-Ollah published a dialogue between himself and "Abu Yasir," a fictional member of a Fundamentalist Islamic sect close to Muslim Brotherhood who believes that Al Qaeda's September 11 attacks have done a lot of harm to the Muslims and that Jihad should not be prompted against the West. The dialogue form is rather unusual among Jihadist intellectuals, although Maqdisi wrote a pamphlet in which he addressed prisoners and explained the legitimacy of his actions. Atiyat-Ollah is much more modern in outlook, since he creates imaginary conditions realistically; he enters a gentlemanlike discussion (rare among the Jihadists) with a Muslim Fundamentalist, without any tendency toward ostracism or declaring him an infidel (*takfir*). He shows some tolerance without a trace of animosity or aggressiveness. A summary of this dialogue is instructive about the Jihadists' state of mind in comparison to that of the Fundamentalists.

In the dialogue the character of Yasir, representing the Fundamentalists, claims that Jihad cannot be reduced to its fighting dimension. He distinguishes between the "fighting Jihad" (*jihad al qitali*) and the cultural Jihad (*jihad al hizari*, or civilizational Jihad). The latter should be promoted in a situation where the Umma's weakness makes it impossible to win a military war. America's power is not only military but material, economic, scientific, and industrial. Muslims cannot match it. The cultural Jihad enables the Umma to unify its efforts, spread awareness, and satisfy its needs in different fields of knowledge. Muslims live at the margins of civilization and should not jump the gun, leaping suddenly to Jihad. From this viewpoint Bin Laden's goal could not be implemented and was not reasonable. Bin Laden made a personal decision based on a whim, whereas global decisions concerning the umma should be taken by competent, nonpartisan specialists among the thinkers and intellectuals. Muslims should put their energy into throwing out the enemy out of Islamic countries rather than fighting America.

Atiyat-Ollah's answer is that Islam rules through "fighting Jihad" and that "Bin Laden makes history, conquers the hearts of the people, and becomes a pole in the fight against the West."[20]

Yasir treats Bin Laden and his group as a "band of intrepid people" (*mutihawereen*) who act recklessly. Atiyat-Ollah claims that this is precisely the viewpoint of the Western media. Abu Yasir returns to the question of September 11 and expresses the view that the bombings were not the deeds of Al Qaeda, because of their complexity and the fact that they were beyond the scope of Bin Laden. This type of operation can only be executed by CIA, Mossad, or the like. Therefore, "there are strong reasons to believe that the Event [September 11] was not the deed of Bin Laden and Al Qaeda."[21] Atiyat-Ollah responds that Muslims are able to carry out complex operations and that denying them this capacity means undervaluing their capacity. Denouncing conspiracy theories, he challenges the idea that "America is behind all the [major] events and that it is impossible to realize anything against its wishes."[22] According to Atiyat-Ollah, the September 11 operations needed Allah's assistance (*towfiq rabbani*), because of the financial resources needed for their accomplishment, their logistics, and the secrecy that surrounded them, divulged by no one.

Yasir responds that Allah assists operations that are to the profit of the Umma and the fact that the fourth plane was downed without attaining its goal shows that Allah did not facilitate the operation. In the same vein, he expresses the view that the September 11 operations were against Muslim interests and therefore could only be performed by the CIA or a Mossad type of organization. Atiyat-Ollah answers:

> The September 11 events were very positive for the Muslims. One major positive consequence of it has been to take the cover off the false peace between the West and the Muslims. This peace is not genuine since under its guise the West succeeded in fragmenting the Muslim world into small states, dividing them into republics they traced and countries of dung, dates, oil and others. They submitted them and created in them military bases or sent armies to warrant their own hegemony over them, perpetuating thus their domination. After that, they dictated a false peace to them, legalizing thus Muslims' submission and their domination over them. Bin Laden and Al Qaeda reject this peace and address an appeal to the Muslims, and claim the right for them to take hold of their own destiny. That peace is nothing but the falsification of genuine Islam (*tadhyif islam al haqiqi*) which demands proselytizing it without the intervention of the rulers, the emirs or the kings. What Al Qaeda did was to begin the Jihad in order that all religion becomes Allah's religion.[23]

For Atiyat-Ollah, Abu Yasir is a nationalist since he makes the *watan* (home, country) the center of gravity of the Muslims' interests in order to renounce Jihad. According to Atiyat-Ollah, "Bin Laden loves his home country more than you do, but this home is not the one militarily defended by the United States to support the rulers of oil and their groups. This is not a real home but a vast prison. The home we defend is the one in which the voice of justice and truth (*haq*) is sung all over. The first soil to defend is the country of the two sacred mosques [Saudi Arabia] that our ancestors defended through their blood and is now occupied by the United States."[24]

Yasir's understanding of the United States is not fundamentally different from that of Atiyat-Ollah. He simply believes that "Muslims are weak and downtrodden (*mustadh'afun*) on all the earth, and it is not wise to push them toward fighting Jihad before they improve the means to do so."[25] From this perspective, Muslims should address their urgent problems that are related to their geography, rather than fighting against an enemy that is far away. To which Atiyat-Ollah rejoins that one should not disconnect local and worldwide problems. American imperialism has to be fought back with the utmost energy:

"Allah the Creator put the oil in our soil, and the Americans came, occupied our lands and separated us from the rest of the world, violently or peacefully. By behaving in your way, you are desecrating Islam through your version [giving prominence to the] region and country [over Islam]. You thus deceive when you talk about the worldwide Islam. Inviting people for a civil society [within one's own country] is to deny that Islam is a world religion and is not restricted to the fake frontiers built up by the colonizers."[26] To which Yasir replies: "I don't deny that America supports and helps Israel and fights against Muslims and encircles them in many ways and bases its domination on the Islamic rulers and extends it through the so-called international organizations. But we believe that fighting America is not the priority."[27] Lewis's reply is that this interpretation is based on the perception of the self as inferior (*istisqar al dhat*) and that behind the view of the priority lies this self-denial. The difference between Yasir and Atiyat-Ollah is what goal is prioritized and not intrinsically on the essentials.

Yasir does not lose his self-control and insists on educating Muslims so that they can "confront the world's impiety *(al kufr al alami)* by fighting against it or through political means."[28] One problem raised by Yasir is that important decisions involving the future of the Umma should be taken through consultation with the ulama—that is, the people with religious competence (*ahl al mashvera*)—and Bin Laden did not so in his acts against America. Atiyat-Ollah believes that the definition of "people with religious competence" does not encompass those who disagree on the principle of military Jihad. Those ulama who advise the people not to take part in Jihad should not be consulted. Yasir comes back to the question of Muslims' problems after September 11. Atiyat-Ollah is quick to point to the fact that the Twin Towers demolition shattered the prestige of the United States worldwide. Since Muslims are devoid of modern military means and nuclear bombs, they have to take this type of action. Muslims should also deal another blow to the prestige of America for the sake of the Palestinians and other Muslims. Since America was powerless to prevent September 11, this means a new move toward equality of power with the United States. Bin Laden is the champion of this reversal: from deep inequality to at least symbolic equality of power. This entails the ascension of Al Qaeda as a new challenger to U.S. might: "Al Qaeda set an explicit goal with a clear representation of the means to achieve it. Then it decided early that America will be in difficulty facing Islam as a power and all the illegitimate Arab and Muslim governments will be paralyzed in the face of the American weakness or its breaking away. It is obvious that Al Qaeda's aim was separating America [from the Muslim world], or its destruction or at least its being frightened, forcing it to get away from the Islamic world."[29]

Yasir again raises the question of the ability of Al Qaeda to carry out the September 11 attacks, when so many Muslim states have been unable to carry out any similar action. Atiyat-Ollah 's answer is purely organizational this time: "This is your problem with your bureaucracy. Al Qaeda was able to solve the problem in two ways; first, by rejecting the idea of a pyramidal organization and organizational relationship in a single body; second, it put an end to the idea that belonging to the organization means getting separated from the society. Al Qaeda assists its members to find out solutions within the society."[30]

Yasir believes that before getting involved militarily with the United States, Muslims should become strong in terms of culture and civilization, to which Atiyat-Ollah answers back that this strategy is doomed to failure since Muslim organizations have attempted it in countries like Sudan, Algeria, Turkey, and Egypt without any success. All these attempts, based on renouncing Jihad and finding peaceful ways of promoting Islam, have been doomed to failure. For Atiyat-Ollah, Al Qaeda's success is precisely due to its rejecting the prevailing rules and inventing new patterns of conduct that confuse the Americans: "Al Qaeda played a new role outside the realm of the well-known rules of the game, and Americans and the others cannot imagine it because they are, like you, programmed to imitate the rules of the calculations of strength and weakness. The kind of war Al Qaeda is waging is called by the Americans asymmetric war (*harb qeyr al motewaziyah*). . . . America will be beset by a state of economic weakness and doubt about itself. Europe and the supporters of America will retreat from fear of becoming the future targets of Al Qaeda. The godless systems in the Muslim countries will be possibly the weakest because of the weakness of the first master."[31]

Atiyat-Ollah believes that the new strategy set up by Al Qaeda will throw America into an economic crisis on top of a crisis of doubt about its own power and this will induce Europe not to follow America, lest it become Al Qaeda's target. Here Atiyat-Ollah is purely rational: God plays no role in his argument, and his aim is to establish new roles breaking the deadlock of Muslims' inferiority to America and the West in general. Yasir questions this reasoning. He says, "I don't intend to defend America, but this country is democratic, it has solid institutions that can cope with the challenges of any kind because they act according to social rationality and they look at the problems in a scientific manner, and I don't believe they have difficulties awakening after any attack."[32]

Atiyat-Ollah, on the contrary, believes that America's self-confidence has been shattered by Al Qaeda and has no other recourse than to yield to Bin Laden's demands, which are manifold: to stop supporting Israel, end the occupation of Iraq, evacuate Saudi Arabia, and stop helping the godless Muslim governments (*tawaqit*, plural of *taqut*).

After the strategic discussion, Atiyat-Ollah embarks on an intellectual debate about the two major social theories in America after the collapse of the Soviet Union: "The two most significant topics that the West devoted itself to it after the Cold War are the theory of the End of History by Francis Fukuyama and Samuel Huntington's theory of the Clash of Civilizations. The September 11 events blew up Fukuyama's theory about the end of history and confirmed Huntington's theory's rightness and its wrongness regarding its conclusion, since one can say: the Western civilization won't win, and there is a new civilization [Islam], and it is the time of its revival."[33]

Normally, theorists of Jihad evoke Islamic thinkers like Ibn Taymiya or their modern representatives like Maqdisi, Tartusi, and the others. Atiyat-Ollah changes the parochialism of the Islamic radicals. He refers to the two major American theorists of global change, namely Huntington and Fukuyama, confirming the former's theory of the clash of civilizations, declaring the West's defeat and the rise of Islam, rejuvenated by Bin Laden and the Al Qaeda combatants who restored the Islamic principle of Jihad, restored Islamic reason (implicitly referring to the French social scientist Mohamed Arkoun, who wrote a book on the critique of Islamic reason), and reshaped Islamic public opinion through its agency (e.g., September 11). All this is due to the return to Jihad, as the keystone of Islam: "Jihad is the soul of the genius that pushed a group of the disciples whose number was at most a thousand as a unified community to fight the apostasy. Through it two empires, the Persian and the Roman, were fought against simultaneously. Through it the combatants of faith (*mujahid*) overthrew the Soviet Empire and now Bin Laden monitors the war against the American Empire and in less than ten years they have been able to reduce to ashes its splendor."[34]

In his subsequent analysis of Al Qaeda's success against the background of other Islamic organizations' failures, Atiyat-Ollah mentions the traditional sincerity and devotion toward God (*ikhlas*) as a major component and the readiness to die as a martyr (traditionally called upon by Jihadists), but also, in an effort to think strategically, the two new components of Al Qaeda's action:

> The first is the initiative. Al Qaeda has been able to take the initiative in the history of the Muslims in modern times: it acts and

the others react to its actions. All the Islamic movements as well as the Arab governments act by merely reacting, except Al Qaeda, who acts, the reaction belonging to the others. Reading the history of the war between Al Qaeda and America, one can clearly distinguish this feature: it is Al Qaeda that defines the timing and the place of action and America reacts to it. The second element is surprise, the behavior of Al Qaeda outside the realm of America's thought. America does not think that its ships will be hit on the sea, for instance! And then September 11 was the apogee of those operations, and the American mind could not grasp how they could succeed, and in spite of it, they succeeded with Allah's assistance. Al Qaeda's conduct was beyond the scope of America's thinking capacity. Dick Cheney and Georges Bush could do nothing but warn against the future dangerous operations of Al Qaeda. Besides it, they could not imagine either its content or its form.

What is new in Al Qaeda, besides its nonpyramidal organization, is its ability to dictate to the American enemy its own conditions and its own line of conduct, based on surprise and the refusal to react. This has entailed a major symbolic victory: dethroning America as the "goddess" for the rest of the world: "Al Qaeda proved to the Muslims that they can be superior and can innovate in thought, organization, and action beyond the level of America's thought who is a goddess (or better said, the goddess of impiety) and technology for the rest of humanity."[35] But the major victory for Al Qaeda has been to set the tone in the world media, dominated by the United States, by using "publicity, communication, politics, and public relations. I look at some of CNN's words about the ability of Al Qaeda to use chemical weapons. And I wonder at the subjugation it exerts on them, which is in accordance with the Prophet's words: I was victorious through the awe [in the enemy's heart], and I imagine the American scenery where people look with dread and anxiety the death of the dogs and relate it to our awesome power. They are anguished at the sight of the Sheikh Usama [Bin Laden]."[36] According to Atiyat-Ollah, Al Qaeda changed the mental situation of Muslims, who can now envisage the destruction of America as a realistic project, whereas before September 11 it was an unrealizable dream.

Combining modern thought with Islamic tradition, Atiyat-Ollah gives a modern picture of Ibn Taymiya, the medieval Muslim radical thinker: "Ibn Taymiya threatened the King of Cyprus that among the Muslims there are groups of devotees whom he described as killing the kings in their communities. And he was discussing a form of

organization like Al Qaeda in his time."[37] Atiyat-Ollah uses Fukuyama, Huntington, and Ibn Taymiya as references for his argument:
"The history ends in the sense that the history of the Western world
is ending and the Western civilization is bankrupt and our Islamic
history of the [Muslim] East begins now, through Allah's assistance."[38]
He thus blends Fukuyama and Huntington, one predicting the end
of history (which is the end of the West's history from Atiyat-Ollah'
view), the other foreseeing the clash of civilizations (which means the
victory of Islam and the defeat of the West).

September 11 has infused a new hope into the Jihadists' souls.
It is more than revenge; it is the dawn of a new world in which Islam takes its revenge against an arrogant West. It is the beginning
of a new era in which Western military might reveals its impotence
against a new strategic mode of action that inverts the Muslims'
weakness in the face of a militarily superior West. The dream of a
hegemonic Islam as a world religion is renewed by the Jihadists. But
this dream is not shared by other Muslims, and even though Yasir
shares Atiyat-Ollah's ideas about the domineering West, he does not
share Atiyat-Ollah's optimism about the defeat of the West and the
efficiency of Al Qaeda–type organizations' in bringing the West to
its knees. Realistically, Yasir believes that Al Qaeda's violent action is
to the detriment of the Muslims all over the world.

This imaginary dialogue sets the tone for a new type of Jihadist
ideology and intellectual. The references are as much the Western as
the Islamic intellectuals. The clash of civilizations the new Jihadist
intellectuals promote is, at its root, a new hybridity—namely, a re-
shaping of Jihad in light of modern ideologies. Atiyat-Ollah is a new
type of ideologue, at ease in the traditional Islamic field of knowledge
and reference as well as modern, Western social and political thought.
He is not within the framework of an exclusively Islamic civilization,
contrary to the famous radical theologian Maqdisi, but a new kind of
political thinker, using references from both the West and the Islamic
world, thinking strategically according to new theories of warfare
(the asymmetric war), elaborating plans to surpass the Americans in
their own tactics of psychological warfare, and setting new ideals for
Muslims, based on a renewed vision of Jihad. He sincerely believes
that Al Qaeda is able to smash American power into pieces. He is
utterly optimistic, unlike other Muslims, who feel overwhelmed and
victimized by Western domination. Jihadism opens up a horizon of
hope to a new generation of activists who are no longer psychologically
overpowered by the prestige and invincibility of America. Against a
background of disenchantment and political alienation in the Muslim

world, Al Qaeda uses destructive tactics to make hope once again possible. Culturally speaking, Atiyat-Ollah is a blend of the West and the East. Psychologically, he is in a merciless war with the West.

NEW WARFARE THROUGH GLOBAL MEDIA: THE PROMINENCE OF THE SYMBOLIC DIMENSION

Right from the beginning, modern terrorism has been linked to modern technology, not only explosives (Nobel invented dynamite in 1867, and the Russian anarchists used it from the end of the nineteenth century onward) but also communication. The Russian Decembrists' attacks against the chief of states in the world were amplified by burgeoning journalism and the new technology of photography.

The social and revolutionary movements in the Muslim world have made broad use of communication technologies. The Islamic Revolution in Iran was boosted by the technology of small tape recorders and their cassettes, which allowed the revolutionaries to spread the speeches of Ayatollah Khomeini throughout Iran and the world and put them at the disposal of the media. Bin Laden's talks have been sent to Al Jazeera network on videotapes. The most spectacular means is still the television for the purpose of propaganda and publicity. TVs all over the world put on display a thousand times the apocalyptic images of the falling Twin Towers for weeks on end after September 11.

Jihadists are fascinated by the images of apocalypse. Since they cannot constructively accomplish a grandiose deed, they are intent on destructively performing awe-inspiring acts. Their mind-set, based on a Manichean vision (right versus wrong, good versus bad[39]), their inclination for overgeneralization (everything is explained through a rigid belief system that denies any role to reality other than confirming their hypotheses), their sense of mission (they are the vanguard, the heroes, the self-proclaimed representatives of True Islam), and their intransigent attitude toward the prescriptions of religion make them the most appropriate people to carry out massive destruction without the slightest guilt. Their impatience with the world as it is and their apocalyptic view make them the messengers of destruction, the more so as their ideology operates as a substitute for a personal code of ethics that prohibits murder under normal conditions in Abrahamic religions (all the religions besides the apocalyptic sects).

Fascination with death and destruction finds its best outlet in the symbolic dimension of images. Even the Twin Towers destruction did not have any real dimension of Apocalypse. Their collapse killed 2,750 people.[40] In the same year the total number of people killed in highway crashes in the United States was 42,116,[41] around fifteen times higher than the Twin Towers deaths. What gives the Twin Towers' destruction its iconic sense is based on the simultaneity of the number of deaths (car accidents kill 114 people every day, dispersed over the year), the geographic concentration of the incident (car accidents occur in different places with a few number of dead each time), the intentional character of the killings (car accidents are largely unintentional and are perceived almost as akin to natural disasters), and the virtually recurrent dimension of the Twin Towers' explosions. They were integrated within Al Qaeda propaganda that foretold other incidents of the same nature, premeditated and planned consciously; it was revealed in documents confiscated later that many other buildings were targets.

At any rate, in real terms, September 11 was not an apocalyptic event, but symbolically it was. Several explanations have been propounded: unlike Great Britain (recurrent Northern Ireland bombings and explosions), it was the first major terrorist attack on American soil. The attack on Pearl Harbor was waged against an American port, not at the financial heart of Manhattan; the Lone Bomber or other types of extreme right incidents or violent anti-abortion acts cannot be compared to September 11 either, because of its sheer dimensions and the implication of foreign involvement. The September 11 attacks were seen as a major victory of the terrorists against the American superpower, even by many Americans; it was the opposite of what many people expected after the fall of communism, which should have brought world peace (the "end of the ideology" implying the end of massive violence worldwide). The Jihadists called "Black Tuesday" (September 11) "Blessed Tuesday."[42] It was the victory of a brand of Islam synonymous with a religion alien to Western civilization and aimed at combating it in a battle that shook the self-confidence of the American people.

The major result of this symbolic catastrophe was the quest for a scapegoat. The American public faced a new enemy, stateless, with no normal army, without a government, and with no might comparable to the Soviet Union or former enemies like Germany in the Second World War. The ideal scapegoat became Saddam Hussein, chosen by the Bush administration and followed by most American media. His bloody record of mass murder of the Kurds and his attempt at killing the father of the US president, as well as his invasion of Kuwait in 1991, gave some legitimacy to the claim that he was in touch with Al Qaeda (which proved wrong later on) and that he was building up weapons of mass destruction (also proved wrong after the invasion of Iraq). Without September 11 American public opinion would probably not have "bought" the idea of attacking Iraq by ground forces. The Vietnam Syndrome was rubbed off by the September 11 attacks:

one recent harrowing memory washed off another, dating back to the 1960s, which resulted in the repugnance of the American people to engage in massive military attacks against a faraway enemy. The new war was, in a sense, the symbolic triumph of Al Qaeda: it forced the only superpower in the world to become involved in a real war in Iraq that resulted in another upsurge of Jihadism.

The relationship between the media and the Jihadists is ambivalent at best. The high "exposure effect" of September 11, perhaps the most publicized world event in the last decade, has given a symbolic prominence to Al Qaeda it could never have otherwise dreamed of. Al Qaeda has done everything to be publicized throughout the world. Its attempts to provoke large damage and the highest number of casualties are part and parcel of this strategy. Without the media, Al Qaeda would have been perceived as a major threat but not as important as it is considered now, in spite of the low number of casualties it has caused in the West in the last few years. Some scholars speak of a symbiotic relationship and even mutual benefits between the terrorists that are provided with a pulpit for expressing their views and the media, in search of sensational news and stories.[43] It is well-known that the print but particularly the electronic media are crucial for spreading terrorist propaganda. The indoctrination of many new Jihadists is carried out through the Internet. Scholars speak of a post–September 11 Jihad in which the Internet clusters different people together through its virtual communication means in an electronic Jihad.

All the major terrorist groups have Web sites. There were some 4,800 terrorist or terrorist-related sites identified in 2006. Among them the global Jihad movements were present on more than 50 different sites.[44] They use the Internet for various purposes, including propaganda for recruitment but also fund raising, terrorist training and instruction (especially explosive manuals and behavior guides to avoid kindling the suspicion of intelligence services), and operational planning for attacks through e-mail.[45] Other ways the Jihadists use the Internet include psychological warfare, publicity, data gathering, mobilization, networking and information sharing, and planning and coordination.[46] In Great Britain, five major uses of the Web by Islamists can be enumerated: information provision, financing, networking, recruitment, and information gathering.[47] The Web has become the online university for radicalizing Muslims by offering them a comprehensive Jihadist curriculum.[48]

One of the tools the Jihadists use is intimidation and horrifying videos presenting hostages (Americans among others) mostly blindfolded, asking in a humiliating way for help, and imploring their respective governments to comply with the Jihadists' demands in order to save their lives. Hooded militants, armed with a Kalashnikov or a sword, announce that the hostage will be executed unless the government complies with their demands. English (and sometimes French or another language) is added to make the entire message understandable to non-Arab visitors.[49] Inspiring horror in the "unbelievers" or to "fake Muslims" gives self-confidence and pride to many Muslims all over the world, who feel despised, mistreated, and, in Europe, second-class citizens with no future prospects. The videos are symbolic occasions for them, who find solace in the suffering of those who make them suffer and are usually in a dominant position. The feeling of having "revenge" through the courage of the Jihadists comforts many young men who are not Jihadists themselves and would not approve of the hyper-puritanical policies of the Jihadists within their own society.

Jihadist cyberwar can bring to a momentary standstill those Web sites seen as enemies of Islam. The Internet site of the Danish daily *Jylands-Posten*, which outraged Muslims by publishing caricatures of the Prophet Mohammed on September 30, 2005, was overloaded with viruses that brought it to a temporary halt.[50] After the pope's remarks in September 2006 calling Islam a violent religion in reference to the words of a Byzantine ruler,[51] Jihadists launched a new Web site called Electronic Jihad.[52] Its purpose was to help organize an electronic holy war against Web sites that insult Islam and Islamic sacred figures. The site was publicized on established Jihadist Web sites. Furthermore, postings from August 2006 on the Electronic Jihad site claimed that they had successfully shut down an Israeli website.[53] The site works by coordinating and organizing its users and sympathizers and offers programs for downloading by those willing to engage in the electronic Jihad. Two main programs are offered: the first, the Electronic Jihad Program 1.5 (Silver Edition), is used for hacking attacks, and the second, when installed, places a toolbar on the user's computer that connects automatically to Electronic Jihad and acquires data containing the specific date, time, and target site for the attack. When that time arrives, the user simply has to run the first hacking program, select the target site to be attacked, and then allow the program to do the rest. The key to these attacks is that they have to be waged simultaneously by many different users to overload the target site.[54]

Jihad on the Internet is beginning to gain momentum. Some sites promote it and aim at targeting specific IP addresses that are deemed anti-Islamic. Since the number of Muslim Internet users is constantly on the rise, those able to take part in the Electronic Jihad might increase as well. Electronic Jihad sites serve also as forums for learning attack techniques. Jihadists learn in particular how to organize synchronized mass cyber attacks on Web sites they deem as anti-Islamic.[55]

Besides clandestine or "illegal" sites, there are nowadays legal ones, within the West, that spread Jihadist messages without infringing on the law. Western media detect some of them: "Terrorism experts at West Point say there are as many as 100 English language sites [in the US] offering militant Islamic views, with Mr. Khan's—which claims 500 regular readers—among the more active. While their reach is difficult to assess, it is clear from a review of extremist material and interviews that militants are seeking to appeal to young American and European Muslims by playing on their anger over the war in Iraq and the image of Islam under attack."[56]

On the whole, the Internet enhances a sense of a global, universal Umma through its anonymity and easy links to other people. The cyber Umma does not need actual meetings and mutual personal knowledge. It makes communication easy on the basis of shared views and common concerns on the screen. The Jihadist Internet becomes a means to achieve the goal of a transnational neo-Umma through the involvement of Islamic youth, who are more aware of the virtual world and participate in a plurality of cultures. The young man who helped Al Qaeda gain access to cyberspace after the fall of the Taliban, code named Irhabi007 (*Irhab* means terrorism in Arabic, 007 referring to James Bond) is Younis Tsouli, the twenty-two-year-old son of a Moroccan tourism board official and a student of information technology. Two of his collaborators, Waseem Mughal, a British-born graduate in biochemistry (Aka Abuthaabit), and Tariq al-Daour, a law student born in the United Arab Emirates, were only in touch through the Web and seem not to have known each other personally. They were condemned to long prison terms in the United Kingdom.[57] Within the Muslim diasporas in Europe, Jihadist Web sites build up a "wall of resentment," opposing integration and pushing toward rancor and violence. The messages also abet obedience to Jihadist authorities.[58]

In addition to the Internet, there are other means by which Al Qaeda and associated groups tend to impose a style on their attacks in order to be recognized as such by mass communications and in this way forge an identity, a "brand." One method is multiple attacks. Al Qaeda and their branch offices tend to make their bombings multiple, within short spans of time. The September 11 attacks aimed at three different sites: the World Trade Center in New York City, the Pentagon in Arlington County, Virginia, and a third target (the last aircraft crashed into a field near the town of Shanksville in rural Somerset County, Pennsylvania, after passengers and members of the flight crew attempted to take control of their plane). The Madrid bombings aimed at four commuter trains during the peak of Madrid's rush hour on the morning of Thursday, March 11, 2004. The London bombings purported to destroy a bus and at least two metro stations: three bombs on the London Underground exploded within fifty seconds of each other at 8:50 in the morning on July 7, 2005.

Another symbolic dimension many Al Qaeda–inspired attacks try to follow is the eleventh day of a Christian month. After the September 11 attacks, there are also the Djerba, Tunisia, attacks on April 11, 2002, then the Madrid bombings on March 11, 2004, and the latest being the December 11, 2007, bombings in Algiers. The striking fact is that the Islamic days are not taken as the yardstick but the Christian ones. The lunar Hegira months are mostly shorter than the solar Christian months, but the eleventh day of the latter are chosen (there are exceptions, like the London bombings of July 7, 2005) to send a message to the Western world.

Another peculiarity of Al Qaeda that has a direct bearing on the media is the attempt at making a spectacle through maximizing the number of the dead. In the West, Al Qaeda's capacity has been eroded, as already mentioned, but in Muslim countries it can still mount deadly operations in which dozens or more people die, like the 2007 Algerian explosions, in which more than forty people died and many more were injured. This "apocalyptic" dimension of death shows that Muslims, let alone non-Muslims, are not protected any more by the taboo of killing the innocent, even in times of peace. Jihadists change the nature of "peace." For them, we are in the time of an all-out war between Islam and the idolatrous powerholders all over the world, and this applies to the societies in which everyone takes part in the effort to suppress Muslims, the West as much as Muslim countries themselves. Peace is therefore rejected. Only temporary respite (*hudna*) is acceptable at the price of the West's renouncing its hostile attitude toward Muslims. Since this is not the case, the language of death is the only one to have legitimacy. It becomes universal and recognizes no boundary. To gain currency, it needs the media to spread it worldwide. The more horrendous the spectacle, the more glorious the action.

Indiscriminate violence is multiplied and "sacralized" by the awe it inspires through the media, which are the indispensable tools for Jihadist action. An action is more "successful" as it kills a higher number of the people, which entitles it to a larger place in the media. In this respect, Al Qaeda is different from classical terrorists, who usually do not intend to blindly kill or maim and maintain a balance between material destruction and human casualty. In the Al Qaeda case, dehumanization combined with spectacular action aimed at the world media makes the arithmetic of the killed the major symbolic dimension of the operation. The heightening horror contributes to the self-confidence of the organization and its prestige through the mainly Western communication system. Global media are the target: they unwittingly give prominence to the Jihadist organization through their coverage of the horror. Dominant Western civil culture is based on avoidance of violence. Jihadists believe that this is sheer hypocrisy. By heightening the violence they aim to attract the media (which depict horror as a countercultural fact) and push the American government to use violence, showing its own inability to hold on to the culture of nonviolence it publicizes as being its official stance. If it does not act violently, it displays its own weakness and the denial of its own military superiority. In both cases, the Western power is put in a double bind: either acting violently (not being true to the culture of nonviolence) or acting nonviolently (thus revealing its own powerlessness).

Jihadists' tactics especially play a role in relation to the global media. Among the tactics used by terrorists in general and Jihadists in particular, bombing is prominent. It is spectacular; it attracts many people, namely cameramen and journalists; it kills indiscriminately large numbers of people; and the technique is easy to manipulate:

> The role of the bomb as an element of terrorists' tactical repertoire reaches back into the earliest history of modern terrorism. Anarchist terrorists adopted the use of explosives in the 1800s, and the attractiveness of the weapon was symbolic as well as functional—"dynamite made all men equal and therefore free."[59] In the period covered by the RAND-MIPT data sets, bombing incidents represent the majority of terrorist attacks (57 percent of all incidents). In most individual years, bombings account for more than half the terrorist attacks (except in 1994, 1996, and 1997) and have reached as high as 70 percent of attacks in 1999. The prevalence of bombings as a tactic of choice for terrorist organizations is reinforced by the many ways explosives can be used and applied. . . . Examination of incidents in the database range from the use of small letter bombs for targeting individuals to large-scale vehicle bombs designed to produce mass casualties and destroy structures and property.[60]

Suicide attacks have also undergone steep increases during the recent years:

> This tactic was not popularly used prior to the early 1980s, but it received widespread media attention from the 1983 suicide

car bombing of the U.S. Marine Corps barracks in Lebanon. Subsequently, several terrorist groups adopted the tactic. Suicide bombings have been an effective tactic for assassinations, for attacks on military targets, and for creating mass casualties and terror. In addition, the dedication of the individuals willing to sacrifice their lives for the cause of the group lends to the credibility and legitimacy of the group in the eyes of other members and possible recruits. As a result, suicide bombings have become increasingly popular with terrorist groups during the 1990s and early 2000s. The MIPT Terrorism Knowledge Base indicates a steep spike in the number of suicide incidents in recent years, with the Iraq war contributing to much of this increase.[61]

Global media induce global Jihad in its symbolic dimension. In them, a new sense of virtual life and death develops that amplifies imaginary reproaches and mythical recriminations. The frontiers between the virtual and the real world become fuzzy, increasing the sense of victimization that is, in part, based on the imaginary and the mythical comparison of the self with other Muslims out of cultural context. The new electronic media largely facilitates decontextualization, mythologization, and fortuitous identifications. Jihadism has become the icon of a modern anti-modernity that blurs the frontiers between life and death in the same fashion as the boundaries are dimmed in the cyber world between the real and the virtual.

A new generation of Jihadists is on the rise, hardly socialized through traditional Islamic channels, bearing their grudge against the West or Muslim societies by focusing their frustrations on imaginary enemies, acquiring their warrior culture through the Internet and video games, and seeking revenge against a world where it is easier to feel like a victim than like an actor, particularly in the Muslim world, populated with tyrants and autocrats. They turn their spite against America, this symbol of arrogant success in a world where Muslims are more often on the loser's side than on the winner's. America's feckless policy toward the Middle East, combined with the search for a scapegoat for Muslims' failures in social and political development, makes the United States the ideal enemy for the Jihadists.

NOTES

1. "*Taqut* is the Tatars' rules and the 'Yasiq' set up by Chingiz Khan. He drew his laws from many sources, namely the Jews, the Christians, the Islamic people, and the others. There is no difference between the Chingiz

Khan's Yasiq and the laws nowadays promulgated in the Muslim countries. In a way the Yasiq was better because it contained some inspirations from the Islamic religion contrary to the laws set up nowadays derived from the Western laws or the arbitrary inspirations of the people." See Abu Basir Tartusi, *Taqut* (Idolatry), *Minbar al Tawhid wal Jihad.*

2. Abu Basir Tartusi, *Al Tariq ila isti'naf hayat islamiya wa qiam khilafa rashida ala dhow' al kitab wal sunna* (The Way for the Revival of the Islamic Life and the Rise of the Well-Guided Caliphs in Light of the Koran and the Prophetic Tradition), *Minbar al Tawhid wal Jihad.*

3. Abdullah el-Faisal was jailed in 2003 after being convicted of soliciting murder and inciting racial hatred. See Jamie Doward, "Cleric Who Urged Jihad to Be Freed from Prison," [London] *Observer,* August 20, 2006.

4. Born in 1934 and the founder of a group of "those who seek martyrdom" (*istishhadiyun*), living in Qom, Yazdi has a Web site in English, www.mesbahyazdi.org/english, in which he proclaims his radical views worldwide.

5. Abu Qatada was forty-five years old when he arrived in the UK in September 1993 on a forged United Arab Emirates passport. He was allowed to stay in June 1994 after claiming asylum for himself and his family. He was ordered to be deported in February 2007 by a British judge.

6. Abu Hamza, forty-seven in 2006, who preached at Finsbury Park Mosque, London, was found guilty of eleven of the fifteen charges he faced. He had already been in jail since May 2004. US authorities are seeking the cleric's extradition for terror-related matters. He is wanted on charges of trying to set up a terrorist training camp in the state of Oregon.

7. Born in Egypt in 1938, Sheik Omar Abdel Rahman is a blind Egyptian Muslim cleric. He is considered to be the spiritual leader and role model of Bin Laden and Ayman al Zawahiri. He holds a degree in Qur'anic studies from Al-Azhar University in Cairo. In the 1970s Rahman developed close ties with two of Egypt's most militant organizations, Egyptian Islamic Jihad (EIJ) and *Al-Gama'a al-Islamiyya* (the Islamic Group). In 1990 Rahman brought his brand of radical Islam to the United States, and in 1996 the sheik was sentenced to life in prison.

8. Mustafa Setmariam Nasar, also known as Abu Mus'ab al Suri and Umar Abd al-Hakim, was a key figure in Al Qaeda before his apparent capture in Pakistan in November 2005. Nasar was born in 1959 in Syria, where he joined the Muslim Brotherhood. He became a Spanish citizen by marriage, and directed and taught at terrorist training camps in Afghanistan, where he met with Osama Bin Laden. In 1995 Nasar moved to the United Kingdom, where he served as a European intermediary for Al Qaeda. He traveled widely around Europe and Afghanistan during the late 1990s before finally moving his family to Afghanistan in 1998. Prior to September 11, 2001, Nasar tried to organize his own extremist group, but following the attacks, he pledged his loyalty to Osama Bin Laden as a member of Al Qaeda. In November 2005, Nasar was reportedly captured in Pakistan. He is believed to be in US custody.

9. See his Web site, http://www.altartosi.alqannas.net.

10. See Rudolph Peter, "Dutch Extremist Islamism: Van Gogh's Murderer and His Ideas," in *Jihadi Terrorism and the Radicalisation Challenge in Europe*, ed. Rik Coolsaet (London: Ashgate, 2008).

11. In an interview, a young Frenchman of Algerian origin said, "Here we are dirty Arabs and in Algeria, dirty Frenchmen." See Farhad Khosrokhavar, *L'islam des Jeunes* (Paris: Flammarion, 1997), and idem, *Quand Al Qaeda parle* (Paris: Grasset, 2006).

12. For instance, in France, the Moroccan-born imam Tareq Oubrou defends this idea. See T. Oubrou, "La shari'a de minorité: Réflexions pour une intégration légale de l'islam," in *Lectures contemporaines du droit islamique: Europe et monde arabe*, ed. F. Frégosi (Strasbourg: PUS, 2004).

13. Quoted in Tartusi, *Taqut.*

14. In 1979, at the head of a group of Islamic militants, Jahiman al Oteibi took over the Grand Mosque in Mecca and held hundreds of pilgrims. The movement was repressed, and he was later condemned and executed.

15. In 1977 agricultural engineer Shukri Mustafa became the leader of the cultist, Jihadist group Takfir wal Hijra in Egypt. He had begun to build the group after his release from prison in 1971. In 1977 the group decided to battle mainstream society by kidnapping a Muslim cleric. After Mustafa was captured and executed in 1978, former members were linked to the assassination of the Egyptian president Anwar Sadat in 1981.

16. He is a Salafi cleric in Kuwait, among major opinion makers in the Arab world, and forty-seven years old; he declares Muslim governments as heretical (*Kuffar*) and extensively comments on current events and political issues. See Chris Heffenfinger, "Kuwaiti Cleric Hamid al Ali: The Bridge between Ideology and Action," *Terrorism Monitor* (Jamestown Foundation) 5 (April 26, 2007).

17. He was a Salafi intellectual and member of Al Qaeda in Saudi Arabia when he was killed by the Saudi forces in 2003 in street battles.

18. He is a soldier-theologian, combining both skills like Yusuf al Uyari. He escaped the Bagram air base in Afghanistan in July 2005 with other Al Qaeda fighters, and since then, he is active in the ideological front, against the Saudi government, Hamas in Palestine, and the Shi'ites.

19. See Lewis Atiyat-Ollah, *Min Baridah ila Manhattan, havar Saudi salafi howle al qaeda wa tafjirat* (From a letter to Manhattan, the Saudi Salafi, about Al Qaeda and the bombings)(London: Dar arriadh, 2003).

20. Atiyat-Ollah, *Min Baridah*, 31.

21. Atiyat-Ollah, *Min Baridah,* 33.

22. *Min Baridah,* 37.

23. *Min Baridah*, 44.

24. *Min Baridah,* 44.

25. *Min Baridah,* 45.

26. *Min Baridah,* 46.

27. *Min Baridah,* 48.

28. *Min Baridah,* 49.

29. *Min Baridah*, 61.

30. *Min Baridah*, 62.

31. *Min Baridah*, 72.

32. *Min Baridah*, 73.

33. *Min Baridah*, 78.

34. *Min Baridah*, 79.

35. *Min Baridah*, 87.

36. *Min Baridah*, 88–89.

37. *Min Baridah*, 90.

38. *Min Baridah*, 97.

39. Manichaeism has also become the ideology of the Bush administration, in its radical form after September 11 and in its milder form in his second term as president after 2005.

40. "Governor Pataki, Acting Governor Di Francesco Laud Historic Port Authority Agreement to Privatize World Trade Center," Port of New York and New Jersey press release, July 21, 2001.

41. See http://www.unitedjustice.com/death-statistics.html.

42. See Mathieu Guidère and Nicole Morgon, *Le Manuel de Recrutement d'Al Qaeda* (Paris: Seuil, 2007).

43. See Brigitte L. Nacos, "Communication and Recruitment of Terrorists," in *The Making of a Terrorist: Recruitment, Training, and Root Causes*, vol. 1, ed. J. Forest (Westport, CT: Praeger Security International, 2006).

44. G. Weimann, *Terror on the Internet: The New Agenda, The New Challenges* (Washington, DC: United States Institute of Peace, 2006); "Virtual Disputes: The Use of the Internet for Terrorist Debates," *Studies in Conflict and Terrorism* 29, no. 7 (October–November 2006).

45. See B. Hofman, *The Use of the Internet by Islamic Extremists*, Rand Corporation Testimony Series, May 4, 2006.

46. See Weimann, *Terror*.

47. M. Conway, "Terrorism and the Internet: New Media—New Threat?" *Parliamentary Affairs* 59, no. 2 (April 2006).

48. Stephen Ulph, *The Next Stage in Counter-Terrorism: Analysing Jihadist Radicalization on the Web*, 2006, http://www.jamestown.org/docs/JR-Slides.pdf.

49. See for instance the case of Paul Marshal Johnson in Jeffrey Donovan, *Middle East: Islamic Militants Take Jihad to the Internet*, June 17, 2004, http://www.terrorisme.net/p/article_107.shtml.

50. "Electronic Jihad's Cyber Soldiers," *Middle East Times*, November 23, 2006, http://www.metimes.com.

51. In his speech in September 2006 in Germany, Pope Benedict the XVI quoted a fourteenth-century Christian emperor who said the Prophet Muhammad had brought the world only "evil and inhuman" things. That led to uproar among the Muslims all over the world.

52. The electronic Jihad was located at http://www.al-jinan.org.

53. The Israeli website claimed to have been brought to a standstill was located at http://www.haganah.co.il.

54. See Abdulhameed Bakier, "New Website Incites Electronic Jihad," *Terrorism Focus* 3, no. 38 (October 3, 2006).

55. The "Electronic Jihad Program" is part of the long-term vision of Jihadist Web site Al-jinan.org, which uses the Internet as a weapon and can affect any organization that relies on the Web. The application even includes a Windows-like interface that lets users choose from a list of target Web sites provided via the Al-jinan site, select an attack speed (weak, medium, or strong), and then click on the "attack" button. See Larry Greenemeier, "'Electronic Jihad' App Offers Terrorism for the Masses," *Information Week*, July 2, 2007, http://www.informationweek.com/story/showArticle .jhtml?articleID=200001943.

56. See "An Internet Jihad Aims at U.S. Viewers," *New York Times*, October 15, 2007.

57. See "A World Wide Web of Terror," *Economist*, July 12, 2007.

58. C. Bernard, *Cybermullahs and the Jihad-Radical Websites Fostering Estrangement and Hostility among Diaspora Muslims*, working paper presented at Rand's Conference on Middle Eastern Youth, September 22–23, 2005.

59. Walter Laqueur, *A History of Terrorism* (Brunswick, NJ: Transaction Publishers, 2001).

60. The Memorial Institute for the Prevention of Terrorism (MIPT), *Terrorism Annual*, 2006.

61. MIPT, *Terrorism Annual*.

Conclusion:
Toward an Islam of Hope

Three major conclusions can be drawn from this study. The first is that a subculture of violence has mutated into a subculture of death through contemporary Jihadism. Jihadism has been, from the inception of Islam, a subculture of violence within the much larger Islamic culture. Its main proponents, after the demise of the Prophet, were the Kharijites. It indirectly survived through "revivalist movements" resulting in a return to the "purity of the origins" in different Fundamentalist shapes throughout the history of Islam.

In modern times, particularly in reaction to late modernity in the second half of the twentieth century, Jihadism became a subculture of death. Within it, violence was turned against the self and the other. In Shi'ism Jihadism turned the utmost violence (death) mainly against the self, and only in a secondary manner against the other (the Iraqi enemy, but also the West as such). In Sunnism, particularly in the Algerian case, Jihadism turned the cruelest violence against the other (Algerian society) during the period of civil war (1992–2001). Al Qaeda generalized the violence and turned it against the world at large.

Of course, fascination with death is not the monopoly of modern Jihadism.[1] But within the Jihadist framework it has attained intensity and a scope that will be groundbreaking for similar movements in the future: the underlying purpose is killing on the largest scale at the price of getting killed oneself. Late modernity has induced a crisis within Muslim societies that has changed a subculture of violence into a subculture of death. International politics, the Soviet Union's attack against Afghanistan in 1979 and the Jihadists' awakening as a result, flawed American policy in the Middle East, and stalemate in the auto-

294

cratic political structures within most Muslim societies also played key roles in the advent of Jihadism as a major actor in the world.

The second conclusion is about the nature of Jihadism in the West and in the Islamic world. There are, of course, many connections within the Jihadist movement between the West and the Muslim world through networks, friendships, professional as well as ethnic ties among Jihadist actors, and ideological commonalities, all reinforced by the globalization of communication and economics.

Still, there are two distinct types of movements in the East and in the West. In the Muslim world, a deep ideological movement underlies Jihadism. In the West, Jihadism is mainly related to the predicament of Muslims in European societies and the plight of Muslims all over the world as imagined by Western Muslims. In this part of the world, Jihadism is primarily a social movement—that is, a phenomenon mainly related to the present-day situation. The historical and cultural aspects are not as significant as the current social and political situation of Muslims in the West (mainly Europe). Unlike the West, in the Muslim world Jihadism is a movement with deep roots in the cultural and historical dimensions of Islam. The ideological dimension is of paramount importance; its sources in the traditions and self-understanding of Muslims are undeniable. As a global movement, Jihadism in the Muslim world has its credentials in the history of Islam within a subculture of violence. The crisis of the Muslim world has increased its attraction vis-à-vis many new generations that have been educated and therefore are able to read the Koran and the inherited texts directly themselves without the moderating influence of the traditional ulama.[2]

Globalization creates nexuses between the two movements in an unprecedented way: besides the Internet there are the migration of Jihadist intellectuals and ulama all over the world, the emergence of Muslim diasporas in the West, and the birth of new generations of Muslims who identify much more with religion than their predecessors, who were under the spell of secular modernization as the key to progress. All these factors give a symbolic advantage to Jihadism as a mythical solution to deep-seated cultural and political problems in the land of Islam.

A sociological and anthropological understanding of these two movements helps us grasp more easily the capacity of their proponents to link to each other but also the limits to these relations. Looking for common ground between the two movements is one of the tasks of Jihadist intellectuals and scholars. Their success so far has been tremendous, yet they cannot continue indefinitely. The West and the East should both attempt to mend the major fissures within each world and create new venues for mutual understanding between the two worlds. Otherwise, Jihadist logic will prevail in spite of its major weaknesses and limits. One of their limitations is that they are not open to everyone, and as Muslim movements, Jihadist groups can only enroll converts, not non-Muslims. Still, they can disrupt societies and create enough anguish and malaise to make life more difficult in both worlds, with human rights being among the universal values that might suffer most.

The third conclusion is that Jihadism, like all movements, has its apogee and will have its decline. Like many Islamic chiliastic movements that erupted every now and then in the Muslim world in the past and progressively died down, modern Jihadism will abate in the next Muslim generations. Globalization has given it major opportunities, coupled with the end of the bipolar world that held it within the two-world system, before the collapse of the Soviet Union and in part in reaction to it (mainly in Afghanistan, after the Soviet invasion). For more than a decade, Jihadism has held free rein. Disenchanted with it, the new Muslim generations will look for other ways than holy war to cope with the crisis of Muslim societies.

In its history, Islam spread through wars, but also by its merchants[3] and Sufis. The new Muslim diasporas have opened up a fourth way, different in its nature from the three others. Diaspora communities are giving Islam a new impetus in the West, without—for the overwhelming majority of them—recourse to violence. But the new expansion of Islam has also induced a deep sense of frustration among Muslims, particularly in Europe and Australia.[4] Among them "Westernization" has spread more quickly, and for many their Muslim identity is endangered. The same phenomenon of secularization has happened in the Muslim world and has caused a sense of deep anxiety among many Muslims. The remedy to secularization is, for the Jihadists, the fight to the death against the fake religion of democracy and religious pluralism, which includes the West and the moderate or even Fundamentalist Muslims who disagree with their methods and, at least in part, their ideology. The Jihadist solution to the malaise is a reactionary, resentment-laden response against the secularization process. It is creative only through self-destruction and the destruction of the other. Jihadism as a counter-secularization tendency is doomed to failure, but as an ideological and social movement in the world it will survive. It will do so only in a more marginal fashion in the next generations of Muslims, if new solutions to the global crisis of Muslim societies and Muslims in Europe are devised.

PERVERSE MODERNIZATION
AND THE FOUNDATIONS OF RENEWAL

In many respects, Jihadism is a regressive, repressive, and dangerous trend within the Muslim world. Its enemies are not only Western societies but also Muslims themselves, besides a tiny minority of Islamic radicals. Jihadism is also overwhelmingly a modernization vis-à-vis traditional Islam, but a perverse one. It puts into question the traditional distinctions within Islam in the name of a rigid, and intolerant, universalism that transcends all ethnic, regional, and political bonds among nations and races. It revitalizes the utopia of a "pure" society, devoid of the double dealings of traditional Muslims. But it is a dangerous holistic ideology, akin to totalitarian ones, while it is the only one that challenges democracy at a large scale in the post-Soviet era.

Still, Islamic radicalism is a perverted modernization that can end up, within the next decade or two, with a new attitude toward religion and modernity. This can happen in two distinct but related ways. First of all, many of today's Jihadist actors will, in the long run, become conscious of the impossible realization of the Jihadist utopia, not only because of the resistance of the outside world, but also because of its very nature, its intrinsic utopia, which is unrealizable. The experience of many young Iranian revolutionaries, imbued with the Shi'ite version of Jihad, is there to militate in favor of this idea: many of them are now proponents of a tolerant version of Islam, some have turned nonviolent in principle, while others denounce through art (cinema, theater, novels, poetry, Islamic theology, mysticism) the holistic, even totalitarian ideology of Islamic theocracy in the name of a new conception of religion, one that is friendly toward open society.

The second way Jihadism will loose its stamina is the reaction of Muslim societies themselves. Mortification, frustration, political deadlock, and biased American policies beget the reaction approving Jihadism as a way of restoring a sense of dignity among Muslims, but this "symbolic" compensation cannot indefinitely serve as a substitute for reality. Again, the example of Iranian society can serve as a hypothetical model: societies succumb to radicalism, populism, and other demagogueries, but the life span of these ideologies is always limited. The mental, intellectual, and spiritual resources of many Muslim societies with sophisticated pre-Islamic civilizations going back to the dawn of humanity like Egypt and Iran make radical Islam a provisional episode in their history.[5] Other Muslim societies, younger and latecomers in the history of modern countries, are more fragile, like Pakistan, Iraq, or Afghanistan. But radical Islam has no real solution for them either. With the modernization of the other societies and the inability of Jihadism to provide them with real solutions, they might awaken through the help of other, more developed societies and build up a reaction of their own to radical Islam. This won't be necessarily democratic but less harmful than Islamic radicalism. It will be a moderate oligarchy instead of the intolerant autocracies in the Muslim world.

Beside these two components, there are some ingredients in Jihadism that can lead, in the future, to its own denial. The first ingredient is the idea of the universal Islamic community, the world-wide Umma. Pushed to its extreme limits, this can lead to a fascist ideology in which the individual is sacrificed on the altar of a mythical collectivity in the name of religion. But the universalistic dimension of this Umma can be used to put into question any repressive system that would impose a "particularistic" political view on it. True universalism is loath to any particular pretension to legitimacy in its name. It is in this way that many Iranian reformist Muslim intellectuals nowadays question the legitimacy of Islamic theocracy: since Islam is a universal Umma, any specific political system imposed on it disfigures its content, be it even in the name of Allah's religion. Many of these reformist Muslims were radical Jihadists at the dawn of the Islamic Revolution in Iran. In Algeria, some of the old guard Jihadists of the1990s have become politically less violent and in search of political solutions to the malaise of their society rather than indulging in bloody violence against it.

Another ingredient of Islamic radicalism that can turn against it is the idea of sacrifice and abnegation to the utmost degree through martyrdom, for the sake of Jihad. The person who accepts the supreme sacrifice is a modernized individual—and not the traditional Muslim person—who voluntarily subscribes to death in the name of the community. The "individual" dimension is essential. Traditional Muslims did not usually accept dying for the sake of the community as easily as do individual Jihadist Muslims today. Many verses in the Koran excoriated them for their lack of enthusiasm for holy death "in the way of Allah."[6] Muslims never died as cheerfully as they do today for the sake of Islam, even in comparison to the first century of Islam. The reasons why they so wantonly subscribe to death are manifold, among which are failed modernization and the advent of the individual who needs to fulfill his wishes. Unable to find a "horizon of hope" extending to the future, he chooses death, for lack of any other perceived alternative.

At the root of the ease with which so many Muslims embrace martyrdom is the crisis of individuation. Mythical solutions cannot be an ersatz for reality in the long run. The process of individuation has induced many new generations in Iran to reject martyrdom as a solution to social ills, after the first enthusiasm for holy death. They have returned to life to answer the questions related to the crisis of modernization. Moroccans do not accept Jihadist martyrdom as a solution to social ills, in spite of their misgivings about the political structure of their country. Martyrs are "individuals in death" within the Jihadist version of Islam. The "mortiferous" (enticement for death) dimension of this individual will not resist the ordeal of reality in the future, and the sheer individual will emerge, seeking down-to-earth solutions to his problems rather than looking for lofty answers through martyrdom. But this will not be easy if Muslims are not more respected by the West, in particular America. The paradox is that Muslims are much more respected as a religious group within the United States than in Europe, but outside America, they are not sufficiently taken into account in terms of international politics. Jihadism is a politics of failed individualization. The old communities with their social bonds and mutual assistance have been disbanded without the promotion of a "positive individualism" in which the individual can assert his own rights and recognize his duties within a framework of a just society. Jihadism promotes individualism in a perverse way, through the invitation to die through the "individual duty" (*fardh al ayn*),[7] not a "collective duty" (*fardh al kifayah*), as was the rule in the dominant Islamic tradition. By pushing the Muslim to accept holy war as his own irretrievable duty, Jihadism contributes, in a destructive fashion, to the individualization of the believers. In the future, this individualization can be put at the service of a positive construction of society rather than demolishing it. "Individual duty" will enhance life instead of doing away with it in the name of a violent Jihad, if Muslim societies open up and the West reconsiders its denial of their legitimate demands.

Jihadism rejects the traditional Islamic view on politics, based on obedience to the powerholders (*vali amr, ulul amr*). It refers to some Koranic verses legitimizing the revolt against non-Islamic rule or an oppressive ruler, but in its essence it is a modern reaction against politics that denies the individual's participation in the name of a sacred principle and at the same time asks this individual to behave in a modern way by acting on his or her own, against others. Jihadism prospers on the grounds of failed individualism within the Muslim world, asking the new malaise-ridden individual to proceed against individualism in a contradictory manner. Jihadism makes Islam a champion of political egalitarianism by stating that being the creature of Allah means that one is subservient to no one else but Him. This is undoubtedly a modernization regarding the traditional anthropology of power in Islam, where subservience to the ruler (even the unjust one) has been generally the norm. But it is destructive and denies the equality hypothesis: it regressively views politics as a new caliphate that is nothing but a totalitarian political system in the modern world, where the only person whose opinion counts is the mythical new caliph and a close circle of Jihadist ulama and intellectuals. The egalitarian side of Jihadism can be put at the service of a pluralist political system that denies servitude toward any power other than that willed by the entire Muslim community through "Islamic consultation" (*shura*), setting thus the premises for political pluralism in Islamic garb.

Jihadism is based on an anthropology of modern impatience: impatience in the face of the desperate situation of most of the Muslim world, in the face of the injustice in the world (couched in the Islamic idiom of the *mustadh'afin*, those reduced to powerlessness, the downtrodden), in the face of nepotism and nonmeritocratic political systems in Islamic societies, in the face of the stigma Muslims suffer in Europe as a result of Islamophobia. This impatience is itself one of the offshoots of modernization and individualization. Until the time Muslims yielded their traditional worldview, the overwhelming majority of them were tempted to have a quietist or fatalist attitude, leaving to the powerholders (emirs, sultans, caliphs, and the like) the ultimate decisions to be made. Jihadism at such a large scale, encompassing groups of radical Muslims all over the Muslim world, puts into question this distribution of power. In its essence, Jihadism is anti-quietist and anti-fatalist. Its impatience is of a destructive nature though. A modern type of patience, devoid of fatalism and quietism,[8] can be proposed to Muslim youth in reference to the Koranic Sayings.[9] This patience will be of an active, creative, and positive essence. It makes possible to set up in the long run one's promotion as an accomplished person within the framework of an entire life and not in the dazzling moment of a glorifying death exhibited in the coverage of the world media. Jihadists' impatience is one of their tender spots .The new version of patience, relieved of its traditional defects (mainly passive surrender to the powerful, quietism, a static worldview, and fatalism) can be made an essential ingredient of a new anthropology of Islam of hope against the negative version of Allah's religion publicized by the Jihadists. The models of the Japanese, South Korean, and other societies can be promoted where positive patience along programmed development has yielded undeniable results. The Japanese, deeply humiliated by their defeat in the Second World War and still able to have a "peaceful revenge" on the West by becoming one of its economic pillars, can inspire many Muslims.

Women's participation in Jihadist bombings has been on the rise. The fact that many women in the West had to work like men during the two World Wars made women aware of their citizenship rights in the public sphere. Martyrdom operations have put women on parity with men in regard to death (but not within the hierarchy of the Jihadist movements). Because of this, in the long run Muslim women will claim more rights in society. If women can die like men in voluntary ways, they can also live like men, equal to them in the public sphere. Martyrdom operations, still a minority phenomenon in the case of women, are the beginnings of a new era in which men and women can be equals not only in holy war and sacred death, but also in daily life, within the family and politically. In the Muslim world women's place is still so marginal as to promote Jihadism among many Muslim women who despair of having their voices heard in the public sphere. Their modernization in terms of education (access to higher education) has not been matched by their access to the political and economic spheres. They suffer from a lack of participation in public life. Islamic radicalism is all the more enticing to them as it provides a heroism in an implicitly death-centered feminism in their eyes. Jihadism provides them as well with a means to assert the values of a virtuous Umma, devoid of the fallacies of the modern Islamic world, where the traditional bonds of the Umma have been broken down and women's protection through the patriarchal system has been weakened without their recognition as full-fledged individuals in the public sphere. Women should be provided the opportunity, through the reinterpretation of Islam, for equality with men, by questioning the patriarchal reading of the Islamic Holy Writ. A new generation of female Islamic jurists (*fuqahat*) is necessary to challenge the patriarchal vision of gender within Islam. Reformists, almost exclusively made up of men, have been at best inept in providing this new gender-oriented *fiqh* (Islamic jurisprudence).

Another dimension of Islamic radicalism that might put it into question in the future is the charismatic aspect of its leadership (the Jihadist stars, like Bin Laden, al Zawahiri, and a few others of lesser stature). Charisma operates for some time, in the name of Bin Laden or his surrogates. The routinization will set in and a less idealized picture of the leadership, desacralized and humanized, will emerge. Of course, there is nothing mechanical in these processes, nor any intrinsic necessity in them. But Muslim societies, in the throes of many deep problems, have to find creative answers to their problems rather than looking for inspiration through sacred stardom. Many intellectuals are at work within the new generations of Muslims, who are much better educated than before. Up to now, because of the conservatism of religious institutions in the Muslim world, the modernization of new generations has benefited the radical Islamists more than the Reformists, mostly reduced to silence or to minor religious positions. In the future, better-educated Muslims will also be better citizens and individuals rather than strict followers of those who speak in the name of the Umma and who entice those who still do not believe in themselves as autonomous individuals.

Jihadism is directly related to the politics of recognition. Too many Muslims have been excluded from the political, economic, and cultural arenas at home and internationally, and the demand for recognition is in part motivating their action. But the claim for recognition is so far based on violence and death. The latter is directed much more toward other Muslims than the West in the sheer number of people killed or maimed.

The West plays a major symbolic role in this violence. Not to be recognized in their dignities by the West (and particularly by America in regards to the Palestinian, Afghan, and Iraqi questions) is a deep wound that induces a movement of absolute violence and the praise of death as the only solution to the dilemma of this denial. The push to extreme violence, inducing death of the self and the other, has to be fought not only through political and economic means, but also through the promotion of a "peaceful recognition." Designing a culture of life able to confront the culture of death of the Jihadists cannot be achieved without the recognition of Muslims' rights in the Middle East and "Muslim particularism" in the West, be it France, England, or America, each in different ways.

Jihadism is also in part the result of the failure of modernizations from above in postindependence Muslim regimes and in Muslim societies where the new secular state was set up in an authoritarian way by the Westernized elites. For them modernity meant centralization, secularization, and bureaucratization minus democratization. Most modernization happened against the Islamic culture in a contemptuous way that did not encourage the participation of the societies in their own modernization. The ruling elites in the Muslim world have always been, with few exceptions, deeply suspicious of society; they have been inspired by vanguard ideology that would push society forward against its own will in a leftist fashion or by fascist ideology (the Ba'th parties were influenced by Fascism). The denial of autonomy to Muslim societies, let alone the slightest respect for them, was (and still is) the characteristic of their modernizing elites. Total disrespect for society has been transmitted to Jihadists, who share this patronizing attitude toward other Muslims, referring to Islam in order to subjugate an "impure society" that has to be forced back to purity. Jihadism looks for meta-political solutions through violence. Once politics has been restored in its own right, the spell of Jihadism will dissipate.[10]

Jihadism, in particular Al Qaeda as its paragon, has opened a new horizon of hope among disgruntled Muslims. This hope challenges American supremacy, inaugurates a new era of imaginary glory for the Muslim neo-Umma, and provides disenchanted and desperate Muslims with an ideal that blends destruction, hope, warfare, heroism, and a glamorous future.[11] This dimension of hope and positive expectations (restoration of the past Muslim glory and a new era of Islamic pride in rupture with the present times, which are engulfed in a deep sense of frustration and despair) is a symbolic dimension that should not be overlooked. Against this "destructive optimism" one should oppose a "constructive optimism," based in a sense of collective achievement through peaceful means. The major problem for Muslims is to find out new ways of creating a horizon of hope without indulging in an apocalyptic vision of destruction and annihilation. Al Qaeda (and Jihadist movements more generally) provide their recruits with this proud sense of optimism through death. To counter them means inventing a promising future that would free the collective imagination from the hegemony of death and destruction. This is not possible other than by promoting real economic and cultural development in the Muslim world. The new religious culture, a positive version of Islam, will function as a therapeutic response opposing the Jihadist fascination for demise and annihilation by inventing a religion of hope and virtue without indulging in victimization and distrust of the future. Protestantism invented a new culture of hard work and deferred gratification. An Islamic Protestantism can achieve the same goals, blended with a renewed sense of patience and self-accomplishment through positive entrepreneurship in a new social setting that does not discourage incentives and optimistic individualism. The subculture of death is the scourge of the Muslim world. Only an Islamic culture of trust in life can supplant it.

Two categories of people play a major role in the subculture of death and distrust of life: the "oppressed" (in Islamic terminology, the *mustadh'afin*) and the new lower-middle classes. The first is made up of people who suffer from the dislocation of social bonds, in the West as much as in the East, in a context of unbalanced urbanization (the French *banlieues* and more generally the poor districts in Europe, the debased neighborhoods like the Kasbah in Algiers, and so forth). They are without future perspective and believe that societies are against them. They harbor a deep sense of victimization by the West and by the unpopular political regimes in the Muslim world. They have to be reconciled with society in terms of opportunities and social justice. They have to be integrated culturally as well by fighting against their sentiment of victimization and by helping them overcome their overriding feeling of resentment-laden despair and distrust toward the values of life.

The second group is made up of the lower-middle classes. In the West, some of their members join Jihadist groups because they feel the Islamic community is endangered by Western arrogance and enmity toward the Muslims. They have to become citizens able to help integrate the downtrodden (*mustadh'afin*) within the social framework through affirmative action and cultural means, among which the capacity for dialogue and communication is paramount. These middle classes in the Muslim world have to be reconquered by democracy. Many have been alienated by the authoritarian modernization of their societies in the nineteenth and the twentieth century. For them democracy is another hypocrisy under the aegis of the Western imperial powers. Many subgroups among the lower-middle classes are ready to be opened up to democratization: students, women (in particular feminist women who fight for equal rights within the framework of Islam or simply in a secular manner), new intellectuals who strive to promote secular politics in the name of Islam (the so-called "Islamic Protestants"), the new Reformist theologians who look for a non-Jihadist, non-Fundamentalist interpretation of Islam, and the artists and new cultural actors (journalists, film directors, writers, movie stars, university teachers, etc.) who would like to shake the yoke of intolerant political regimes, be they secular or Islamic.

These new groups are in their gestation but they are becoming more and more conscious of their own existence. The heydays of Islamic radicalism are linked to the repression of these groups by authoritarian governments. Islamic radicalism will be waning in the future, and the role of these groups will inevitably increase if they are given the opportunity to assert their ideas without being persecuted by despotic governments. The West should not help them in a too visible way. They should be discreetly defended because within their own societies they should be considered as "indigenous" and "autochthonous" rather than dependent on the West. As new groups aspiring for a new freedom, they will be the main actors of democratization in the Muslim world. They are the best bulwarks against Jihadism, even though part of them, for historical reasons, have cooperated and keep on cooperating with radical Muslims.

THE SUCCESS AND FAILURE OF JIHADISM

Jihadism has a dangerous social and political project for Muslims and non-Muslims alike. Its implementation in the Muslim world would be at best a Taliban-like political regime and, in the worst case, an Islamic Pol Pot. In the West, the consequence would be a closed and less democratic society, in reaction to Jihadists' excesses and boundless violence.

As already said, the major anthropological ingredient of Jihadism in the Muslim world is offended dignity (a complex web of humiliation, denial of autonomy, damaged honor, and lack of freedom against a background of nostalgia for a glorified Umma). Too many disasters have befallen the Muslim world since the beginning of the twentieth century. Up to the first half of that century, Islam was considered by anthropologists as friendly to modernity, open to the world, able to adapt to the vicissitudes of change, and congenial to pluralism and democracy, perhaps more than other non-Western religions and cultures. The picture has radically changed since then. What could have been a large capacity for dialogue and mutual exchange between the West and the Muslim world has been transformed into a heinous mutual misunderstanding and, on top of it, a chasm within the Muslim world itself. In this chasm secular people and moderate Muslims are, besides a few countries, intimidated or persecuted by radical Muslims or by autocratic governments.

Jihadism is mainly based on the alliance of two types of actors, the modernized and the traditionalist hyper-conservatives, both turned radical because of the lack of any positive perspective on the future. In the West, the major rift is between a minority of radicalized Muslims on the one hand and the other Muslims and the non-Muslims on the other.

Offended dignity is rooted in a deep sense of humiliation and the desire to inflict humiliation on the "overbearing" Westerners who keep on oppressing Muslims.[12] Lack of self-esteem based on a sense of degradation is the backdrop of this complex web of victimization upon which Jihadism builds up its legitimacy. Islamic radicalism has succeeded in mobilizing large minorities in the Muslim world and small ones among Muslims within their diasporas in the West. This success is based on an unflinching feeling of victimization. To fight Islamic radicalism one has to resolve the major problems besetting the world of Islam (the Palestinian, Chechen, Iraqi, and Afghan questions among others), but beyond that, one has to fight against the victimization that suffocates many believers in Allah's faith. Be it in the French, English, or German prisons, in the ethnic ghettoes in the poor suburbs of France, or in the poor ethnic neighborhoods of England, be it among the Egyptian engineers or Algerian "trabendists," the problem is the sense of helplessness and victimization that is not exclusively related to reality but is based on a dark vision of the world and the inability to challenge it in a positive manner. Jihadism is the Islamic version of inverted victimization with a horizon of hope that results in fascination with heroic death and self-righteous killing.

Islam is an old civilization, and political structures within its ambit have always been defined in relation to it, in a much closer way than in Christianity, at least in the last half a millennium. Modernization has broken down this major element shaping the Muslim worldview by the despotic secular regimes, ungainly copied from the West, without presenting a positive substitute for what they destroyed. An alternative to the hollow nationalism of the 1960s and subsequent abasements caused by the successive Muslim defeats at the hands of Israel in the Middle East as well as America and the West (in Iraq, Afghanistan, etc.) should be one major pillar of any future solution.

Islamic radicalism has succeeded in raising the "Muslim question" in a world that used to be utterly blind to the extent of the crisis within the orbit of Islam, in the two worlds, the West and the South. The West has ignored Muslims and their problems for a long time, within its own ambit (Muslim diasporas) and without it (mainly the Middle East). It cannot ignore its wrath and the irrational but predictable reach and scope of its desperate reaction. Repressive measures by Western governments will have a transitional effect. Real solutions to the harrowing problems remain to be found, in terms of fighting racism, Islamophobia, and colonial prejudice. The unbalanced American policies in the Middle East must be reviewed. The Palestinian problem (symbolically much more important than the Chechnyan or the Kashmiri in Muslims' eyes) has to be addressed.

The success of radical Islam is to have given to the Muslims some solace for the "lost dignity" and a taste of "revenge." The very same Muslims, who applaud Al Qaeda's misdeeds in the West, do not otherwise share the violence and the fanaticism of its followers. Still, rancor has never solved any real problem, and the major challenge facing the Muslim world is to overcome the deep resentment accumulated through the last century. The latter is one of the most redoubtable obstacles to a positive self-appraisal among the new generations of Muslims from all walks of life, in the West as well as in the old Islamic countries. This feeling cannot be combated exclusively through economic or political means, although these aspects are of the utmost importance. The fight against the denial of self-esteem, the cultural rehabilitation of the self, and new ways of looking at Islam in a peaceful and politically open way are necessary. Resentment prevents the revitalization and revisiting of Islam in light of an optimist self-appraisal and relating to the modern world through means other than heroic death. A renewal of the promises of Islam in terms of tolerance and the multiplicity of readings of the Koran,[13] as was the implicit message of many Muslim thinkers in the ninth and tenth centuries, combined with the advent of new Reformist intellectuals, might help fight the scourge of rancor in its extreme forms in today's Muslim societies.

Another success of radical Islam is to have proven that Muslims can master the sense of life and death in the modern world: the Promethean Western individual can solve problems within the realm of life. Being denied this capacity, radicalized Muslims become Promethean by pushing the frontiers of action beyond death. Hitherto, they supersede the Westerners through the alchemy of self-transcendence through death. This ability (going beyond the values set by life) can be used to challenge the despair that underlies much of martyrdom. If Muslims can defy life, they can even better challenge the predicaments within the sphere of life by improving their own lots and those of their societies. The "death ordeal" can be transformed through building a better world by channeling the energy of despair at the service of a constructive project.

Another success of Jihadism is questioning the self-righteousness of the West. After a time of incrimination and condemnation on both sides, dialogue among Muslims and the West on equal footing becomes possible. The Western world is still far from being able to have a critical attitude toward itself and an uncomplacent one toward Muslims worldwide, be it in politics or culture. The example of the United States up to today is instructive. It shows the major difficulty in a critical reassessment of national policies toward Muslims worldwide, particularly in the Middle East. After the trauma of September 11, a new critical dialogue with the world of Islam might be at hand. On the other side, in their overwhelming majority, the next generation of Muslims will have to overcome the "Jihadist syndrome" and its symbolic, emotional, heroic, and counter-humiliation posturing. A positive opening to the other might be within reach.

Radical Islam has had a tremendous capacity for destruction and death. It has even yielded a stronger symbolic power of enacting Apocalypse through global media. Its iconic power display has been by far superior to its real might. The conversion of this wild violence, symbolic and real, into a constructive ability is possible, if the West becomes aware of its own bias toward the other, in the name of ethical and universal values that it has, at best, applied with a deep ambivalence, if not insincerity, for the sake of domination in the colonial period and then, by imposing unilateral political stances. Once Jihadist violence is stabilized, it would be necessary to build up a politics in which subaltern cultures and societies should not be deemed as the great absents on the world scene. Jihadism has shown that Muslim identity is not a void word. Now that the parenthesis of despotic nationalism of the 1950s and 1970s is over in the Muslim world, a new era is opening in which compromises between Islamic and Western culture on the one hand, the modern international political system on the other, are on the agenda. In the Muslim world, political systems will not remain untouched by the forthcoming change. If not discussed and mastered, the direction of change will be toward intolerance and closure in the name of Islam.

The major success of Jihadism, as already mentioned, is in its symbolic ability to put on display "Apocalypse Now." Its major failure is its inability to convince majorities in the Muslim world or in the Muslim diasporas of its legitimacy to rule. Its skill in denouncing Western imperialism, the illegitimacy of Muslim governments, and their submissiveness to America in the name of Allah has been tremendous, but no Muslim society has adhered to its utopia of a new Muslim caliphate. Authoritarian Muslim governments face hitherto a dilemma: if they open up to society, it implies sweeping electoral victories for Muslim Fundamentalists, and if they don't, their attitude legitimizes Jihadists in the long run. Still, framed Fundamentalism is by far a better solution than unfettered Jihadist violence.

Another failure of the Jihadists has been their inability to profit from the deep cultural and political crisis in the world of Islam to gain a foothold in a country (the only country where they were openly present was Afghanistan under the Taliban). Their internationalist stance prevents them from espousing any geographically limited hegemony, and this reduces them to dependence on some organizations or elites (for example the intelligence service in Pakistan and part of the economic elites in Saudi Arabia) or ethnic groups (the tribal groups in Pakistan's Waziristan) within Muslim countries. In fact, this failure gives them some resilience as well, since they cannot be targeted in a single country or institution.

The main tenet in the ideology of Jihadism is the unity of the Muslim world, the Umma. Its attitude has, on the contrary, sharpened the divide between Sunnis and Shi'ites and among the former, between Fundamentalists and moderate Muslims on the one hand, radical Muslims on the other. Promoting tolerance and dialogue among different religious groups within Islam is, in the long term, a significant means to fight Jihadism. Based on a subculture of intolerance within the Muslim world, Jihadism lacks a culture of compromise and leans on an autocratic view of Allah's religion. Reformist and Fundamentalist intellectuals are the most appropriate people to propose Islamic alternatives to their rigid and intolerant reading of Islam. To this end, old religious institutions should be opened up to them and new ones should be erected, within which the new culture of Islamic dialogue and toleration ought to be developed. To bring this task to fruition, the alliance between Fundamentalist and Reformist intellectuals against Jihadist and hyper-Fundamentalist thinkers and ideologues is essential. The new hermeneutics of Islamic toleration exists but needs to be publicly endorsed and institutionalized. Within new religious institutions, the rapprochement between the two groups could be implemented. Insistence on human dignity and respect for human rights should take precedence over democracy, seen at best as the privilege of the Westernized secular elites, at worst the symbol of subservience to imperial America.

In the West, appropriate means should be taken to spread the culture of Islamic forbearance in the Muslim diasporas, and beyond that, Islam should be accessible to Muslims, mainly in the secular European societies where religion has been marginalized and Islam ignored. A new sense of citizenship combined with a subculture of Islamic tolerance would marginalize the Islamic radicals who find vindication through the alarming situation of the excluded Muslims within European ghettoes.

The fight against Jihadism in the West needs continuity over time and long-term policies of persuasion, combined with short-term repressive measures to fight Jihadists' actions (without repression of the Jihadists, the entire Muslim diaspora in the West runs the risk of stigmatization). One component without the other is doomed to failure. Governments are able to provide for short-term repression, but a policy of promoting tolerance and cultural communication in the long run is beyond their scope. International and civil society organizations should be substituted for them for this new task, helping to foster new actors who would defend an Islamic *ahimsa* (nonviolence in Gandhian terms), couched in terms of Islamic spirituality, Sufism, or Islamic philosophy, in reference to its rich legacy.

Jihadist groups are attracting young people because they incorporate three dimensions. The first is based on the readiness of minority groups within Muslims to die for the sacred cause of Islam, out of a sentiment of hopelessness and despair, in a world that does not leave them any positive opportunity according to their victimized view. Organized groups and networks that put this readiness to die at the service of ideological motives are manipulating this calling.

The second dimension, as already mentioned above, is that this death is not simply a desperate death; it is fostered by a deep sense of revenge based on rancor and gall. Death is not only self-inflicted but also imposed on the enemy. The problem is that the enemy who is clearly defined in the national Jihad (Palestinian, Chechnyan, and Kashmiri contexts) lacks any precise definition in transnational Jihadism. The face of the new adversary is fuzzy; it encompasses almost everyone, through a conspiratorial vision that includes the entire world. This new face of enmity is related to a global malaise resulting from the late secularization of Islam, one that induces a sentiment of threat among sizeable minorities in the Muslim world as in its Western diasporas.[14] Against the background of this "negative secularization," a "positive secularization" should be endorsed by Muslim intellectuals and reformist ulama, proving its compatibility with the main tenets of Islam and modernization's requirements. Jihadism has shown Muslims' capacity for modernization by its creative use and sophisticated manipulation of the most modern technologies. It has transformed an ideological and social movement into an online movement. This achievement paradoxically points to the fact that Muslims can become hypermodern by mastering the most up-to-date technologies. The transfer from the destructive creativity of the Jihadists to the constructive know-how of modern Muslims can happen if they are given the opportunity to act as sovereign individuals. This is not possible except within a framework of more meritocratic, more pluralist, and less clientelist political systems within the Muslim world, even though in the short term, this might result in the political hegemony of Fundamentalists who are critical or even inimical toward the West.

The third dimension is utterly modern. Martyrdom does not occur between the self and the enemy, but in front of the world conceived as scenery promoted by the global media. Killing, getting killed—all of it exhibited on the world stage in a way that ensures the symbolic supremacy of the neo-Umma is an important part of the message. The relationship is not binary but triangular and involves world media as its essential ingredient. A modern, narcissistic dimension is ubiquitous in the new martyrdom, symbolically extended to the entire community of the "elected," namely the Jihadists. The inversion of life into death is the major event in a world where otherwise the dominant West monopolizes all the values of life. By promoting martyrdom, Jihadists intend to monopolize the values of death as a counterculture to life and worldly values where the West is paramount. But even the values of death are contaminated by the globalized West, in spite of the denials of the Jihadists, mainly through the culture of exhibitionism that infests holy death. Martyrdom through global Jihad displays, on the fairyland of global TV screens, the death of the Jihadist as well as the bystander in a juggernaut that annihilates, in an indiscriminate manner, three sets of people: the enemy, the bystanders (they could be TV watchers as well), together with the candidate for holy death. Those who watch the horrendous spectacle of apocalypse on TV feel as if they could be among those who died in the explosion. The symbolic strength of Jihadism is that on the one hand, it promotes the values of death, extended not only to the foe but also to the spectators, be they Muslims or non-Muslims; on the other hand, the very same spectator who is supposed to die as a bystander is called upon to witness the collective death in a theatrical exhibition in the world theater, this time as a spectator. The Occident that is to die is summoned to take part in the ceremonies of killing and dying as an audience. This is the task unwittingly fulfilled by global media.

What should be done to oppose this narcissistic seduction of the world stage is to point out that martyrs are nothing but walkers-on in a piece whose main star is paradoxically the spectator, not the martyr. Jihadists' power to inflict death can be matched and even largely surpassed by the West, but their hopeless attempt to infuse life with new values is their major weakness. In the long run, the spectacle of death reveals its inability to build up positive values, and this will be the death of the Jihadist spectacle. The fight through generalized martyrdom leaves life to the dominant West; it does not fundamentally change the domination relationship. It enhances domination through its own hideousness and its inability to promise anything but mere obliteration. Death as the ultimate message of Jihadism will still seduce many young, desperate, and disoriented or disenfranchised Muslims or converts to Islam from all social strata, those who seek justice, those who seek revenge, or simply those who aspire to exhibit their stardom on the stage, in a battle that leaves no issue for their survival. Since the seduction of Jihadism resides in its capacity for annihilation, not in its positive contribution to life, it exhibits its Achilles' heel, its scope but also its limit. The time will come when the attraction of death will give way to the renewed charms of life in a new generation, one that is less victimized and living in a world not so dominated by biased and one-sided imperial powers that reject a multipolar world.

Last but not least, one of the major achievements of the Islamic Reform movement in the twentieth century was to disconnect Islamic mysticism (Sufism) from Jihad. Unlike Christian mystics, who did not have much to do with just war, the Muslim Sufis, historically, were mostly connected to violent Jihad. Their major Jihad (or Greater Jihad, *jihad akbar*), based on internal purification and spirituality, was not contradictory to minor Jihad (or Lesser Jihad, *jihad asqar*). They were mostly complementary. Many Sufi mystics were staunch fighters in the violent Jihad (*lesser Jihad*). The new Islamic mysticism, be it in Shi'ism or in Sunnism, disconnects the two, with the spiritual Jihad becoming exclusively spiritual and leaving the social realm to the human beings who can autonomously legislate in the name of revisited Islamic themes. Neo-Sufism has not benefited from the attention of Muslims and the West because of the domination of Islamic institutions of higher learning and teaching by Islamic conservatives and Fundamentalists. This trend should be reversed and free voice given to the Neo-Sufis and Reformists who express the new aspirations of the modern Muslim middle classes, marginalized by the despotic Islamic regimes and by the autocratic secular governments in the Muslim world (such as the Tunisian government).

The voice of moderation, be it from the modern Islamic mystics, secular Muslims, Reform-minded Muslims, or even peaceful Fundamentalists should be heard more often, to help promote a new version of Islam, full of promise for this-world and other-world lives, not opposing it, not promoting death as central to faith, and not seeing in every non-Muslim a potential enemy. The new hermeneutics of Islam is on the move. To be successful it simply needs the opening up of the old institutions and a new human agency in Islamic civilization in the name of hope for a better life.

NOTES

1. The aesthetics of death was developed in the First World War, by, among others, the German poet Ernst Jünger (1895–1998), an officer of the German Imperial Army, who wrote in 1920 *Storm of Steel* (German title: *In Stahlgewittern*), which glorified war. The glorification of death through violence in war was largely shared by the German *junker* elite. In the Second World War, the German SS saw in death the ultimate value of life through exaltation of absolute violence. The Japanese kamikaze culture had a flavor of death, which was seen as ennobling heroic people who accepted death in the name of Japanese nationalism.

2. The traditional ulama mostly interpreted in a moderating way the so-called Medina suras, in which violence is generally more present than in the Mecca suras. They did so either consciously—among the Shi'ite, through reference to *ijtihad*, the revisiting of the tradition in light of the current situation—or unconsciously—among the majority of Sunnis. Among the latter, after the first three centuries, *ijtihad* was banned until it was revived by the Reformists in the late nineteenth century, without being adopted by the majority of the Sunni ulama up to now.

3. The Indonesian Islamization occurred by peaceful means as well, mainly through merchants.

4. In the United States white Muslims' frustration mainly dates to the post–September 11 period, when they were exposed to racism and Islamophobia.

5. Islamic Fundamentalism is, on the contrary, deeply entrenched in the history of these societies. It is the transformation of traditionalism in the context of rapid change. It can be peaceful and attract in the future many of those who are fascinated, nowadays, to Jihadism.

6. One can find these reprimands in the sura al Tawba (Repentance): "O ye who believe! What is the matter with you, that, when ye are asked to go forth in the cause of Allah, ye cling heavily to the earth? Do ye prefer the life of this world to the Hereafter? But little is the comfort of this life, as compared with the Hereafter" (verse 38).
"Unless ye go forth, He will punish you with a grievous penalty, and put others in your place; but Him ye would not harm in the least. For Allah hath power over all things" (verse 39).

7. Of course, in the traditional Islamic jurisprudence, "individual duty" did not refer to the individual in the modern sense of the word. Nowadays, Jihadists implicitly use the modern sense of "individual," implying that he should act consciously and obey to the utmost his own personal sense of sacrifice, to promote the Islamic cause against the unbelievers.

8. Fatalism and quietism are related to the history and geography of Islam and not to a so-called "essence" of Islam, as some Orientalists and the modern interpreters of it suggest. Among Shi'ites fatalism was related to the oppression of the Sunni majority. In the Sunni world, it was the consequence of the constitution of empires, where the person could not assert himself, like the Roman Empire, in which Stoicism developed a form fatalism because the individual was overcome and overawed by the Empire. Recent studies show that in Indonesia, Christians have a higher level of fatalism than Muslims because of their situation as "dominated" people within a Muslim society. Huntington's emphasis on Islamic fatalism as an inherent characteristic of Islamic religion cannot be defended in light of empirical, social scientific data. See Gabriel A. Acevedo, "Islamic Fatalism and the Clash of Civilizations: An Appraisal of a Contentious and Dubious Theory," *Social Forces* 86, no. 4 (June 2008).

9. One can quote, for instance, the Sura al Anfal (the Spoils of War), verse 46, among others: "Be patient, since Allah is with those who are patient."

10. See Hamit Bozarslan, *Une Histoire de la Violence au Moyen-Orient* (Paris: La Découverte, 2008).

11. The case of Lewis Atiyat-Ollah is characteristic. See my analysis in chapter 7.

12. For a comparative perspective, see James W. Jones, *Blood That Cries Out from the Earth: The Psychology of Religious Terrorism* (Oxford: Oxford University Press, 2008).

13. The Mu'tazila believed that the Koran is the Prophet's utterances, inspired by God, expressing in a human (and therefore fallible) way Allah's

commandments. This opened up the possibility for multiple interpretations of the Koran. The Mu'tazila were repressed under the late Abbasid caliphs, and their major premise (human expression of godly injunctions) was rejected in the later dominant Islamic tradition. The Murji'a believed that no one can ostracize a Muslim out of the Umma, Allah being the only judge in this matter. This excluded the possibility for *takfir* (declaring someone infidel), widely used by the Kharijite and today by the Jihadists. The word *Murji'a* is used in a derogatory way in the Muslim tradition. All these traditions can be revitalized and revisited through a new reading of the Koran and the religious traditions. This brings a tolerant and positive reappraisal of Muslims through their own eyes.

14. American policy in the Middle East has overwhelmingly increased this dimension of insecurity and threat among Muslims around the world.

Index

ABOUT THE AUTHOR

Farhad Khosrokhavar is Professor at the École des Hautes Études en Sciences Sociales in Paris and author of fourteen books translated in ten languages. Khosrokhavar continues his travels and work on Islam, Muslim radicalization, and postrevolutionary Iranian society. His most recent books in English include *Suicide Bombers: Allah's New Martyrs* (Pluto 2005).